MACROMEDIA® DIRECTOR® MX
DESIGN PROFESSIONAL

Steve Johnson

THOMSON

COURSE TECHNOLOGY

Macromedia® Director® MX—Design Professional

Steve Johnson

Executive Editor:
Nicole Jones Pinard

Product Managers:
Rebecca Berardy and Jane Hosie-Bounar

Associate Product Manager:
Elizabeth Harris

Production Editors:
Megan Belanger, Kristen Guevara, and Summer Hughes

Development Editor:
Holly Lancaster

Composition House:
GEX Publishing Services

QA Manuscript Reviewers:
Burt LaFountain, Danielle Shaw, Chris Kunciw, Tom Pedrick, Susan Whalen, Andy Smith, Chris Carvalho

Text Designer:
Ann Small

Illustrator:
Philip Brooker

Cover Design:
Philip Brooker

Credits:
Some of the images used in this book are the property of Atlas Image [or Atlas Image mosaic] obtained as part of the Two Micron All Sky Survey (2MASS), a joint project of the University of Massachusetts and the Infrared Processing and Analysis Center/California Institute of Technology, funded by the National Aeronautics and Space Administration and the National Science Foundation; and material was also created by STScI under contract for NASA.

Design Professional Series Vision

The Design Professional Series is your guide to today's hottest multimedia applications. These comprehensive books teach the skills behind the application, showing you how to apply smart design principles to multimedia products, such as dynamic graphics, animation, Web sites, software authoring tools, and video.

A team of design professionals including multimedia instructors, students, authors, and editors worked together to create this series. We recognized the unique learning environment of the digital media or multimedia classroom and have created a series that:

- Gives you comprehensive step-by-step instructions
- Offers in-depth explanation of the "why" behind a skill
- Includes creative projects for additional practice
- Explains concepts clearly using full-color visuals

It was our goal to create a book that speaks directly to the multimedia and design community—one of the most rapidly growing computer fields today.

This series was designed to appeal to the creative spirit. We would like to thank Philip Brooker for developing the inspirational artwork found on each unit opener and book cover. We would also like to give special thanks to Ann Small of A Small Design Studio for developing a sophisticated and instructive book design.
—The Design Professional Series

Author Vision

The Macromedia Director MX Design Professional book gives you hands-on experience using the powerful authoring tools in Macromedia Director MX to create interactive multimedia software for distribution on CD/DVD-ROM, kiosks, and the Web. The book directs you through the development of an interactive software product for a fictional company called SpaceWorks. You'll learn the fundamentals of software development in Director from the design process to the final delivery of the product.

With this book, I hope you learn to do all the things you wanted to do with Director MX, discover how to do things you didn't know you wanted to do with Director MX, and enjoy doing them all. The best way to learn is by doing, and that's what I hope you'll get from this book.

The task of creating any book requires the talents of many hardworking people pulling together to meet short schedules and difficult demands. I would like to especially thank Holly Lancaster for making this book easier to read, understand, and follow. For their helpful feedback during the writing process, I would also like to thank the manuscript reviewers: Cindy Young from Langara College, Vancouver, B.C. Canada; Grethel Gomez from Miami Dade Community College; and Larry Gonzales and Marni Sweetland from Macromedia whose efforts were coordinated by Alisse Berger.

At Course Technology, I would like to thank Rebecca Berardy and Jane Hosie-Bounar for keeping this book on track, and the entire QA staff for testing the book on every conceivable computer system.

And, most importantly, I would like to thank my wife Holly and our three children, JP, Brett, and Hannah, for their support and encouragement during the project.

Introduction

Welcome to *Macromedia® Director® MX—Design Professional*. This text is organized into thirteen units that offer creative projects, concise instructions, and complete coverage of basic to intermediate Director MX skills, helping you to create interactive multimedia software. Use this book both in the classroom and as your own reference guide.

1. Attach built-in behaviors.
2. Create a behavior.
3. Add and modify a behavior.
4. Open a movie with a behavior.
5. Create a dropdown list with a behavior.
6. Add keyboard navigation with a behavior.
7. Change text to speech with a behavior.

301

LESSON 5

APPLY COLOR EFFECTS TO A BITMAP

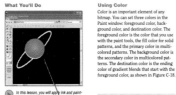

What You'll Do

In this lesson, you will apply ink and painting effects to a bitmap.

Using Color

Color is an important element of any bitmap. You can set three colors in the Paint window: foreground color, background color, and destination color. The foreground color is the color that you use with the paint tools, the fill color for solid patterns, and the primary color in multi-colored patterns. The background color is the secondary color in multicolored patterns. The destination color is the ending color of gradient blends that start with the foreground color, as shown in Figure C-18.

Applying Ink Effects

You can use Paint window inks to create color effects for bitmap cast members. You can select an ink effect from the Ink pop-up menu at the bottom of the Paint window, as shown in Figure C-18. The result of the ink you choose depends on if you are working in color or black and white. In addition, some inks work better when painting with patterns, and others work better when painting with solid colors. For example, the Transparent ink effect works best with patterns in black

Selecting colors with the Eyedropper tool

The Eyedropper tool is commonly used with a paint tool; it selects a color from the artwork, which you can then use as the foreground, background, or destination color. To select a color as the foreground, click the Eyedropper tool on the Tool palette, position the bottom tip of the eyedropper pointer over the color you want to select, then click the color. To use the eyedropper pointer to select a background color, press [Shift], then click a color. To select a color as the destination color, press [Alt] (Win) or [option] (Mac), then click a color. After you select a color, you can

96

Creating Graphical Cast Members Unit C

What You'll Do

A What You'll Do figure begins every lesson. This figure gives you an at-a-glance look at the skills covered in the unit and shows you the completed data file for that lesson. Before you start the lesson, you will know—both on a technical and artistic level—what you will be creating.

iv

Comprehensive Conceptual Lessons

Before jumping into instructions, in-depth conceptual information tells you "why" skills are applied. This book provides the "how" and "why" through the use of professional examples. Also included in the text are tips and sidebars to help you work more efficiently and creatively, or to teach you a bit about the history behind the skill you are using.

Step-by-Step Instructions

This book combines in-depth conceptual information with concise steps to help you learn Director MX. Each set of steps guides you through a lesson where you will apply tasks to a Director MX data file. Step references to large colorful images and quick step summaries round out the lessons.

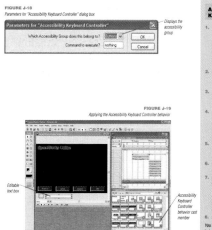

FIGURE J-18
Parameters for "Accessibility Keyboard Controller" dialog box

Displays the accessibility group

FIGURE J-19
Applying the Accessibility Keyboard Controller behavior

Editable text box

Accessibility Keyboard Controller behavior cast member

Lesson 6   Add Keyboard Navigation With a Behavior

321

Apply the Accessibility Keyboard Controller behavior

1. Click frame 1 in channel 21 in the Score, click the Text tool on the Tool palette, drag to create a text box in the gray area at the bottom next to the rectangle sprite, as shown in Figure J-19, name the text sprite **Keyboard Controller**, then extend the text sprite to frame 70 in the Score. A

2. Expand the docking channel (Win) or open the grouped panel (Mac) with the Property inspector.

3. Select the Keyboard Controller sprite if necessary, click the Text tab in the Property inspector, then select the Editable check box.

4. Drag the Accessibility Keyboard Controller behavior from the Library palette onto the text sprite off the Stage to open the Parameters for "Accessibility Keyboard Controller" dialog box.

5. Click the Which Accessibility Group does this belong to? list arrow , then click Buttons if necessary, as shown in Figure J-18.

6. Click OK to attach the behavior to the sprite and place the behavior in the Cast window .

7. Minimize the docking channel (Win) or close the grouped panel (Mac) with the Property inspector.

The Accessibility Keyboard Controller behavior appears in the Cast window , as shown in Figure J-19.

8. Save your work.

You applied the Accessibility Keyboard Controller behavior to a text sprite.

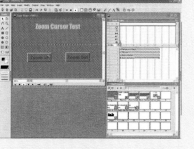

PROJECT BUILDER 1

You are a freelance computer programmer and want to create a game in Director that allows the user to zoom in and zoom out of the current scene. You are at the beginning stages of development and want to test the Change Cursor behavior with the two different zoom cursors. You use Director to change the cursor to the Zoom In or Zoom Out cursor.

1. Start Director and save the movie as **Zoom**.

2. Create a text cast member with the text **Zoom Cursor Test** and drag it to the top of the Stage.

3. Using the Filled Rectangle tool on the Tool palette, draw a filled rectangle the size of the Stage to create a background.

4. In the Paint window, create a button cast member with the text **Zoom In**, then add the cast member to the Stage.

5. In the Paint window, create a button cast member with the text **Zoom Out**, then add the cast member to the Stage.

6. Attach a behavior to the Zoom In button on the Stage that changes the cursor to the Zoom In cursor.

7. Attach a behavior to the Zoom Out button on the Stage that changes the cursor to the Zoom Out cursor.

8. Attach a behavior to the filled rectangle on the Stage that restores the cursor.

9. Play the movie, click the Zoom In button, then compare your screen to Figure J-27.

FIGURE J-27
Completed Project Builder 1

10. Click the filled rectangle, click the Zoom Out button, then click the filled rectangle again.

11. Save the movie, then exit Director.

326

Attaching Behaviors   Unit J

Projects

This book contains a variety of end-of-unit materials for additional practice and reinforcement. The Skills Review contains hands-on practice exercises that mirror the progressive nature of the lesson material. The unit concludes with four projects: two Project Builders, one Design Project, and one Group Project. The Project Builders require you to apply the skills you've learned in the unit to create multimedia projects. Design Projects explore design principles, and let you use your knowledge of Director to create or modify Director projects. Group Projects encourage group activity as students use the resources of a team to create a multimedia project.

What Instructor Resources are Available with this Book?

The Instructor Resources CD-ROM is Course Technology's way of putting the resources and information needed to teach and learn effectively into your hands. All the resources are available for both Macintosh and Windows operating systems, and many of the resources can be downloaded from *www.course.com*.

Instructor's Manual

Available as an electronic file, the Instructor's Manual is quality-assurance tested and includes unit overviews and detailed lecture topics for each unit, with teaching tips. The Instructor's Manual is available on the Instructor Resources CD-ROM, or you can download it from *www.course.com*.

Syllabus

Prepare and customize your course easily using this sample course outline (available on the Instructor Resources CD-ROM).

PowerPoint Presentations

Each unit has a corresponding PowerPoint presentation that you can use in lectures, distribute to your students, or customize to suit your course.

Figure Files

Figure Files contain all the figures from the book in bitmap format. Use the figure files to create transparency masters or use them in a PowerPoint presentation.

Data Files for Students

To complete most of the units in this book, your students will need Data Files. Put them on a file server for students to copy. The Data Files are available on the Instructor Resources CD-ROM, the Review Pack, and can also be downloaded from *www.course.com*. Instruct students to use the Data Files List at the end of this book. This list gives instructions on copying and organizing files.

Solutions to Exercises

Solution Files are Data Files completed with comprehensive sample answers. Use these files to evaluate your students' work. Or, distribute them electronically or in hard copy so students can verify their work. Sample solutions to all lessons and end-of-unit material are provided.

Test Bank and Test Engine

ExamView is a powerful testing software package that allows instructors to create and administer printed, computer (LAN-based), and Internet exams. ExamView includes hundreds of questions that correspond to the topics covered in this text, enabling students to generate detailed study guides that include page references for further review. The computer-based and Internet testing components allow students to take exams at their computers, and also save the instructor time by grading each exam automatically.

Additional Activities for Students

We have included **Macromedia Fundamentals** interactive training tutorials to help students learn the basics of each of the applications in Macromedia Studio MX.

BRIEF CONTENTS

BRIEF CONTENTS

UNIT A — GETTING STARTED WITH MACROMEDIA DIRECTOR MX

UNIT B — CREATING A MOVIE

UNIT H   ADDING AUDIO, VIDEO, AND OTHER MEDIA

UNIT I   MANAGING COLOR

Intended Audience

This text is designed for the beginner or intermediate student who wants to learn how to use Director MX. The book is designed to provide basic and in-depth material that not only educates, but also encourages the student to explore the nuances of this exciting program.

Approach

The text allows you to work at your own pace through step-by-step tutorials. A concept is presented and the process is explained, followed by the actual steps. To learn the most from the use of the text, you should adopt the following habits:

- Make sure you understand the skill being taught in each step before you move on to the next step.
- After finishing a skill, ask yourself if you could do it on your own, without referring to the steps. If the answer is no, review the steps.

Icons, Buttons, and Pointers

Symbols for icons, buttons, and pointers are shown in the step each time they are used.

Creating a Portfolio

The Group Project and the Project Builders allow students to use their knowledge and creativity to create interactive multimedia software. You might suggest that students create a portfolio in which they can store their work.

Director Settings

Each time you start Director, the program remembers previous settings, such as program preferences, open or closed windows, and Control Panel options, to name a few. When you start Director, your initial screen might look different than the ones in the book. For purposes of this book, make sure the following settings in Director are in place before you start each unit:

- Toolbar and Tool Palette are turned on from the Window menu.
- Stage, Score, Cast window, and Property inspector are turned on from the Window menu.
- Cast window is set to Thumbnail view; click the Cast View Style button in the Cast window if necessary.
- Loop Playback is turned off on the Control Panel.
- Tempo Mode and Actual Tempo Mode are set to fps (frames per second) on the Control Panel.
- Show Info is turned off on the Sprite Overlay submenu from the View menu.

- The Snap To check boxes are deselected in the Guides and Grid sections on the Guides tab in the Property inspector.
- The Visible check box is selected in the Guides section and deselected in the Grid section on the Guides tab in the Property inspector.

Director for Windows and Macintosh

This book is written for the Windows version and the Macintosh version of Macromedia Director MX. Both versions of the software are virtually the same, but there are a few platform differences. When there are differences between the two versions of the software, steps written specifically for the Windows version end with the notation (Win) and steps for the Macintosh version end with the notation (Mac). In some instances, lessons are split between the two operating systems.

Director for Windows 98

For Units J, K, and M, the Data and Solution Files use new speech-to-text features in Director MX. These features take advantage of the speech technologies in Windows 2000 and Windows XP, or later. If you are using Windows 98 or Windows Me, you might receive script errors when you run the Data and Solution Files for the units.

Fonts

Whenever fonts are used in Data Files, they are chosen from a set of common typefaces that you will most likely have available on your computer. If any of the fonts in use are not available on your computer, please make a substitution. In the Solution Files, we have used non-standard typefaces; however, we have embedded those fonts in the Director movie, so they appear on the screen.

QuickTime Player

To play QuickTime movies in Director, you need to install the QuickTime player on your computer. The QuickTime player is a software product developed by Apple Computer, Inc. for Macintosh and Windows computers. You can download the latest version of the QuickTime player for free and QuickTime Pro (a combination movie creator, editor, and player) for a price, from the Apple Computer Web site at *www.apple.com/quicktime*. Follow the instructions on the Web site to download and install the software.

UNIT

GETTING STARTED WITH
MACROMEDIA DIRECTOR MX

1. Showcase Director.

2. Start Director.

3. Examine the Director windows.

4. Open and save a movie.

5. Work with panels.

6. Play a movie.

7. Find information using Director Help.

8. Close a movie and exit Director.

MACROMEDIA DIRECTOR MX

Learning About Director MX

Macromedia Director MX is a software program that allows you to create your own software. It's often referred to as an **authoring tool** or a **development platform**. In Director, you can use a combination of graphics, images, 3D models, digital video, sound, text, and animation, known as **multimedia**. Director includes user feedback and navigation, known as **interactivity**, to develop virtually any type of software you want to deliver. Thus, the term **interactive multimedia** is often applied to the software produced by Director. Using Director, you can create fully self-contained, self-running interactive multimedia software for distribution on CD-ROM or on the Web. For example, you can easily create animations, movies, interactive training, online learning, marketing and kiosk presentations, software prototypes, technical simulations, and multiuser games. Because Director is available in both Macintosh and Windows versions, it's relatively easy to produce software that runs on both platforms. Director operates virtually the same on both, except for a few keyboard commands that have equivalent functions. You use the [Ctrl] and [Alt] keys in Windows, and the [command] and [option] keys on a Macintosh computer.

Royalty-Free Distribution

All software created with Director can be freely sold and distributed without having to pay Macromedia a royalty for the privilege. That may be something you take for granted, but some development platforms actually have licensing agreements stipulating that you have to pay to market anything created with the product. Macromedia doesn't require you to pay any fees, but they do ask that you place a special "Made with Macromedia" logo, as shown in Tools You'll Use, on your software packaging. The logo is included with the data files that accompany this book.

Tools You'll Use

New		▶
Open...	Ctrl+O	
Close	Ctrl+F4	
Save	Ctrl+S	
Save As...		
Save and Compact		
Save All		
Revert		
Import...	Ctrl+R	
Export...	Ctrl+Shift+R	
Create Projector...		
Publish Settings...		
Publish	Ctrl+Shift+S	
Preview in Browser	F12	
Page Setup...	Ctrl+Shift+P	
Print...	Ctrl+P	
Send Mail...		
Recent Movies		▶
Recent Casts		▶
Exit	Alt+F4	

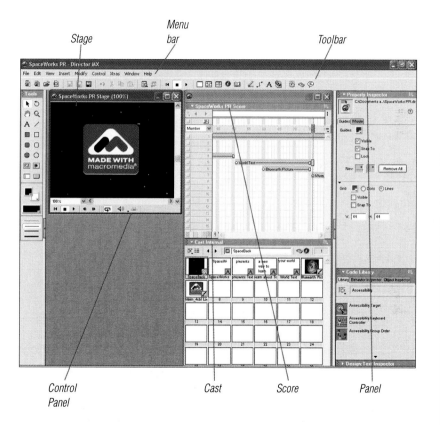

Menu bar

Stage

Toolbar

Control Panel

Cast

Score

Panel

SHOWCASE DIRECTOR

What You'll Do

In this lesson, you will view Director examples on the Web.

Showcasing Director on the Web

After you create and fine-tune multimedia content in Director, you can deliver it on the Web as Shockwave content. **Shockwave** content is a compressed Director file viewable within a browser with Shockwave Player. **Shockwave Player** is a software product developed by Macromedia for browsers on the Macintosh and Windows platforms. To play Shockwave content within a browser, you need to install Shockwave Player on your computer. Shockwave Player is free, easily accessible, and widely distributed over the Web. You can download the latest version from the Macromedia Web site at *www.macromedia.com*. Shockwave Player installs as a shared system component and includes an automatic updating feature. Over 300 million users have Shockwave Player installed, and approximately 200,000 users install it daily.

Learning from Examples

The best way to learn about Director is to view examples of Shockwave content on the Web. These examples can give you ideas on how you can create Shockwave content with Director. Macromedia provides two Web sites that show off Shockwave's many multimedia multiuser features: the Macromedia showcase Web site (*www.macromedia.com*) and the Shockwave Web site (*www.shockwave.com*). The Macromedia showcase Web site displays descriptions and links to Web sites with Shockwave content, and the Shockwave Web site displays Shockwave examples of 2D and 3D games, animation, music, and MP3 audio.

FIGURE A-1

Macromedia's Director showcase Web page

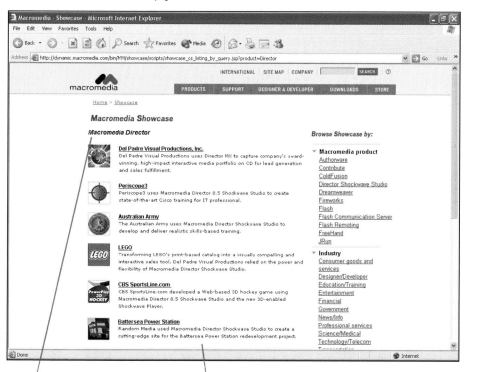

Macromedia
Director showcase

Your Web page
might differ

1. Start your browser.

2. Go to the Macromedia showcase Web site at *www.macromedia.com/showcase*.

3. Browse case studies by Director (click Macromedia Products, then click Director), as shown in Figure A-1.

   > TIP   Web sites change, so your links might differ.

4. Explore and view the case study examples.

5. Go to the Shockwave Web site at *www.shockwave.com*.

6. Explore and view the examples.

7. Close your browser.

You viewed Director examples on the Web.

Understanding the difference between Macromedia Flash and Shockwave Players

Like Shockwave Player, Flash Player is a free Web player from Macromedia; both players display rich multimedia content on the Web, and each player has a distinct purpose. Shockwave Player displays multimedia Web content, such as interactive product training and demonstrations, e-commerce programs, music, multiuser games, and communication, developed in Director. Flash Player displays fast-loading high-impact Web animation, such as advertising and promotion, developed in Macromedia Flash. By installing both players, you can ensure that you can display the widest variety of animated and interactive Web content.

START DIRECTOR

What You'll Do

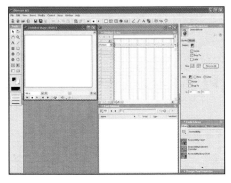

In this lesson, you will start Director for Windows or Macintosh, depending on the platform you are using.

Starting Director

You can start Director in several ways, depending on the platform you are using. When you start Director, the computer displays a splash screen and then the Director window. The first time you start Director, a Welcome to Director window appears, displaying tutorial options to help you get started. Director displays a set of blank windows and panels ready for you to create a new file, which is a collection of information stored together as an individual unit. A file in Director is called a movie.

Starting Director and Opening a Movie

You can also start Director and open a movie at the same time. Simply double-click the Director file icon in Windows Explorer or My Computer (Win) or in a Macintosh folder (Mac). You can identify a Director movie by the file icon or .dir file

Displaying file extensions

If you do not see file extensions in Windows or Macintosh, your system is set to hide them. For Windows, you can show them by performing the following steps: open My Computer, click View or Tools on the menu bar, click Folder Options, click the View tab, deselect the Hide file extensions for known file types check box in the Advanced settings list box, then click OK. For Mac OS 10 or later, you can show file extensions by performing the following steps: view the Finder, click Finder on the menu bar, click Preferences, select the Always show file extensions check box, then click the Close button.

extension. A **file extension** is a three-letter suffix at the end of a filename that identifies the file type for the operating system, as shown in Figure A-2. Macintosh doesn't need to use file extensions, but added the feature to promote cross-platform use. In the Mac Operating System (OS) 10 or later, you have the option to show or hide file extensions. When you are working on both platforms, using file extensions on Macintosh allows Windows and Director to recognize and open the files.

FIGURE A-2

Showing file extensions for Windows and Macintosh

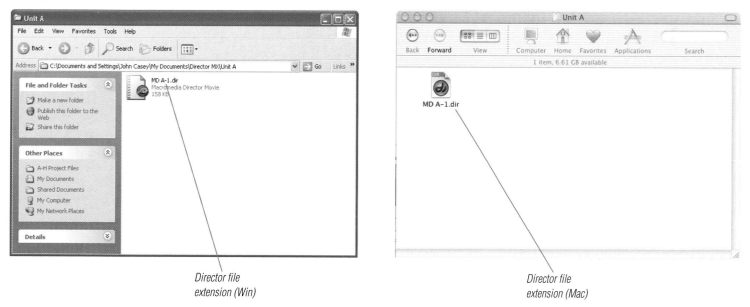

Director file
extension (Win)

Director file
extension (Mac)

Start Director (Windows)

1. Click the Start button on the taskbar.
   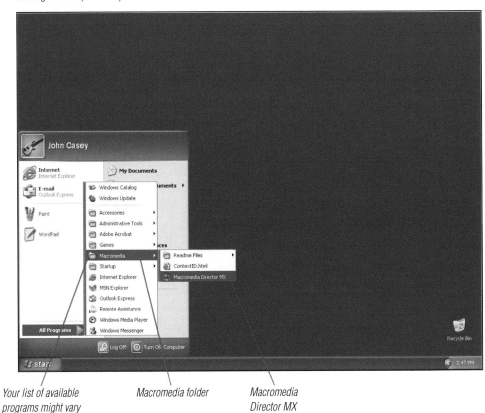 **start**

2. Point to All Programs or Programs, then point to Macromedia.

3. Click Macromedia Director MX, as shown in Figure A-3.

   Director opens, displaying the workspace for a new file.

4. If the Welcome to Director window appears, click the Close button.

   | TIP To open the Welcome to Director window later, click Help on the menu bar, then click Welcome.

You started Director for Windows.

FIGURE A-3
Starting Director (Windows)

Your list of available programs might vary *Macromedia folder* *Macromedia Director MX*

FIGURE A-4

Starting Director (Macintosh)

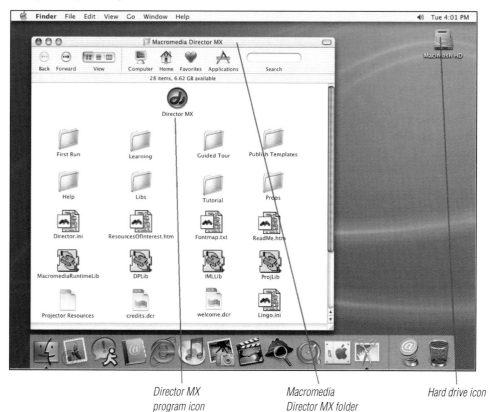

Director MX
program icon

Macromedia
Director MX folder

Hard drive icon

1. Double-click the hard drive icon.

2. Double-click the Macromedia Director MX folder.

3. Double-click the Director MX program icon shown in Figure A-4.

   Director opens, displaying the workspace for a new file.

4. If the Welcome to Director window appears, click the Close button.

   > TIP   To open the Welcome to Director window later, click Help on the menu bar, then click Welcome.

You started Director for Macintosh.

EXAMINE THE DIRECTOR WINDOWS

What You'll Do

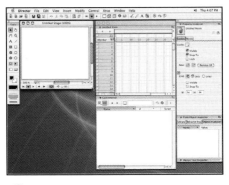

In this lesson, you will close, open, resize, and move windows.

Identifying Elements of the Director Window

When you start Director, four main windows of varying sizes appear in the Director (or program) window: the Stage, the Score, the Cast, and the Property inspector. Depending on your installation and previous program usage, not all of these windows may appear, or additional ones may be visible. You'll do the bulk of your work in Director with these four windows.

In Director, windows appear in the workspace with a title bar, such as the Stage window, or in a panel. A **panel** is a window you can collapse, expand, and group with other panels, known as a **panel group**, to improve accessibility and workflow. A panel appears with a shaded header bar, which includes the window title and additional accessibility options. A panel group

consists of either individual panels stacked one on top of the other, such as the Score and Cast, or related panels organized together with tabs, such as the Code and Design panels, to navigate from one panel to another. Refer to your screen and Figure A-5 as you locate the main elements of the Director window described below. The size and location of your windows might differ.

The Director window **title bar** displays the filename of the open file and the program name, Director MX. The title bar also contains a Close button and resizing buttons.

A **menu** is a list of commands that you use to accomplish specific tasks. You've already used the Start menu to open Director. A **command** is a directive that accesses a feature of a program. Director has its own set of menus, which are located on the **menu bar** along the top of the Director window. On a menu, a **check mark** identifies a feature that is currently selected (that is, the feature is enabled or on). To disable (turn off) the feature, you click the command again to remove the check mark. A menu can contain several check-marked features. A **bullet** (Win) or **diamond** (Mac) also indicates that an option is enabled, but a menu can contain only one bullet-or diamond-marked feature per menu section. To disable a command with a bullet or diamond next to it, you must select a different option in the section on the menu.

When you perform a command frequently, it's faster and sometimes more convenient to use a **shortcut key**, which is a keyboard alternative to using the mouse. When a shortcut key is available, it is listed beside the command on the menu, such as Ctrl+1 (Win) or [command]+3 (Mac) for the Stage command on the Window menu.

The **toolbar** contains buttons for the most frequently used commands. Clicking a button on a toolbar is often faster than clicking a menu and then clicking a command. When you position the pointer over a button, a **tooltip** appears, displaying the button name.

The **Tool palette** contains a set of tools you can use to create shapes, such as lines, rectangles, rounded rectangles, and ellipses, and to create simple buttons, such as radio, check box, and command buttons. You can fill shapes with a color, pattern, or custom tile. The shapes and buttons you create in Director are saved as media elements in the Cast window.

The **Stage** is the visible portion of a movie, on which you determine where your media elements appear. The Stage window title bar displays the movie name and the zoom factor. When you start Director or create a new movie, the default values are Untitled

FIGURE A-5
Director window

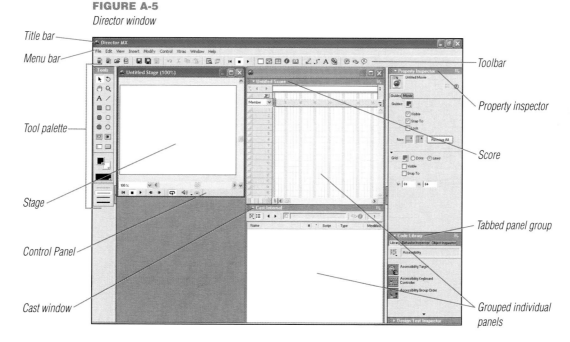

Lesson 3   Examine the Director Windows

Stage (100%). You can define the properties of your Stage, such as its size and color. At the bottom of the Stage window is the **Control Panel**, which provides DVD-type control over the playback of your movie, including Rewind, Stop, and Play buttons. You can also modify volume and playback settings.

The **Cast window** is the storage area that contains your media elements, such as graphics, images, digital videos, sounds, animations, text, color palettes, film loops, and scripts. The media elements in the Cast window are called **cast members**. In the Cast window, you can view your cast members as a list or as **thumbnails**, or small images. You can create your own cast members, and you can import existing media to include in your cast. You can also open or create casts to organize sets of cast members. When you open Director with a new movie, the Cast window is called **Internal Cast**.

The **Score** organizes and controls media elements over a linear timeline in rows called **channels** and in columns called **frames**. The Score displays a movie's time-line and monitors the playback frame by frame. A frame represents a single point in a movie. The Score includes special channels that control the movie's tempo, sound, transitions, and color palettes.

The **Property inspector** provides a convenient way to view and change attributes of any selected object or multiple objects, such as cast members on the Stage, in your movie. After you select an object, relevant category tabs and associated fields for it appear in the Property inspector. Below the Property inspector are the **Code** and **Design** tabbed panel groups, predefined sets of related tools, which allow you to view additional object properties, add and create programming-related functionality, and change text formatting and align objects directly on the Stage.

Working with Director Windows

As you work with Director windows, sometimes it is necessary to change the size of a window, move it to a different location, or close it altogether. Each window is surrounded by a standard border that you can drag to change the size of the window. Each window has one or more buttons in the upper-right corner that allow you to close or change a window's size. The Maximize button (Win) or Zoom button (Mac) resizes the window to take up the available screen. When a window is maximized, the Restore Down button (Win) appears so you can return a window to its previous size. To open and close a window, you can use buttons on the toolbar (such as the Stage button), the Window menu, or shortcut keys. To close a window, you can also use the Close button on the title bar. When you close a window, you can open the window again at any time. When you reopen a window, it appears in the same position in which it was last closed.

FIGURE A-6
Window menu for Windows and Macintosh

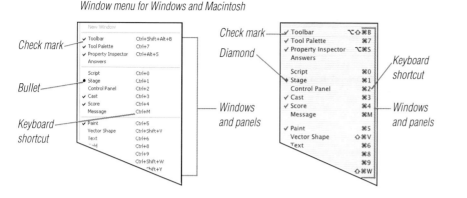

Check mark

Bullet

Keyboard
shortcut

Check mark

Diamond

Keyboard
shortcut

Windows
and panels

Windows
and panels

FIGURE A-7
Resizing a window (Macintosh)

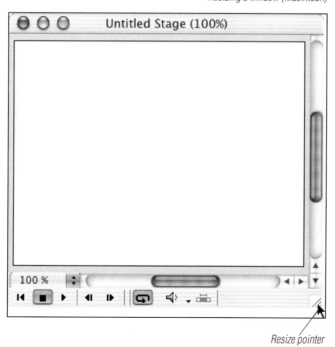

Resize pointer

Close and open a window

1. Click the Stage title bar to select it, if necessary.

2. Click Window on the menu bar.

3. On the Window menu, as shown in Figure A-6, click Stage to close the window.

4. On the toolbar, point to the Stage button to display a tooltip. □

5. Click the Stage button on the toolbar to open the window.

   TIP To quickly close a window, click the Close button.

You closed and opened the Stage window.

Resize and move a window

1. Position the pointer on the bottom-right corner of the Stage window, then drag the border to the right to expand the window, as shown in Figure A-7. (Win) (Mac)

   TIP To maximize a window, click the Maximize button (Win) or the Zoom button (Mac).

2. Position the pointer on the Stage window title bar, then drag the title bar to an empty area of the Director window.

You resized and moved a window.

OPEN AND SAVE A MOVIE

What You'll Do

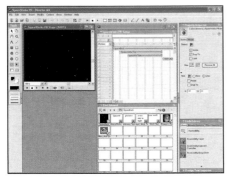

 In this lesson, you will open a movie file and save it with a new name.

Opening and Saving Files

A movie is the product you create using Director. When you start Director, the program displays a set of blank windows. You can insert new information to create a new movie and save it as a file, or you can open an existing movie and save the file with any changes. You can use the Open button on the toolbar or the Open command on the File menu, as shown in Figure A-8, to open movies created in Director MX or 8. If you have movies from earlier versions of Director (5, 6, or 7), you use the Update Movies command on the Xtras menu. If you recently opened a movie, you can use the Recent Movies command on the File menu to instantly locate and open a movie.

The first time you save a new movie, you need to give it a name and specify where you want to store it. After that, Director automatically updates the file in that location each time you save it. You can save

Multiple Save commands

In addition to the typical Save and Save As commands you already learned about in this lesson, the File menu and the Director toolbar include other Save commands. For example, you use the Save and Compact command on the File menu to save and compress the size of a movie file before you publish it. The Save All command on the File menu and button on the Director toolbar saves the movie file and all open external cast files linked to the movie. **External cast files** allow you to store and manage media in separate locations for use in multiple movies.

files to a hard disk, a removable disk, or a network drive. Windows and Macintosh let you save files using names that have up to 255 characters, including spaces. When you open or save a file, its name appears on the Director window's title bar.

When you save a movie with Director, the .dir file extension is automatically added to the filename, even if the system doesn't show it. For Windows, this functionality is standard. However, for Macintosh, this functionality is new with Mac OS 10 or later. The addition of the .dir file extension on Director files for Macintosh makes it easier to open the same files on Director for Windows. When you transfer a Macintosh Director file with the .dir file extension to a PC, Windows and Director recognize the file type as a Director file. Without the extension, Windows and Director can't open the Macintosh Director file.

Using Save versus Save As

You use the Save command to save the changes you make to an open movie and the Save As command to name an untitled movie or to save an existing movie with a new name. Sometimes it's more efficient to create a new movie by modifying an existing one or prevent any accidental changes to the original movie by saving it with a new name. The Save As command on the File menu, as shown in Figure A-8, makes a copy of the movie, so you can make changes to the new movie and leave the original file unaltered. For example, throughout this book, you will be instructed to open a file from a drive and folder where your data files are stored and use the Save As command to create a copy of the file with a new name. Saving the files with new names keeps your original data files intact, in case you need to start the lesson over or want to repeat an exercise.

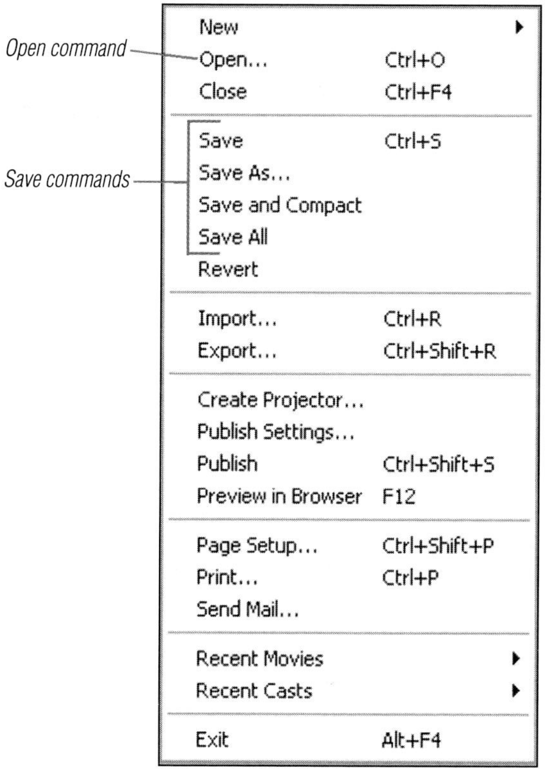

FIGURE A-8
File menu with Open and Save commands

Open a movie file

1. Click the Open button on the toolbar.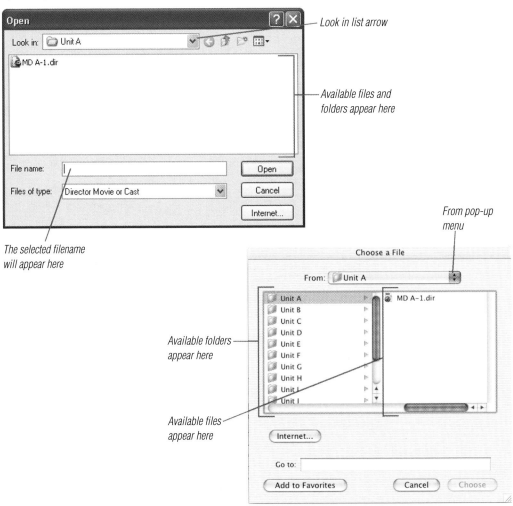

   TIP To open Director 5, 6, and 7 movies, click Xtras on the menu bar, click Update Movies, select one of the Action options, select one of the Original Files options, click OK, select the movies and casts you want to update, then click Update.

2. Click the Look in list arrow (Win) or From pop-up menu (Mac), shown in Figure A-9, then navigate to the location where your Unit A data files are stored.

3. In the file list, click MD A-1.dir.

4. Click Open (Win) or Choose (Mac).

5. If asked to save your work, click No (Win) or Don't Save (Mac).

You opened a movie file.

FIGURE A-9

Open dialog box for Windows and Macintosh

Look in list arrow

Available files and folders appear here

The selected filename will appear here

From pop-up menu

Available folders appear here

Available files appear here

Save Movie dialog box

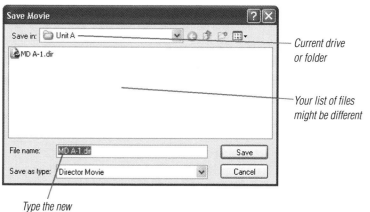

Current drive
or folder

Your list of files
might be different

Type the new
filename here

FIGURE A-11
Movie with a new filename

New filename

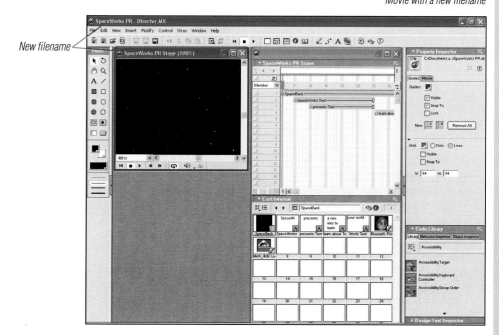

Save a movie file

1. Click File on the menu bar, then click Save As.

   TIP To quickly save a movie, click the Save button on the toolbar. ⊟

2. If the drive containing your data files is not displayed in the Save Movie dialog box, click the Save in list arrow (Win) or Where pop-up menu (Mac), then navigate to the location where your Unit A data files are stored.

3. Select the current filename in the File name text box, shown in Figure A-10, if necessary, then type **SpaceWorks PR** as the new filename.

4. Click Save, then compare your screen to Figure A-11.

   TIP To open the last saved version of your current movie, click File on the menu bar, then click Revert.

You saved a movie file with a new name.

WORK WITH PANELS

What You'll Do

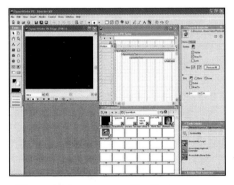

In this lesson, you will collapse, expand, undock, dock, group, and ungroup panels, and save, switch, and delete a panel layout.

Working with Panels

In Director you work with several windows at one time. Instead of continually moving, resizing, or opening and closing windows, you can collapse or expand individual panels within a window with a single click to save space. You can also group panels together to improve organization and workflow. Director includes two types of panels: document panels and tool panels. Panels related to a movie, such as the Score and Cast, are called **document panels**. Panels related to tools and options settings, such as the Tool palette and Property inspector, are called **tool panels**. A panel appears with a header bar, which includes the window title and three accessibility options: the panel gripper, the expander arrow, and an Options menu, as shown in Figure A-12. You use the panel gripper to group or ungroup and dock or undock panel windows. You use the expander arrow to collapse or expand panels. The Options menu provides you with commands to group, rename, maximize, and close a panel, and use the Help system. When you group panels together, you can stack one on top of the other, such as the Score and Cast panels in Figure A-12, or group related panels together as a tabbed panel group, such as the Code and Design panels.

Docking and Undocking Panels

You can dock and undock, or temporarily attach and detach, panels or panel groups in docking channels. A **docking channel** is a region located on the left and right side of the Director window, as shown in Figure A-13, to which you can temporarily attach and detach panels. You can only dock tool panels in a docking channel. Document panels and the Stage cannot be docked to a docking channel. When you drag a panel over a dockable area, an outline around the target dock appears. When you release the mouse button, the panel snaps to the dockable area and stays there until you move it. If you attempt to dock a panel over an undockable area, no outline appears. When a docking channel doesn't have any panels, the channel disappears until it is needed again.

Minimizing a Docking Channel

If you use Windows and need more workspace, you can use the Drawer button on the **channel separator bar** (a thin line along the edge of a docking channel) to quickly minimize a docking channel, as shown in Figure A-13. When you click the Drawer button, the docking channel collapses to increase the size of the workspace. When you click the Drawer button again, the docking channel reopens. If you need to increase or decrease the size of a docking channel, you can drag the channel separator bar to resize the docking channel as you would any window.

Saving and Switching Panel Layouts

As you work with Director, you'll open, close, and move around windows and panels to meet your individual needs. After you customize the Director workspace, you can save the location of windows and panels as a custom panel layout set, which you can display using the Panel Sets command on the Window menu. You can create custom panel sets, or use the default panel set provided by Director. If you no longer use a custom panel set, you can remove it at any time.

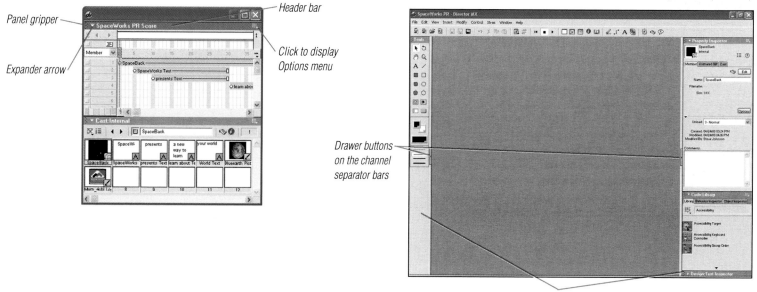

FIGURE A-12
Individual panels in a group

Panel gripper

Expander arrow

Header bar

Click to display Options menu

Drawer buttons on the channel separator bars

FIGURE A-13
Docking channels (Windows)

Docking channels with panels

Collapse and expand a panel

1. Click the expander arrow or window title on the header bar of the Score panel.

   The Score panel collapses down to the header bar, as shown in Figure A-14.

2. Click the expander arrow or window title on the header bar of the Score panel again.

   TIP   To hide and show all panels, click Window on the menu bar, then click Hide Panels or Show Panels.

You collapsed and expanded the Score panel.

FIGURE A-14

Collapsed Score panel

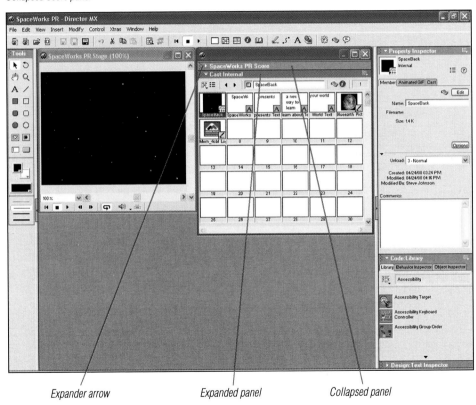

Expander arrow   Expanded panel   Collapsed panel

FIGURE A-15

Undocking a panel

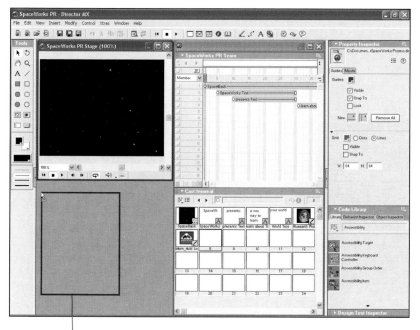

Outline of panel

FIGURE A-16

Undocked panel

Undocked panel in
a separate window

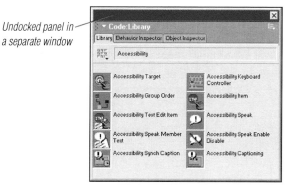

Undock and dock a panel

1. Position the pointer (which changes to a four-headed arrow ✛ [Win] or 🖑 [Mac]) on the panel gripper in the Code panel.

2. Drag the window away from the panel (an outline of the panel appears as you drag) to an empty area of the Director window, as shown in Figure A-15.

3. Release the mouse button, then resize the window, if necessary.

   The panel appears undocked in its own window with a title bar, as shown in Figure A-16.

4. Position the pointer on the panel gripper in the Code panel, and then drag the panel to the right channel (at the bottom of the Property inspector) until a thick black border appears around the channel.

5. Release the mouse button to dock the panel.

You undocked and docked the Code panel.

Ungroup and group a panel

1. Position the pointer on the panel gripper in the Cast panel. ✛ (Win) or 🖐 (Mac)

2. Drag the Cast panel (which changes to an outline of the panel) to an empty area of the Director window.

3. Release the mouse button.

   The panel windows appear ungrouped, as shown in Figure A-17.

4. Position the pointer on the panel gripper in the Cast panel. ✛ (Win) or 🖐 (Mac)

5. Drag the Cast panel (which changes to an outline of the panel) onto the lower area of the Score panel so that a thick, black line appears, which indicates the location of the panel.

6. Release the mouse button to group the panels.

   > TIP To move a panel within a group, drag the panel gripper (which changes to a thick black bar) to a new location in the panel window.

You ungrouped and grouped the Cast panel.

FIGURE A-17
Ungrouped panels

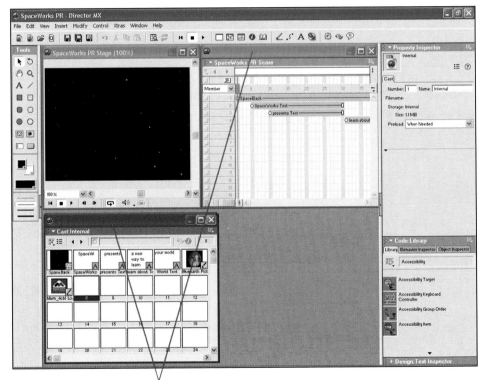

Ungrouped panels in separate windows

Switching between panel sets

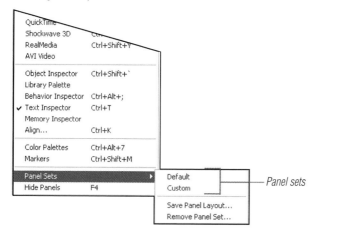

— *Panel sets*

Default panel set

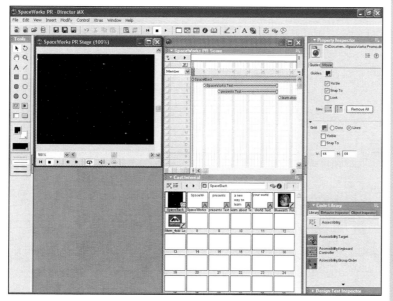

Save, switch, and delete a panel layout

1. Click the expander arrow in the Design panel to expand it.

2. Click Window on the menu bar, point to Panel Sets, then click Save Panel Layout to open the Save Panel Set dialog box.

3. In the Name text box, type **Custom**, then click OK.

4. Click Window on the menu bar, then point to Panel Sets, as shown in Figure A-18.

5. Click Default, then compare your screen to Figure A-19.

6. Click Window on the menu bar, point to Panel Sets, then click Remove Panel Set to open the Remove Panel Set dialog box.

7. Click the Panel Set list arrow, click Custom (if necessary), then click Remove.

You saved, switched, and deleted a panel layout.

PLAY A MOVIE

What You'll Do

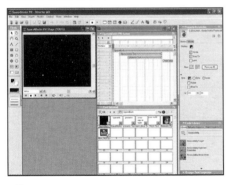

In this lesson, you will play a movie.

Viewing the Score

While the movie is displayed on the Stage, the Cast window stores the media elements, or cast members that play in the movie. You use the Score to instruct the cast members where to appear on the Stage, what to do, and where to exit, as shown in Figure A-20. The Score resembles a spreadsheet with lots of individual cells divided into rows and columns. The rows are used as channels; the columns are used as frames. A **channel** stores and controls the playback of cast members on the Stage. Each column has a number associated with it; they are marked off in shaded, five-column intervals, and each channel begins with either a number or a distinctive icon. When you first view the Score, all the channels might not be visible. The upper channels are called the **effects channels,**

FIGURE A-20

Cast, Score, and Stage interaction

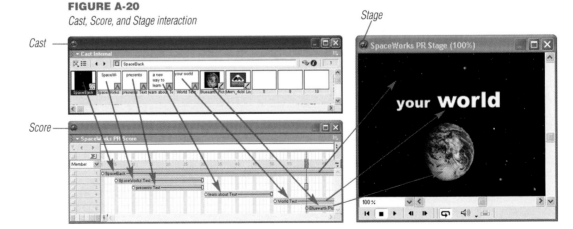

which control the movie speed, color, audio, and transition effects. You can display and hide the effects channels using the Hide/Show Effects Channels arrows on the right side of the panel.

Describing Channel Types

The Score contains seven channel types, each designed to hold different types of data. Refer to your screen and Figure A-21

as you locate the channels in the Score panel described below.

- The **tempo channel** allows you to adjust the speed or time of a movie as it plays. The tempo determines how many frames per second are displayed in a movie.
- The **palette channel** allows you to set the available colors for a movie.

- The **transition channel** allows you to set screen transitions, such as fades, wipes, dissolves, and zooms.
- The two **sound channels** allow you to add music, sound effects, and voice-overs.
- The **behavior channel**, or **script channel**, provides a place to write frame scripts. **Frame scripts** provide one way to add interactivity and extended functionality to a movie.

FIGURE A-21
Score window

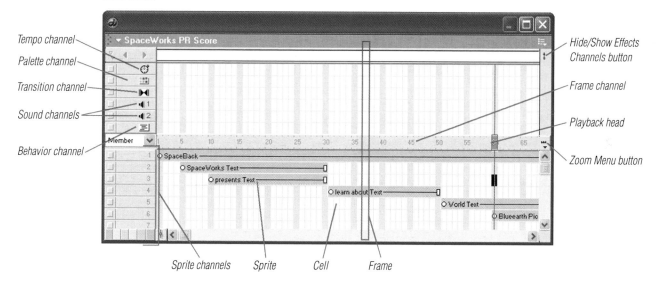

- The **frame channel**, or **timeline**, is the shaded area that contains the numbers 5, 10, 15, 20, and so on. These numbers identify the frame number. An individual frame represents a single point in a movie.
- The **sprite channels** are numbered channels at the bottom of the Score panel. You use these channels to assemble and synchronize all the cast members in the Cast panel. A **sprite** is a representation of a cast member that has been placed on the Stage or in the Score. Director provides 1000 available sprite channels.

Playing a Movie

The Control Panel gives you control over the playback of your movie and displays important information about your movie's performance. You can use the buttons on the Control Panel at the bottom of the Stage to play a movie or to adjust the volume. An expanded Control Panel with additional buttons is also available to monitor the speed, or **tempo**, at which a movie plays. As you play your movie, the playback head automatically moves through your Score. The **playback head** moves through the Score to show the frame currently displayed on the Stage. A frame in the Score represents a single point in a movie, much like a frame in a traditional celluloid film. You can click any frame in the Score to move the playback head to that frame, and you can drag the playback head backward or forward through frames.

As Director plays a movie, the playback head moves from left to right across the frame channel in the Score according to the current tempo setting, which is set to the number of frames displayed per second (fps) or the number of seconds displayed per frame (spf). As the playback head enters a frame, Director draws the sprites that it finds in the sprite channels for that frame. When the playback head moves to another frame, Director redraws the Stage with the sprites in the frame it enters. When sprites change or move from frame to frame, animation effects are created. When drawing each frame on the Stage, Director draws the contents of each sprite channel starting with channel 1 at the top of the Score and continuing down the channel list. As Director draws, it overdraws any sprites on the lower-numbered channels wherever they might overlap. As a result, the highest-numbered sprite will always be visible, and the lower-numbered sprites will be visible only if no higher-numbered sprite appears at the same location. For this reason, the background image is usually kept in sprite channel 1, the lowest-numbered sprite.

Step Backward
and Step Forward
buttons

Rewind   Stop   Play
button   button   button

FIGURE A-23

Positioning the playback head

Playback head
at frame 1

Play a movie

1. Click the Play button on the Control
   Panel. ▶

   TIP You can also access many of the
   same commands on the Control Panel using
   the Control menu.

2. Before the end of the movie, click the Stop
   button on the Control Panel, as shown in
   Figure A-22. ■

3. Click Window on the menu bar, then click
   Control Panel to display a detached
   Control Panel.

4. Click the Rewind button on the Control
   Panel. ◀

5. Click the Step Forward button on the Control
   Panel 10 times. ▶

6. Click the Step Backward button on the
   Control Panel 6 times. ◀

7. Click number 1 on the frame channel in
   the Score.

   TIP To go to a specific frame number,
   you can also enter a number in the frame
   counter on the expanded Control Panel.

8. Click Window on the menu bar, then click
   Control Panel to close the detached
   Control Panel.

9. Compare your screen to Figure A-23, then
   save your work.

You played a movie using Control Panel buttons.

FIND INFORMATION USING DIRECTOR HELP

What You'll Do

▶ In this lesson, you will find information using Director Help.

Finding Information Using Help

Director features an extensive Help system that you can use to access definitions, explanations, and useful tips. The Help system information is displayed in a separate window, as shown in Figure A-24. You can resize the Help window and set it to appear onscreen so you can refer to it as you work. The Help window for the Macintosh uses the standard Help system that comes with the operating system, which provides you with a list of topics, an index, and the Ask a Question search feature to help you find the information you need. The Help window for Windows has three tabs that you use to find information about Director commands and features: Contents, Index, and Search. The Contents tab provides you with a list of Help categories. Each book icon has several "chapters" (topics) that you can see by clicking the book icon or the name of the Help category next to the book. The Index tab provides you with an alphabetical list of all the Help topics that are available, much like an index at the end of a book. You can find out about any Director feature either by entering the topic in the text box, or by scrolling down to the topic for which you want help, selecting a topic, and then clicking Display. The Search tab allows you to enter keywords as your search criteria. When you select a topic using any of the three methods, information about that topic appears in the right pane of the Help window. When you find a topic that you may want to reference later, you can add the topic to a favorites list for easy access. The Favorites tab allows you to add, remove, and display your favorite help topics. While you are working in Director for Windows, you can also access **context-sensitive help** that specifically relates to what you are doing. For example, when you are working in a dialog box, you can click the Help button, and then click any item in the dialog box to get more information about the item.

FIGURE A-24

Director Help window (Windows and Macintosh)

Help tabs   Help toolbar

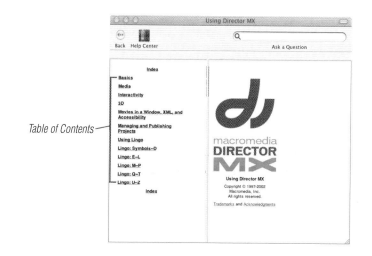

Table of Contents

Getting answers when you still have questions

When you are looking for more information about Director than the Help system provides, you can open the Answers panel to discover and access links to new resources, such as Director new features, release notes, and tutorials. To access the Answers panel, click Window on the menu bar, then click Answers. In the Answers panel, you can click the Update Panel button, as shown in Figure A-25, to get the latest Director information from the Macromedia Web site. You can also get additional information using the Director Support Center on the Web. The Director Support Center Web site contains the latest information on Director, plus additional topics, examples, tips, and updates, which explain how to get the most out of the program. Click Help on the menu bar, click Web Links, then click the Director Support Center Web site link. To find additional sites on the Web with Director information, you can use a search engine. Some of the links require a browser to display the information.

FIGURE A-25

Answers panel

View information in Help

1. Click Help on the menu bar, then click Director Help.

    TIP You can also open the Help window by pressing [F1] (Win only).

2. Click the Contents tab (Win only if necessary), then click the Basics category.

3. Click the Director Basics category, then click the Introducing the Director workspace subcategory (Win only).

4. Under the Introducing the Director workspace subcategory, click The Stage in the left pane (Win) or right pane (Mac), as shown in Figure A-26, to display the help topic.

5. Read the topic.

6. Click the Back button on the Help toolbar until you reach the Table of Contents (Mac only).

You opened Director Help and viewed a topic in Help Contents.

FIGURE A-26

Selecting a topic in Help Contents (Windows and Macintosh)

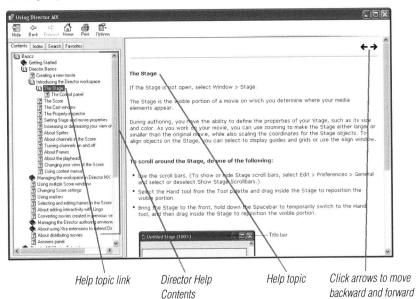

Help topic link   Director Help Contents   Help topic   Click arrows to move backward and forward

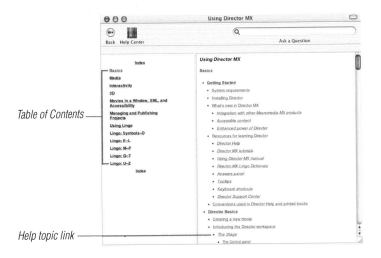

Table of Contents

Help topic link

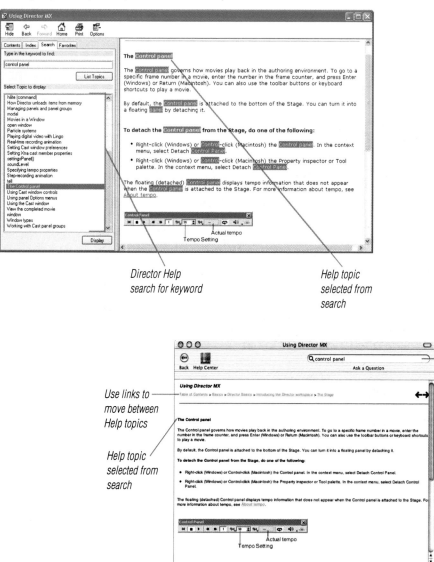

Director Help
search for keyword

Help topic
selected from
search

Use links to
move between
Help topics

Help topic
selected from
search

Ask a Question
text box

Find information using Help

1. Click the Index tab (Win) or Index (Mac) in the Help window.

2. Type **score** in the keyword text box (Win) or click S (Mac).

3. Under the Score index, click basics of, then click Display (Win only) to show the Help information.

4. Click the Search tab in the Help window (Win) or Ask a Question (Mac).

5. Type **control panel** in the search text box, then click List Topics (Win) or press [return] (Mac).

6. Double-click The Control panel in the results list, as shown in Figure A-27.

7. Read the topic.

   TIP   You can move back and forth between Help topics you have already visited by clicking the Back button and the Forward button (Win) on the Help toolbar.

8. Close the Help window when you are done reading the topic.

You searched for information in Director Help.

CLOSE A MOVIE AND EXIT DIRECTOR

What You'll Do

```
New                          ▶
Open...              Ctrl+O
Close                Ctrl+F4
─────────────────────────────
Save                 Ctrl+S
Save As...
Save and Compact
Save All
Revert
─────────────────────────────
Import...            Ctrl+R
Export...            Ctrl+Shift+R
─────────────────────────────
Create Projector...
Publish Settings...
Publish              Ctrl+Shift+S
Preview in Browser   F12
─────────────────────────────
Page Setup...        Ctrl+Shift+P
Print...             Ctrl+P
Send Mail...
─────────────────────────────
Recent Movies                ▶
Recent Casts                 ▶
─────────────────────────────
Exit                 Alt+F4
```

▶ *In this lesson, you will close a movie and exit Director.*

Closing versus Exiting

After you work on a movie, you can close the movie by creating a new movie, by opening an existing movie, or by exiting Director. You should save the movie before closing it. Creating a new movie or opening an existing movie closes the current movie and leaves the Director window open. Exiting Director closes the current movie and the Director program, and returns you to the desktop. You can use the Exit command on the File menu (Win) or the Quit command on the Director menu (Mac) to close a movie and exit Director, or you can use the Close button on the Director window title bar (Win). Unlike the Close command in other Windows programs, the Close command on the File menu doesn't close the movie file; it only closes the active Director window. If you try to close a movie without saving your final changes, a dialog box opens, asking if you want to do so.

Setting preferences

When you start Director and work with the program, you'll notice default settings in the Director window. Default settings include open and closed panels, window and panel position, colors in the toolbox, units of measurement, and tooltip display. As you use Director, make changes and exit, the program automatically saves your settings. You can control some of Director's default settings by selecting options in one of several preference dialog boxes. You can set preferences relating to general program usage, network and Internet connections, the Paint window, the Score, the Script window, sprites, and external editors. For example, you can save the position of windows as you exit Director. To select the save window position option, you use the General Preferences dialog box. Click Edit (Win) or Director (Mac) on the menu bar, point to Preferences, then click General. Select the Save Window Positions On Exit check box, then click OK to complete the operation.

Exit or Quit Director

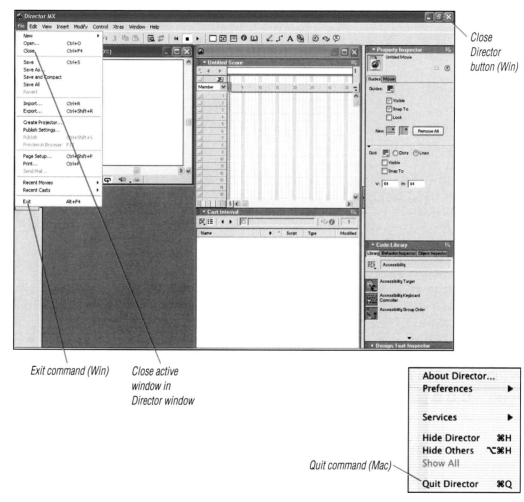

Close Director button (Win)

Exit command (Win)

Close active window in Director window

Quit command (Mac)

Close a movie and exit Director

1. Click the New Movie button on the toolbar.
2. If asked to save your work, click Yes (Win) or Save (Mac).

   Director closes the current movie and creates a blank new one.
3. Click File (Win) or Director (Mac) on the menu bar, as shown in Figure A-28.
4. Click Exit (Win) or Quit Director (Mac).
5. If asked to save your work, click No (Win) or Don't Save (Mac).

You closed a movie by opening a new one, then exited Director.

Showcase Director.

1. Start your browser.
2. Go to the Shockwave Web site at *www.shockwave.com*.
3. Explore and view the examples, then close your browser.

Start Director.

1. Use the Start button to open Macromedia Director MX (Win) or use the Director MX program icon to open Director (Mac).

Examine the Director windows.

1. Open the Stage window if necessary.
2. Resize the Stage to a larger size.

3. Drag the Stage window title bar to another area of the Director window.

Open and save a movie.

1. Open MD A-1.dir from the location where your Unit A data files are stored.
2. Save it as **SpaceWorks Promo** where your Unit A data files are stored.

Work with panel groups.

1. Collapse the Cast panel.
2. Undock the Tools panel from the left channel (Win only).
3. Dock the Tools panel to the left channel (Win only).

4. Using the panel gripper, ungroup the Score and Cast panels into separate windows.
5. Group the Cast panel with the Score panel in a panel group.
6. Display the default panel set.

Play a movie.

1. Using the Control Panel, play the movie.
2. Before the end of the movie, stop it.
3. Rewind the movie.
4. Start at frame 50 and step forward 10 frames.

Find information using Director Help.

1. Open Director Help.
2. Using the Contents, find information about docking panels under Director basics.
3. Using the Index, find information about the playback head in the Score.
4. Using the Search, find information about channels in the Score.
5. Close Help.

Close a movie and exit Director.

1. Compare your screen to Figure A-29.
2. Exit Director without saving your work.

FIGURE A-29

Completed Skills Review

You are new to Director and still unsure how to use the product. Director provides extensive Help. At any time, you can select Director Help from the Help menu and get the assistance you need. You use the Help options to learn about the topics listed below.

1. Locate and read the Help information on zooming your view of the Stage.

2. Locate and read the Help information on the basics of sprites.

3. Locate and read the Help information on using the panel Options menus.

4. Locate and read the Help information on panel groups.

5. Compare your screen to Figure A-30 (Win only).

6. Locate and read the Help information on the Director Support Center.

7. Print one or more of the Help topics you located using the Print button on your browser window.

8. Close the Director Help window.

FIGURE A-30

Completed Project Builder 1

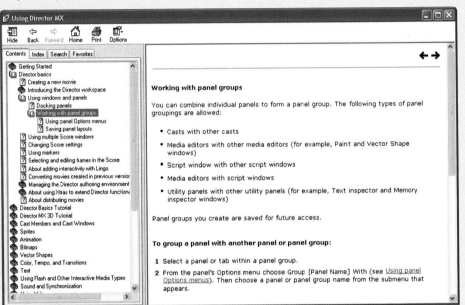

You want to learn how to use Director, so you decide to take a Director class. After working through the first tutorial in class, the instructor asks you to open the completed tutorial file, play the movie to determine if your file is correct, and save the movie so you can take it back to the office.

1. Open Fun.dir from the location where your Unit A data files are stored.
2. Using the expanded Control Panel on the Stage window, play the movie until it reaches frame 139, then step forward until it reaches frame 180, then continue to play the movie.
3. Compare your screen to Figure A-31.
4. Save the movie as **Fun Tutorial** in the location where your Unit A data files are stored, then exit Director.

FIGURE A-31
Completed Project Builder 2

Your boss has sent your entire department to a class on Director MX. After completing the first tutorial, the instructor asks you to open the completed tutorial file that comes with Director, play the movie, and describe the Cast window, Score, and Stage interaction. Your instructor tells you that the sample and instructional movies installed with the Director program are typically located in a subfolder inside the Director MX folder.

1. Open the Magic_finished.dir file from the 3d folder. For the typical Director MX installation, the folder is located in the Program Files folder, Macromedia folder, Director MX folder, and Tutorial folder (Win) or Director MX and Tutorial folder (Mac).
2. Using the Control Panel on the Stage window, play the movie, then view the Cast window, Score, and Stage interaction as you click each table on the Stage.
3. Compare your screen to Figure A-32.
4. Open a document in a word processor, describe what's happening in the movie, print and save the file as **Magic_Doc**, then exit the word processor.
5. Exit Director and don't save the movie.

FIGURE A-32
Completed Design Project

Your group can assign elements of the project to individual members or work collectively to create the finished product.

Now that you are somewhat familiar with Director and its Help system, you decide to see what kind of information is available on the Macromedia Web site. This Web site has important product information, including a feature tour, upgrade guide, system requirements, Frequently Asked Questions (FAQs), support and training, and a showcase of what others are creating with Director. As a Director user, you should become familiar with this site.

1. Start your browser and go to the Macromedia Web site at *www.macromedia.com*.
2. Click the Products link, then click the Director MX link.
3. Search the Director MX area for the following:
   - Why you would want to use Director, then print any relevant pages.
   - What makes it different than Flash, another Web design product developed by Macromedia, then print any relevant pages.
   - Real-world Director examples in the Showcase and describe how the software was used to solve a problem or meet a need, then write a brief summary of your finding or print any relevant pages.
4. Compare your screen to Figure A-33.
5. Exit your browser.

FIGURE A-33
Completed Group Project

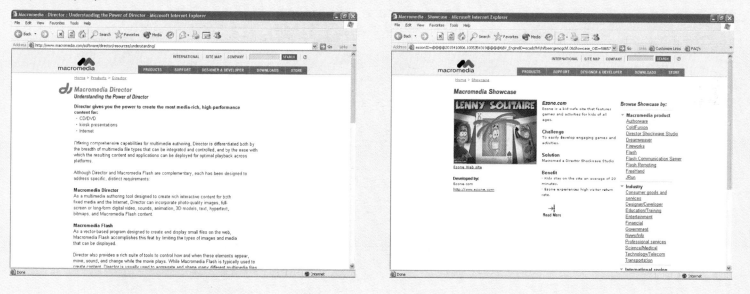

UNIT

CREATING B A MOVIE

1. Plan a movie.

2. Set up a movie.

3. Import cast members.

4. Create and name cast members.

5. Create and modify sprites.

6. Create animation using keyframes.

7. Print a movie.

UNIT B
CREATING A MOVIE

Planning a Movie

Before you begin to create a movie in Director, it's important to develop a project plan first. The project plan provides a road map for you to follow as you build your project in Director. Without a project plan, you'll inevitably hit road blocks, which will cause you to waste time redesigning all of or portions of the movie. Planning a movie project involves determining its purpose, identifying the audience, logically developing the content, organizing the structure of the content, developing the layout and design, and identifying the delivery computer system. As part of the project plan, it's also important to include details about the look and feel of your production, its length and size, how it will interact with the viewer, and how and for whom it will be distributed. With a project plan in place, you'll be ready to create a movie in Director.

Creating a Movie

After you develop a project plan, you can use Director to create a movie according to the plan. Creating a movie involves six main steps: setting up movie properties, assembling media elements in the Cast window, positioning the media elements on the Stage and sequencing them in the Score, adding custom functionality and interactive elements, previewing and testing the movie, and finally packaging the movie for distribution on CD-ROM or over the Internet.

Tools You'll Use

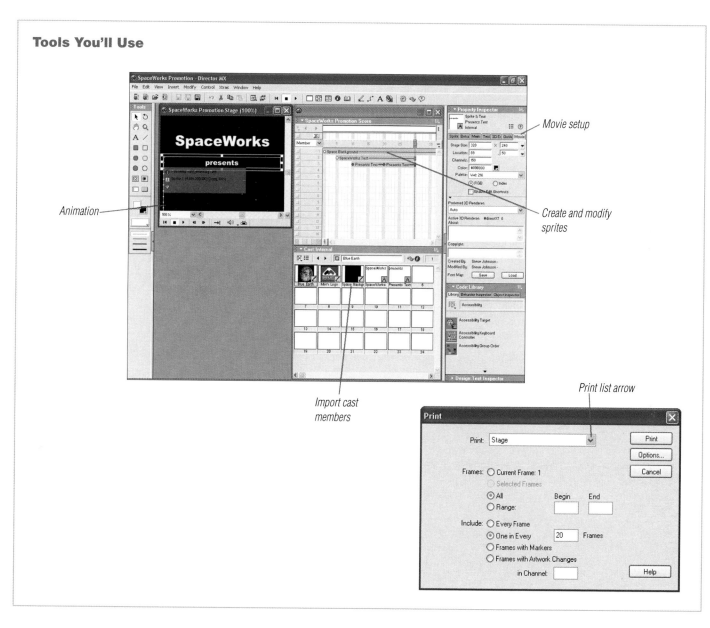

Movie setup

Create and modify sprites

Animation

Import cast members

Print list arrow

PLAN A MOVIE

What You'll Do

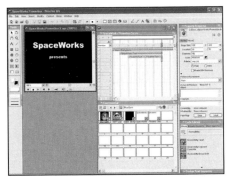

In this lesson, you will learn how to plan a movie.

Planning a Movie

Creating a movie can take a long time; it's worth the effort to plan carefully. The tendency for most first-time Director developers is to start creating a movie without carefully planning the project. Before you begin, you need to develop and follow a plan. Otherwise, you might end up spending a lot of time fixing or completely changing parts of the movie, which you could have avoided from the beginning. You need to figure out the goal of the project, the look and feel of your production, its length and size, how it will interact with the viewer, and how and for whom it will be distributed.

When planning a movie, it's important to accomplish the following:

- Determine the purpose

Is it for training? Promotion? Sales? Marketing? Entertainment? Informing? The answer will determine the types of features you may want to include or exclude in the movie. If the purpose is to create a self-paced training product, you might want to include simple navigation, easy-to-use instructional material, and a help system. On the other hand, if the purpose is to create a sales promotion, you might want to include eye-catching graphics and videos to get users' attention and draw them into the presentation.

- Identify the audience

How you create your movie will depend on how you classify the intended audience. If the intended audience consists of novice computer users, you will have to concentrate on making the navigational controls and layout as simple to use as possible. If the users are experienced computer users, you can include more advanced features and interactions.

- Develop the content and organize the structure

The most beneficial planning tools for the multimedia developer are the script and schematic flowchart. The **script** tells the story of your movie production in text form, as shown in Figure B-1. Just as in the movies, a script is used to describe each section, to list audio or video, and to provide a basis for the text that will appear onscreen or will be read by a voice-over talent. **Schematic flowcharts** are the best way to sketch the navigational structure of a movie and make sure that each of the sections is properly connected, as shown in Figure B-2. After you have the script and schematic flowchart mapped out on paper, you will quickly see the correlation between what you have developed and what you will begin to set up in Director.

- **Develop the layout and design of the movie**

The **storyboard** tells the story of your movie in visual form. It helps you design the layout of each screen in your movie. The storyboard follows the script and develops visual frames of the movie's main transitional points, which help you develop the Director media elements that you will use to create your movie. A storyboard can take a long time to develop, but the media elements you assemble and create in the process will shorten the overall development time.

- **Identify the delivery computer system to be used for playback**

Some computers are more up to date than others. You need to determine the minimum computer hardware and software requirements in which your movie will be delivered. The hardware and software requirements will determine what types of media you can use and how the movie will play back. Some hardware requirements you need to consider are the CPU (central processing unit), which determines the speed with which your computer can compute data; RAM (system memory), which determines how fast files load and how smoothly they run; sound cards, which determine if you can use sound files; video cards, which determine the quality and speed of the graphic and video display; and monitor resolution, which determines the color display, size, and overall look of your movie. Some software requirements you need to consider are the delivery platform—Macintosh, PC, or both (cross-platform)—and operating system (Windows 98/2000/XP or Macintosh OS 8/9/10). Each platform and operating system will determine which types of image files will work on which types of systems.

FIGURE B-1

Project planning script

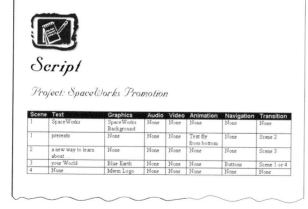

FIGURE B-2

Project planning schematic flowchart

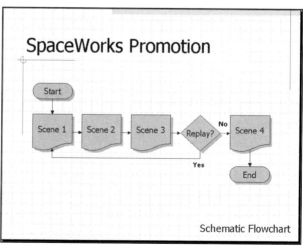

Developing a Movie with Director

Before you start creating a movie using Director based on your project plan, it's important to understand the process of developing software. The basic steps for developing interactive multimedia software with Director are shown in Figure B-3 and listed below.

- **Step 1: Set up movie properties**

Before you start a movie project, you need to set up initial movie properties for how your movie looks and operates. It is important to specify movie property settings that affect the entire movie at the beginning of the project, such as how colors are defined, and the size and location of the Stage, so you don't have to redesign the movie later.

- **Step 2: Assemble the media elements in the Cast window**

Media elements include graphics, images, digital videos, animations, sounds, and text. You can create new media elements in Director or import ones that have already been developed and store them in the Cast window. Director provides several tools for creating media elements, including a paint tool and text creation tools.

- **Step 3: Position the media elements on the Stage and sequence them in the Score**

The Stage is the viewing area you use to display where media elements appear in a movie, and the Score is the timeline you use to organize what you want to occur at the time and duration you specify. You use the Stage to create the look and feel for your production; you use the Stage and Score together to arrange the media elements from the Cast window in space and time. The Stage represents the media elements' position in space (where) and the Score represents the media elements' position in time (when).

- **Step 4: Add scripting and interactive behaviors**

FIGURE B-3
Developing interactive software with Director

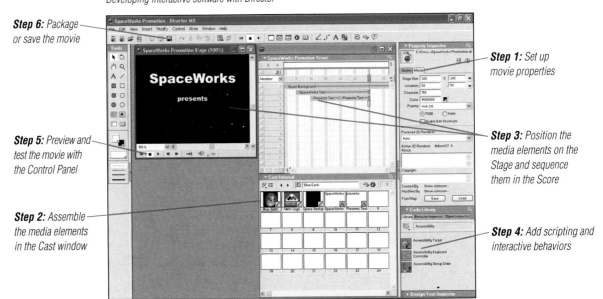

Step 6: Package or save the movie

Step 5: Preview and test the movie with the Control Panel

Step 2: Assemble the media elements in the Cast window

Step 1: Set up movie properties

Step 3: Position the media elements on the Stage and sequence them in the Score

Step 4: Add scripting and interactive behaviors

You can add scripting and behaviors to your production. **Scripting** allows you to add custom functionality to your movie, such as moving objects on the Stage, formatting text, storing and managing information, performing mathematical operations, and controlling the movie in response to specific conditions and events, such as a mouse click. In Director, scripts are written in **Lingo**, a Director-specific programming language. To help you get started scripting and save you some time, Director comes with ready-made scripts called **behaviors**. For example, interactive behaviors can include buttons, arrows, or other navigation elements that move the viewer to different parts of a movie or to different locations on the Web.

- Step 5: Preview and test the movie with the Control Panel

After you create your movie, you use the Control Panel to preview and test the movie to make sure it runs the way you want it to. It's important to test the functionality of your movie early and often during the development process to catch problems while they are still minor. As needed, you make refinements and adjustments in the Score.

- Step 6: Package the movie as a stand-alone projector file, or save the movie as a Shockwave file for use over the Internet

When the movie runs the way you want it to, you can package your production as a stand-alone projector movie that viewers can run from a CD-ROM or hard drive. When you distribute your movie in projector form, viewers can run the movie without using Director. You can also save your production as a Shockwave movie that viewers can play on a Web page, using a browser. Viewers can't change the movies; they can only play them.

Computer requirements for developing and playing a movie

Developing a movie requires a computer with an increased level of hardware and software capabilities. The minimum requirements to develop Director movies are an Intel Pentium II 300 processor running Windows 98 Second Edition or 2000/XP or later, or a Power PC G3 Macintosh running System 10.1.2 or later 128 MB of installed RAM plus 100 MB of available disk space, a sound card, 1024× 768 16-bit color display, and a CD-ROM drive. The increased CPU requirements provide the necessary speed to preview and test your movie on the Stage. The additional disk space requirements for the development computer provide the necessary storage space to store large media elements, such as graphics, animation, video, and sound. For a playback computer with a slower CPU (Intel Pentium 166 processor running Windows 95/98 or NT 4.0 or later [Win], or a Power PC 120 Macintosh running System 8.6 or later [Mac]), the movie is optimized to achieve the same results as the development computerIn addition, to view Shockwave movies, you need to have a browser with Microsoft Internet Explorer 4.01 or later or Netscape Navigator 4.0 or later.

SET UP A MOVIE

What You'll Do

In this lesson, you will set up a movie.

Setting Up a Movie

When you start Director, the Director window appears with a set of blank windows ready for you to create a new movie. Before you start, however, you need first to set up the movie properties. You set movie properties at the beginning of the project to make basic decisions about how your movie looks and operates. You use the Property inspector's Movie tab to specify movie property settings that affect the entire movie, such as how colors are defined, the size and location of the Stage, the number of channels in the Score, author and copyright information, and font mapping. These settings apply only to the current movie unless you set Director preferences to apply to every movie. The Movie tab appears only if you do *not* have an object selected on the Stage or in the Score. If you do have an object selected, the Property inspector displays category tabs associated with the object. To display the Movie tab, you simply click a blank area of the Stage or Score or use the Property Inspector command on the Window menu. Table B-1 describes the movie properties available in the Property inspector.

QUICKTIP

For additional information about these movie properties, click the Help button in the Property inspector.

Working with Color

Director manages colors as sets of colors, or palettes. A **color palette** is a set of colors used by a movie or cast members. For example, the Web 216 color palette provides a set of colors that can be properly displayed on the Web. Director offers a choice of two basic color modes: RGB (Red, Green, Blue) and palette index. The **RGB color mode** identifies a color by a set of **hexadecimal numbers**, an internal computer numbering scheme that specifies the amounts of red, green, and blue needed to create a color. The **palette index color mode** identifies a color by the number (0 through 255) of its position in a color palette.

Director comes with two color palette displays. One is a color pop-up menu, and the other is a color palettes window. The color pop-up menu provides quick access to colors in the color palette and other color options, while the color palettes window allows you to select or create a color palette, define new colors, or change foreground, background, and fill colors. For example, when you click the color box on the Property inspector's Movie tab, a color pop-up menu appears that allows you to select a background color for the Stage. When you display a color palette, the colors that appear are based on the current color mode, which is labeled at the top of the color palette. When you select a color in the color palette, the color is applied to the selected item and appears in the color box. In some cases, like on the Movie tab, a corresponding color value (for example, #000000) appears next to the color box.

TABLE B-1: Movie Properties in the Property Inspector

movie property	allows you to
Stage Size	Change the size of the Stage by choosing a monitor size from the pop-up menu, or by entering the width (in pixels) in the first text box and the height in the second text box
Location	Select Stage location, either Centered, Upper Left, or Other from the pop-up menu; you enter the left value (in pixels) in the first text box and the top value in the second text box to specify how far away you want the Stage to be from the upper-left corner of the screen
Channels	Set the number of channels available for sprites in the Score
Color	Select the color of the Stage from a color pop-up menu
Palette	Set the default color palette for your movie; select a color mode option, either RGB (assign all color values as absolute RGB values) or Index (assign color according to its position in the current palette)
Enable Edit Shortcuts	Cut, copy, and paste editable text boxes while a movie is playing
Expander arrow	Expand the Property inspector to display all settings or collapse to hide settings
Preferred 3D Renderer	Select the software or control to display 3D objects
About	Specify information about your movie
Copyright	Specify copyright information for your movie
Save	Save current font map settings in a specific text file
Load	Load font map settings from a file

Set a movie property

1. Start Director and save the new file as **SpaceWorks Promotion** in the location where your Unit B data files are stored.

2. Click the Stage window to display the Property inspector.

   TIP You can also click Window on the menu bar, then click Property Inspector, or [Ctrl][Alt][S] (Win) or [option] ⌘ [S] (Mac) to display the Property inspector.

3. Click the Movie tab in the Property inspector, as shown in Figure B-4, and view the movie properties.

   TIP If you prefer to view the Property inspector options as a list, click the List View Mode button at the top of the panel. To switch back to a graphical view, click the List View Mode button again.

4. Click the Stage Size list arrow, then click 320 × 240 if necessary.

You viewed movie properties and set the Stage size.

FIGURE B-4

Movie tab in the Property inspector

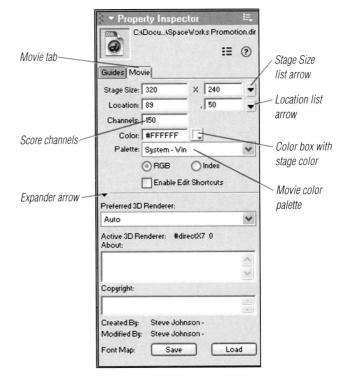

Movie tab

Stage Size list arrow

Location list arrow

Score channels

Color box with stage color

Movie color palette

Expander arrow

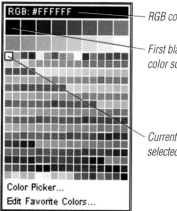

RGB: #FFFFFF ——— *RGB color palette*

——— *First black color square*

——— *Current color selected*

Color Picker...

Edit Favorite Colors...

Select movie colors

1. Click the Palette list arrow, then click Web 216 if necessary.

2. Click the RGB option button if necessary.

3. Click the color box next to the Color text box to display the color palette on the color pop-up menu, as shown in Figure B-5.

   You may have to hold down the mouse button a bit longer than usual to display the color pop-up menu.

   > TIP To open the Color Palettes window, double-click the color box (Win), or click Window on the menu bar and then click Color Palettes.

4. Click the first color square (black) in the first row of the color palette to select a background color for the Stage, then compare your screen to Figure B-6.

5. Save your work.

You selected a color palette for a movie and set the Stage color.

FIGURE B-6

Movie color properties

Property Inspector

C:\Docu...\SpaceWorks Promotion.dir

Guides | Movie

Stage Size: 320 X 240

Location: 89 . 50

Channels: 150

Color: #000000

Palette: Web 216

⦿ RGB ○ Index

☐ Enable Edit Shortcuts

Preferred 3D Renderer:

Auto

Active 3D Renderer: #directX7 0
About:

Copyright:

Created By: Steve Johnson -
Modified By: Steve Johnson

Font Map: Save | Load

Black Stage color

Color value

Web color palette

RGB color mode

IMPORT CAST MEMBERS

What You'll Do

In this lesson, you will import media elements into the Cast window.

Importing File Types

If you've already developed animations and multimedia content, images, sounds, video, or text in other programs, you can import these media elements as cast members into the Cast window. Because most movie content is developed in graphics programs, importing media elements is an important part of creating a movie with Director. Before you can import a media element into Director, you need to know the different types, or formats, Director can import. You can view a list of file types in the Import Files dialog box, as shown in Figure B-7 (Win). Table B-2 provides a summary of the formats and objects that you can import into Director.

From the Import Files dialog box, you can select files individually or as a group and import them into the active, or currently selected, cast. The active cast name appears in quotation marks in the title bar of the Import Files dialog box. The selected files are imported into the Cast window according to the order of the files in the File List

from top to bottom. The top file in the list will be imported into the next available location in the Cast window. You can change the import order by selecting a file and using the Move Up or Move Down buttons (Win), as shown in Figure B-7.

Using Additional Media Elements

If you have a media element in a format not included in the supported list of formats, you need to convert the media element to one of the supported formats or use an Xtra to insert the media element. An **Xtra** is a software module you can add to Director, which extends the capabilities of Director. Director comes with built-in Xtras on the Media Element submenu on the Insert menu, and you can also install third-party Xtras developed by other companies.

Understanding Color Depth

As Director imports images into the Cast window, the program checks that the images are compatible with the current movie property settings. If an incompatibility arises, Director prompts you on how to resolve it. A common incompatibility arises when an imported image and your computer system have a different **color depth**, which is the number of colors that an image or a computer monitor and display adapter can display. The higher the color depth value, the greater the number of colors that can be displayed, which necessitates greater system memory. An image with a 1-bit color depth appears only in black and white; similarly, a monitor with a 1-bit color depth setting displays only black-and-white images. The most common color depth display settings are: 2-bit, which displays 4 colors; 4-bit, which displays 16 colors; 8-bit, which displays 256 colors; 16-bit, which displays 32,768 colors; and 24-bit and 32-bit, both of which display 16.7 million colors.

Selecting Image Color Depths

When you specify the color depth of your computer, you set the maximum color depth for a movie and the maximum number of colors for all the images it contains. When you import a graphic that has a different color depth from the computer, the Image Options dialog box opens, asking you to select a color depth. The Stage option value reflects the color depth set for your computer, so a 24-bit or 16-bit Stage setting reflects a 24-bit or 16-bit monitor setting. In most cases, you should transform an image with a higher color depth setting (displayed next to the Image option button) to the lower setting displayed next to the Stage option button so that the color depth setting for the Stage and the image will be the same. If you don't change an image to the Stage color depth when you import it, you might experience color flashes or conflicts when the image appears on the Stage.

FIGURE B-7
Import file types

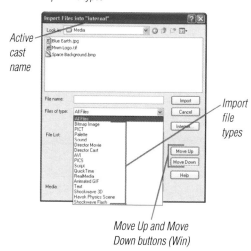

Active cast name

Import file types

Move Up and Move Down buttons (Win)

TABLE B-2: Import File Types

type of file	supported formats
3D	Shockwave 3D, Havok Physics Scene
Animation and multimedia	Animated GIF, Flash movies, Director movies, Director External Cast files
Image	BMP, GIF, JPEG, LRG (xRes), Photoshop 3.0 (or later), MacPaint, PNG, TIFF, PICT, Targa
Multiple-image file	PICS, Scrapbook (Mac)
Sound	AIFF, WAV, MP3 audio, Shockwave Audio, Sun AU uncompressed, IMA compressed (Win)
Video	QuickTime 2, 3, 4, and 6; AVI (Win); RealMedia
Text	RTF, HTML, ASCII (often called Text Only), Lingo scripts
Palette	PAL, Photoshop CLUT

Import cast members

1. Click the Import button on the toolbar or [Ctrl][R] (Win)/[control][R] (Mac).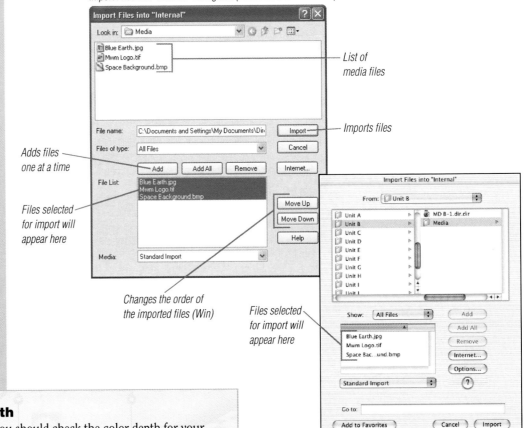

2. Navigate to the location where your Unit B data files are stored, then double-click (Win) or click (Mac) the Media folder.

3. In the list of media files, click a file (Mac), click Add All, then compare your screen to Figure B-8.

   TIP To import one file, click the file, then click Import. To import more than one file at once, click the file, click Add, repeat until you're done adding to the list, then click Import.

4. In the File List, click Mwm Logo.tif, then click Move Down or Move Up to display the media elements in the same order shown in Figure B-8 if necessary (Win).

(continued)

FIGURE B-8
Import Files into "Internal" dialog box (Windows and Macintosh)

List of media files

Imports files

Adds files one at a time

Files selected for import will appear here

Changes the order of the imported files (Win)

Files selected for import will appear here

Changing computer color depth

Before you import images into a movie, you should check the color depth for your computer monitor to make sure the current color settings are high enough for the project. Changing the color depth during the development of the movie can produce color problems, so it is a good idea to decide the maximum color depth at the start of the project, and import images at a consistent color depth. To change a computer monitor's color setting, right-click the desktop, click Properties, click the Settings tab, click the Color quality list arrow, click a color depth, then click OK (Win); or click the Apple menu, click System Preferences, click Displays, then choose 256, Thousands or Millions from the Color pop-up menu (Mac).

FIGURE B-9

Image Options dialog box

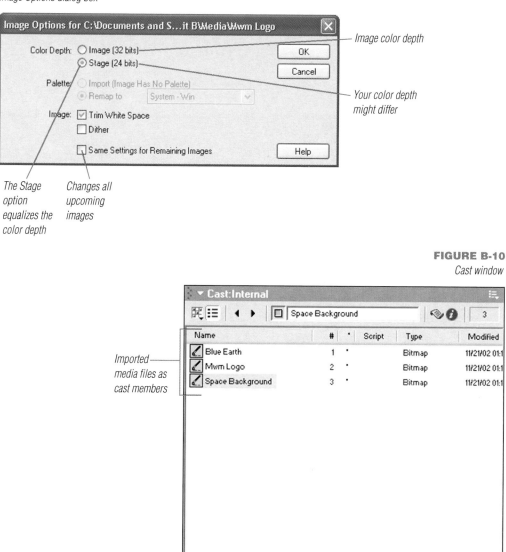

Image Options for C:\Documents and S...it B\Media\Mwm Logo

Color Depth: ○ Image (32 bits) ——— Image color depth
○ Stage (24 bits)

Palette: ○ Import (Image Has No Palette)
○ Remap to ⌄ System - Win ⌄ ——— Your color depth
might differ

Image: ☑ Trim White Space
☐ Dither

☐ Same Settings for Remaining Images

OK
Cancel
Help

The Stage option equalizes the color depth

Changes all upcoming images

FIGURE B-10

Cast window

▼ Cast:Internal

Space Background   3

Name	#	·	Script	Type	Modified
Blue Earth	1	·		Bitmap	11/21/02 01:1
Mwm Logo	2	·		Bitmap	11/21/02 01:1
Space Background	3	·		Bitmap	11/21/02 01:1

Imported media files as cast members

5. Click Import.

   If your computer color depth is set to 32 bits, the same color depth as the image, the Image Options dialog box might not open. Skip steps 6 and 7.

6. In the Color Depth section in the Image Options dialog box, click the Stage (24 bits) option button, as shown in Figure B-9, or the Stage (16 bits) option button if it's available.

7. Select the Same Settings for Remaining Images check box.

8. Click OK, then compare your screen to Figure B-10.

9. Save your work.

You imported cast members.

CREATE AND NAME CAST MEMBERS

What You'll Do

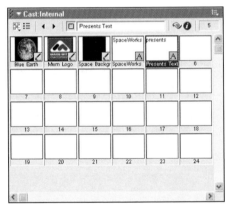

In this lesson, you will create and name cast members.

Creating Cast Members

In addition to importing media elements into Director, you can create new media elements in Director itself. Director provides several tools for creating media elements, including a vector shape tool, paint tool, and text creation tools. With the vector shape tool, you can create simple shapes, such as circles, squares, and polygons. With the paint tool, you can create simple or detailed graphics. With the text creation tool, you can quickly and easily create normal 2D text and 3D text.

Creating Text Cast Members

Almost every movie requires some text, either titles or credits. You can use the Text Window button on the toolbar to create a text cast member in a separate window with complete text formatting controls, or you can use the Text tool on the Tool palette to create a text cast member directly on the Stage. When you use the Text Window button on the toolbar, the Text window opens with the Text tab displayed, as shown in Figure B-11. The Text window is a predefined tabbed

Changing text alignment

On the Text tab of the Text window, you can change the alignment for each paragraph in a text cast member. A **paragraph** is a new section of text. To create a new paragraph on the Text tab, press [Enter] (Win) or [return] (Mac). You can align paragraph text relative to the margins on the Text tab. Although you can vary the width and placement of the margins, the right margin cannot exceed the length of the text cast member. By default, text is left-aligned, or flush with the left margin. However, you can also right-align text flush with the right margin, center text between the margins, or justify text so that both the left and right edges are evenly aligned. To align multiple paragraphs, you need to select the paragraphs, then select an alignment button on the toolbar on the Text tab. ≣ ≡ ≡ ≣

panel group, which provides a convenient way to access Director text tools that you can use to create and modify text. The text formatting and alignment controls available in the Text window work in the same way as similar features in a word processing program.

Working with Cast Members in the Cast Window

When you create or import a media element, it is stored in the Cast window. A Cast can contain up to 32,000 cast members, each one represented by a thumbnail image and identified by its position number and an optional name. A small icon associated with each cast member identifies its type. In the Cast window, cast members appear in either List view or Thumbnail view, as shown in Figure B-12. List view works best for organizing cast members, while Thumbnail view works best for

visually finding cast members. You can name a new cast member or rename an existing one. When you name a cast member, it's important to use a name that identifies its purpose so that you can quickly find it in the Cast window. You can also copy, paste, delete, duplicate, relocate, and modify a cast member. Any changes you make to a cast member are reflected in its appearance on the Stage. You don't have to use every cast member in your movie; however, saving your movie with all of the unused cast members increases the file size.

FIGURE B-11
Text window

FIGURE B-12
Cast members in different views

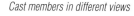

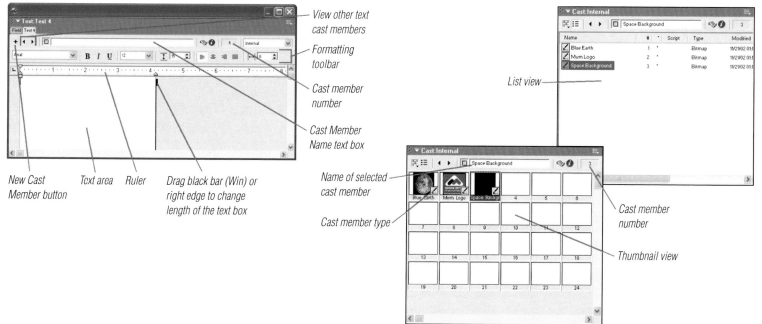

View other text cast members

Formatting toolbar

Cast member number

Cast Member Name text box

New Cast Member button   Text area   Ruler   Drag black bar (Win) or right edge to change length of the text box

List view

Name of selected cast member

Cast member type

Cast member number

Thumbnail view

View cast members

1. If Thumbnail view appears in the Cast window, click the Cast View Style button in the Cast window to change to List view, as shown in Figure B-13.

2. Click the Previous Cast Member button until the first cast member is selected. ◀

3. Click the Cast View Style button in the Cast window to change to Thumbnail view.

4. Click the Next Cast Member button until the last cast member is selected, as shown in Figure B-14. ▶

You viewed cast members.

FIGURE B-13
Cast members in List view

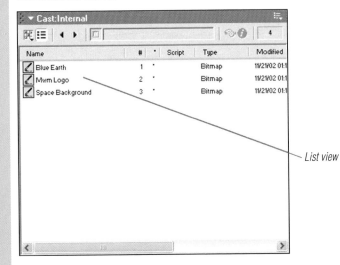

List view

FIGURE B-14
Cast members in Thumbnail view

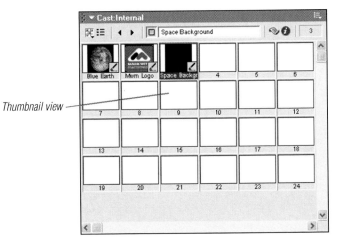

Thumbnail view

Text cast member in Text window

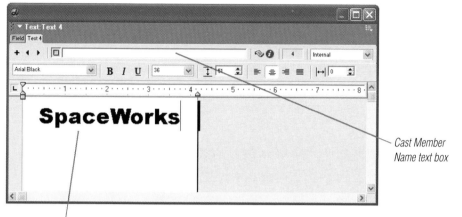

Cast Member
Name text box

Cast member text

Create and name cast members

1. Click the Text Window button on the toolbar. A

2. Position the pointer on the lower-right corner of the Text window, then drag the border to display the text area and the toolbar if necessary.

3. Click the Font list arrow, scroll if necessary, click Arial Black, click the Size list arrow, then click 36.

4. Click the Align Center button. ≣

5. Type **SpaceWorks**, then compare your text to Figure B-15.

> TIP If the text doesn't fit on one line, drag the black bar in the upper-right corner (Win) or the right edge of the text area until the text fits. If you make a mistake, press [Backspace] (Win) or [delete] (Mac) to delete the incorrect text, then retype the text.

6. Click the Cast Member Name text box, type **SpaceWorks Text**, then press [Enter] (Win) or [return] (Mac).

7. Click the New Cast Member button in the Text window. ✚

8. Click the Size list arrow, click 18, type **presents**, click the Cast Member Name text box, type **Presents Text**, then press [Enter] (Win) or [return] (Mac).

9. Click the Close button in the Text window, then compare your screen to Figure B-16.

10. Save your work.

You created and named text cast members.

FIGURE B-16

New text cast members in the Cast window

Text cast
member type

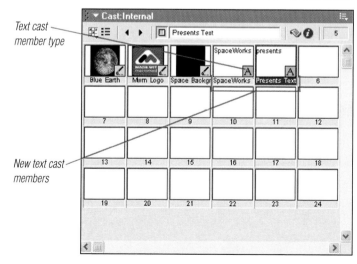

New text cast
members

CREATE AND MODIFY SPRITES

What You'll Do

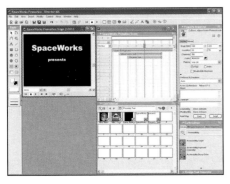

▶ *In this lesson, you will create, reposition, and modify sprites.*

Creating Sprites

A sprite is an object that consists of a cast member and a set of properties and behaviors. The properties and behaviors control how, where, and when cast members appear in a movie. You can create sprites by placing cast members either on the Stage or in the Score; regardless of where you create the sprite, it will appear in both locations. You can create many sprites from a single cast member. You use the Stage to control *where* a sprite appears, and you use the Score to control *when* it appears.

Sprites appear on the Stage, layered according to the corresponding channel in the Score. Sprites in higher-numbered channels appear in front of sprites in lower-numbered channels.

Each new sprite you create has a default duration of 28 frames, called the **span duration**. The range of frames in which the sprite appears is called the **sprite span**, as shown in Figure B-17. You can change the duration of the sprite anytime. Placing a sprite over a range of frames indicates when the sprite appears during the movie.

Changing sprite preferences

You can use the Sprite Preferences dialog box to control the way sprites appear and behave in the Score and on the Stage. You can change sprite options that control Stage selection, span defaults, and span duration. To change preferences for sprites, click Edit (Win) or Director (Mac) on the menu bar, point to Preferences, then click Sprite. In the Stage Selection section, you can customize how you select a sprite on the Stage; you can select the entire span of the sprite or only the current frame in the sprite. In the Span Defaults section, you can determine the appearance and behavior of sprites you'll create in the future. In the Span Duration section, you can determine the length of sprites in frames, indicating either a specified amount or the visible width of the Score.

When you place a cast member in the Score, such as an image, the sprite appears in the center of the Stage with a selection rectangle. Attached to the bottom of the sprite selection rectangle is the Sprite Overlay panel. The **Sprite Overlay panel** displays important sprite properties directly on the Stage, as shown in Figure B-17.

Repositioning and Modifying Sprites

You can reposition sprites on the Stage and in the Score and make other changes to them without affecting the original cast members. To move or modify a sprite, you must select it first. You use the Arrow tool on the Tool palette to select one or more sprites. You can also select a certain frame or range of frames within a sprite in the score instead of the entire sprite. The first frame in a sprite is called a **keyframe** and the last frame is called an **end frame**, as shown in Figure B-17. A keyframe is denoted in a sprite by a circle, while an end frame is denoted by a small bar. The line that connects the circle and the small bar is called the **sprite bar**.

When you create a sprite, the colors of the sprite may not match your movie color scheme on the Stage. You can use tools on the Tool palette, such as the Foreground color box and the Background color box, which are similar to those found in drawing programs, to change the color of the sprites, as shown in Figure B-17.

FIGURE B-17

Stage and Score with new sprites

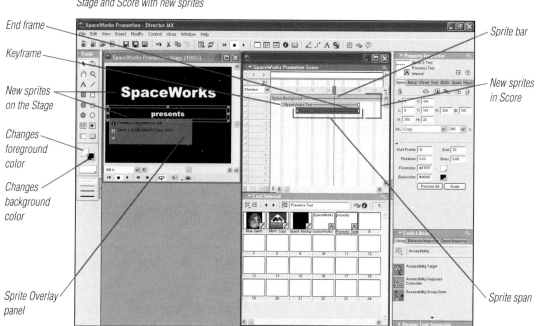

End frame

Keyframe

New sprites on the Stage

Changes foreground color

Changes background color

Sprite Overlay panel

Sprite bar

New sprites in Score

Sprite span

Create sprites

1. Resize the Stage, Score, and Cast windows to match the windows in Figure B-18 if necessary.

2. Click cast member 3 (Space Background) in the Cast window.

3. Drag the cast member from the Cast window to frame 1, channel 1 in the Score, as shown in Figure B-18.

4. Click frame 5 in the frame channel to move the playback head to frame 5.

5. Drag cast member 4 (SpaceWorks Text) from the Cast window to the upper-center of the Stage, then click the gray area around the Stage or an empty area of the Stage to deselect the sprite.

6. Drag cast member 5 (Presents Text) from the Cast window to the Stage below cast member 4 (SpaceWorks Text), then click the gray area around the Stage or an empty area of the Stage to deselect the sprite.

7. Compare your screen to Figure B-19, click the Rewind button ◄ on the toolbar, then click the Play button on the toolbar. ▶

   TIP If the playback head loop is turned on, click the Stop button, then click the Loop Playback button on the Control Panel.

You created sprites.

FIGURE B-18
Score window with a new sprite

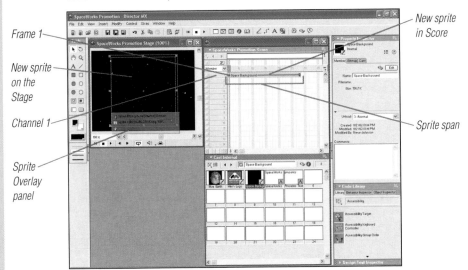

Frame 1

New sprite on the Stage

Channel 1

Sprite Overlay panel

New sprite in Score

Sprite span

FIGURE B-19
Stage and Score with new sprites

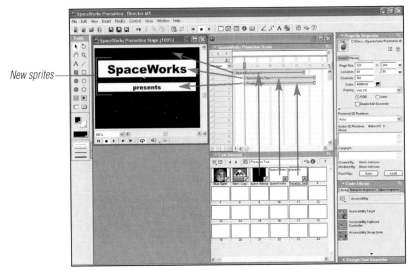

New sprites

FIGURE B-20

Sprite repositioned in the Score

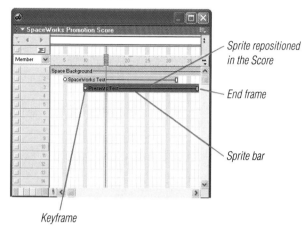

Sprite repositioned in the Score

End frame

Sprite bar

Keyframe

FIGURE B-21

Stage with new foreground and background colors

Arrow tool

Foreground color of the text changes to white

Foreground color box

Background color box

Background color of the text changes to black

Reposition and modify sprites

1. Verify that the Arrow tool is selected, then click anywhere in the Space Background sprite in channel 1 in the Score.

2. Position the pointer over the end frame in the Space Background sprite in channel 1, then drag the end frame to frame 75 (as you drag, the Score scrolls to the right).

3. In the Score, scroll to the left, position the pointer over the Presents Text sprite in channel 3 (not over the keyframe or end frame), then drag the sprite to the right so that the sprite starts at frame 10, as shown in Figure B-20.

4. Drag the end frame for the SpaceWorks Text sprite in channel 2 back to frame 30, then drag the end frame for the Presents Text sprite in channel 3 back to frame 30.

5. Click the SpaceWorks Text sprite in the sprite bar, press and hold [Shift], then click the Presents Text sprite within the sprite bar to select both sprites.

6. Click and hold the Foreground color box on the Tool palette to display the color palette, then click the last large color square (white) in the second row on the color palette.

7. Click and hold the Background color box on the Tool palette, click the first large color square (black) in the first row on the color palette, then click the gray area around the Stage to deselect the sprites, as shown in Figure B-21.

8. Rewind and play the movie, then save your work.

You repositioned and modified sprites.

CREATE ANIMATION USING KEYFRAMES

What You'll Do

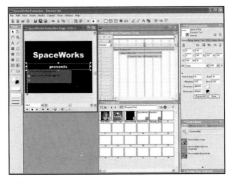

▶ *In this lesson, you will create an animation using keyframes.*

Creating Animation Using Keyframes

The simplest way to make a sprite move from one position to another is through tweening. In traditional animation, **tweening** describes the process in which an animator draws all the frames *in between* the frames where major changes take place, which creates the impression of movement. To tween the animation using Director, you need to set the frames in the Score that correspond to the major change points on the Stage where the sprite will move. The major change point frames are the keyframes in the animation. A keyframe is the first frame in a sprite (the starting point for the animation) and the selected frames in the Score where a sprite appears in a new location or changes appearance in some other way.

As you place keyframes in the sprite, Director automatically tweens the sprites between the keyframes to create an animation path. The **animation path** is a track the sprite moves along to create an animation. The green dot on the animation path represents the animation start point, the white dots represent the tweens, and the red dot represents the end point. You can set as many keyframes in a sprite as there are frames in its span. By changing the number of frames between keyframes, you can control the smoothness of the animation. When you insert a keyframe, Director places a **keyframe indicator** in the sprite. After every keyframe, Director inserts a sprite label in the sprite so you can identify what appears after the keyframe, as shown in Figure B-23.

FIGURE B-22
Start position for animation

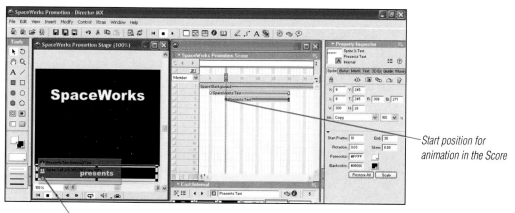

Start position for animation in the Score

Start position for animation on the Stage

FIGURE B-23
Score with a keyframe indicator

Sprite label

Start animation at frame 10

Keyframe indicator; end animation at frame 20

FIGURE B-24
Stage with an animation

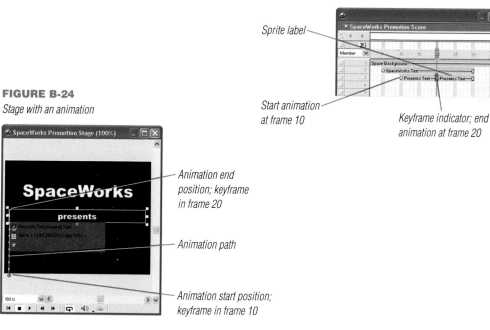

Animation end position; keyframe in frame 20

Animation path

Animation start position; keyframe in frame 10

Create an animation using keyframes

1. Increase the size of the Stage window to the size shown in Figure B-22 to display the gray area around the Stage, then select the Presents Text sprite on the Stage.

2. On the Stage, press and hold [Shift], then drag the Presents Text sprite in a straight path to the gray area at the bottom of the Stage, as shown in Figure B-22.

   TIP When you press and hold [Shift] as you move a sprite, the object is constrained to move in a straight line right to left or up and down.

3. Click frame 20 in channel 3 to select the keyframe insertion point for the animation end point.

4. Click Insert on the menu bar, click Keyframe, then compare your screen to Figure B-23.

   TIP Instead of using the Keyframe menu command, you can also drag the red dot in the sprite on the Stage to create an animation path.

5. Press and hold [Shift], then drag the Presents Text sprite in a straight path from the gray area at the bottom of the Stage to an area below the SpaceWorks text.

   The animation path appears as you move the text sprite on the Stage from the start point (keyframe in frame 10) to its end point (keyframe in frame 20), as shown in Figure B-24.

6. Rewind and play the movie, then save your work.

You created an animation using keyframes.

PRINT A MOVIE

What You'll Do

In this lesson, you will print a movie for review.

Printing a Movie for Review

Sometimes the best way to review different parts of your movie content and mark changes is to print it. You can print a movie in a variety of ways. You can print an image of the Stage in standard or storyboard format, print the Score, the cast member number and contents of text cast members in the Cast window, all scripts or a range of scripts (movie, cast, Score, and sprite scripts), the comments in the Markers window, the Cast window artwork, or the entire Cast window. After you print a movie, the print settings stay in effect until you change them.

QUICKTIP

If you have printing problems, you may need to adjust the graphics intensity and mode settings of your printer. Click File on the menu bar, click Page Setup, then click Properties.

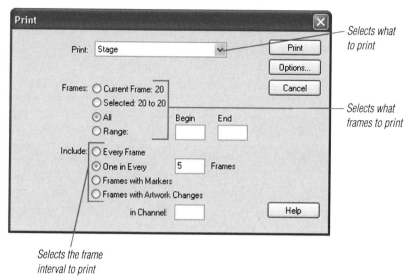

Selects what
to print

Selects what
frames to print

Selects the frame
interval to print

FIGURE B-26
Print Options dialog box

Your number
of frames may
be different

This option only
appears when Scale
is 50% or 25%

Print a movie

1. Click File on the menu bar, click Print, click the Print list arrow, then click Stage if necessary.

   TIP You can also press [Ctrl][P] (Win) or ⌘[P] (Mac) to open the Print dialog box.

2. Click the All option button, click the One in Every option button, click the Frames text box, then type **5** in the Frames text box, as shown in Figure B-25.

3. Click Options, click the 50% option button in the Scale section, then select the Storyboard Format check box, as shown in Figure B-26.

4. Select the Custom Footer check box, click the text box below it, then type your name.

5. Click OK to close the Print Options dialog box, click Print, then click OK (Win) or Print (Mac) to print the storyboard.

6. Click File on the menu bar, then click Page Setup, click the Landscape option button, then click OK.

7. Click File on the menu bar, click Print, click the Print list arrow, click Score, click Print, then click OK (Win) or Print (Mac).

8. Save your work, then exit Director.

You printed a storyboard and Score of a movie for review.

Plan a movie.

1. Write down the basic steps involved in planning a movie.

Set up a movie.

1. Start Director.
2. Change the movie's color palette to Web 216 if necessary.
3. Change the Stage color to black if necessary.

Import cast members.

1. Import all the media elements from the Media folder, which is located in the Unit B folder where your data files are stored.
2. Change the color depth to match the Stage setting and use this setting for any remaining images.

Create and name cast members.

1. Open the file MD B-1.dir, and save it as **SpaceWorks Promo Rev**. Don't save the untitled movie.

2. Open the Text window, resize it if necessary, then drag the black bar (Win) or right edge of the text area to 3½" on the ruler if necessary.
3. Change the font attributes to the font Arial Black, size 24, and center alignment.
4. Change the foreground color to white and the background color to black.
5. Type **a new way to learn about …**, then name the cast member **Learn About Text**.
6. Create a new text cast member.
7. Type **your**, press the spacebar, change the font size to 36, then type **World**.
8. Name the cast member **World Text**, then close the Text window.

Create and modify sprites.

1. Position cast member 6 (Learn About Text) in the Score starting at frame 31 in channel 4, then drag the sprite to the center of the Stage if necessary.
2. Select frame 60 in the frame channel.
3. Drag cast member 7 (World Text) from the Cast window to the top-center of the Stage.

4. Drag cast member 1 (Blue Earth) from the Cast window to the Stage below the World text.
5. Rewind and play the movie.
6. Adjust the Learn About Text sprite in channel 4 to end at frame 50.
7. Move the World Text sprite to channel 5, then adjust it to start at frame 51 and end at frame 75.
8. Move the Blue Earth sprite to channel 6, then adjust it to start at frame 60 and end at frame 75.

Create animation using keyframes.

1. Start the animation at frame 60, channel 6 (Blue Earth sprite).
2. Resize the Stage to the right to display the gray area if necessary.

3. Move the Blue Earth image to the gray area directly to the right. (*Hint*: Do not grab the dots in the center of the earth.)
4. Insert a keyframe at frame 70, channel 6, to end the animation.
5. Move the Blue Earth image in a straight path from the gray area to the center of the Stage.
6. Rewind and play the movie.
7. Save your work, then compare your screen to Figure B-27.

Print a movie.

1. Create a custom footer with your name in it, then print the entire storyboard at 25% scale in portrait orientation. (*Hint*: If you have problems printing, you may need to adjust the graphics intensity and mode settings of your printer.)
2. Print all the cast members as thumbnails in landscape orientation.
3. Save your work and exit Director.

FIGURE B-27
Completed Skills Review

As the public relations manager for an international charity, you want to create a multimedia presentation that celebrates the 50th anniversary of the organization and promotes increased participation in charitable events. The charity wants to hire a multimedia development company to create the presentation. To get funds for the project, you need to create a project plan.

1. Create a project plan in a word processor and save the document as **Charity Project Plan**.
2. Develop a project plan containing the following:
   - Purpose
   - Target audience
   - Content and structure
   - Layout and design
   - Delivery computer system
3. Print the project plan, save your work, then compare your screen to Figure B-28.

FIGURE B-28

Completed Project Builder 1

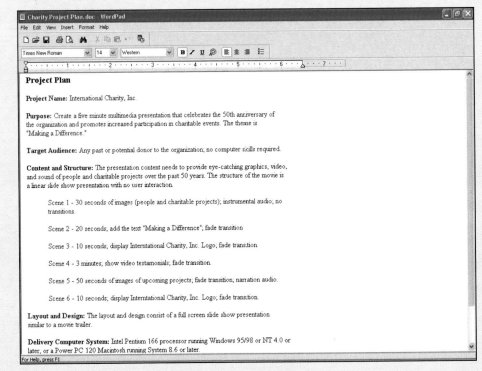

As the lead designer for BannerAD Designs, you regularly use Director to create the designs. A new client recently met with you about creating a banner ad for a company called ABC123 Learning. You use the media creation tools in Director to create a banner ad with some animation.

1. Create a movie and save it as **ABC123**.
2. Set up the Stage to be 300 × 100 pixels with a blue background and a Web 216 color palette.
3. Create a text sprite for the letters **A**, **B**, and **C**.
4. Create a text sprite for the numbers **1**, **2**, and **3**.
5. Create a text sprite with the phrase **Where learning counts!**
6. Animate the text sprites.
7. Create a custom footer with your name in it.
8. Print all of the cast members and all of the Stage frames.
9. Play and save the movie, then compare your screen to Figure B-29.

FIGURE B-29
Completed Project Builder 2

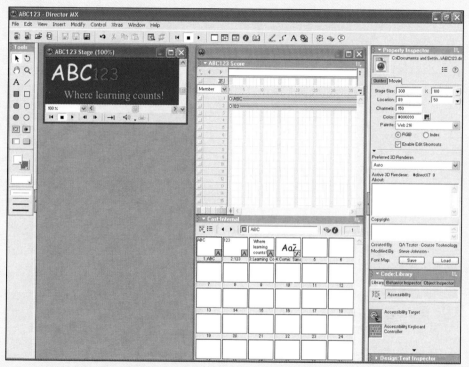

You're putting together a portfolio to showcase your multimedia skills. You use the import and media creation tools in Director to create a résumé with some animation.

1. Create a movie and save it as **Resume**.
2. Set up the Stage to be 500 × 330 pixels with any background color and Web 216 color palette.
3. Import a picture.
4. Create text sprites highlighting accomplishments.
5. Animate the text and graphic sprites.
6. Create a custom footer with your name in it.
7. Print the last frame of the Stage.
8. Play and save the movie, then compare your screen to Figure B-30.
9. Create a portfolio for your completed Design Project movies. See the Read This Before You Begin section at the beginning of this book for steps on how to set up a portfolio.
10. Put a copy of this movie in your portfolio.

FIGURE B-30
Completed Design Project

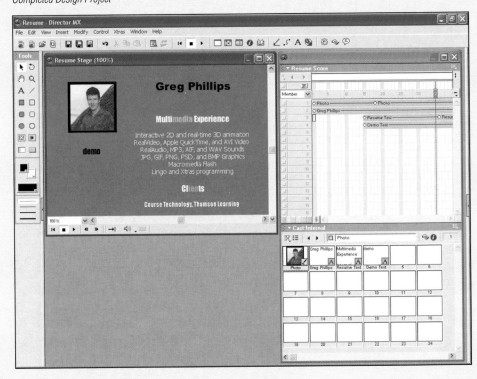

Your group can assign elements of the project to individual members, or work collectively to create the finished product.

You are a member of an astronomy research team at your university. Your team has been asked to create a self-running slide presentation on the topic of your choice for a booth at an upcoming space exploration convention. You use media elements from the Web and the media creation tools in Director to create a movie.

1. Work as a group to develop a written project plan, which includes the purpose, target audience, script, flowchart, storyboard, and minimum requirements for the delivery computer system.
2. Use images from the Web that are free for both personal and commercial use (check the copyright information for any image before downloading it).
3. Create a new movie and save it as **Space Pres**.
4. Develop a movie, containing the following:
   ■ A Stage, any size, with a black background
   ■ Imported images from the Web
   ■ Sprites from the cast members to create a slide show
   ■ Animated text sprites for titles and credits
   ■ A custom footer with a group name

5. Print all the cast members and the Score.
6. Play and save the movie presentation, then compare your screen to Figure B-31.

FIGURE B-31
Completed Group Project

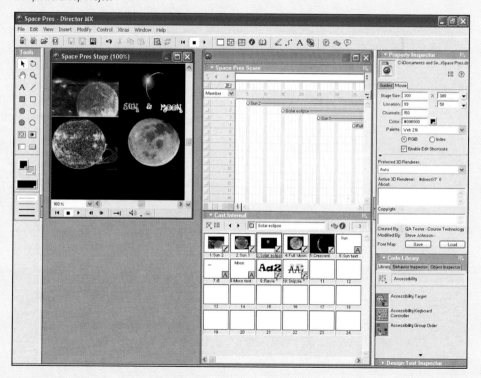

CREATING GRAPHICAL CAST MEMBERS

1. Draw a vector shape.

2. Modify a vector shape.

3. Draw a bitmap.

4. Apply special effects to a bitmap.

5. Apply color effects to a bitmap.

6. Add text to a bitmap.

Understanding Vector Shapes and Bitmaps

In Director, you can create new graphical media elements for the Cast window or import ones that have already been developed. Director provides several tools for creating graphical cast members. With Director's graphical tools, you can create vector shapes or bitmaps. A **vector shape** is a mathematical description of a geometric form, which is composed of line thickness, line color, line shape, fill color, corner points, and so on, while a **bitmap** is a pixel-by-pixel representation of a graphic. A **pixel** is an individual point in a graphic with a distinct color. To understand the difference between a vector shape and a bitmap, imagine a simple line. You can draw a line pixel-by-pixel as a bitmap, or you can draw a line from point A (the starting point) to point B (the ending point) as a vector shape. The simple line looks the same on the screen using either method, but the vector shape is more versatile. If you need a simple shape with minimal detail, a vector shape is the best choice. A vector shape also uses less drive storage and memory space than a bitmap and requires less download time from the Internet or other network. A vector shape can also be resized without incurring any loss of image quality, unlike a bitmap. If you need a more complex graphic in which you can edit individual pixels, a bitmap is the right choice.

Tools You'll Use

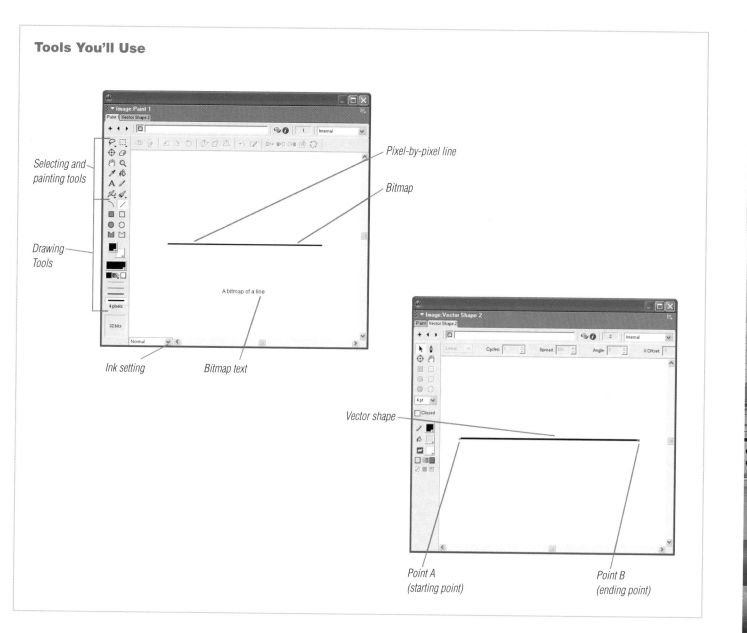

Selecting and painting tools

Drawing Tools

Ink setting

Bitmap text

Pixel-by-pixel line

Bitmap

A bitmap of a line

Vector shape

Point A (starting point)

Point B (ending point)

DRAW A VECTOR SHAPE

What You'll Do

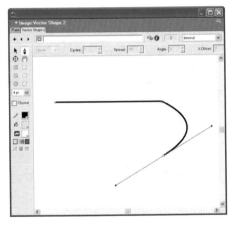

In this lesson, you will draw a regular and irregular vector shape.

Drawing a Vector Shape

A vector shape can be a line, a curve, or an open or closed shape that you can fill with a color or gradient. An **open shape** is one in which the starting point and the ending point do not connect. A **closed shape** is one in which the points do connect. A shape can be **regular**, such as an oval, rectangle, or rounded rectangle; or **irregular**, such as a free-form object, as shown in Figure C-1. You can fill the inside of a closed vector shape with a solid color, two-color pattern, or **gradient** blend, which is shading from one color to another color, as shown in Figure C-2. You can also vary the thickness of the vector shape's outline.

You create a vector shape in the Vector Shape window by plotting points to define a path and by controlling the curvature of the line between the points. When you create a vector shape, you create **vertices** (also called points), which are fixed points,

Drawing on the Stage

With Director's Tool palette, you can create text, shapes, and buttons directly on the Stage. The shapes you create with the Tool palette are called **QuickDraw graphics**. These graphics are neither vector shapes nor bitmaps. You can resize and edit the QuickDraw shapes on the Stage, but you cannot edit them in the Paint window or in the Vector Shape window. QuickDraw graphics use a lot less memory than bitmaps, and print much better on laser printers, but animate more slowly than bitmaps or vector shapes.

and **control handles**, which determine the degree of curvature between the vertices, as shown in Figure C-1. This type of curvature is known as a **Bézier curve**. The vertices allow you to resize a vector shape without losing sharpness and detail, unlike a bitmap. Every vector shape you create becomes a cast member.

QUICKTIP

You can create a vector shape entirely with Lingo (a scripting language specific to Director) and control it while a movie is playing.

Anti-Aliasing a Vector Shape

When you create a vector shape with thick lines, the edges can look jagged around the curves. You can anti-alias a vector shape to blur the edges, which makes the jagged edges appear smooth. You can apply anti-aliasing to a vector shape by selecting the vector shape in the Cast window and the Anti-Alias check box on the Vector tab in the Property inspector. Anti-aliasing is turned on by default when you create a vector shape.

FIGURE C-1
Vector shape

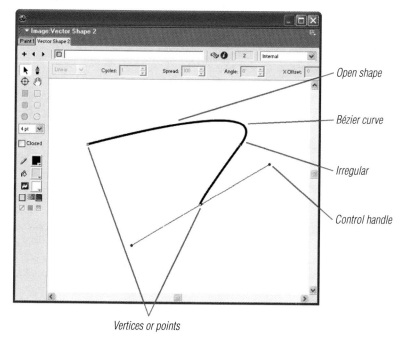

Open shape

Bézier curve

Irregular

Control handle

Vertices or points

FIGURE C-2
Vector shape with gradient

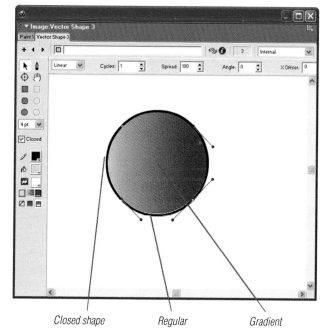

Closed shape

Regular

Gradient

Draw a regular vector shape

1. Start Director and save the new movie as **Space Graphics** where your Unit C data files are stored.

2. Click the Stage window, click the Movie tab in the Property inspector, click and hold the color box until the color palette appears, then click the last square (white) in the second row of the color palette.

3. Click the Vector Shape Window button on the toolbar. $\mathbf{5}$

   TIP   To create a vector shape quickly, click a shape tool on the Tool palette, then click a blank area in the Vector Shape window.

4. Click the Filled Ellipse tool  on the Tool palette in the Vector Shape window, then position the Drawing pointer in the drawing area, as shown in Figure C-3. +

5. Press and hold [Shift], then drag the Drawing pointer in a right downward diagonal to create the proportional shape shown in Figure C-4. +

   TIP   To move a vector shape, click the Arrow tool, then drag any part of the shape, except a point.

6. Click the Cast Member Name text box, type **Jupiter**, then press [Enter] (Win) or [return] (Mac).

You created a regular vector shape.

FIGURE C-3
Vector Shape window

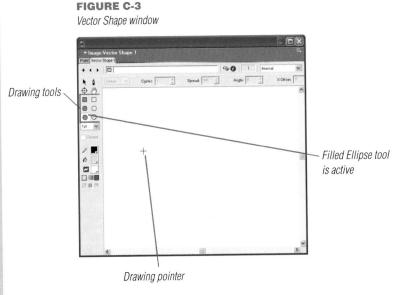

Drawing tools

Filled Ellipse tool
is active

Drawing pointer

FIGURE C-4
Vector shape of a circle

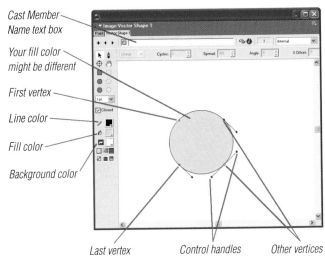

Cast Member
Name text box

Your fill color
might be different

First vertex

Line color

Fill color

Background color

Last vertex   Control handles   Other vertices

FIGURE C-5

Vector shape of an irregular free form

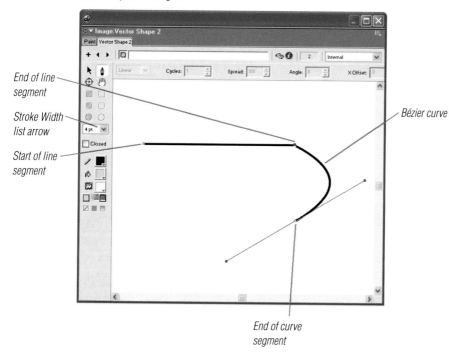

End of line segment

Stroke Width list arrow

Start of line segment

Bézier curve

End of curve segment

1. In the Vector Shape window, click the New Cast Member button. ✚

2. Click the Stroke Width list arrow, then click 4 pt.

3. Click the Pen tool 🖊 on the Tool palette, then position the Drawing pointer in the Vector Shape window. ┼

4. Click the upper-left side of the Vector Shape window to start the first line segment, press and hold [Shift], then click the right side of the window to create the first line segment.

5. Position the drawing pointer approximately halfway down the Vector Shape window, even with the end of the line segment, then click and drag to the left to create a curve similar to the one shown in Figure C-5.

   > TIP If you release the mouse button before you drag the angle that you want, press [Delete] and drag again.

6. Click the Cast Member Name text box, type **Dipper**, then press [Enter] (Win) or [return] (Mac).

7. Close the Vector Shape window, then view the two new cast members in the Cast window.

8. Save your work.

You created an irregular vector shape.

MODIFY A VECTOR SHAPE

What You'll Do

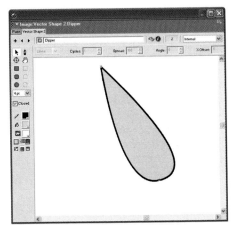

In this lesson, you will add a gradient to a vector shape and edit a vector shape.

Adding a Gradient to a Vector Shape

After you create a vector shape, you can modify it by adding and changing the color, pattern, or gradient blend. A gradient can be **linear** (shading from one color on one side to another color on the other side) or it can be **radial** (shading from one color in the center to another color on the outside), as shown in Figure C-6. After you add a gradient, you can change the cycle value, the spread value, the angle value, and the stroke width using toolbar buttons at the top of the Vector Shape window. The **cycle value** determines how many times the gradient repeats from the start color to the end color within the vector shape. The **spread value** controls whether the gradient is weighted more toward the start color or the end color. A value of 100 distributes

Adjusting the registration point

When you place a vector shape on the Stage, the shape is placed relative to its registration point. You use the **registration point**, which is initially set to the center of the shape, to position the shape, bitmap, or cast member accurately on the Stage. Director uses the registration point to determine a shape's position when you animate the shape. To adjust the registration point for a vector shape, open the vector shape in the Vector Shape window, then click the Registration Point tool on the Tool palette. The default registration point appears as crosshairs at the center of the vector shape. Click a new location in the window to set a new registration point. To reset the registration point to the center of the vector shape, you can double-click the Registration Point tool. You can change the registration point for a bitmapped cast member in the same way.

the gradient evenly between starting and ending colors. Values greater than 100 weight the gradient toward the starting color, and values less than 100 weight it toward the ending color. For a linear gradient, the **angle value** controls the direction of the gradient. The **stroke width** determines the thickness of lines and outlines.

Editing a Vector Shape

In addition to inserting a gradient, you can edit a vector shape by moving, adding, or deleting control points and by changing the way the control points affect control curves. To edit a vector shape, you need to open the vector shape in the Vector Shape window. You use the Arrow tool to select the point you want to edit. After you select a point on a vector shape, you can press [Delete] or [Backspace] to remove it, or you can drag the point to a different location to change a curve. When you view a vector shape, selected points are unfilled, and unselected points are filled. For curves in a vector shape, the first point is green, the last point is red, and all other points are blue, as shown in Figure C-6. If you want to close the path to create a shape that you can fill, select the Closed check box on the Tool palette. You can click anywhere in an open shape to add end points or click anywhere on a line in a closed shape to add points. You can also use buttons at the bottom of the Tool palette to change a line, fill, and background color, change a shape solid, and remove a fill.

FIGURE C-6
Radial gradient in a vector shape

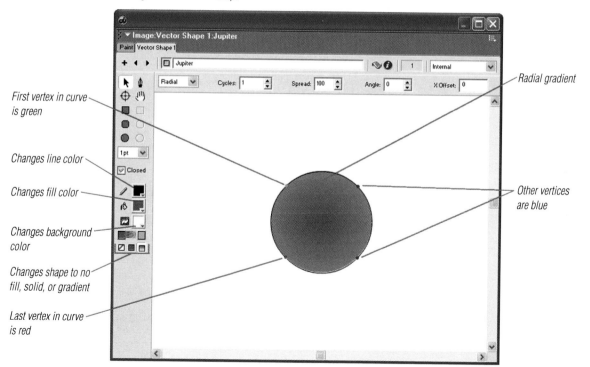

First vertex in curve is green

Changes line color

Changes fill color

Changes background color

Changes shape to no fill, solid, or gradient

Last vertex in curve is red

Radial gradient

Other vertices are blue

Add a gradient to a vector shape

1. Double-click the Jupiter vector shape cast member in the Cast window.

2. Click and hold the starting Gradient Colors color box until the color palette appears, click the first color square (orange-red) in the seventh row on the color palette, click and hold the ending Gradient Colors color box, then click the last color square (yellow) in the fifth row on the color palette.

3. Click the Gradient tool on the Tool palette in the Vector Shape window.

4. Verify that the gradient type is Linear, as shown in Figure C-7, then click the Gradient Cycles up arrow until it reaches 7.

5. Double-click the Gradient Spread text box, type **200**, then click a blank area of the Vector Shape window.

6. Double-click the Gradient Angle text box, type **75**, then click a blank area of the Vector Shape window.

7. Click the Stroke Width list arrow, click 0 pt, then compare your screen to Figure C-8.

   TIP To resize and keep the proportions of a vector shape, click the Arrow tool, press and hold [Ctrl] [Alt] (Win), or press and hold [⌘] [option] (Mac), then drag a point to the size you desire.

You added a gradient to a vector shape and modified it.

FIGURE C-7

Adding a gradient to a vector shape

Gradient type

Starting gradient color

Gradient button   Ending gradient color

FIGURE C-8

Modifying a gradient

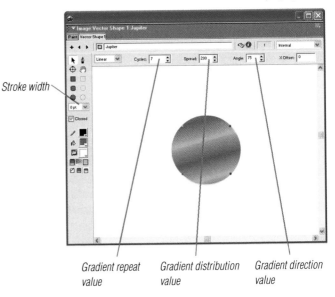

Stroke width

Gradient repeat value   Gradient distribution value   Gradient direction value

FIGURE C-9

Adjusting the curvature of a vector shape

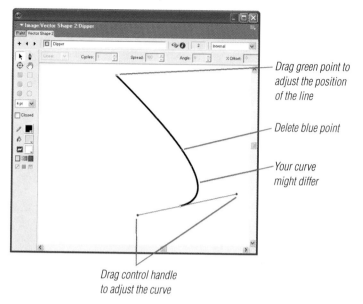

Drag green point to
adjust the position
of the line

Delete blue point

Your curve
might differ

Drag control handle
to adjust the curve

FIGURE C-10

Closing a vector shape

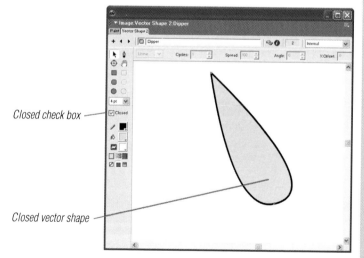

Closed check box

Closed vector shape

Lesson 2   Modify a Vector Shape

Edit a vector shape

1. In the Vector Shape window, click the Next Cast Member button. ▶

2. Click the Arrow tool on the Tool palette in the Vector Shape window if necessary. ▶

3. Drag the green end point to the top-middle area of the Vector Shape window, as shown in Figure C-9.

4. Click the red end point, then drag a control handle to adjust the curve, as shown in Figure C-9.

5. Click the blue point in the middle of the shape, then press [Backspace] or [Delete] to delete it.

    > TIP   To change a corner point to a curve point, press and hold [Alt] (Win) or [option] (Mac), then click the corner point and drag the control handle.

6. Select the Closed check box on the Tool palette, as shown in Figure C-10.

7. Close the Vector Shape window, select the Dipper cast member in the Cast window, then press [Backspace] or [Delete] to delete it.

8. Save your work.

You edited a vector shape.

DRAW A BITMAP

What You'll Do

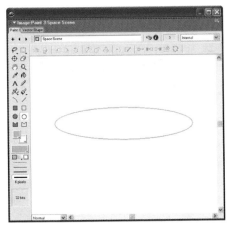

In this lesson, you will draw a bitmap in the Paint window.

Learning About Bitmaps

A bitmap can consist of any arrangement of pixels, connected or disconnected. You can edit single pixels, groups of pixels, or all the pixels in a bitmap. When you resize a bitmap, the image will lose some quality. You can alleviate part of the problem by using the anti-aliasing feature. Anti-aliasing blends the bitmap's colors with background colors around the edges to make the edge appear smooth instead of jagged. A bitmap requires more drive storage and memory space than a vector shape. The larger the bitmap, the greater the amount of storage and memory space required.

Drawing a Bitmap

Director includes a simple paint program known as the Paint window to allow you to create and edit bitmapped cast members without having to use another program, such as Adobe Photoshop. Every bitmap you create in the Paint window becomes a cast member. You create and modify a bitmapped cast member by using the tools on the Tool palette along the left side of the Paint window, as shown in Figure C-11. For example, you can select a color or pattern, a line width, and a drawing tool, then drag to draw a bitmapped shape. A small arrow in the lower-right corner of a tool indicates that pop-up menu options are available for that tool. To display the pop-up menu, you click a tool, then press and hold the mouse button. The toolbar at the top of the Paint window contains buttons you can use to apply effects to bitmapped cast members. You can use the Paint Window Preferences dialog box to modify the settings of several tools, such as setting a brush tool to display the last color used and setting line thickness for the line tools.

Changing the View of the Paint Window

Sometimes when you are drawing a picture with the drawing or painting tools or modifying artwork with the Eraser tool, you need to view individual pixels. The Magnifying Glass tool allows you to zoom in to view artwork pixel by pixel and zoom out to return to normal view. To zoom in, you click the Magnifying Glass tool on the Tool palette, then click the artwork (the Magnifying Glass pointer will contain a plus sign). Click again to increase the magnification. As you gain in magnification, a miniature shape appears in the corner of the Paint window. You press [Shift] and click the artwork (the Magnifying Glass pointer will contain a minus sign) to zoom out.

FIGURE C-11

Tool palette in the Paint window

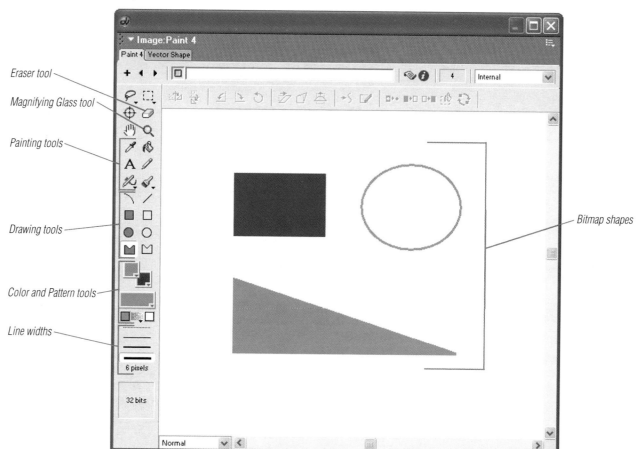

Eraser tool

Magnifying Glass tool

Painting tools

Drawing tools

Color and Pattern tools

Line widths

Bitmap shapes

Change Paint window preferences

1. Click Edit (Win) or Director (Mac) on the menu bar, point to Preferences, then click Paint.

   The Paint Window Preferences dialog box opens, as shown in Figure C-12.

2. Click the "Other" Line Width right or left arrow until it reaches 6 to change the default line thickness for the line tools.

3. Click OK.

You changed the default line width preference for the Paint window.

FIGURE C-12
Paint Window Preferences dialog box

Custom line width

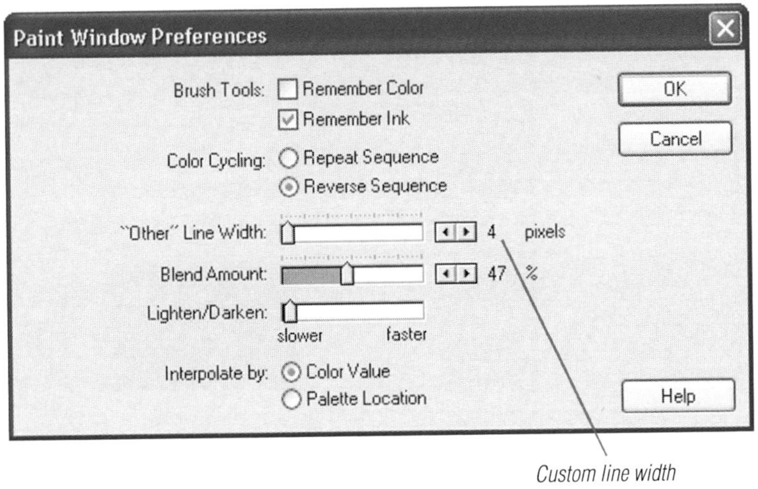

FIGURE C-13

Drawing an elliptical shape

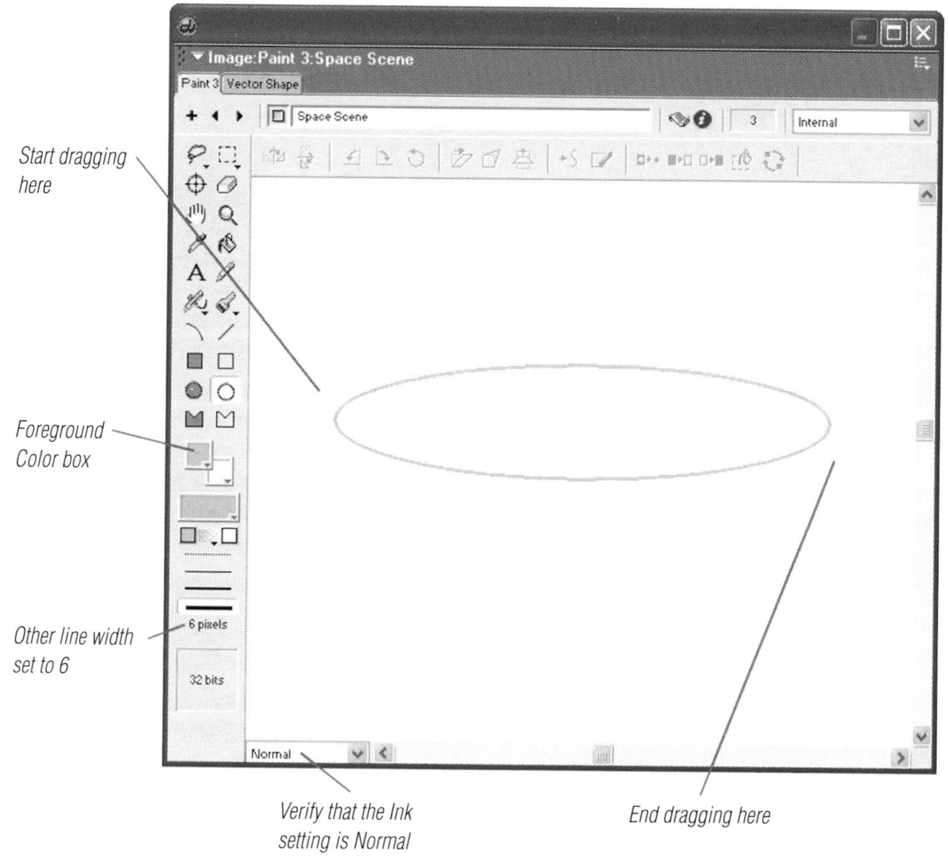
Start dragging here
Image:Paint 3:Space Scene
Paint 3
Vector Shape
Space Scene
3
Internal
Foreground Color box
Other line width set to 6
6 pixels
32 bits
Normal
Verify that the Ink setting is Normal
End dragging here

Draw a bitmap

1. Click the Paint Window button on the toolbar, then verify that the Ink setting (displayed at the bottom of the Paint window) is Normal.
2. Click the Cast Member Name text box, type **Space Scene**, then press [Enter] (Win) or [return] (Mac).
3. Click and hold the Foreground Color box, then click the ninth light gray color square in the third row of the color palette.
4. Click the Ellipse tool on the Tool palette, position the Drawing pointer on the left side of the window, then drag to draw an elliptical shape, as shown in Figure C-13.

   TIP If the shape doesn't match the figure, double-click the Eraser tool to erase it, then repeat step 4.
5. Click the Magnifying Glass tool on the Tool palette, then click anywhere on the elliptical shape.
6. Press [Shift], then click anywhere in the Paint window to return to normal view.
7. Close the Paint window, then save your work.

You created a bitmap in the Paint window.

APPLY SPECIAL EFFECTS TO A BITMAP

What You'll Do

In this lesson, you will rotate and apply effects to a bitmap.

Applying Effects to a Bitmap

The toolbar at the top of the Paint window contains buttons you can use to apply effects to bitmapped cast members, as shown in Figure C-14. These effects allow you to flip, rotate, skew, and warp the contents of a selection. You can also create a perspective effect and an outline around the edges of a selected bitmap. The Paint window also includes tools for controlling the color and pattern of cast members. You can apply color effects to soften edges, reverse colors, increase or reduce brightness, fill solid or pattern, or switch colors.

Before you can apply an effect, you need to select all or part of the bitmap. Director has two main tools that you use to make selections: Lasso and Marquee, as shown in Figure C-14. You use the **Lasso tool** to select irregular areas or polygons. You use the **Marquee tool** to select rectangular areas. You can apply effects, such as flip, rotate, skew, warp, and perspective, to areas selected by the Marquee tool. You can use either tool to apply color effects to a selection.

Using Auto Distort to create animation

After you apply a special effect, such as rotate, skew, warp, and perspective, to a bitmap, you can use Auto Distort to generate intermediate cast members to create a frame-by-frame animation. After you use the Free Rotate, Skew, Warp, or Perspective buttons in the Paint window, select the Auto Distort command on the Xtras menu, enter the number of intermediate cast members that you want to create in the Auto Distort dialog box, then click Begin. Director creates new cast members in the Cast window with gradual changes, showing the entire special effect. You can use the individual cast members to create a frame-by-frame animation.

Selecting with the Lasso and Marquee Tools

To select an irregular area with the Lasso tool, click the Lasso tool, then drag to enclose the area you want to select. To select a polygon area with the Lasso tool, press and hold [Alt] (Win) or [option] (Mac) while you click to create anchor points to enclose the shape. The Lasso tool selects only those pixels that are of a different color than the ones you select when you first drag the selection. To select a rectangular area with the Marquee tool, drag the tool to enclose the area you want to select.

You can press and hold the Lasso tool or Marquee tool to display a pop-up menu of settings, such as Shrink (Marquee tool only), No Shrink, Lasso, and See Thru Lasso. Shrink tightens the selection rectangle around the selected object, while No Shrink selects the entire selection area. Lasso tightens the selection around the selected object. See Thru Lasso tightens the selection around the selected object and changes your selection to transparent (pixels with the same color as the first pixel selected are not included in the selection).

FIGURE C-14
Bitmap special effects

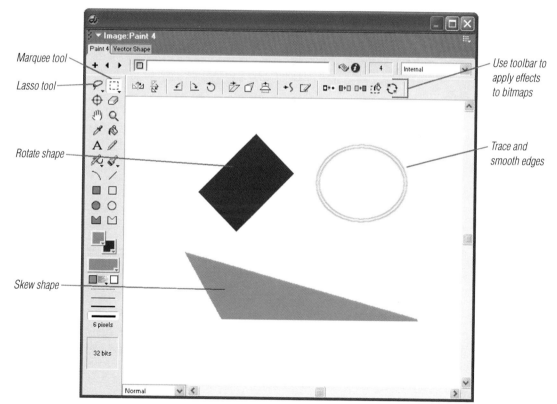

Marquee tool

Lasso tool

Rotate shape

Skew shape

Use toolbar to apply effects to bitmaps

Trace and smooth edges

Apply special effects

1. Double-click the Space Scene cast member in the Cast window.

2. Click and hold the Marquee tool, click No Shrink if necessary, then drag a selection rectangle around the ellipse.

   > TIP To select the entire drawing, double-click the Marquee tool; to size the selection proportionately, press and hold [Shift] while you drag.

3. Click the Trace Edges button on the Paint toolbar.

4. Click the Smooth button on the Paint toolbar.

5. Click the Skew button on the Paint toolbar.

6. Position the Drawing pointer on the upper-left corner handle, drag right to skew the ellipse, as shown in Figure C-15, then click a blank area of the window (outside the selection).

   > TIP To make a copy of the area that is selected with the Marquee tool, press and hold [Alt] (Win) or [option] (Mac), then drag the selection.

You applied special effects to a bitmap.

FIGURE C-15
A bitmap with special effects

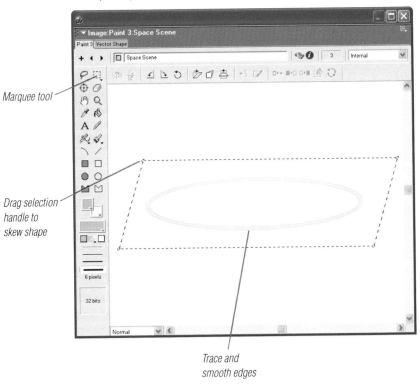

Marquee tool

Drag selection handle to skew shape

Trace and smooth edges

FIGURE C-16
Rotating a bitmap

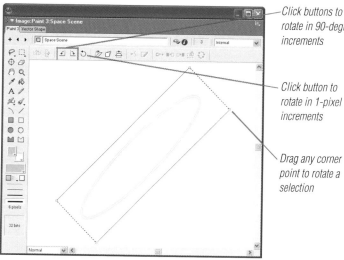

Click buttons to rotate in 90-degree increments

Click button to rotate in 1-pixel increments

Drag any corner point to rotate a selection

FIGURE C-17
Moving a bitmap

Lasso tool

Move shape here

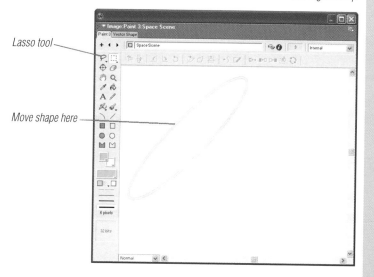

Lesson 4   *Apply Special Effects to a Bitmap*

Rotate a bitmap

1. Use the Marquee tool to drag a selection rectangle around the ellipse.

   TIP After you select an area with the Marquee tool, you can press and hold [Ctrl] (Win) or [command] (Mac), then drag a border of the selected area to resize the selection.

2. Click the Free Rotate button on the Paint toolbar.

3. Position the drawing pointer on a corner rotate handle, drag to rotate the ellipse approximately 45 degrees, as shown in Figure C-16, then click a blank area of the window (outside the selection).

4. Click and hold the Lasso tool until the pop-up menu appears, then click Lasso if necessary.

5. Position the Lasso pointer near the ellipse in the Paint window, then drag an outline around the ellipse (try to end the selection at the point where you started it).

   TIP If you did not entirely enclose the selection, Director connects its starting and ending points when you release the mouse button.

6. Drag the ellipse to the upper-left corner of the visible Paint window (don't scroll), then click a blank area of the window (outside the selection) to deselect the shape, as shown in Figure C-17.

7. Close the Paint window, then save your work.

You rotated, selected, and moved a bitmap.

APPLY COLOR EFFECTS TO A BITMAP

What You'll Do

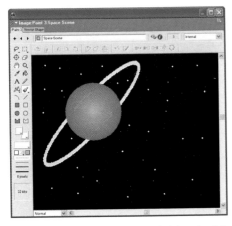

In this lesson, you will apply ink and painting effects to a bitmap.

Using Color

Color is an important element of any bitmap. You can set three colors in the Paint window: foreground color, background color, and destination color. The foreground color is the color that you use with the paint tools, the fill color for solid patterns, and the primary color in multicolored patterns. The background color is the secondary color in multicolored patterns. The destination color is the ending color of gradient blends that start with the foreground color, as shown in Figure C-18.

Applying Ink Effects

You can use Paint window inks to create color effects for bitmap cast members. You can select an ink effect from the Ink pop-up menu at the bottom of the Paint window, as shown in Figure C-18. The result of the ink you choose depends on if you are working in color or black and white. In addition, some inks work better when painting with patterns, and others work better when painting with solid colors. For example, the Transparent ink effect works best with patterns in black

Selecting colors with the Eyedropper tool

The Eyedropper tool is commonly used with a paint tool; it selects a color from the artwork, which you can then use as the foreground, background, or destination color. To select a color as the foreground, click the Eyedropper tool on the Tool palette, position the bottom tip of the eyedropper pointer over the color you want to select, then click the color. To use the eyedropper pointer to select a background color, press [Shift], then click a color. To select a color as the destination color, press [Alt] (Win) or [option] (Mac), then click a color. After you select a color, you can use the Paint Bucket tool to fill an area of pixels.

and white or color and makes the background color in patterns transparent, while the Reverse ink effect works best with both patterns and solids in black and white and changes any color to its mirror color at the opposite end of the color palette. In addition to working well with solids and patterns, some ink effects work well with specific painting tools. For example, the Gradient ink effect works well with Brush, Bucket, and shape tools in black and white or color and paints a blend of colors, starting with the foreground color and ending with the destination color. Ink effects are permanent.

Applying Painting Effects

The Paint window includes tools for applying painting effects to your artwork. The main paint tools are the Pencil, Paint Bucket, Brush, and Air Brush tools, as shown in Figure C-18. You use the Pencil tool to draw lines pixel by pixel. You use the Paint Bucket tool to fill all adjacent pixels of the same color with the foreground color. You use the Brush tool to brush strokes with the current foreground color, ink, and fill pattern. The Brush tool displays a pop-up menu in which you can define five different brush sizes and shapes. You use the Air Brush tool to spray the current foreground color, ink, and fill pattern. The longer you spray the Air Brush tool in one spot, the more it fills in the area. You can define the following spray settings in the Air Brush Settings dialog box: flow rate, spray area, dot size, and dot options.

Using Patterns

Instead of using a solid fill color in a bitmap, you can use a pattern. A pattern consists of a small image that is repeated continuously to fill in a shape, such as a rectangle, ellipse, or polygon. The current foreground and background colors are the primary and secondary colors, respectively, in a multicolored pattern, as shown in Figure C-18. To display a palette of patterns, click and hold the Pattern tool on the Tool palette. The pattern palette includes preset patterns, but you can also click Pattern Settings to add your own patterns. When you create your own pattern, the Pattern Settings dialog box displays an enlarged version of any pattern you select, which you can edit.

FIGURE C-18
Ink effects

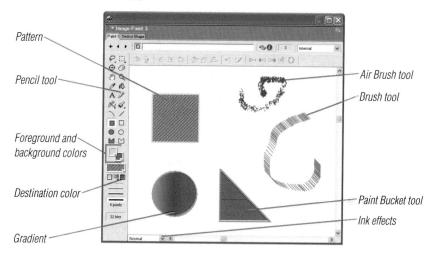

Pattern

Pencil tool

Air Brush tool

Brush tool

Foreground and background colors

Destination color

Paint Bucket tool

Ink effects

Gradient

Apply ink effects

1. Double-click the Space Scene cast member in the Cast window.

2. Click and hold the starting Gradient Colors color box, click the first color square (orange) in the fifth row on the color palette, click and hold the ending Gradient Colors color box, then click the last color square (yellow) in the third row on the color palette.

3. Click the middle Gradient Colors box, then click Sun Burst.

   > TIP To create a custom gradient, click the middle Gradient Colors color box, click Gradient Settings, then specify the method, direction, cycles, spread, and range for the gradient.

4. Click the Pattern tool, click the first pattern in the first row, if necessary, then click the Filled Ellipse tool on the Tool palette.

5. Click the Ink list arrow, then click Gradient if necessary.

6. Press and hold [Shift], position the Drawing pointer beneath the ellipse, then drag to draw a circle, as shown in Figure C-19.

7. Click and hold the Marquee tool, click Lasso, then drag a selection rectangle around the circle.

8. Click the Ink list arrow, click Reverse, then drag the circle over the ellipse, as shown in Figure C-20.

9. Click a blank area of the window (outside the selection).

You applied ink effects to a bitmap.

FIGURE C-19
Applying a gradient ink effect

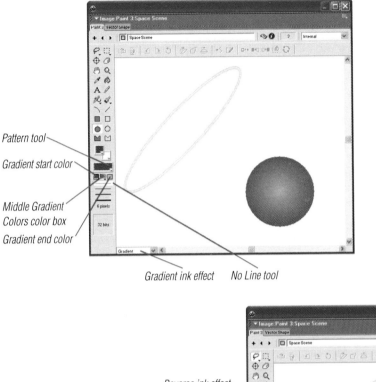

Pattern tool

Gradient start color

Middle Gradient
Colors color box

Gradient end color

Gradient ink effect   No Line tool

FIGURE C-20
Applying a reverse ink effect

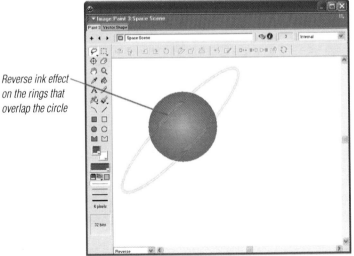

Reverse ink effect
on the rings that
overlap the circle

FIGURE C-21

Applying the Paint Bucket effect

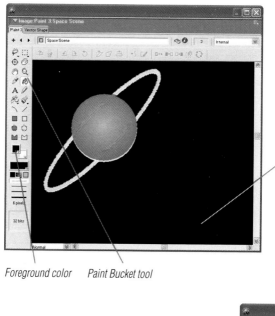

Foreground color
applied to background

Foreground color   Paint Bucket tool

FIGURE C-22

Applying the Brush effect

Brush tool

Arrow indicates a
pop-up menu is
available

Brush tool used
to create dots

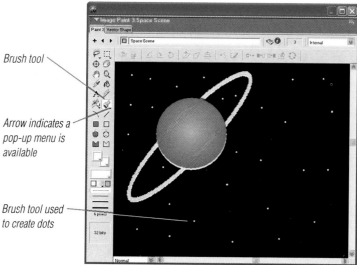

Apply painting effects

1. Click and hold the Foreground Colors box, then click the first black color in the first row on the color palette.

2. Click the Paint Bucket tool on the Tool palette, then click the white area of the Paint window, as shown in Figure C-21.

   TIP If the inside of the ring or other areas do not fill with black, click inside a white area to fill the entire area black.

3. Click and hold the starting Gradient Colors color box, then click the last white color square in the second row on the color palette.

4. Click and hold the Brush button on the Tool palette, then click Brush 1 if necessary.

5. Click and hold the Brush button on the Tool palette, then click Settings.

   TIP To open the Brush Settings dialog box quickly, double-click the Brush tool.

6. Click the dot in the lower-left corner of the dialog box, then click OK.

7. Click several times in the Paint window, as shown in Figure C-22, to create stars.

8. Close the Paint window, then save your work.

You applied painting effects to a bitmap.

ADD TEXT TO A BITMAP

What You'll Do

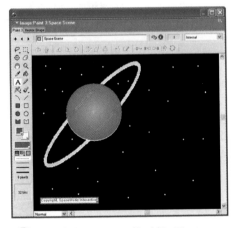

In this lesson, you will add text to a bitmap.

Adding Text to a Bitmap

When the Paint window is open, you can add text to a bitmap. When you add text to a bitmap, the text becomes part of the bitmap and is difficult to edit, so you should carefully consider the text you want to include. You must choose the font, font style, text spacing, and color before you finish creating the text. If you need to edit these items after you create the text, you must erase the original text and start over again. However, you can use effects in the Paint window to transform and change bitmapped text just as you would any other bitmap. You can flip, rotate, skew, and warp bitmapped text. Text created in the Paint window is not anti-aliased.

Creating a custom tile

A tile is a graphic that you can repeat in a pattern to create backgrounds, textures, or fillers. Custom tiles provide an effective way to create a background without using a lot of memory or increasing the download time for movies on the Web. A custom tile uses the same amount of memory no matter what size area it fills. You can create tiles from an existing cast member. To create a custom tile, display a bitmap cast member in the Paint window, click and hold the Pattern tool, click Tile Settings, click an existing tile to edit, click Cast Member, drag the dotted rectangle to the area of the cast member you want tiled, specify the size of the tile, then click OK. The new tile appears at the bottom of the Pattern palette. You can use the custom tile as a fill pattern. To do so, click and hold the Pattern tool, then click the custom tile at the bottom of the Pattern palette. You can use one of the Filled drawing tools or the Paint Bucket tool to fill an area with the custom tile.

FIGURE C-23

Font dialog box

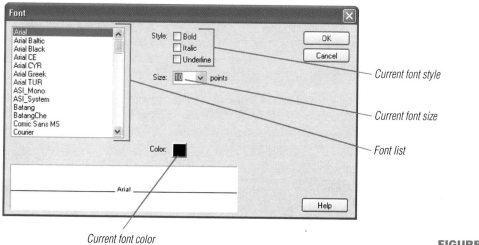

Current font style

Current font size

Font list

Current font color

Add text to a bitmap

1. Double-click the Space Scene cast member in the Cast window.

2. Click the Text tool on the Tool palette in the Paint window. **A**

3. Click Modify on the menu bar, then click Font.

   | TIP You can also double-click the Text tool to open the Font dialog box.

4. In the Font list, click Arial (scroll if necessary), click the Size list arrow, click 10, as shown in Figure C-23, then click OK.

5. Click and hold the Foreground Color box, then click the first color square (orange) in the fifth row on the color palette.

   | TIP You can also select a color by clicking the color box in the Font dialog box.

6. Click the lower-left corner of the Paint window, type **Copyright, SpaceWorks Interactive**, then drag any edge of the text box to move it to the place shown in Figure C-24.

7. Click the Marquee tool to deselect the text box. :⁻:

8. Close the Paint window, save the movie, then exit Director.

You added text to a bitmap.

FIGURE C-24

Adding text to a bitmap

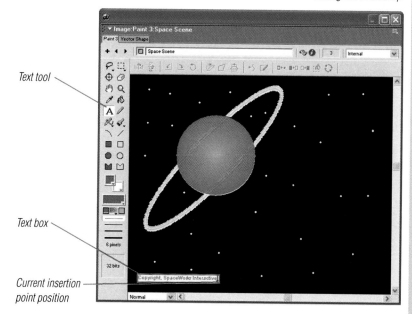

Text tool

Text box

Current insertion
point position

Lesson 6   Add Text to a Bitmap

101

Draw a vector shape.

1. Start Director, open MD C-1.dir, then save it as **Space Graphics Final**.
2. Open the Vector Shape window.
3. Create a new cast member if necessary.
4. Draw a circle, then name the cast member **Sun**.
5. Close the Vector Shape window.

Modify a vector shape.

1. Open the Sun vector shape cast member, then add a gradient to the circle.
2. Change the starting Gradient Colors color box to a bright yellow.

3. Change the ending Gradient Colors color box to a bright red.
4. Change the gradient type to Radial, then change the gradient cycles to 2.
5. Change the stroke width to 0 pt.
6. Create a new cast member in the Vector Shape window.
7. Change the stroke width to 4 pt.
8. Draw a line and add a curve to it.
9. Adjust the line to a longer length, then change the curvature of the line.
10. Close the Vector Shape window.

Draw a bitmap.

1. Open the Paint window.

2. Change the foreground color to red and the background color to orange.
3. Click the Pattern box, click the seventh pattern square in the seventh row, then draw a circle.
4. Select the circle shape and move it to the center of the window.
5. Name the cast member **Planet Scene** and close the Paint window.

Apply special effects to a bitmap.

1. Open the Planet Scene cast member in the Paint window.
2. Change the skew of the circle shape.

3. Flip the circle shape horizontally.
4. Move the circle shape to the lower-left corner of the window.
5. Change the Pattern box so that it displays the first square in the first row.
6. Close the Paint window.

Apply color effects to a bitmap.

1. Open the Planet Scene cast member in the Paint window, then change the line width to No Line.
2. Change the foreground color to black.
3. Fill the background of the Paint window with black.
4. Change the brush setting to the dot in the fourth row and fourth column.
5. Change the foreground color to white.
6. Change the ink effect to Blend, then click individual dots in the window.
7. Change the ink effect to Normal.
8. Close the Paint window.

Add text to a bitmap.

1. Open the Planet Scene cast member in the Paint window, then select the Text tool.
2. Verify that the font is Arial, that the font size is 10, and that the color is orange.
3. Add your initials to the lower-left corner of the Paint window, then compare your screen to Figure C-25.
4. Close the Paint window, save the movie, then close Director.

FIGURE C-25
Completed Skills Review

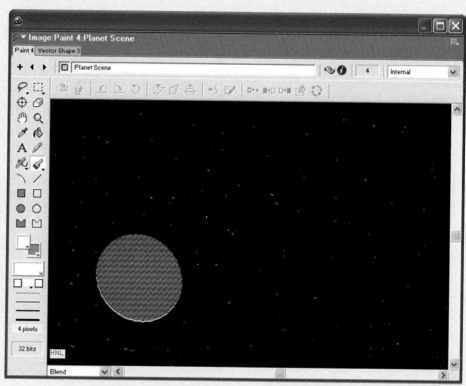

You are the chief designer and owner of Unique Pools, a company that designs uniquely shaped swimming pools. The owner of Gourmet Jelly Beans asks you to design the corporate swimming pool in the form of a jelly bean, which he wants to display on their Web site to promote the company. You use Director's Vector Shape tools to create the jelly bean shape and add a blue gradient to represent water.

1. Start Director and save the movie as **Unique Pools**.
2. Open the Vector Shape window.
3. Draw a large circle and change the curves to form a jelly bean.
4. Add a blue gradient from left to right to represent water.
5. Change the stroke width to 2 pt and the stroke color to dark blue.
6. Name the cast member **Jelly Bean Pool**, and close the Vector Shape window.
7. Create a text cast member with the text **Pool Designed by Unique Pools**.
8. Place both cast members on the Stage and add a color background.
9. Compare your screen to Figure C-26.
10. Print the Stage, save the movie, then exit Director.

FIGURE C-26
Completed Project Builder 1

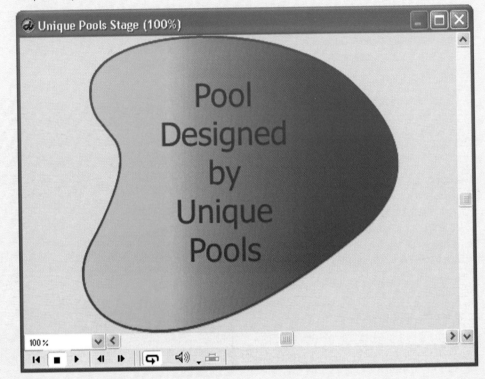

You are a student at the state university. Your history professor gives you an assignment to create a multimedia presentation on your home state. You use Director's Vector Shape tools to create the shape of your state and add a gradient to represent the terrain.

1. Start Director and save the movie as **US State**.
2. Open the Vector Shape window.
3. Draw a free-form shape with lines and curves to represent any state in the U.S. (*Hint*: If you live in Colorado, Kansas, Nebraska, North Dakota, South Dakota, New Mexico, or Wyoming, try to pick another state.)
4. Modify the lines and curves to display the outline of the state.
5. Add a gradient that represents the terrain of the state.
6. Change the stroke width to 1 pt and the stroke color to black if necessary.
7. Name the cast member **US State**, and close the Vector Shape window.
8. Create a text cast member with the text **US State presentation by [Your Name]**.
9. Place both cast members on the Stage and add a background color.
10. Compare your screen to Figure C-27.
11. Print the Stage, save the movie, then exit Director.

FIGURE C-27
Completed Project Builder 2

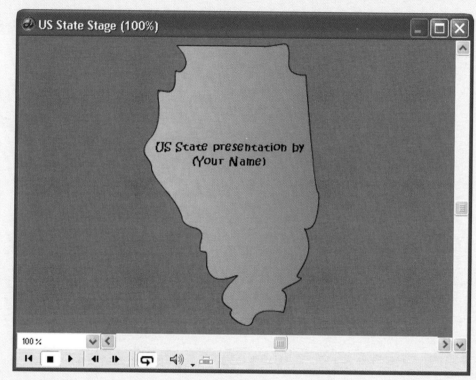

You are the chief designer at Borderlines, a company that designs company logos and advertising banners. The president of Garfield Graffiti Removal, Inc. asks you to design a company logo for use on their company Web site and in Web advertising banners. You use Director's Paint tools to create a company logo.

1. Start Director and save the movie as **Borderlines**.
2. Open the Paint window, draw a large unfilled rectangle with a gray 2 pt border for the logo, then use other drawing and painting tools to create a background (similar to the one shown in Figure C-28) within the gray border.
3. Add the text **Garfield Graffiti Removal** to the logo, using the Text tool.
4. Add different color graffiti to the logo, using the Airbrush tool. (*Hint*: Do not cover the text with the Airbrush tool.)
5. Name the cast member **GGRI Logo**, and close the Paint window.
6. Create a text cast member with the text **GGRI LOGO DESIGNED BY BORDERLINES**.
7. Place both cast members on the Stage, then compare your screen to Figure C-28.
8. Print the Stage, save the movie, then exit Director.
9. Put a copy of this movie in your portfolio.

FIGURE C-28
Completed Design Project

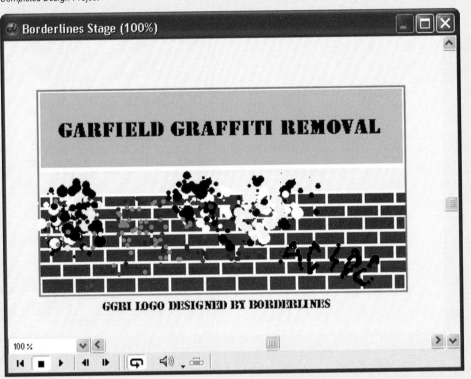

Your group can assign elements of the project to individual members, or work collectively to create the finished product.

You are a member of the graphics design team at Fifth Avenue Advertising & Design. The president of the New York City Olympic Committee asks your team to create an Olympic logo for a multimedia presentation they are developing for the International Olympic Committee. You use Director's Paint tools to create the Olympic logo.

1. Start your browser and go to *www.olympic.org*. Review past Olympic logos for ideas.
2. Assign each member of the group to create a design for the Olympic logo.
3. Start Director and save the movie as **NYC Olympics**.

4. Develop a movie with several logo designs using the Paint tools; include the Olympic rings and the text **New York**, then name each cast member.
5. Create a text cast member with the text **New York Olympic Logo designed by Fifth Avenue Advertising and Design**.

FIGURE C-29
Completed Group Project

6. Place the cast members on the Stage and add a color background.
7. Compare your screen to Figure C-29.
8. Print the Stage, save the movie, then exit Director.

MANAGING AND MODIFYING CAST MEMBERS

1. Create and save a cast.

2. Change the Cast window.

3. Organize cast members.

4. Change cast member properties.

5. Transform a bitmap cast member.

6. Add and modify a text cast member.

7. Create and modify 3D text.

8. Link and unlink a cast.

Managing Cast Members

A complex Director movie can often require a large number of cast members. When you assemble a large number of cast members in a Cast window, it can sometimes be difficult to locate the one you want. You can use management and organization tools in Director to help alleviate the hassle of scrolling through a long list of cast members.

Organizing Cast Members

Organizing your cast members from the beginning will ensure that both your movie-making process and your movie run smoothly. You can use several techniques to organize and manage cast members: name each cast member with a unique identifier, group similar cast members together, and create multiple casts. Lingo, Director's programming language, identifies cast members in scripts by their name, so the naming convention should identify the media element's function or purpose. Help button, Space background, Blue Earth graphic, or Welcome text are good examples of cast member names and are more descriptive than simply Button,

Graphic, Text, or no name at all. When grouping similar cast members together, you can move cast members around to any location in the Cast window; they are not required to be in consecutive order. You can leave a few blank cast member windows between each group to separate each section of the Cast window visually. If you decide to organize your cast members by creating multiple Cast windows, you can create ones that contain cast members by type, such as buttons and navigation, text, pictures, sounds, videos, transitions and effects, and behaviors and scripts.

Modifying Cast Members

After you import or create a cast member, you might need to modify it to meet your design goals. Sometimes you might need to resize a graphic cast member or change its color setting to match the movie, while other times you might need to convert a text cast member to a bitmap, customize its alignment and spacing, or change it to 3D text. You can use graphic and text tools in Director to help transform and customize cast members.

Tools You'll Use

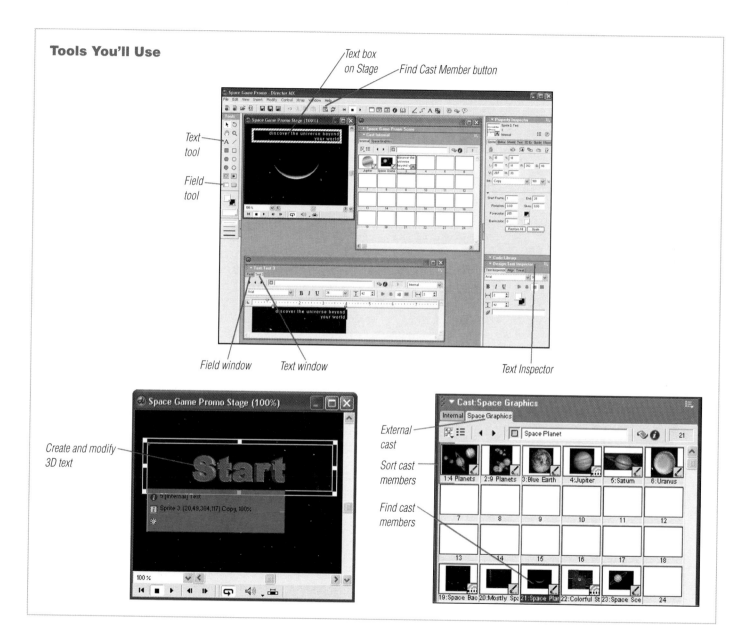

Text box on Stage

Find Cast Member button

Text tool

Field tool

Field window

Text window

Text Inspector

Create and modify 3D text

External cast

Sort cast members

Find cast members

CREATE AND SAVE A CAST

What You'll Do

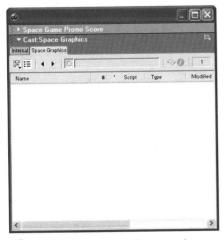

In this lesson, you will create and save a cast.

Creating a Cast

In Director, your movies literally can have a cast of thousands—you can include up to 32,000 cast members in a Cast window. Before you create and assemble a large number of cast members for a movie, you should think about how you want to organize them. Director allows you to create and work with multiple casts in a movie. If you notice that you use certain media elements in more than one movie, you can organize them into separate casts. Separating them saves the time and inconvenience of importing them individually for each movie. When you create a new cast, you need to decide whether to create an **internal cast**, which is saved as part of the movie, or an **external cast**, which is saved in a separate file outside the movie. If you plan to use cast members in one movie only, then use an internal cast. If you plan to share cast members in more than one movie, then use an external cast. When you use cast members from an external cast, it's easiest if you first link

the cast to the movie so it's always available for use. However, even if you don't link an external cast to the movie, you can still open the external cast and add, remove, and modify cast members. When you distribute a movie that uses an external cast, you need to include the external cast file. You can add as many internal or external casts as you want; each cast is viewed as a tabbed panel in the Cast window.

Saving a Cast

You can use the Save All or Save button on the toolbar to save an external cast. The Save All button on the toolbar allows you to save the movie and all open casts, linked or unlinked. When you select the Stage window before you use the Save button, Director saves the movie and all linked Cast windows; when you select an unlinked External Cast window, Director saves just the external cast. The external cast file is saved with a .cst extension.

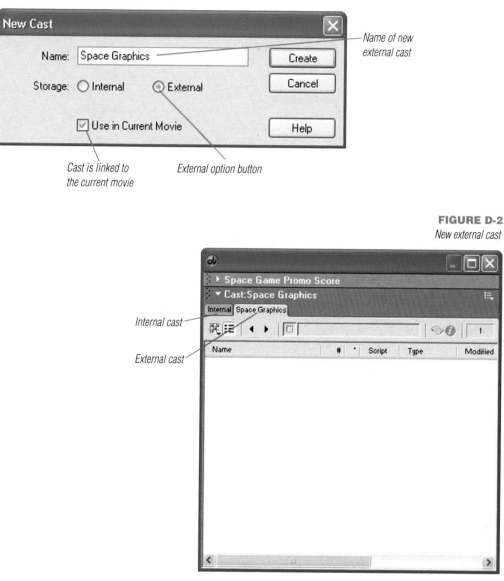

Name of new
external cast

External option button

Cast is linked to
the current movie

Internal cast

External cast

Create and save a cast

1. Start Director, open the file MD D-1.dir from where your Unit D data files are stored, save it as **Space Game Promo**, then change the background to black if necessary.

2. Click the expander arrow in the Score to collapse the panel.

3. Click and hold the Choose Cast button in the Internal Cast window, then click New Cast to open the New Cast dialog box.

4. In the Name text box, type **Space Graphics**.

5. Click the External option button, as shown in Figure D-1.

6. Click Create to display a tabbed panel with two casts in the Cast window, as shown in Figure D-2.

   TIP To open an unlinked external cast, click File on the menu bar, click Open, select an external cast file, then click Open.

7. Click the Save button on the toolbar to open the Save Cast "Space Graphics" dialog box.

   TIP To save an external cast with a new name, click the Cast window, click File on the menu bar, then click Save As.

8. Navigate to the location where your Unit D data files are stored, then click Save to save the external cast and the movie.

You created and saved an external cast in the Cast window.

CHANGE THE CAST WINDOW

What You'll Do

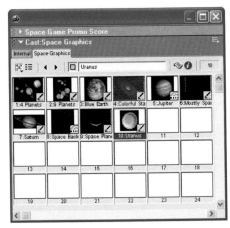

In this lesson, you will view and switch between casts and change Cast window preferences.

Viewing and Switching between Casts

When you create or open a cast, it appears as a tabbed panel labeled with the cast name in the Cast window. You can use the Choose Cast button or select a tab in the Cast window to switch between open casts easily, as shown in Figure D-3. In the Cast window, you can view the cast in List view or Thumbnail view. List view works best for organizing cast members, while Thumbnail view works best for visually finding cast members. You can use the Cast View Style button in the Cast window to toggle between the List and Thumbnail views easily.

Changing Cast Window Preferences

You can use the Cast Window Preferences dialog box, as shown in Figure D-4, to control the appearance of the current cast or all open casts. When you open the Cast Window Preferences dialog box, the title bar of the dialog box displays the name of the selected Cast window and the dialog box displays the current preference settings for the Cast window, which you can change. In the Cast View section, you can select the default cast view style, either List or Thumbnail, for the selected cast or all open casts. In the List Columns section, you can select the type of information, such as the cast member type or size, you want to display in List view. Table D-1 describes the display features of List view. At the bottom of the Cast Window Preferences dialog box, you can select options that control the appearance of thumbnails in Thumbnail view, including the maximum number of thumbnails visible in the Cast window and for each row, the thumbnail size (Small, Medium, or Large) and label type (Number, Name, or Number:Name), and whether to display a media type icon in the lower-right corner of each cast member. If you want to apply your preferences to all open casts in the Cast window, select the Apply to All Casts check box. If you want to make your preferences the default settings for all casts, open or not, use the Save As Default button.

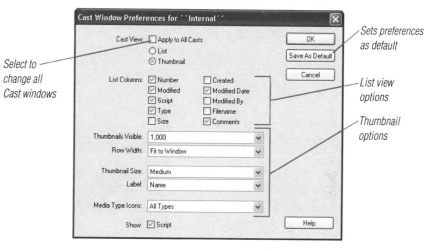

Tabbed panels

Choose Cast button

Select to change all Cast windows

Sets preferences as default

List view options

Thumbnail options

TABLE D-1: List View Display Features

column	title description
Number	Number assigned to the cast member (appears as (#) in the Cast window)
Modified	Cast member changes need to be saved (appears as (.) in the Cast window)
Script	Script type: *Member* means the cast member is a script; *Movie* means the cast member is a movie script; *Behavior* means the cast member is a behavior
Type	Cast member type
Size	Size in bytes, kilobytes, or megabytes
Created	Date and time the cast member was created
Modified Date	Date and time the cast member was changed
Modified By	Name of the person who modified the cast member
Filename	Full path to the cast member if it is a linked asset
Comments	Comments field on the Member tab of the Property inspector

View and switch between casts

1. Click the Space Graphics tab in the Cast window if necessary.

2. Click the Import button on the toolbar navigate to the location where your Unit D data files are stored, then open the Media folder 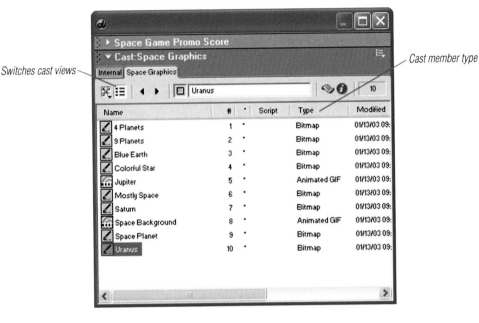

3. In the list of files, click a file, click Add All, click Import, then click OK to accept the selected graphic settings for each of the images and files.

4. If the Image Options dialog box or Select Format dialog box opens, use the selected settings, select the Same Settings for Remaining Image check box and the Same Format for Remaining Files check box (if available), then click OK as necessary.

5. Click the Cast View Style button in the Cast window (if necessary) to display the Cast window in List view.

6. Click the Internal tab in the Cast window to display the internal cast in Thumbnail view.

7. Click the Space Graphics tab in the Cast window, as shown in Figure D-5.

You imported cast members and viewed and switched between casts in the Cast window.

FIGURE D-5

External Cast window in List view

Switches cast views

Cast member type

FIGURE D-6

Cast Window Preferences dialog box

Current setting for
Space Graphics
Cast window

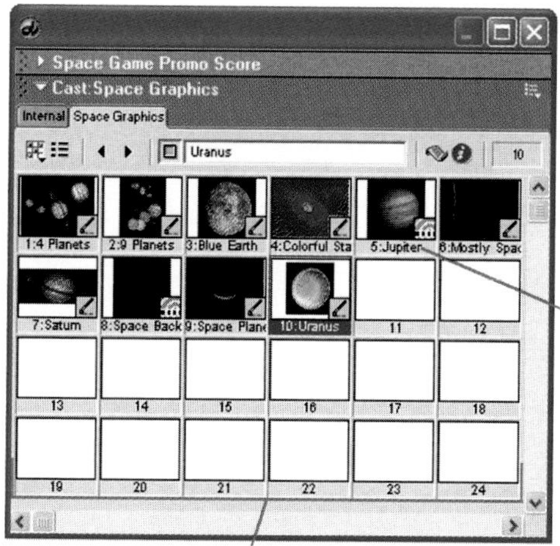

Change Cast window preferences

1. Click Edit (Win) or Director (Mac) on the menu bar, point to Preferences, then click Cast to open the Cast Window Preferences dialog box, as shown in Figure D-6.

   TIP You can also open the Cast Window Preferences dialog box by right-clicking a cast member (Win), or pressing and holding [control] and clicking a cast member (Mac), then clicking Cast Preferences.

2. Click the Thumbnail option button, then select the Apply to All Casts check box.

3. Click Save As Default, then click OK.

4. Click Edit (Win) or Director (Mac) on the menu bar, point to Preferences, then click Cast.

5. Deselect the Apply to All Casts check box, then select the Size check box.

6. Click the Label list arrow, then click Number:Name to change the label under the cast member in Thumbnail view.

7. Click OK to display the Space Graphics Cast window, then resize the Cast window to display six cast members in a row (if necessary), as shown in Figure D-7.

8. Click the Save All button to save the external cast and the movie. 💾

You changed Cast window display preferences.

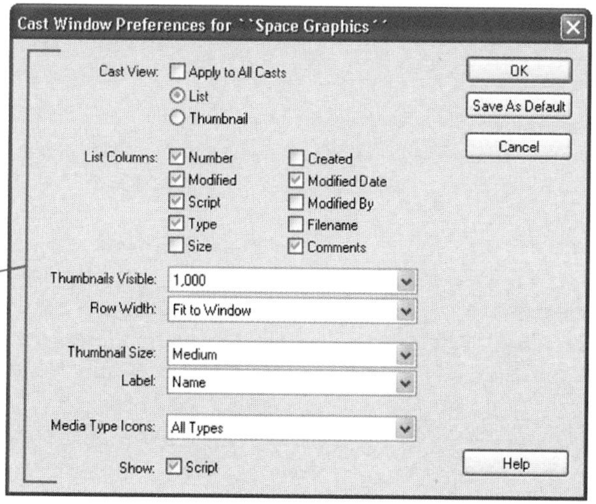

FIGURE D-7

External Cast window with new preferences

Number and name

External Cast window
in Thumbnail view

ORGANIZE CAST MEMBERS

What You'll Do

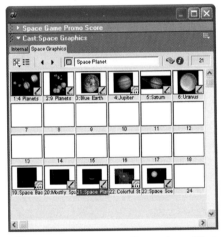

In this lesson, you will organize and find cast members.

Organizing Cast Members

Director allows you to move, copy, delete, and sort cast members. For example, you can click the column titles in List view to toggle easily between ascending and descending sort order, as shown in Figure D-8. When you click a column title, List view changes the display of the cast member information, but it doesn't change the cast member's original number or location on the Stage or the Score. You can use the Sort command to arrange cast members by their media type, name, size, or usage in the Score. You can also use the Sort command to remove empty cast member locations in a Cast window.

Deleting unused cast members

If you import or create a cast member that you don't end up using in the movie, you should delete it. When you delete unused cast members, your movie's file size becomes smaller and faster to load, and the file uses computer memory more efficiently. To delete unused cast members, click the Find Cast Member button on the toolbar. In the Find Cast Member dialog box, click the Cast list arrow, click a cast with unused cast members, click the Usage option button, click in the cast member list, then click Select All. Director finds and selects all cast members not used in the Score from the selected cast. Before you complete the deletion, make sure that the selected cast members are still not used in the movie. Embedded fonts, movie scripts, rollover-graphics, and fields used as variable containers are all examples of cast members that would not necessarily appear in the Score, yet are essential to the movie. To delete the selected cast members, press [Delete] or [Backspace], or click Edit on the menu bar, then click Clear Cast Members.

You can easily move or copy a cast member within the same Cast window or to another one. You might want to create copies of a cast member with minor differences, such as color or position, to create an animation effect. When you move a cast member to a new location, Director assigns it a new location number and updates all references to the cast member in the Score, but it does not update references to the cast member number in Lingo scripts, which is why it is best to name your cast members and then refer to them by name in Lingo.

You can also organize your cast members by deleting the ones that you don't need. When you delete a cast member, it is removed from the movie, even if it is being used on the Stage and in the Score. However, there still may be blank sprite references on the stage.

Finding Cast Members

If your movie contains several cast members, it may be difficult to locate a particular one. You can use the Find feature to locate cast members by name, type, color palette, or usage in the Score as shown in Figure D-9. When you name your cast members logically, you make it easy to find them. You can find multiple cast members with similar names. For example, cast members with the names Space Background and Space Scene share the common word "space." When you search by name, Director finds all the cast members with the common word at the beginning of the name. After Director completes the search, you can specify which cast members to select in the Cast window.

FIGURE D-8
Sorting columns in List view

Column titles

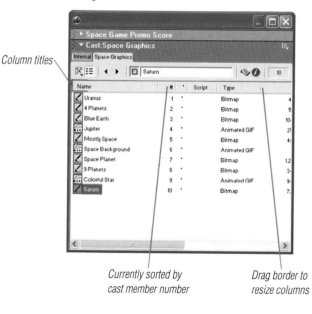

Currently sorted by cast member number

Drag border to resize columns

FIGURE D-9
Finding cast members

Changes casts

Options to find cast members

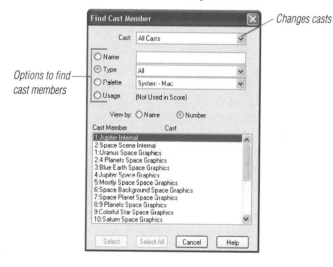

Organize cast members

1. Click the Cast View Style button in the Cast window to display the window in List view, then click the Name column title (Win) to sort the cast members by name in descending order, as shown in Figure D-10.

   TIP To resize the columns in List view, position the Column Resize pointer over the column title border, then drag the column to the desired size.

2. Click the Cast View Style button in the Cast window again to display the Cast window in Thumbnail view sorted by number.

3. Click the Internal tab in the Cast window, click the Jupiter cast member (if necessary), press and hold [Shift], then click the Space Scene cast member to its right to select both cast members.

4. Click the Copy button on the toolbar, click the Space Graphics tab in the Cast window, click the empty cast member 11, then click the Paste button on the toolbar.

5. Drag the Space Background cast member in the Space Graphics Cast window to empty cast member 19, then drag the cast members to the locations shown in Figure D-11 to separate space- and planet-related cast members.

   TIP If you drag a cast member to a location that already contains a cast member, the selected cast member will move where you place it, and the existing one will move one location to the right. However, if you paste a cast member into a location that already contains a cast member, the pasted cast member will overwrite the existing one.

   (continued)

FIGURE D-10
Sorting the Name column in List view

Sorted by cast member name in descending order

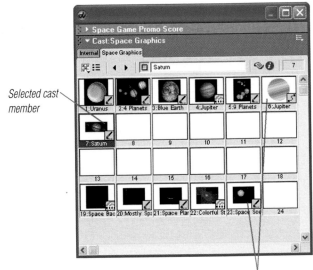

FIGURE D-11
Organizing cast members in the Cast window

Selected cast member

Cast members copied from the Internal Cast window

FIGURE D-12
Find Cast Member dialog box

Find criteria

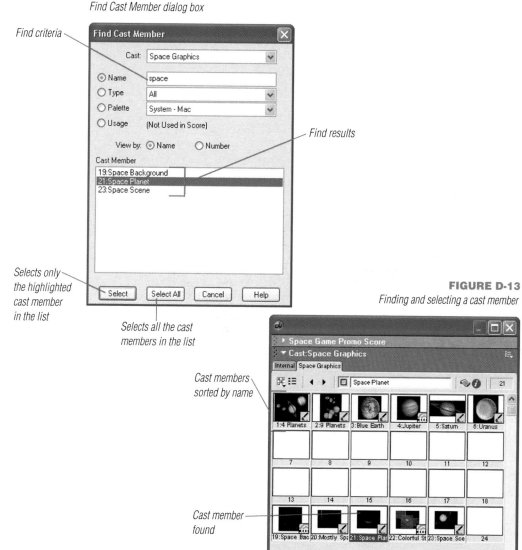

Find results

Selects only the highlighted cast member in the list

Selects all the cast members in the list

FIGURE D-13
Finding and selecting a cast member

Cast members sorted by name

Cast member found

6. Click the orange Jupiter cast member in the Space Graphics Cast window, then press [Delete] or [Backspace].

7. Click the Saturn cast member in the Space Graphics Cast window, press and hold [Shift], then click the Uranus cast member to select all of the cast members in the first two rows.

8. Click Modify on the menu bar, then click Sort to open the Sort dialog box.

9. Click the Name option button, then click Sort to sort the selected cast members by name.

You organized cast members in the Cast window.

Find cast members

1. Click the Find Cast Member button on the toolbar to open the Find Cast Member dialog box.

2. Click the Cast list arrow (Win) or pop-up menu (Mac), then click Space Graphics.

3. Click the Name option button in the View by section to display selected cast members in alphabetical order.

4. Click the Name option button that has an accompanying text box.

5. Click the text box to the right of the Name option button, then type **space**.

6. Click Space Planet in the list of cast members, as shown in Figure D-12.

7. Click Select to select the Space Planet cast member in the Cast window, as shown in Figure D-13.

8. Save all your work.

You found a cast member.

CHANGE CAST MEMBER PROPERTIES

What You'll Do

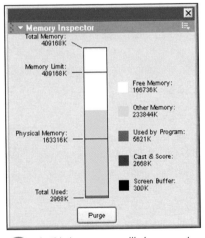

In this lesson, you will change cast member property settings.

Changing Cast Member Properties

You can view and change cast member properties for one or more cast members. If you select multiple cast members with different types, the information common to all the selected cast members appears. When you view cast member properties, a tab labeled with the cast member's type appears in the Property inspector. For example, if you click the Blue Earth cast member in the Cast window, the Bitmap tab in the Property inspector appears, as shown in Figure D-14. The Bitmap tab displays options for selecting a color palette, highlighting a bitmap when you click it (such as a button), dithering a bitmap (color matching when a color is not available), selecting alpha settings (the transparent area of a bitmap), trimming white space around a bitmap, and compressing a bitmap with a range of quality settings (the higher the quality, the lower the compression amount). The Bitmap tab also displays the dimensions and color depth of the cast member. The property

information available depends on the type of the selected cast member.

Setting Cast Member Priorities in Memory

You can also use cast member properties to manage memory usage in a movie. If Director determines that memory is running low while you play a movie, it unloads some cast members from memory so that other ones can be loaded. Director loads and unloads cast members to keep the movie playing as smoothly as possible. When memory is limited on the playback computer, the priority setting for loading and unloading cast members becomes crucial to the movie's performance.

Setting an Unload Value

You can set unload values to determine which cast members stay in memory and which ones are removed. You can use the Member tab in the Property inspector, as shown in Figure D-15, to set a cast member's unload value in memory. The **unload value** determines which cast members stay in memory and which ones are removed when the movie plays. The unload value ranges from 0 to 3, where 0 means never to remove the cast member from memory, and 3 means to unload the cast member from memory first (before cast members that have a 2 or 1 value assigned to them). You should assign heavily used cast members, such as a background, a 0 value, moderately used cast members a 2 or 1 value, and sparingly used cast members a 3 value.

Setting a Preload Value

In addition to the unload value, you can also set a cast member's preload value in memory using the Cast tab in the Property inspector (Win) or Lingo commands. The **preload value** determines when cast members are loaded into memory as the movie plays. The When Needed preload value loads each cast member into memory when it is needed by the movie as quickly as possible in the order in which it is used. The After Frame One preload value loads the cast members for the first frame as quickly as possible and then loads other cast members in the order in which they are used in the Score, up to the limit of available memory. The Before Frame One preload value loads all cast members into memory (up to the limit of available memory) before the movie plays the first frame.

Using the Memory Inspector

If you are about to perform a memory-intensive operation in Windows, you can use the Memory Inspector to monitor usage and purge all removable items from memory. The **Memory Inspector** displays information about how much memory is available to Director for your movie and indicates how much memory different parts of the current movie use and the total disk space the movie occupies.

FIGURE D-14
Property inspector with bitmap settings

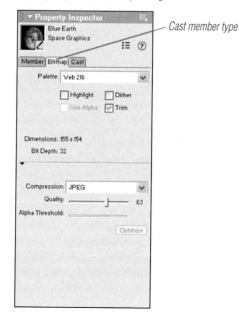

Cast member type

FIGURE D-15
Property inspector with cast member settings

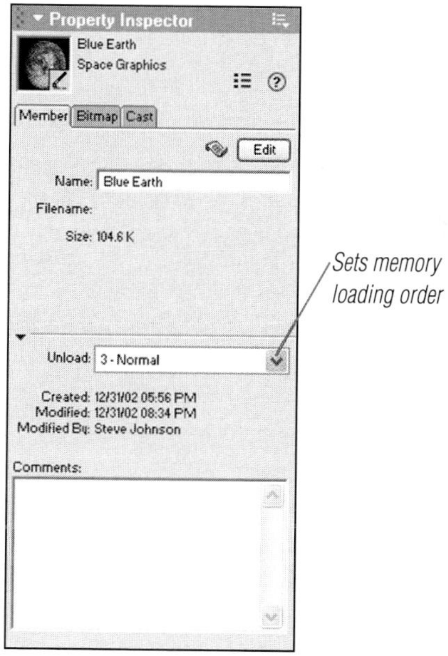

Sets memory loading order

Change cast member properties

1. Verify that the Space Planet cast member is selected in the Space Graphics Cast window.

2. Click the Cast Member Properties button in the Space Graphics Cast window to display the Bitmap tab in the Property inspector, as shown in Figure D-16. *ⓘ*

   TIP To get help using and setting cast member properties, click the Help button in the Property inspector.

3. Select the Dither check box to provide color matching.

4. Drag the Quality slider to 75 to increase the compression quality.

You changed cast member properties for a bitmap.

FIGURE D-16
Property inspector with Bitmap tab

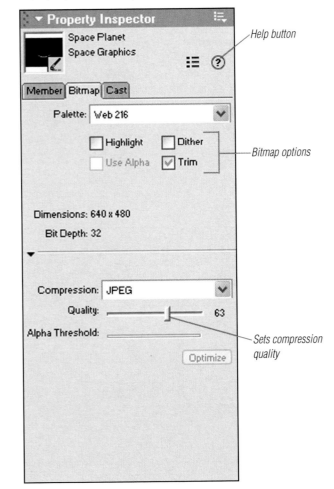

Property inspector with Cast tab

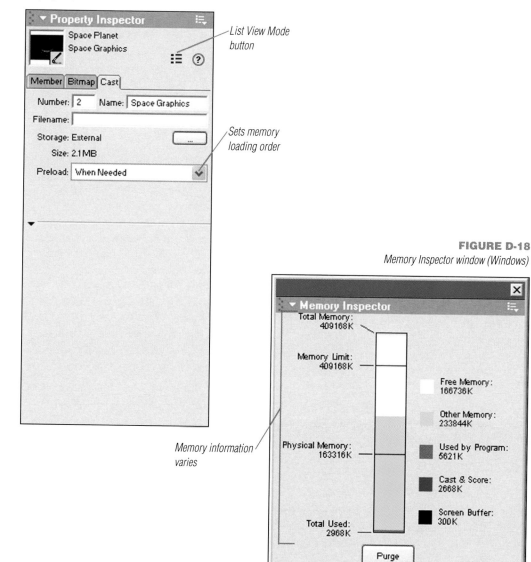

Memory Inspector window (Windows)

Change cast member memory properties

1. Verify that the Space Planet cast member is selected in the Space Graphics Cast window.

2. Click the Member tab in the Property inspector

3. Click the Unload list arrow, then click 1 – Last.

4. Click the Cast tab in the Property inspector, as shown in Figure D-17.

   TIP To change the view mode in the Property inspector from Graphical view to List view, click the List View Mode button in the Property inspector.

5. Click the Preload list arrow, then click After Frame One (Win).

6. Click Window on the menu bar, then click Memory Inspector to open the Memory Inspector window, as shown in Figure D-18 (Win).

7. Click Purge, then close the Memory Inspector window (Win).

8. Save all your work.

You changed memory settings for a cast member.

TRANSFORM A BITMAP CAST MEMBER

What You'll Do

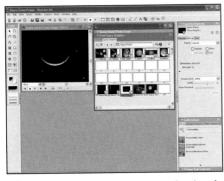

In this lesson, you will change the size of a bitmap.

Transforming a Bitmap Cast Member

Sometimes, after you import a bitmap into a cast, you may need to resize it or change its color settings to match the movie. You can use the Transform Bitmap command to change the size, color depth, and palette of selected cast members. You cannot undo the changes you make to a cast member after using the Transform Bitmap command, so make sure you have a duplicate of the original cast member. You can change the physical dimensions of a cast member by setting the Scale value as a percentage of the cast member's current size or by entering width and height values in pixels. The color depth option allows you to reset the number of colors used in the cast member, while the palette option allows you to assign a new color palette to the cast member. When you change to a new palette, you need to choose a method to match current colors with the ones in the new palette. You can either remap or dither the colors. **Remapping** replaces the original colors in the bitmap with the most similar solid colors in the new palette. This is the preferred option in most cases. **Dithering** blends the colors in the new palette to approximate the original colors in the bitmap.

Converting text to a bitmap

You can use the Convert to Bitmap command to change a text or field cast member to a bitmap. Converting text to bitmap avoids font issues, such as embedded fonts and differences in type sizes from one system to another. To convert text to a bitmap, select the text cast member, click Modify on the menu bar, then click Convert to Bitmap. The cast member type changes from text to bitmap. After you convert a cast member to a bitmap, you cannot undo the change and edit the text. Make sure you have a duplicate of the original cast member before making the change. You can modify the converted bitmap in the Paint window.

FIGURE D-19
Transform Bitmap dialog box

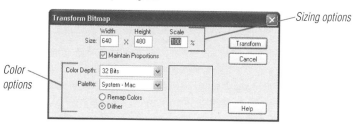

Sizing options

Color
options

FIGURE D-20
Sizing a bitmapped cast member

Resized bitmapped
cast member

Bitmapped cast
member

Dimensions of the
bitmapped cast member

1. Verify that the Space Planet cast member is selected in the Space Graphics Cast window.

2. Click Modify on the menu bar, then click Transform Bitmap.

3. If an alert box appears, asking you to launch an external editor, click Continue to open the Transform Bitmap dialog box, as shown in Figure D-19.

   > TIP If you click Launch External Editor in the alert box, an imaging program such as Fireworks opens, in which you can modify the bitmap.

4. Deselect the Maintain Proportions check box.

5. Double-click the Width text box, type **320**, press [Tab], then type **240** in the Height text box.

6. Click Transform, then click OK to perform the sizing change.

7. Drag the Space Planet cast member on the Stage, click the cast member on the Stage, press the arrow keys to reposition the cast member in the center of the Stage if necessary, then click the gray area around the Stage (scroll if necessary) to deselect the cast member.

8. Click the Space Planet cast member in the Space Graphics Cast window, then click the Bitmap tab in the Property inspector, as shown in Figure D-20.

9. Save all your work.

You changed the size of the bitmap.

ADD AND MODIFY A TEXT CAST MEMBER

What You'll Do

In this lesson, you will add and modify a text cast member.

Adding and Editing Text

Director provides several ways to create and edit text cast members. You can add text to and edit text directly on the Stage using the Text tool or the Field tool, and format it using the Text Inspector on the Design panel. When you use the Text or Field tools on the Tool palette, you create a text box on the Stage. The text box appears with an insertion point and a slanted-line selection rectangle, which allows you to add or edit text. When you select a text box on the Stage, it appears with a double-border selection rectangle, which means the entire text box is selected and any formatting changes you make will be applied to all the text. You can also use the Text window or the Field window to add or modify text. Figure D-21 illustrates the different ways you can create and edit text. The text you create using the Text tool or Text window is called **regular text**, while the text you create using the

Customizing text alignment using tabs

Numerical information is often easier to read when you align the text with tabs. A tab is used to position text at a specific location in the Text window. You should use tabs rather than the Spacebar to align your text vertically because tabs are more accurate, faster, and easier to change. When you press [Tab], the insertion point moves to the next tab stop. A **tab stop** is a predefined position in the text to which you can align tabbed text. By default, tab stops are located every ½" from the left margin, but you can also create and modify tab stops. You can click the Tab button on the left side of the ruler to select the type of tab you want. The tab marker **L** aligns text to the left, **⌐** aligns text to the right, **⊥** aligns text to the center, and **⊥** aligns numbers to the decimal point. After you select the type of tab you want, click the position on the ruler where you want to place the tab.

Field tool or Field window is called **field text**. Regular text looks good in large sizes because you can use anti-aliasing, which smoothes the jagged edges and curves of text. Field text works best for short passages of small-sized text, which saves space and uses less memory.

Aligning and Spacing Text

In the Text window, you can change the alignment, indentation, tabs, and spacing for each paragraph in a text cast member. The ruler in the Text window contains controls for indentation and tabs. You can change the indentation by dragging the **indent markers** on the ruler, which show the indent settings for the paragraph that contains the insertion point. Dragging the **Left Indent marker** indents the entire text, dragging the **First Line Indent marker** indents only the first line of the text and leaves the remaining lines aligned with the left margin, and dragging the **Right Indent marker** indents the text from the right margin. Because field text is limited, you can't change indentation and tabs in the Field window.

Line spacing controls the vertical spacing between lines of text, while **kerning** controls the horizontal spacing between certain parts of characters, as shown in Figure D-22. Kerning improves the appearance of text in large sizes but does very little to improve small text. You can change kerning for an entire text cast member or for individual text. When you kern individual text, you can refine letter spacing without affecting the kerning for an entire text cast member.

FIGURE D-21
Creating and modifying text

FIGURE D-22
Changing line spacing and kerning

Text tool

Text box on Stage

Field tool

Text Inspector

Field window

Text window

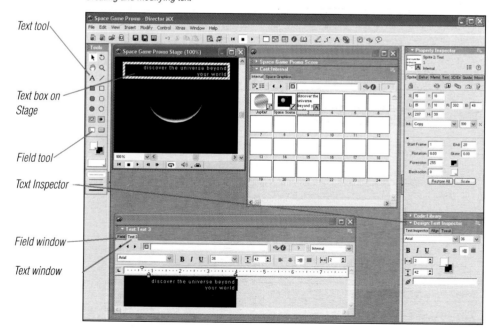

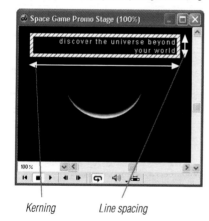

Kerning   Line spacing

Add text to and modify text on the Stage

1. Click the Internal tab in the Cast window, click empty cast member 3, click the Text tool **A** on the Tool palette, then drag the Drawing pointer from the upper-left side of the stage to the right side to create a text box. ╋

2. Verify that the Foreground Color box is white and that the Background Color box is black, then type **discover the universe beyond your world**, as shown in Figure D-23.

3. Click the slanted-line selection rectangle to select the entire text box.

4. Click the expander arrow on the Design panel, then click the Text Inspector tab if necessary.

5. Click the Align Center button in the Text Inspector, click the Font list arrow, click Arial Black, click the Size list arrow, then click 18 if necessary. ☰

6. Drag the right-middle sizing handle and center the text box to match Figure D-24.

7. Click the Field tool ▢ on the Tool palette, then drag the Drawing pointer from the lower-left side of the stage to the right side to create a text box. ╋

8. Click the Align Center button in the Text Inspector, click the Font list arrow, click Arial, click the Size list arrow, then click 12 if necessary. ☰

9. Verify that the Foreground Color box is white and that the Background Color box is black, type **www.spaceworksgames.com**, then drag text box to the center if necessary.

You added and modified text directly on the Stage.

Creating a text cast member on the Stage

Your font attributes might be different

Text box with a slanted-line selection rectangle

Slanted-line selection rectangle

Formatting a text cast member on the Stage

Double-border selection rectangle

Sizing handle

Formatting and spacing options

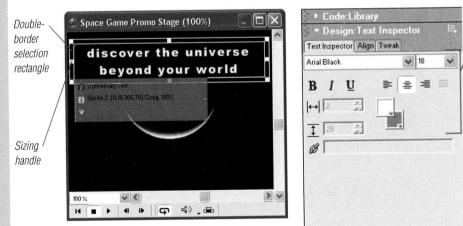

FIGURE D-25

Changing text indentation

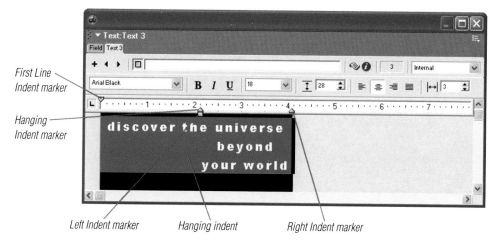

First Line Indent marker

Hanging Indent marker

Left Indent marker   Hanging indent   Right Indent marker

FIGURE D-26

Regular and field text on the Stage

Regular text

Field text

1. Double-click the *discover the universe beyond your world* text on the Stage, then select all the text in the text box.

2. Click the Line Spacing up or down arrow in the Text Inspector until it reaches 28.

3. Click the Kerning up or down arrow in the Text Inspector until it reaches 3.

   TIP To control kerning for a field text cast member, select a field text cast member, click Modify on the menu bar, point to Cast Member, click Properties, click the Kerning list arrow, then select a kerning option.

4. Click the expander arrow on the Design panel to collapse it, then click the expander arrow on the Code panel to expand it (if necessary) to display the default screen settings.

5. Double-click cast member 3 in the Internal Cast window to open the Text window.

6. Drag the Left Indent marker to 1" on the ruler. ☐

7. Drag the First Line Indent marker to 0" on the ruler. ▽

8. Drag the Hanging Indent marker to the position on the ruler to match Figure D-25. △

   TIP If the text doesn't appear as shown in Figure D-25, adjust the Hanging Indent marker to match the figure.

9. Close the Text window, deselect the text on the Stage, as shown in Figure D-26, then save all your work.

You changed text alignment and spacing.

CREATE AND MODIFY 3D TEXT

What You'll Do

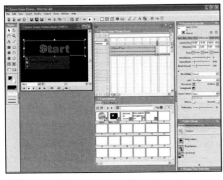

In this lesson, you will create and modify 3D text.

Understanding 3D Cast Members

In Director, you can create a 3D world like those found in many virtual games on CD-ROM or on the Web, or simply create 3D text for buttons and titles. Director uses 3D cast members to create a 3D world where each 3D cast member contains one or more models as well as lights and cameras. **Models** are the objects that users see within the 3D world. A model makes use of model resources, such as the outside surface of a model, known as the **shader** and **texture**. The relationship between a model and a model resource is similar to that between a sprite and a cast member. Multiple models can use the same model resource. Lights illuminate the 3D world and cameras act as windows into the 3D world. The Property inspector includes two tabs for working with 3D cast members: the 3D Extruder tab for text and the 3D Model tab for graphics. You can create 3D text and simple 3D graphics, such as spheres, boxes, and cylinders, in Director, as shown in Figure D-27, and import more complex models developed in 3D modeling programs in the W3D format.

Creating and Modifying 3D Text

Creating 3D text is a simple extension of creating 2D text; just modify the 2D text using the Text tab in the Property inspector to give it 3-dimensional depth. After you create 3D text, you can use the 3D Extruder tab in the Property inspector to modify it, as shown in Figure D-28. The 3D Extruder tab provides you with a comprehensive set of controls to enhance 3D text. The controls allow you to manipulate the following properties of 3D text:

- **Camera position and rotation settings:** These fields located at the top of the tab show the initial position and orientation of the default camera using the X axis, Y axis, and Z axis. The default camera position represents a vantage point looking up through the middle of the scene with the Z axis.
- **Front face, back face, and tunnel options:** These options control which sides of the text are displayed.

- **Smoothness slider:** This option controls the smoothness of the text. The higher the number, the smoother the text.
- **Tunnel Depth slider:** This option controls the length of the tunnel from the front face to the back face. The higher the number, the greater the depth.
- **Bevel options:** These options control the size and type of beveled edge. The beveled edge makes the edges of 3D text rounded or angled.

- **Light options:** These options control the lighting direction and position for a 3D model, known as the directional and ambient light, and the background color. Directional light comes from a particular direction, while ambient light is diffused illumination.
- **Shader Texture options:** These options control shaders and textures of a 3D model. Shaders control how the surface of the 3D text reflects light. The

shader is the surface of a 3D model, and the texture is an image applied to a shader. You can choose shader textures, which are simple 2D images that are drawn onto the surface of 3D text. You can also control the surface highlight color, known as specular; overall color, known as diffuse; and reflectivity.

FIGURE D-27
3D cast members

FIGURE D-28
Property inspector with 3D Extruder tab

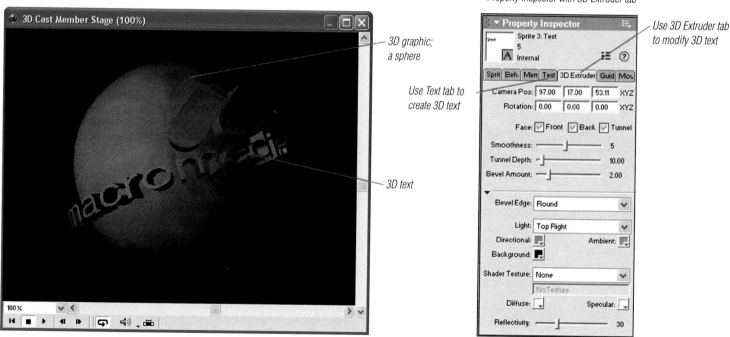

3D graphic; a sphere

Use 3D Extruder tab to modify 3D text

Use Text tab to create 3D text

3D text

Create 3D text

1. Click the expander arrow in the Score to expand the panel, then click frame 29 in channel 3 to position the text in the movie.

2. Click cast member 5 in the Internal Cast window, then click the Text Window button on the toolbar to open the Text window. **A**

3. Verify that the Foreground Color box is white, the Background Color box is black, and the font is Arial Black.

4. Click the Size list arrow, click 48, then type **Start**.

   | TIP If the text doesn't fit on one line, change the margins to adjust the size of the text box.

5. Close the Text window, then drag cast member 5 to the middle of the Stage.

6. Click the Text tab in the Property inspector if necessary.

7. Click the Display list arrow, then click 3D Mode to change the text to 3D, as shown in Figure D-29.

   | TIP You can use the Framing list arrow to modify the text box to fit the size of the 3D text, scroll, or stay fixed.

You created 3D text.

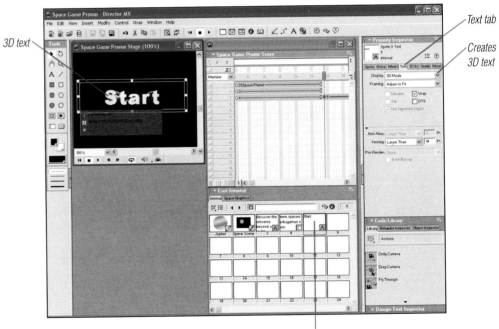

3D text

Text tab

Creates 3D text

3D text cast member

1. Select the 3D text box (if necessary), then click the 3D Extruder tab in the Property inspector.

   TIP When you edit 3D text on the Stage, the 3D effect is temporarily removed.

2. Click the Light list arrow, then click Top Right.

3. Click and hold the Background color box, then click the first square (black) in the first row of the color palette.

4. Click and hold the Directional color box, then click the first square (orange) in the fifth row of the color palette.

5. Click and hold the Ambient color box, then click the last square (orange) in the sixth row of the color palette.

6. Drag the Smoothness slider until it reaches 8, then drag the Tunnel Depth slider until it reaches approximately 10.

7. Click the Bevel Edge list arrow, click Round, then drag the Beveled Amount slider until it reaches 2.00.

8. Save all your work, then compare your screen to Figure D-30.

You modified 3D text.

FIGURE D-30

Modifying 3D text

Modified 3D text

3D text options

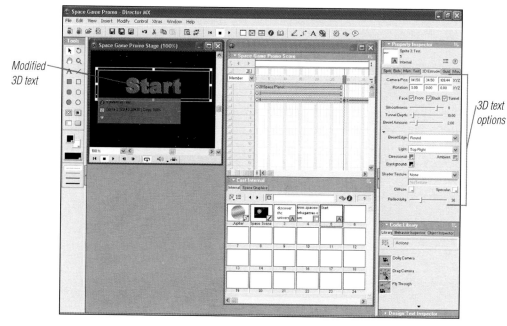

LINK AND UNLINK A CAST

What You'll Do

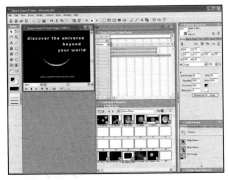

In this lesson, you will link and unlink a cast.

Linking and Unlinking a Cast

Before you can use external cast members in a movie, you need to link the external cast to the movie. After you link an external cast to the current movie, Director opens that cast whenever you open the movie. When you unlink an external cast from a movie, the cast is not available the next time you open the movie unless you open the external cast and relink it. When you make changes to an external cast that is not linked to your movie, you need to save the external cast. Director doesn't save changes to an external cast when you save the movie, because the external cast is not recognized as being part of the movie file. When you want to save an unlinked external cast, you can select the External Cast window and use the Save button on the toolbar. After you save an unlinked external cast, you can use the Save All button on the toolbar to save the unlinked external cast and the current movie. Remember to include the external cast file when you distribute and package a movie.

Creating a cast library

If you save an unlinked external cast in the Libs folder in the Director folder, you create a cast library. A cast library is a special type of unlinked external cast. When you drag a cast member from an external cast library to the Stage or Score, Director copies the cast member to one of the movie's internal casts. Libraries are useful for storing any type of commonly used cast members, especially behaviors. Unlike an external cast, a library cannot be linked to a movie.

Movie Casts dialog box

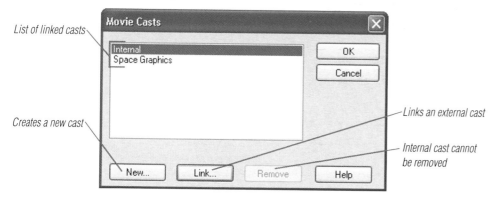

List of linked casts

Creates a new cast

Links an external cast

Internal cast cannot
be removed

Link and unlink a cast

1. Click the Space Graphics tab in the Cast window, then rewind the movie to display the first frame.

2. Click Modify on the menu bar, point to Movie, then click Casts to open the Movie Casts dialog box, as shown in Figure D-31.

3. Click Link, navigate to the location where your Unit D data files are stored, open the file Space Ships.cst, click choose (Mac), then click OK.

4. Click Window, point to Cast, then click Space Ships to display the cast in the Cast window.

    Space Ships is linked to the movie.

5. Click Modify on the menu bar, point to Movie, then click Casts.

6. Click Space Ships in the text box, then click Remove to unlink the cast.

7. Click OK to unlink the cast and display the Director window, as shown in Figure D-32.

8. Save all your work, then exit Director.

You linked and unlinked a cast.

FIGURE D-32
Director window with linked external cast

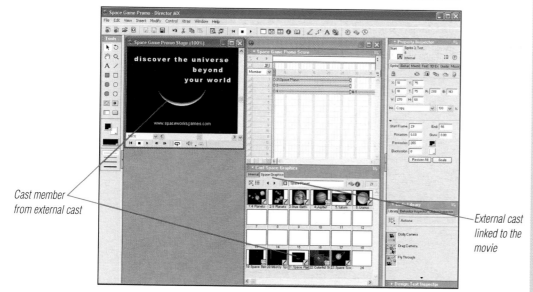

Cast member
from external cast

External cast
linked to the
movie

Create and save a cast.

1. Start Director and save the new movie as **Space Star** where your Unit D data files are stored.
2. Collapse the Score window if necessary.
3. Create a linked external cast as **Space Backgrounds** and save it where your Unit D data files are stored.

Change the Cast window.

1. Import all the files in the Media folder where your Unit D data files are stored into the Space Backgrounds Cast window (select format as Bitmap Image when requested).
2. Change the Cast view to a list.
3. Change the Cast preferences to display number, type, and size if necessary.
4. Switch to the Internal Cast window.
5. Switch to the Space Backgrounds Cast window.

Organize cast members.

1. Sort the list in descending order by size.
2. Change the Space Backgrounds Cast window view to Thumbnail, then resize the Cast window to display six columns (if necessary).
3. Move the cast members into two rows (one and three) by planets (4 Planets, 9 Planets, Blue Earth, Uranus, Jupiter, and Saturn) and backgrounds (Space Background, Mostly Space, Space Planet, and Colorful Star).
4. Sort each row by name.
5. Select the Colorful Star and Mostly Space cast members in the Space Backgrounds Cast window.
6. Copy and paste the cast members in the Internal Cast window (locations 1 and 2).
7. Find the Colorful Star cast member in the internal cast to select the cast member in the Internal Cast window.

Change cast member properties.

1. Select the Colorful Star cast member in the Internal Cast window if necessary.
2. Change the unload value to last and change the preload value to Before Frame One (Win).
3. Purge all removable items from memory (Win).

Transform a bitmap cast member.

1. Select the Colorful Star cast member in the Internal Cast window.
2. Change the dimensions of the cast member to 320 × 240.
3. Drag the Colorful Star cast member in the Internal Cast window onto the Stage.
4. Use the arrow keys to reposition the cast member in the center of the Stage.

Add and modify a text cast member.

1. Select cast member 3 in the Internal Cast window.
2. Use the Text tool to create a text box starting in the upper-middle area of the Stage.
3. Change the Foreground color to white and the Background color to black (if necessary).
4. Type **You can be a STAR!**
5. Change the Ink setting on the Sprite tab in the Property inspector to Background Transparent to make the text box background transparent.
6. Expand the Design panel and display the Text Inspector, then change the text to align right.
7. Change the text to a spacey-looking font and a large font size.
8. Collapse the Design panel.
9. Open cast member 3 (in the internal cast) in the Text window.
10. Create a hanging indent so that *You can* appears on the top line, *be a* appears on the next line, and *STAR!* appears on the next line down.
11. Change the line spacing and kerning to fill the right side of the Stage as shown in Figure D-33.
12. Name the cast member **Shining Star** and close the Text window.

Create and modify 3D text.

1. Change the Shining Star cast member to 3D text.
2. Change the light source to Bottom Left.
3. Change the directional color to the first square (blue) in the third to the last row, and the ambient color to the third square (pink) in the fifth row.
4. Change the smoothness to 10.
5. Change the bevel edge to Round and the bevel amount to approximately 1.80.
6. Change the tunnel depth to approximately 14.50.

Link and unlink a cast.

1. Link the cast file Space Ships.cst from where your Unit D data files are stored to the movie.
2. Open the Space Ships Cast window.
3. Unlink the Space Ships cast from the movie.
4. Expand the Score, then compare your screen to Figure D-33.
5. Save the movie, then exit Director.

FIGURE D-33
Completed Skills Review

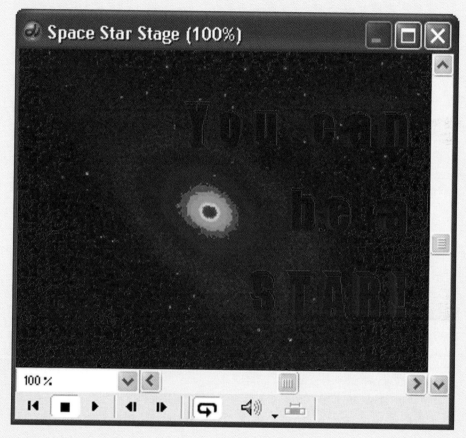

You are an estate planner at Langford Financial Services, an insurance and estate planning company. After years of using a generic company Web site, you decide it's time to create a customizable presentation about company products and services for clients. You use Director's Text and Paint tools to create media elements and an external cast to organize them.

1. Start Director and save the movie as **Langford Financial**.
2. Create a linked external cast and save it as **Financial Symbols**.
3. Using the Text tool, create and name cast members in the Financial Symbols Cast window with numbers and financial symbols.
4. Duplicate cast members in the Financial Symbols Cast window and convert the text to bitmaps.
5. Create a text cast member with the text **Are you confused by all the numbers?** and one with the text **Langford Financial Services**.
6. Change the text cast member Langford Financial Services to 3D text using the following settings: Smoothness 8, Tunnel Depth 19 (or as close as possible), Bevel Edge Miter, Bevel Amount 1.00, Light Top Center, Directional light blue, and Diffuse dark gray.
7. Organize the cast members by type (text and bitmap) in the Financial Symbols Cast window.

8. Resize a bitmap to 320 × 240 and create a background.
9. Print thumbnails of the Financial Symbols window and the Stage.

10. Place the background and the cast members on the Stage, then compare your screen to Figure D-34.
11. Save the movie and the external cast, then exit Director.

FIGURE D-34

Completed Project Builder 1

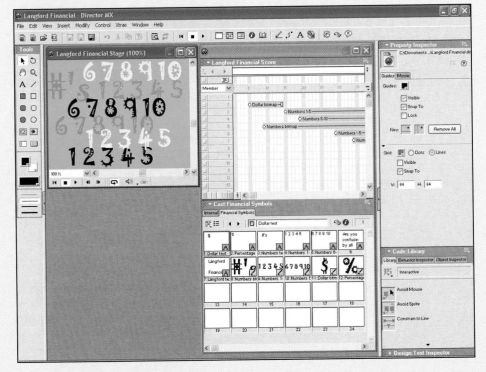

You are a software developer at the Keenen Group, a Web design and development company that was recently selected by your local Professional Web Designers Group as an industry model in Web development. You've been asked to create a multimedia demo of their development process. You use Director's Paint, Vector Shape, and Text tools to create flowcharting shapes and instructions, and an external cast in which to organize them.

1. Start Director and save the movie as **Keenen Group**.

2. Create a linked external cast and save it as **Flowchart Symbols**.

3. Using the Text, Paint, and Vector Shape tools, create and name cast members in the Flowchart Symbols Cast window with flowcharting shapes and connecting lines. (*Hint*: See Figure B-2 for an example of a flowchart.)

4. Organize the cast members by type (shapes and lines) in the Flowchart Symbols Cast window.

5. Create a text cast member with the text **Keenen Group**.

6. Resize a bitmap to 320 × 240 and create a background.

7. Place the background and the cast members on the Stage.

8. Print thumbnails of the Flowchart Symbols Cast window and the Stage, then compare your screen to Figure D-35.

9. Save the movie and the external cast, then exit Director.

FIGURE D-35
Completed Project Builder 2

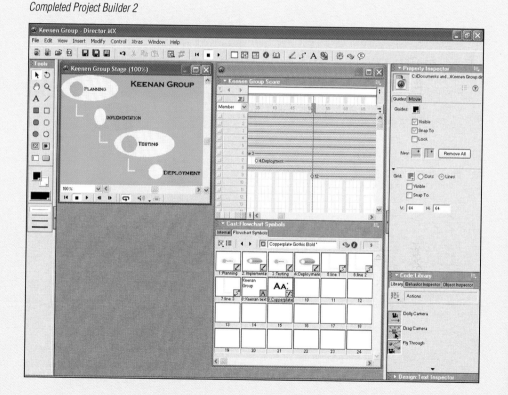

You are the chief designer at Designer Flags, a custom flag company. The manager of Victory Homes, a home development company, asks you to design a company flag for their Web site and other online promotions. You use Director's Paint and Text tools to create a flag with the company name, and an external cast in which to organize them.

1. Start Director and save the movie as **Designer Flags**.

2. Create a linked external cast and save it as **Victory Flags**.

3. Using the Paint and Text tools, create and name cast members in the Victory Flags Cast window with several different flag designs and the company name.

4. Organize the cast members by type (shapes and text) in the Victory Flags Cast window.

5. Create a text cast member with the text **Victory Homes**.

6. Change the text cast member Victory Homes to 3D text and modify the 3D Extruder settings to enhance your design.

7. Create a text cast member with the text **Flag designs by Designer Flags**.

8. Place the cast members on the Stage and add a color background.

9. Print thumbnails of the Victory Flags Cast window and the Stage, then compare your screen to Figure D-36.

10. Save the movie and the external cast, then exit Director.

11. Put a copy of this movie in your portfolio.

FIGURE D-36
Completed Design Project

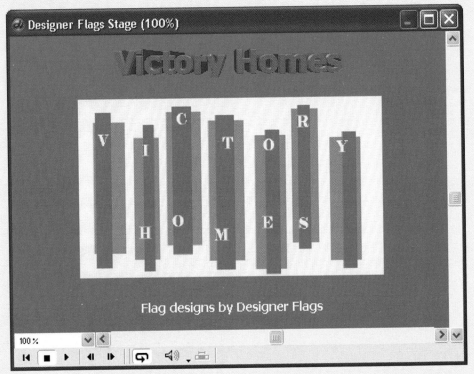

Your group can assign elements of the project to individual members, or work collectively to create the finished product.

You are a member of the graphics design team at WOW! Designs, Inc. The owner and chief baker at Only Desserts, a catering and specialty dessert company, asks you to create an online kiosk with photos and prices of their delicious desserts to help promote the company. You use Director's importing feature to assemble photos, and an external cast to organize them.

1. Assign each member of the group to research catering and dessert companies on the Web for layout ideas and pricing information, and to obtain dessert photos for the kiosk project. Use images from the Web that are free for both personal and commercial use (check the copyright information for any image before downloading it).
2. Start Director and save the movie as **Only Desserts**.
3. Create a linked external cast and save it as **Dessert Photos**.
4. Import the photos into the Dessert Photos Cast window.

5. Organize the cast members by type (photos and text) in the Dessert Photos Cast window
6. Create text titles and prices, using the Text tool.
7. Create a text cast member with the text **Only Desserts**.
8. Change the text cast member Only Desserts to 3D text using the following settings: Smoothness 10, Tunnel Depth 10.00, Bevel Edge Round, Bevel Amount 2.00, Light Middle Center, and Directional light blue.
9. Place the cast members on the Stage and add a color background, or create your own.
10. Print thumbnails of the Dessert Photos Cast window and the Stage, then compare your screen to Figure D-37.
11. Save the movie and the external cast, then exit Director.

FIGURE D-37
Completed Group Project

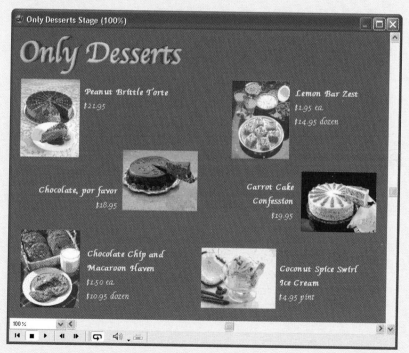

CREATING AND MODIFYING SPRITES

1. Create and select sprites.

2. Layer sprites.

3. Apply sprite inks.

4. Change the sprite display.

5. Change sprite properties.

6. Position and align sprites.

7. Extend, join, and split sprites.

8. Set text for users to change.

UNIT 7

CREATING AND MODIFYING SPRITES

Working with Sprites

A sprite is an object that consists of a cast member and a set of properties and behaviors. The properties and behaviors control how, where, and when cast members appear in a movie. You use the Stage to control where a sprite appears, and you use the Score to control when it appears.

Each sprite includes a set of properties that describe how the sprite looks and behaves in a movie. These properties include a sprite's location on the Stage, its size, blend percentage, ink effect, start frame and end frame, and rotation and skew angles. You can also set sprite properties to add basic user interaction and simple animation, such as allowing users to enter text and move a sprite on the Stage while the movie is playing. You can

change some sprite properties, such as size and Stage location, by directly moving or resizing a sprite on the Stage.

For other sprite properties, you need to use the Sprite tab in the Property inspector. The Sprite tab's main features include the locking, editable, moveable, trails, and ink effect properties. The locking property allows you to lock a sprite on the Stage to prevent you from making any changes to the sprite. The editable property applies to text sprites only and allows you to enter text on the Stage while the movie is playing. The moveable property allows you to drag a sprite on the Stage while the movie is playing. The trails property leaves a trail of images on the Stage behind an image when it is moved. Ink effects change the display of a sprite's colors along with the blend.

Tools You'll Use

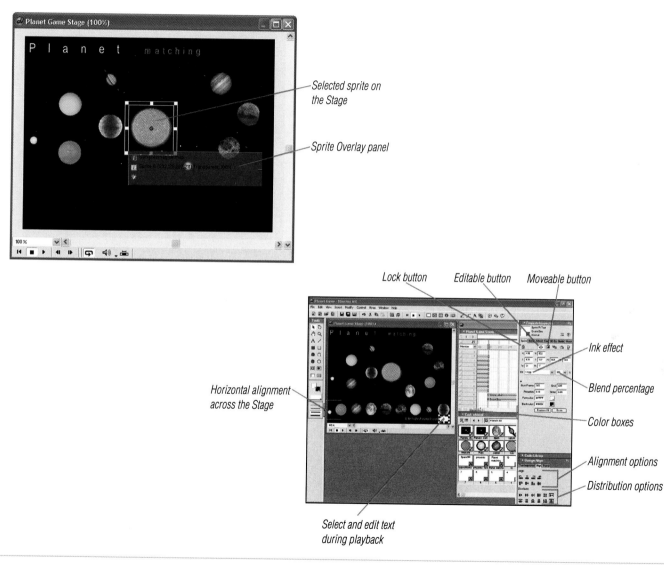

Selected sprite on the Stage

Sprite Overlay panel

Lock button

Editable button

Moveable button

Ink effect

Blend percentage

Color boxes

Horizontal alignment across the Stage

Alignment options

Distribution options

Select and edit text during playback

CREATE AND SELECT SPRITES

What You'll Do

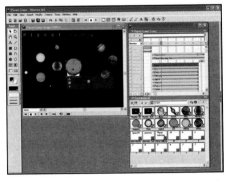

In this lesson, you will create a sprite and select sprites.

Creating Sprites

You can create sprites by placing cast members either on the Stage or in the Score; regardless of where you create the sprite, it will appear in both locations. When you place a cast member in the Score, the sprite appears in the center of the Stage surrounded by a double border. The selected sprite appears in the Score highlighted in dark blue in the sprite bar, as shown in Figure E-1. As you drag a cast member in the Score, an outline of the sprite appears, indicating the current location of the sprite in the Score before you release the mouse button.

Selecting Sprites

Before you can edit, copy, or move a sprite, you need to select it first. You can select sprites either on the Stage or in the Score. To select a sprite, you use the Arrow tool on the Tool palette. If you need to select more than one sprite, you can use the [Shift] key as you click items on the Stage or the [Ctrl] (Win) or [command] (Mac) key as you click items in the Score. If you

need to select a contiguous range of sprites in the Score, you can select a sprite at one end of the range, press and hold the [Shift] key, and then select a sprite at the other end of the range. You can also select all the sprites in a single channel, or frames within sprites. To select all the sprites in a channel, you click a channel number at the left side of the Score. After you finish working with a sprite, you can click a blank area on or around the Stage, or in the Score, to deselect the sprite. When a background sprite takes up the entire Stage area, you should click the gray area around the Stage to deselect a sprite.

Selecting Sprite Frames

Selecting a frame is useful for modifying keyframes and for creating animation. To select a keyframe, you click the keyframe indicator in the Score. You can also select a frame that isn't a keyframe by pressing and holding [Alt] (Win) or [option] (Mac), then clicking the frame you want within the sprite span. When you select a frame (keyframe or not), the sprite appears on the Stage with a single border and the individual frame becomes highlighted in the Score. If you need to change several sprite frames at a time, you might want to change how Director selects a sprite. You can use the Edit Sprite Frames command to display individual frames within a sprite span instead of the entire span in the Score. It is especially useful for changing an animated sprite where each frame contains a different cast member in a different position. After you click Edit Sprite Frames on the Edit menu for a sprite, clicking the sprite selects a single frame (surrounded by a single border), while double-clicking selects the entire sprite (surrounded by a double border). Any change you make to an animation property for a frame defines a new keyframe. To return sprites to their normal state, you click Edit Entire Sprite on the Edit menu.

FIGURE E-1
Creating a sprite

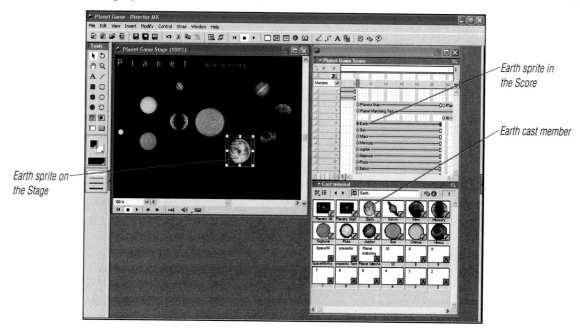

Earth sprite in the Score

Earth cast member

Earth sprite on the Stage

Create and select sprites

1. Start Director, open the file MD E-1.dir from where your Unit E data files are stored, save it as **Planet Game**, then resize the Stage to display the gray area around the Stage.

   TIP To change the Stage view size, click the Zoom list arrow at the bottom-left of the Stage, then click a view percentage.

2. Minimize the docking channel (Win) or close the grouped panel (Mac) with the Property inspector.

3. Click number 31 in the frame channel in the Score.

4. Click the Sun cast member on the Stage, as shown in Figure E-2, to select the sprite.

5. Press and hold [Shift], click a black area on the Stage to select the Sun and Planets Start sprites, then click the gray area around the Stage to deselect the sprites.

6. Click channel number 5 on the left side of the Score to select all of the sprites in channel 5.

7. Click the Zoom Menu button to the right of the frame channel in the Score, then click 25% to view the selected sprites in a reduced view size.

8. Click the Zoom Menu button, then click 100% to return to normal view.

(continued)

FIGURE E-2
Selecting a sprite

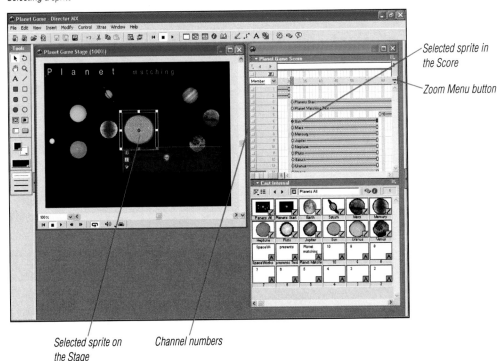

Selected sprite in the Score

Zoom Menu button

Selected sprite on the Stage

Channel numbers

FIGURE E-3

Selecting a sprite frame

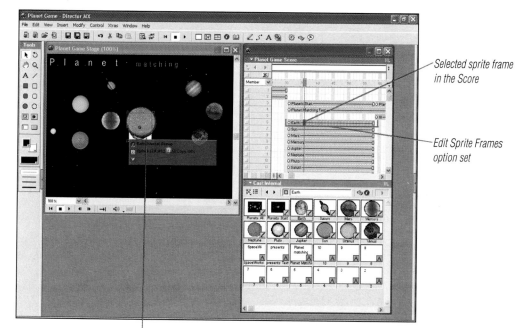

Selected sprite frame in the Score

Edit Sprite Frames option set

Selected sprite frame on the Stage under the Sun sprite

9. Drag the Earth cast member from the Cast window to frame 31, channel 6 in the Score to create a sprite.

The new sprite appears above the Sun sprite in the Score, but behind it on the stage.

   TIP To create a sprite that is one frame long, press and hold [Alt] (Win) or [option] (Mac) as you drag a cast member to the Score.

You selected sprites and created a sprite.

Select sprite frames

1. Click frame 31 in channel 6 to select the Earth sprite's keyframe and display a single border around it on the Stage.

2. Press and hold [Alt] (Win) or [option] (Mac), then click any frame (except the keyframe) within the Earth sprite span to select an individual frame.

   TIP To select a range of frames, press and hold [Shift][Alt] (Win) or [shift][option] (Mac), then click an end frame.

3. Click the Earth sprite (not the keyframe) to select the entire sprite.

4. Click Edit on the menu bar, then click Edit Sprite Frames to display the selected sprites as individual frames.

   TIP You can also right-click a sprite, then click Edit Sprite Frames to set the option.

5. Click any frame within the Earth sprite span to select a frame, as shown in Figure E-3.

6. Click Edit on the menu bar, then click Edit Entire Sprite to return the sprite to its normal selection state.

7. Save your work.

You selected sprite frames.

LAYER SPRITES

What You'll Do

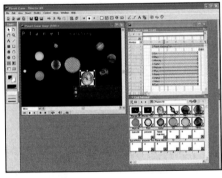

In this lesson, you will layer sprites.

Layering Sprites

A sprite is displayed on the Stage layered according to its channel in the Score. Sprites in higher-numbered channels appear in front of sprites in lower-numbered channels. For example, if the Sun sprite appears in channel 7, and the Earth sprite appears in channel 6, the Sun sprite will appear in front of the Earth sprite. When you position the sprite that contains the background for your movie, you should place that sprite in a lower-numbered channel, generally channel 1, so that the background always appears on the back layer. You can change sprite layering in several ways. If an empty area in a higher-numbered channel is available, you can drag the sprite in the Score to that channel. If no space is available in a channel, you can use Arrange commands from the

Modify menu to switch sprites in channels. For example, the Move Forward command on the Arrange menu moves the sprite to the next highest channel.

When you work with sprites stacked in layers, it is sometimes difficult to view sprites in lower-numbered channels. For this reason, you can hide the contents of any channel on the Stage to make it easier to see and select sprites. To hide or show the contents of a channel, you click the gray button to the left of the channel number in the Score. A light gray button indicates that the channel is displayed. A dark gray button indicates that the channel is hidden. When you hide a channel, the channel will not be hidden when viewed as a projector or Shockwave movie.

Sprite in lower level

Sprite in higher level   Sprite in middle level

Light gray button

Earth sprite in the highest-numbered channel

Earth sprite on the Stage

Layer sprites

1. Verify that the Earth sprite is selected on the Stage and in the Score.

2. Click the light gray button in the first column of the Score to the left of channel 7 to hide the Sun sprite.

3. Position the Arrow pointer over the Earth sprite (not on the colored circle or on the sizing handles on the edge) on the Stage, then drag the Earth sprite to the left partly behind the Mercury sprite.

   TIP If the Snap To features are turned on, a green plus sign appears when you drag the sprite.

4. Click the dark gray button in the first column of the Score to the left of channel 7 to show all the sprites in the channel.

5. Click Modify on the menu bar, point to Arrange, then click Move Forward to move the Earth sprite to channel 7, as shown in Figure E-4.

6. Click Modify on the menu bar, point to Arrange, then click Bring to Front to move the Earth sprite to the top layer.

7. Click the title bar in the Score, then scroll down to display the Earth sprite in channel 15.

8. Position the Arrow pointer over the Earth sprite (not on the colored circle or on the sizing handles on the edge) on the Stage, then drag the Earth sprite over the white dot below the lower-right side of the Sun sprite, as shown in Figure E-5.

9. Save your work.

You layered sprites.

APPLY SPRITE INKS

What You'll Do

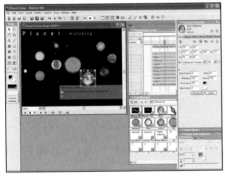

 In this lesson, you will apply sprite inks.

Applying Sprite Inks

Sprite inks change the display of a sprite's colors. Inks can reverse and alter colors, remove backgrounds, and create masks that obscure or reveal portions of a background. The Matte or Background Transparent inks are most useful when you want to hide white backgrounds, and the Ghost or Mask inks create useful and dramatic color effects. When you create a sprite, the Copy ink appears by default and animates faster than sprites with any other ink. The Copy ink displays all the original colors in a sprite with a white background.

Unlike Paint ink effects, which are applied in the Paint window and are permanent, sprite ink effects are applied in the Score and can be changed at any time. For many of the ink effects, you can set a blend value. The **blend value** makes a sprite more or less transparent. A blend value of 100% makes a sprite completely opaque, and a blend value of 0% makes a sprite completely transparent. You can set the keypoints of a sprite to different blend values to create a fading in or fading out effect.

Applying the Mask ink effect

The Mask ink effect allows you to define which parts of a sprite are transparent and which are opaque to reveal or tint certain parts of a sprite. To create a Mask ink effect, you first create or place the cast member that you want to mask (Earth, for example) into the Cast window. Then, create or place the masking cast member (Saturn, for example) in the next cast member position in the Cast window. Drag the cast member you want to mask (Earth) to the Stage or Score, display the Sprite tab in the Property inspector, click the Ink list arrow, then click Mask. The parts of the sprite revealed by the mask appear on the Stage. The black areas of the masking cast member (Saturn) make the masked sprite completely opaque, and white areas make it completely transparent. Colors between black and white are more or less transparent.

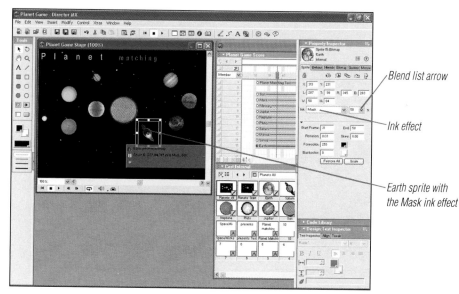

Blend list arrow

Ink effect

Earth sprite with the Mask ink effect

FIGURE E-7

Applying the Background Transparent ink effect

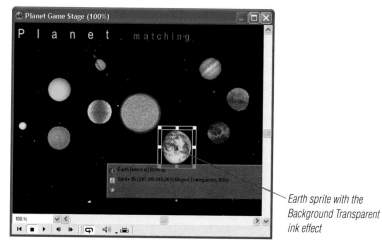

Earth sprite with the Background Transparent ink effect

Apply sprite inks

1. Verify that the Earth sprite is selected on the Stage and in the Score.

2. Display the Property inspector and display the Sprite tab if necessary.

3. Verify that the Ink is set to Copy, click the Ink list arrow, then click Ghost to reverse overlapping colors.

4. Click the Ink list arrow, then click Mask to create transparent effects.

   The Earth sprite appears on the Stage with a mask of the Saturn cast member, which is the cast member that follows the Earth cast member in the Cast window.

   > TIP The Mask ink effect is a memory-intensive feature, so use it sparingly for movies on playback computers that have limited memory.

5. Click the Blend list arrow, then click 50 to create transparent artwork, as shown in Figure E-6.

   > TIP The Blend percentage value affects only Copy, Background Transparent, Matte, Mask, and Blend inks.

6. Click the Blend list arrow, then click 100.

7. Click the Ink list arrow, scroll up if necessary, then click Background Transparent to hide the Earth's white background, as shown in Figure E-7.

8. Minimize the docking channel (Win) or close the grouped panel (Mac) with the Property inspector, then save your work.

You applied sprite inks.

CHANGE THE SPRITE DISPLAY

What You'll Do

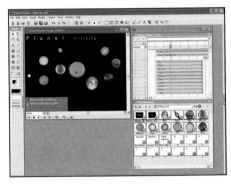

In this lesson, you will change the sprite display and the Sprite Overlay panel display.

Changing the Sprite Display

The text that identifies the sprite in the Score is called a **sprite label**. To make it easier to work with sprites, you can change the display for sprite labels in the Score to show different information about the sprite, such as member name and number or ink effect. Table E-1 describes the display options for sprite labels. For example, the Extended display option for sprite labels can display cast member number (depending on your Director preference settings) and name, ink, blend, and location, depending on what's selected in the Score Window Preferences dialog box in the Extended Display section. Member is the default sprite display setting.

Organizing Sprites Using Color

When you create a sprite, it appears in the Score in blue by default. After you create several sprites, sometimes it is hard to distinguish them without looking intently at each sprite label. You can organize sprites in the Score using color. For example, you

can set all text sprites to gold and all graphic sprites to green. You use the color boxes in the bottom-left corner of the Score to change the color of a sprite label, as shown in Figure E-8. The color boxes only change the appearance of the sprite label in the Score; they do not affect the sprite on the Stage or in the Cast window.

Changing Sprite Overlay Panel Settings

When you select a sprite on the Stage or in the Score, the Sprite Overlay panel appears on the Stage at the bottom of the sprite, as shown in Figure E-9. The Sprite Overlay panel displays important sprite properties directly on the Stage. You can determine when the Sprite Overlay panel appears using the Overlay Settings dialog box. The panel can appear when you move the mouse over, or roll over, a sprite, when you select a sprite, or all the time. If the text in the Sprite Overlay panel is difficult to read, you can change the color of the text or the opacity of the panel.

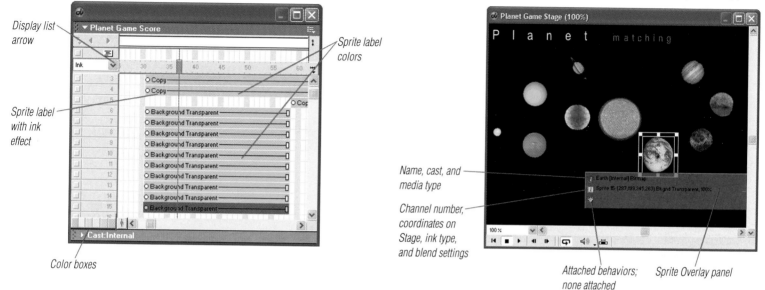

FIGURE E-8

Changing the sprite display in the Score

Display list arrow

Sprite label colors

Ink

Sprite label with ink effect

Color boxes

FIGURE E-9

Sprite Overlay panel

Name, cast, and media type

Channel number, coordinates on Stage, ink type, and blend settings

Attached behaviors; none attached

Sprite Overlay panel

TABLE E-1: Score Window Display Options

format	description
Member	Identifies the number and name of the cast member (depending on your Director settings)
Behavior	Tells you which (if any) behaviors have been assigned to the sprite by number or name
Location	Describes the sprite's registration point relative to the upper-left corner of the Stage
Ink	Displays the ink effect that is applied to the sprite
Blend	Indicates the percentage of the sprite's blend setting
Extended	Displays member, behavior, ink, blend, and location information

Change the sprite display

1. Click the title bar in the Score, click the Display list arrow on the left side of the Score, then click Extended to display the Score with extended sprite display, as shown in Figure E-10.

   TIP To change the extended display in the Score, click Edit (Win) or Director (Mac) on the menu bar, point to Preferences, click Score, then select the Extended Display check boxes in the Score Window Preferences dialog box.

2. Click the Display list arrow on the left side of the Score, then click Ink to display sprite labels that display the sprite ink effect.

3. Click the Display list arrow on the left side of the Score, then click Member.

   TIP To show or hide keyframes in the Score, click View on the menu bar, then click Keyframes.

4. Click the Earth sprite in the Score if necessary.

5. Press and hold [Shift], then click the Sun sprite to select all the sprites in between.

6. Click the gold color box in the lower-left corner of the Score.

7. Click the Earth sprite in the Score, as shown in Figure E-11, to view the new sprite label color.

You changed the sprite display in the Score.

FIGURE E-10
Score window with extended sprite display

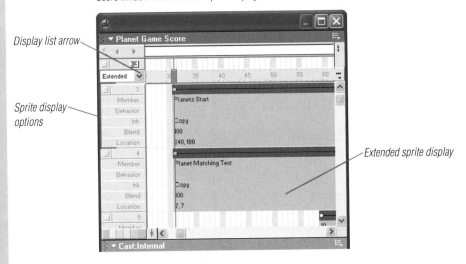

Display list arrow

Sprite display options

Extended sprite display

FIGURE E-11
Changing sprite label colors

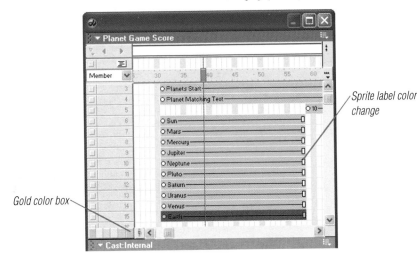

Sprite label color change

Gold color box

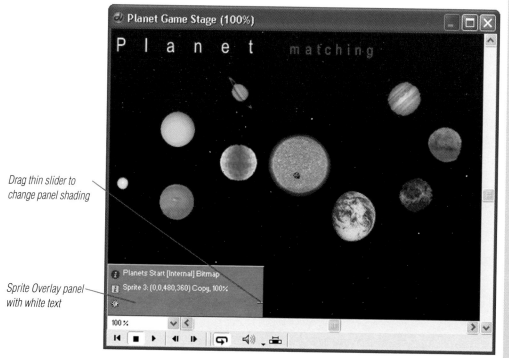

Change the Sprite Overlay panel display

1. Click the Earth sprite on the Stage if necessary.

2. Click View on the menu bar, point to Sprite Overlay, then click Settings to display the Overlay Settings dialog box, as shown in Figure E-12.

3. Click the Selection option button (if necessary), click and hold the Text Color color box, then click the last color square (white) in the second row on the color palette.

4. Click OK, then click the Planets Start sprite (the black background) on the Stage to display the Sprite Overlay panel with the new properties.

   TIP   To open the Bitmap, Sprite, or Behavior tabs in the Property inspector, you can click the corresponding icon in the Sprite Overlay panel.

5. Drag down the slider that appears on the right edge of the Sprite Overlay panel, as shown in Figure E-13, to change the shading of the panel.

6. Click View on the menu bar, point to Sprite Overlay, then click Show Info to hide the Sprite Overlay panel.

7. Save your work.

You changed Sprite Overlay panel display settings.

FIGURE E-13
Changing the Sprite Overlay panel

Drag thin slider to change panel shading

Sprite Overlay panel with white text

CHANGE SPRITE PROPERTIES

What You'll Do

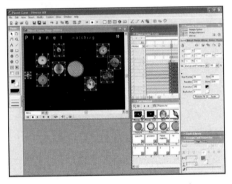

In this lesson, you will change sprite properties.

Changing Sprite Properties

Each sprite includes a set of properties that describe how the sprite looks and behaves in a movie. These properties include the ability to lock a sprite in place, resize a sprite, and add basic user interaction and simple animation, such as allowing users to enter text, move a sprite on the Stage, or leave a trail of images as they move a sprite on the Stage while the movie is playing. When you lock a sprite on the Stage, you can no longer make any changes to the sprite. Locking sprites is not supported during playback. A locked sprite appears with a lock icon in front of its name in the Score and in the upper-right corner of the sprite's selection rectangle on the Stage. If you want to allow users to move sprites around while your movie is playing, you can use the moveable property. This property is useful for creating educational games, such as puzzles or matching exercises. You can also set sprites to leave a trail of images as they move on the Stage. When you use the trail property, the Stage doesn't erase previous versions of the sprite as the playback head moves through the Score. The result is an impression of a continuous string of sprites. This property is useful for fine-tuning animations, because you can determine where motion in an animation needs to slow down, speed up, or smooth out. You can use the trail effect with the moveable property. If you need to resize a sprite, you can use the scale property to set a specific height and width or a percentage. You can change some sprite properties by directly moving or resizing a sprite on the Stage, and change others by using the Sprite tab in the Property inspector, or the Sprite toolbar.

> **QUICKTIP**
>
> To show or hide the Sprite toolbar at the top of the Score, click the Score window, click View on the menu bar, then click Sprite Toolbar.

FIGURE E-14

Locking sprites

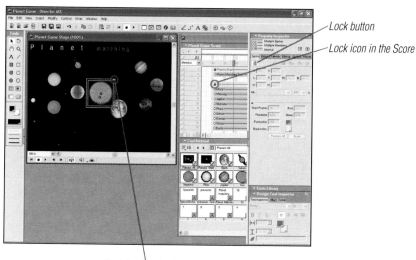

Lock button

Lock icon in the Score

Lock icon on the Stage

FIGURE E-15

Setting sprites to move during playback

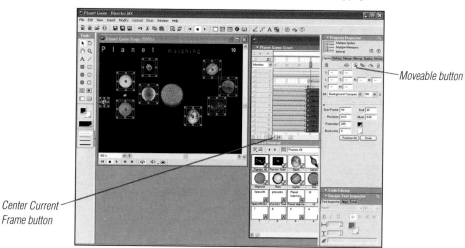

Moveable button

Center Current
Frame button

1. Display the Property inspector if necessary.

2. Click channel number 3 on the left side of the Score to select the planet background sprites, press and hold [Ctrl] (Win) or ⌘ (Mac), then click the Sun sprite in the Score.

3. Click the Lock button in the Property inspector to lock the selected sprites, as shown in Figure E-14.

4. Click the Earth sprite on the Stage, then click Scale in the Property inspector to open the Scale Sprite dialog box.

5. Double-click the Scale text box (if necessary), type **75**, then click OK.

6. Click the title bar in the Score, scroll to the right to display frame 59, scroll up to display channel 6 (if necessary), press and hold [Shift], then click the Sun sprite in channel 6 to select all the planet sprites.

7. Click the Copy button on the toolbar, click frame 59 in channel 6, then click the Paste button on the toolbar.

8. Press and hold [Ctrl] (Win) or ⌘ (Mac), click the Sun sprite in frame 60 of channel 6 to deselect the sprite, then click the Moveable button in the Property inspector to make the selected sprites moveable.

9. Click the Center Current Frame button at the bottom of the Score to center the current frame in the Score, as shown in Figure E-15, then save your work.

You changed sprite properties.

POSITION AND ALIGN SPRITES

What You'll Do

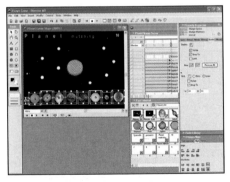

In this lesson, you will position and align sprites.

Positioning and Aligning Sprites

Sometimes you might need to change the position of a sprite or align a group of sprites on the Stage. You can drag a sprite, use the arrow keys, or set coordinates on the Sprite tab of the Property inspector to position sprites on the Stage. You can align sprites on the Stage using the grid or the guides on the Guides tab in the Property inspector, or the Align tab in the Design panel.

The **grid** is a set of rows and columns of a specified height and width that you can use to help place sprites on the Stage, as shown in Figure E-16. When you select the Snap To option, sprites snap to the grid points, whether the grid is visible or not. When you drag a sprite to a grid line, a green plus sign appears, indicating where the sprite will snap to the grid. The position where you drag the sprite determines where the green plus sign appears in the sprite. For example, if you drag the

Tweaking the placement of a sprite

Sometimes you might need to make only minor adjustments to the placement of a sprite. You can drag the sprite with the mouse, use the arrow keys, or use the Sprite tab in the Property inspector to enter specific coordinates, but these techniques can sometimes be time consuming or inefficient in achieving the exact placement you want. The Tweak tab in the Design panel allows you to make an adjustment with the mouse and know the exact distances involved. You can drag the line (or dot) on the Tweak tab to set a specific direction for movement and then use the X Offset (horizontal) and Y Offset (vertical) arrows to make any final adjustments to the sprite's location. When you finish making adjustments, you select one or more sprites and click Tweak to apply the movement. You can apply the Tweak settings to as many sprites as you want. The Tweak settings stay in effect until you change them.

left side of the Earth sprite, the green plus sign appears to the left of a grid line.

The **guides** are horizontal or vertical lines, as shown in Figure E-17. You can either drag a guide around the Stage or lock it in place to help you align sprites in a straight line. As you drag a guide onto the Stage, a tooltip appears, indicating the guide position in pixels starting at zero from the top of the Stage for a horizontal guide or from the left edge of the Stage for a vertical guide. You can add as many horizontal and vertical guides as you want. When you select the Snap To option, sprites snap to the guide. When you are not using the grid or guides, you can hide them.

The Align tab in the Design panel moves sprites not to a specific location on the Stage, but to positions relative to one another. You can align sprites along the left, right, top, or bottom edge of the Stage, or horizontally or vertically in the center. In addition to alignment, you can also distribute sprites an equal distance from each other on the Stage.

FIGURE E-16
Displaying the grid

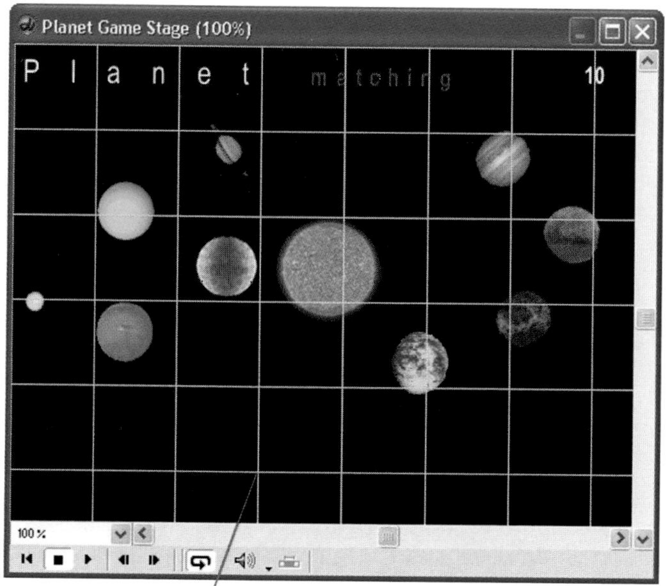

FIGURE E-17
Displaying a horizontal and vertical guide

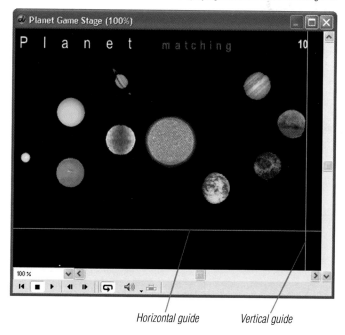

Grid

Horizontal guide   Vertical guide

Position sprites

1. With the playback head positioned between frames 59–89 in the Score, click the black background on the stage, then click the Guides tab in the Property inspector if necessary.

2. Select the Visible and Snap To check boxes in the Grid section if necessary.

3. Position the Arrow pointer over the bottom part of the Earth sprite on the Stage, drag the pointer down to the bottom horizontal grid line, as shown in Figure E-18, then click the Planets Start sprite on the Stage.

   TIP To change the height and width of the rows and columns in the grid, enter a value in the H or W text boxes on the Guides tab in the Property inspector, then press [Enter] (Win) or [return] (Mac).

4. Deselect the Visible check box in the Grid section on the Guides tab in the Property inspector.

5. Select the Visible check box in the Guides section if necessary, then click Remove All.

6. Click and hold the Hand pointer over the New horizontal guide box on the Guides tab in the Property inspector, then drag the guide to the bottom of the Stage at 330 pixels, as shown in Figure E-19.

7. Drag the bottom part of each planet (don't forget Pluto on the far left) to the horizontal guide in any order.

8. Position the Move Guide pointer over the horizontal guide on the Stage, then drag the horizontal guide down off the Stage to remove it.

You positioned sprites.

FIGURE E-18
Positioning a sprite on the Stage using a grid

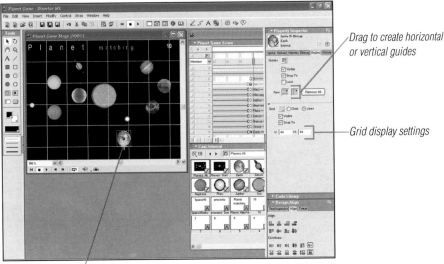

Drag to create horizontal or vertical guides

Grid display settings

Green plus sign for positioning

FIGURE E-19
Creating a guide

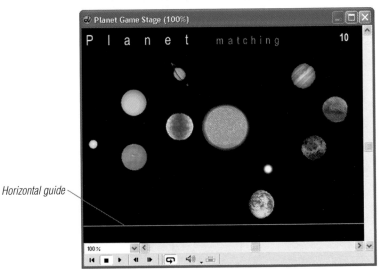

Horizontal guide

FIGURE E-20
Aligning sprites

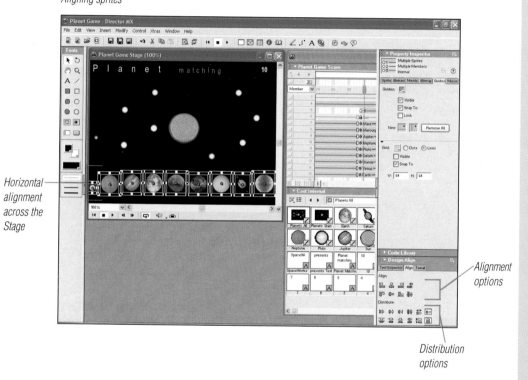

Horizontal
alignment
across the
Stage

*Alignment
options*

*Distribution
options*

1. Click a planet sprite on the Stage if necessary, press and hold [Shift], then click each of the other planet sprites to select all the planet sprites.

2. Click Window on the menu bar, then click Align to display the Align tab in the Design panel.

3. Click the Distribute width button on the Align tab to distribute the sprites evenly across the Stage, as shown in Figure E-20.

4. Minimize the docking channel (Win) or close the grouped panel (Mac) with the Property inspector.

5. Save your work.

You aligned sprites.

EXTEND, JOIN AND SPLIT SPRITES

What You'll Do

In this lesson, you will extend, join, and split sprites.

Extending Sprites

You can change the duration of a sprite on the Stage by adjusting the length of the sprite in the Score. The longer the span of the sprite in the Score, the longer the sprite appears in the movie. You can drag the end frame of a sprite to change the length or use the Extend Sprite command on the Modify menu. The Extend Sprite command provides an easy way to stretch a sprite across numerous frames. You can also use the Extend Sprite command to shorten a sprite.

Joining and Splitting Sprites

Sometimes you might need to split an existing sprite into two separate sprites, or join separate sprites in the Score. For example, if you create a text sprite with a long duration and need to separate it into two sprites to make changes in one of them, you can use the Split Sprite command. Similarly, if you create a complex animation as separate sprites and need to link them together into a single sprite, you can use the Join Sprites command.

Viewing multiple Score windows

You can display different views of the Score window to make it easier to display information or to move a sprite to a different part of the Score without scrolling. If you have a large Score window and want to move a sprite a long distance, you can open the same Score window, scroll to a different portion, then drag the sprite between the two windows. To open a copy of the Score window, click the title bar in the Score, click Window on the menu bar, then click New Score Window. You can change the Score display settings for sprite labels in the new window. When you change the Score display options in one Score window, the other Score window retains its original settings, but if you alter a sprite in either window, both Score windows reflect the change.

FIGURE E-21
Extending sprites

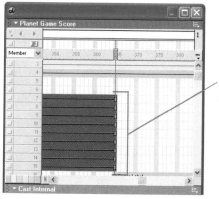

Selected sprites extended
to playback head

FIGURE E-22
Joining sprites

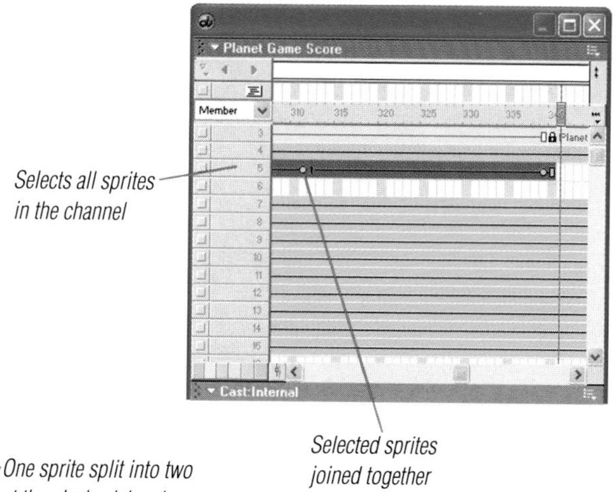

Selects all sprites
in the channel

Selected sprites
joined together

FIGURE E-23
Splitting sprites

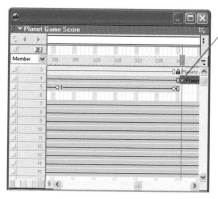

One sprite split into two
at the playback head

Extend, join, and split sprites

1. Click the title bar in the Score, then verify that the copied set of nine planets is selected (channels 7 through 15 starting at frame 59).

2. Scroll to frame 365 in the Score, then click number 365 in the frame channel.

3. Click Modify on the menu bar, then click Extend Sprite to extend sprites to the playback head, as shown in Figure E-21.

   TIP You can also extend and shorten a sprite by changing the Start Frame and End text boxes on the Sprite tab in the Property inspector.

4. Scroll to frame 341 in the Score (if necessary), click 341 in the frame channel, then click the Center Current Frame button at the bottom of the Score.

5. Click channel 5 on the left side of the Score to select all the sprites in the channel.

   TIP You can also adjust the duration of a sprite by changing the movie tempo or modifying a sprite with Lingo.

6. Click Modify on the menu bar, click Join Sprites to join all the sprites together in channel 5 to create one sprite, then scroll to the left to display the joined sprites, as shown in Figure E-22.

7. Click the Planet Matching Text sprite in channel 4 in frame 341.

8. Click Modify on the menu bar, then click Split Sprite to split the sprite into two sprites at the playback head, as shown in Figure E-23.

9. Save your work.

You extended, joined, and split sprites.

SET TEXT FOR USERS TO CHANGE

What You'll Do

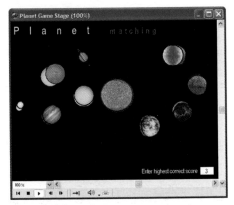

In this lesson, you will set text for users to change.

Setting Text for Users to Change

You can set regular text and field text cast members to be editable as the movie plays. For example, suppose your movie calls for users to enter their names; you can include an editable text or field sprite where users can click a text box to display an insertion point and modify the contents of the text box while a movie is playing. You can use the Editable button on the Sprite tab or the Editable check box on the Text tab or Field tab of the Property inspector to make text and field sprites editable. You can also use the Editable button on the Sprite tab to make a field sprite editable in only a certain range of frames in the Score. If you choose the Edit Sprite Frames command on the Edit menu, you can select individual frames and make a text box editable in one frame but not in another. Keep in mind that any edits you make to a text or field sprite will also affect the original text or field cast member, as well as all subsequent sprites that you create from that cast member.

Changing text and field properties

You can use the Text or Field tab in the Property inspector to view and change settings for selected text sprites. You can select a framing option to determine how Director places text within the boundaries of a text box. The Framing option includes Adjust to Fit, Scrolling, Fixed, and Limit to Field Size (for field text only). The Editable option makes the cast member editable while the movie plays. The Wrap option increases the vertical size of the text box or field on the Stage so that all text is visible. The Tab option advances the insertion point to the next editable sprite on the Stage when the user presses Tab. The DTS (Direct to Stage) option makes text appear more quickly by rendering it directly to the Stage. The Use Hypertext Styles option makes hypertext links appear the same as in a browser

FIGURE E-24

Setting sprites for editing during playback

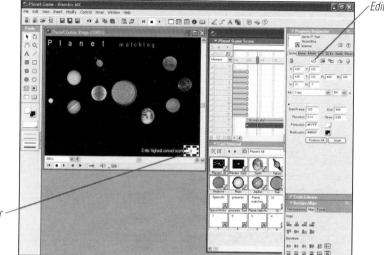

Editable button

Text sprite set for editing during playback

FIGURE E-25

Editing text during playback

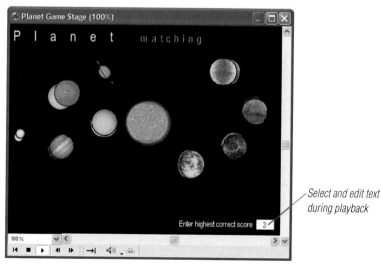

Select and edit text during playback

Set text for users to change

1. Scroll to frame 365 and channel 17 in the Score, then click the Score Box sprite (don't click the keyframe).

2. Display the Property inspector (if necessary), then click the Editable button on the Sprite tab in the Property inspector, as shown in Figure E-24.

   TIP   You can also select the Editable check box in the Text or Field tab of the Property inspector to edit text for an entire sprite.

3. Rewind and play the movie.

4. When the timer in the upper-right corner starts, drag the planets to their original positions around the sun. When the timer reaches 0, count how many planets you placed in the correct position on the screen.

5. Double-click the score box in the lower-right corner, type your score, as shown in Figure E-25, then click a blank area on the Stage.

   TIP   If the playback loop is turned on, stop the movie.

6. Click View on the menu bar, point to Sprite Overlay, click Settings, click and hold the Text Color color box, click the first color square (black) in the first row on the color palette, then click OK to restore default Director settings.

7. Click View on the menu bar, point to Sprite Overlay, click Show Info, click the Score Box sprite on the Stage, then drag the slider to the middle of the Sprite Overlay panel to restore default Director settings.

8. Save your work, then exit Director.

You set text for users to change.

Create and select sprites.

1. Start Director and open the file MD E-2.dir from where your Unit E data files are stored, then save it as **States Game**.
2. Resize the Stage to display the gray area around the Stage.
3. Display the Title cast member on the Stage with a double border and then with a single border.

Layer sprites.

1. Select the Name Title sprite in the Score, then move the sprite forward one channel.
2. Drag the Name Title sprite on the Stage above and aligned with the Name sprite.
3. Hide channel 1 to display the background, then show channel 1 to restore it.

Apply sprite inks.

1. Select the USA Map Blank sprite.
2. Display the Property inspector.
3. Change the ink to Background Transparent.

4. Select the Title sprite, then change the ink to Matte.
5. Select all the state sprites, then change the ink to Matte.

Change the sprite display.

1. Change the display in the Score window to Extended, Ink, and then Member.
2. Open the Sprite Overlay Settings dialog box, then change the text color to blue.
3. Change the shading of the Sprite Overlay panel, then hide the Sprite Overlay panel.

Change sprite properties.

1. Select and lock the USA Map Blank sprite.
2. Select all the state sprites and set them to be moveable.

Position and align sprites.

1. Display the Guides tab in the Property inspector.
2. Drag four horizontal guides on the Stage.

3. Align the state text sprites in four rows at the top of the Stage.
4. Remove the guides.
5. Select each row of state text sprites individually and change the horizontal alignment to Distribute width.

Extend, join, and split sprites.

1. Select all the state sprites.
2. Extend the state sprites to frame 1250. (*Hint*: Depending on the speed of your computer, you might need to wait a few moments for Director to perform this task.)
3. Click 1000 in the Frame channel, select the Title sprite in channel 2, then split the sprite.

Set text for users to change.

1. Select the Name sprite and set it to be editable.
2. Rewind the movie, then play it.
3. Select the text *Your Name* (if necessary), then type your name.

4. Drag the state names for the purple states in the map until the answers appear.

5. Stop the movie, then show the Sprite Overlay panel.

6. Open the Sprite Overlay Settings dialog box and change the text color to black.

7. Change the shading of the panel to the middle, then compare your screen to Figure E-26.

8. Save the movie, then exit Director.

FIGURE E-26
Completed Skills Review

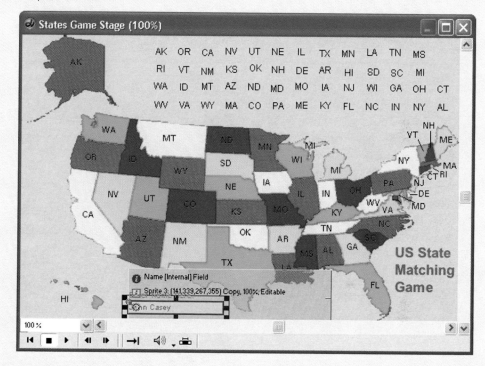

You are a student at Benson Art College. The multimedia department is having a graphic design contest. First prize is $500.00. Recently, you have been experimenting with the ink effects in Director and want to use your newly acquired skills for the contest. You use Director's Paint tool to create two cast members and apply the Mask ink effect.

1. Start Director and save the movie as **Design Contest**.
2. Open the Paint window, then open the Pattern pop-up menu on the Tool palette and select a light color tile at the bottom.
3. Create a filled rectangle with the tile pattern to fit the entire Stage.
4. Create a new cast member, then draw a filled rectangle with a different color tile pattern to fit the entire Stage. If you have a graphic available, you can import it.
5. Create a new cast member, then draw a filled black rectangle to fit the entire Stage.
6. Use the Text tool in the Paint window to create a text box in the filled black rectangle with a white foreground color and black background color and the text **Designs by your name** in the center of the window, then close the Paint window.
7. Transform the last cast member bitmap to 32 bits if necessary. (*Hint*: Use the Transform Bitmap command on the Modify menu.)

8. Drag the first cast member on the Stage, drag the second cast member on the Stage on top of the first, change the ink effect for the second cast member to the Mask ink effect, then compare your screen to Figure E-27.

9. Print the Stage and the cast members, save the movie, then exit Director.

FIGURE E-27
Completed Project Builder 1

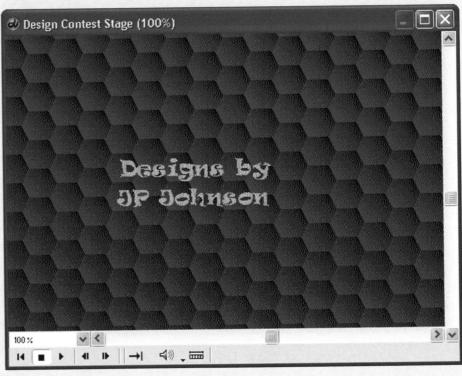

You are a game designer at Freeware Games, a software company that develops memory games for kids. Your boss asks you to create a simple shape matching game for ages three to four. You use Director's Paint tool to create circle, square, and triangle cast members and a background cast member with the outline of the shapes.

1. Start Director and save the movie as **Shape Matching**.
2. Create and name a background cast member with the outline of a circle, square, and triangle.
3. Create and name filled cast members with the circle, square, and triangle shapes.
4. Drag the background on the Stage and lock it.
5. Drag the shapes on the Stage and set them to be moveable.
6. Create a text cast member with the text **Shape Matching Game**.
7. Change the duration and modify the shape sprites to create a matching game, then compare your screen to Figure E-28.
8. Print the Stage and the cast members, save the movie, then exit Director.

FIGURE E-28
Completed Project Builder 2

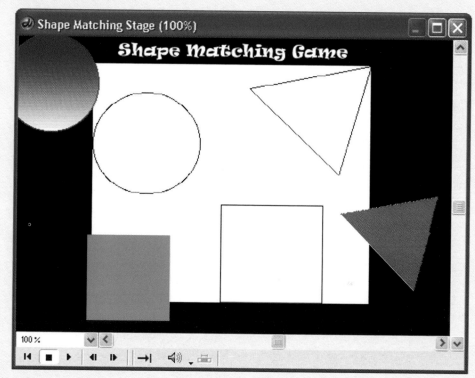

You are a customer service specialist at 24-7 Answers, an online technical support company. You've been tasked with creating a data structure with the information you need from your customers, including different types of information, such as name, e-mail address, and problem. You use Director's Text tool to create text labels and empty text boxes where users can enter text.

1. Start Director and save the movie as **Answers Prototype**.
2. Write down a list of information you might need from a person to provide online technical support.
3. Create and name text label cast members, using the Text tool.
4. Create and name empty text cast members, using the Text tool, and set them to be editable. (*Hint*: To create a check box, use the Check box tool on the tool palette.)
5. Line up the text labels and empty text cast members using guides and a grid.
6. Change at least one empty text cast member to a scrolling frame. (*Hint*: Use the Text tab in the Property inspector.)
7. Extend the sprites in the Score to provide enough time to enter information in the editable text cast members.
8. Create a text cast member with the text **24-7 Answers**.

9. Place and arrange the cast members on the Stage, lock unchangeable sprites, and add a color, pattern, or image background.
10. Play the movie and enter text in the editable text cast members, then compare your screen to Figure E-29.

11. Print the Stage, save the movie, then exit Director.
12. Put a copy of this movie in your portfolio.

FIGURE E-29
Completed Design Project

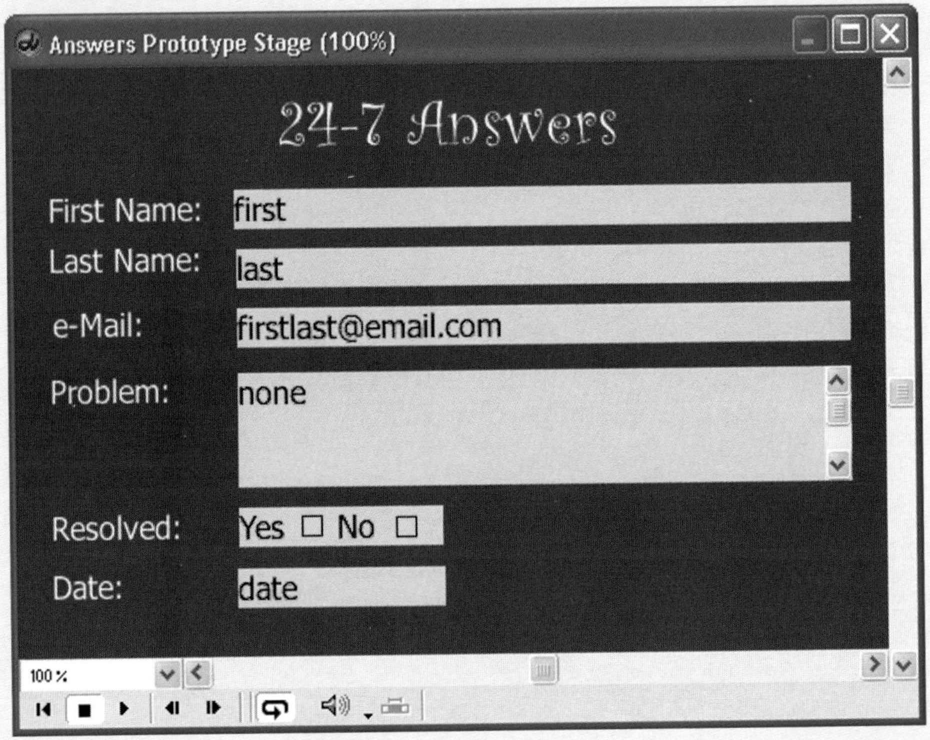

Your group can assign elements of the project to individual members, or work collectively to create the finished product.

You are a member of the graphics design team at WOW! Designs, Inc. The owner of Fun and Games truck, a mobile teaching unit that delivers books and software games to kids in rural areas, asks you to create a new animal matching game for four to five year olds. You use Director's import capabilities to create a cast of animals, and the Paint tool to create a background for matching each animal with its name.

1. Assign each member of the group to research children's game sites on the web for layout ideas and obtain animal images for the project. Use images from the web that are free for both personal and commercial use (check the copyright information for any such clip art before downloading it).
2. Start Director and save the movie as **Animal Matching**.
3. Create and name a background cast member with a text label for each animal name.
4. Drag the background on the Stage and lock it.
5. Drag the animal cast members on the Stage and set them to be moveable.
6. Create a text cast member with the text **Animal Matching Game**.

7. Change the duration and modify the animal sprites to create a matching game, then compare your screen to Figure E-30.

8. Print the Stage and the cast members, save the movie, then exit Director.

FIGURE E-30
Completed Group Project

CREATING ANIMATION

1. Create animation using tweening.

2. Create a circular animation.

3. Record an animation.

4. Animate with a series of cast members.

5. Crcate a film loop.

UNIT E
CREATING ANIMATION

Creating Animation

Animation is the process of creating movement. Director provides several ways to create animation: tweening, step recording, real-time recording, and sequencing cast members frame by frame. You can create animation by moving an object across the Stage or by changing its attributes, such as its position, size, color, or angle, over a series of frames. An important part of animation in Director involves the use of keyframes. A keyframe contains specific information about a sprite, such as its position on the Stage, size, background or foreground color, or rotation or skew angle. The animation occurs when you change the keyframe information about a sprite over a series of frames.

Understanding Animation Techniques

Tweening is a quick way to animate a sprite. The process involves two or more keyframes. These keyframes define a sprite in two or more different locations on the Stage, or define a sprite with different sets of attributes. Tweening fills in the difference between two keyframes to create animation over the length of the sprite in the Score.

Step recording is a manual recording of one frame at a time. The process involves setting up the recording attributes, moving the playback head forward one frame, changing the sprite attributes, and moving the playback head forward again one frame.

Real-time recording records the movement of a cast member on the Stage. The process involves setting up the recording attributes and manually dragging a cast member around the Stage. Director records the motions and saves them as keyframes within the sprite in the Score.

Frame-by-frame animation is a series of cast members placed in the Score one frame at a time. The process involves altering cast members slightly from frame to frame to build an animated sequence. As the playback head moves through each frame, a slightly different cast member is displayed on the Stage, which makes the image appear to move. This technique has been used for years by Walt Disney Studios, among others, to create animation.

Tools You'll Use

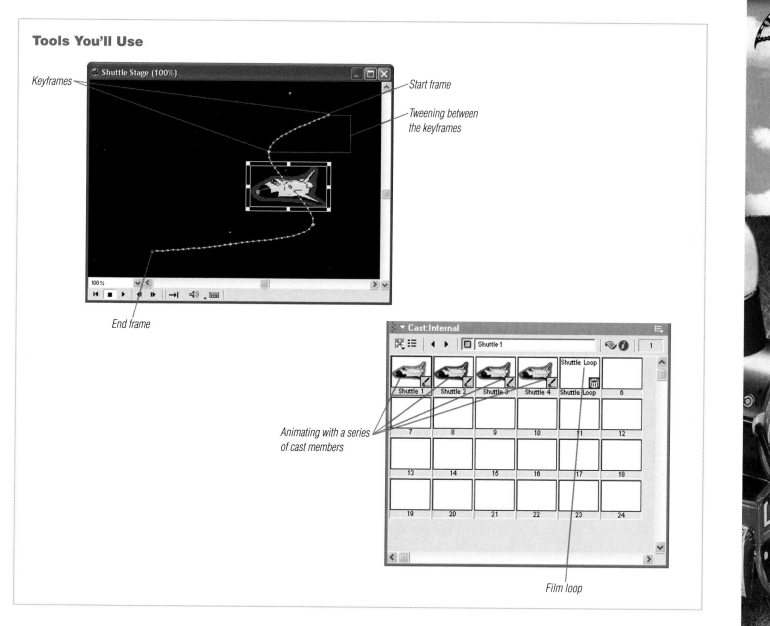

Keyframes

Shuttle Stage (100%)

Start frame

Tweening between
the keyframes

End frame

Cast:Internal

Shuttle 1

Animating with a series
of cast members

Film loop

CREATE ANIMATION USING TWEENING

What You'll Do

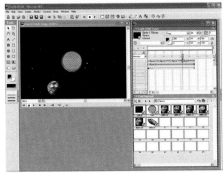

In this lesson, you will create an animation using tweening.

Creating Animation Using Tweening

Tweening is one of the most common types of animation. To tween an animation, you place keyframes in the sprite that correspond to the major schange points in sprite properties. Tweening occurs between two keyframes that contain the before and after property settings of a sprite. As you place keyframes in the sprite, Director automatically tweens the sprites between the keyframes. You can set as many keyframes within a sprite as there are frames in its span. By changing the number of frames between keyframes, you can control the smoothness of the animation.

Changing Tweenable Sprite Properties

After you create and position all the keyframes that you will need within a sprite, you adjust the sprite's initial properties for the tween. You select the first keyframe (in most cases, the first frame) and change one or more tweenable sprite properties, such as position, size, background and foreground color, ink, blend, skew, and rotation. You can change tweenable sprite properties

Repositioning keyframes in the Score

After you insert a keyframe in the Score, you can reposition it at any time. You can reposition a keyframe in the Score by dragging it to another frame in the channel. When you reposition a keyframe, the number of frames between the keyframes changes and Director changes the speed at which the animation plays. When you drag the start or end keyframe of a sprite to shorten or lengthen its span, all keyframes within the sprite move proportionately closer or farther apart. If you want to extend the span of a sprite without moving the keyframes, you can hold down [Ctrl] (Win) or [command] (Mac) while you drag the start or end frame of a sprite.

directly on the Stage by using the Sprite tab in the Property inspector, or by using the Sprite toolbar in the Score. After you adjust the tweenable sprite properties for the first keyframe, you select the next keyframe within the sprite and change its tweenable properties. Director generates all the frames between this keyframe and the first one. If you need to refine tweening in a sprite, you can insert additional keyframes and change properties to create a smoother path, or add frames between keyframes to add a gradual transition. For tweening to work, you need to make sure the properties you want to

tween are selected in the Sprite Tweening dialog box. You can tween one or more sprite properties at the same time by selecting multiple properties in the Sprite Tweening dialog box. Tweenable properties are not available for all sprites. For example, you can't rotate a quickdraw shape made with a drawing tool on the Tool palette.

Creating Effects Using Tweenable Properties

You can create special effects by changing the tweenable sprite properties. You can create the illusion of a sprite rotating in 3D

by changing its skew angle by 90 degrees or more, or create a fade out or fade in effect by changing the blend property of a sprite from a high value to a low value (fade out), or from a low value to a high value (fade in), as shown in Figure F-1. You can also create a zoom out or zoom in effect by changing the size of a sprite from large to small (zoom out) or from small to large (zoom in).

FIGURE F-1

Creating animation by tweening blend properties

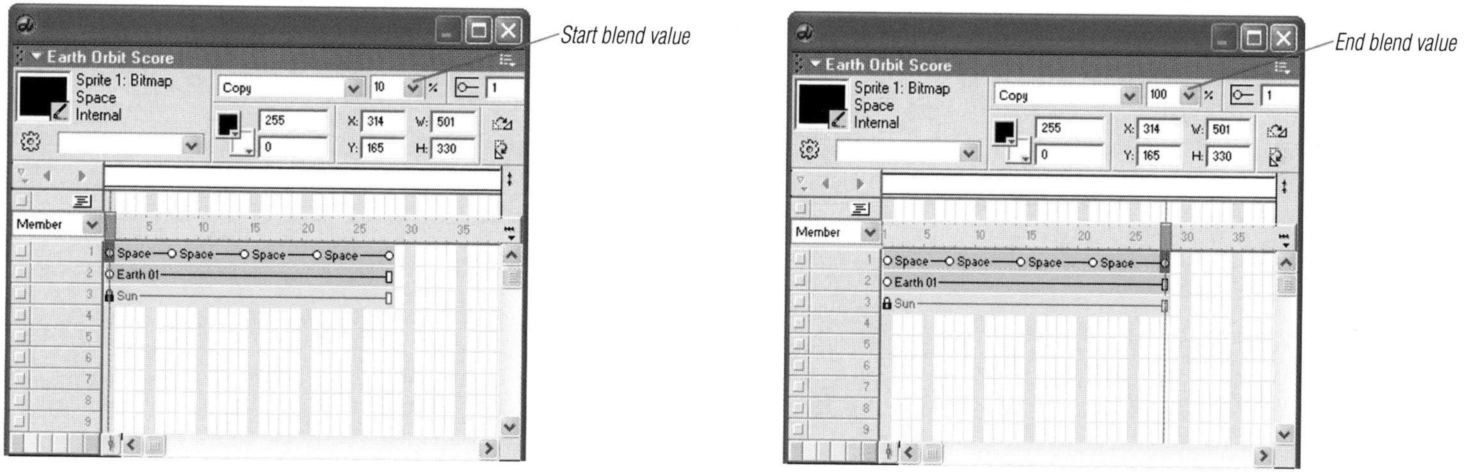

Create animation using tweening

1. Start Director, open the file MD F-1.dir from where your Unit F data files are stored, then save it as **Earth Orbit**.

2. Minimize the docking channel (Win) or close the grouped panel (Mac) with the Property inspector.

3. Click Edit (Win) or Director (Mac) on the menu bar, point to Preferences, then click Sprite to open the Sprite Preferences dialog box, as shown in Figure F-2.

4. Select the Tweening check box, if necessary, then click OK.

5. Click frame 7 in channel 1 to place the playback head at frame 7 and select the sprite.

   TIP To create an animation quickly, on the Stage, drag the red handle within the sprite (in the center [Win] or in the upper-left corner [Mac]) to the place you want the sprite's path to end, then insert keyframes to modify the sprite.

   (continued)

FIGURE F-2
Sprite Preferences dialog box

Select option to turn on tweening

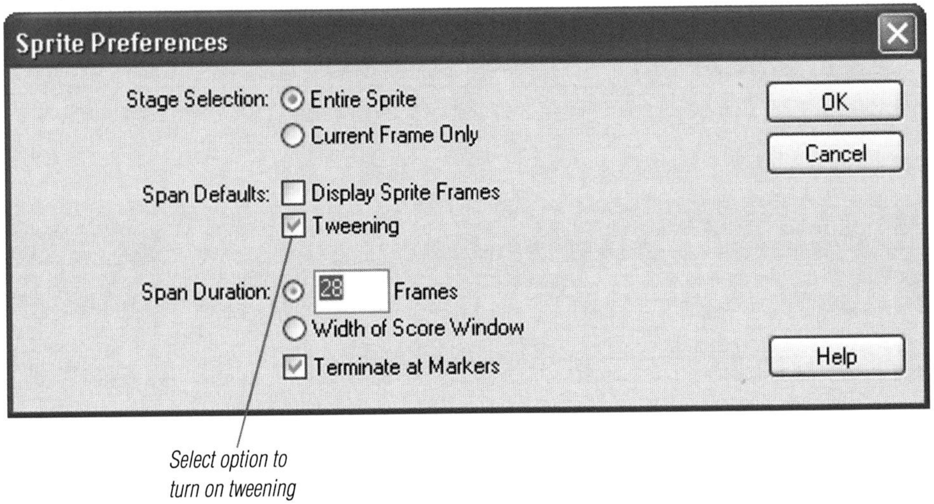

FIGURE F-3

Keyframes in a sprite

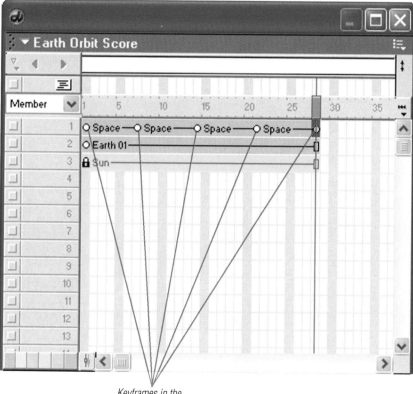

Keyframes in the
Space sprite

6. Click Insert on the menu bar, then click Keyframe to set a change point in the animation at frame 7.

7. Click frame 14 in channel 1, click Insert on the menu bar, then click Keyframe to set a change point in the animation at frame 14.

   TIP To delete a keyframe, click the frame with the keyframe in the Score, then press [Delete].

8. Press and hold [Alt] (Win) or [option] (Mac), then drag frame 14 in channel 1 to frame 21 in channel 1 to copy the keyframe in frame 14 to frame 21.

   TIP To move multiple keyframe positions at the same time, press and hold [Ctrl] (Win) or ⌘ (Mac), click multiple keyframes in the Score to select them, then move the sprite on the Stage.

9. Press and hold [Alt] (Win) or [option] (Mac), then drag frame 21 in channel 1 to frame 28 in channel 1 to copy the keyframe in frame 21 to frame 28, as shown in Figure F-3.

You created animation using tweening.

Change tweenable sprite properties

1. Click Modify on the menu bar, point to Sprite, click Tweening to open the Sprite Tweening dialog box, verify that the Blend check box is selected, as shown in Figure F-4, then click OK.

2. Click the keyframe in frame 1 in channel 1, click View on the menu bar, then click Sprite Toolbar to display it.

3. On the Sprite toolbar, click the Blend list arrow, then click 10.

4. Click the keyframe in frame 7 in channel 1, click the Blend list arrow, then click 30.

(continued)

FIGURE F-4

Sprite Tweening dialog box

Sprite tweenable properties

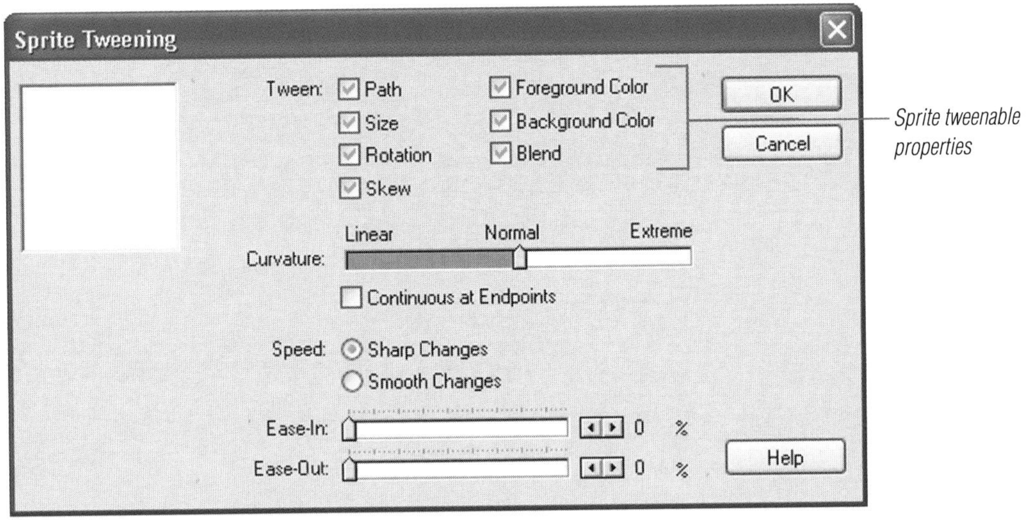

FIGURE F-5
Tweenable blend property

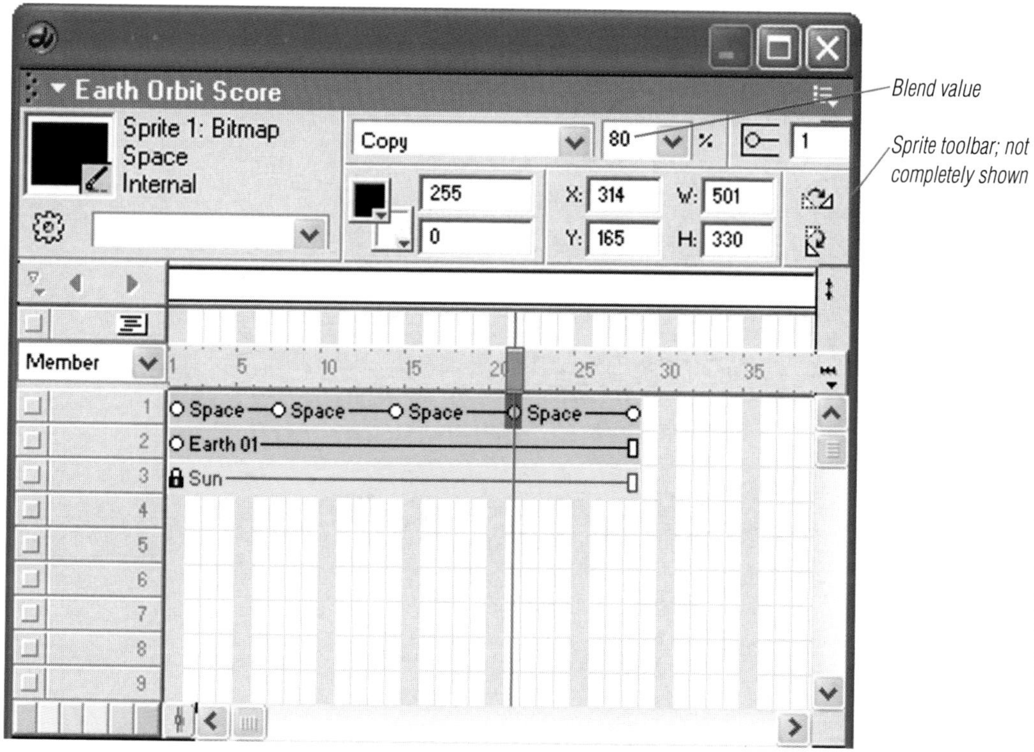

Blend value

Sprite toolbar; not
completely shown

5. Click the keyframe in frame 14 in channel 1, click the Blend list arrow, then click 60.

6. Click the keyframe in frame 21 in channel 1, click the Blend list arrow, then click 80, as shown in Figure F-5.

7. Click Modify on the menu bar, click Lock Sprite to lock the sprite, click View on the menu bar, then click Sprite Toolbar to hide the toolbar.

8. Rewind and play the movie.

   TIP If the movie loops, click Loop Playback on the Control Panel to deselect it.

9. Save your work.

You changed tweenable sprite properties.

CREATE A CIRCULAR ANIMATION

What You'll Do

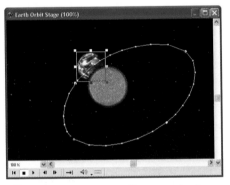

In this lesson, you will create a circular animation.

Creating a Circular Animation

When a sprite uses three or more keyframes, you can make the path between them follow a curve rather than a straight line. You can adjust the path by dragging any keyframe in the path on the Stage or by using the Curvature slider in the Sprite Tweening dialog box, as shown in Figure F-6. As you create a circular path, you can select the Continuous at Endpoints check box in the Sprite Tweening dialog box to cause the animation to begin and end at the same point. When you tween a sprite along any path, you can add a touch of realism by using the Ease-In and Ease-Out sliders in the Sprite Tweening dialog box to control the speed of a sprite at the beginning or end. The Ease-In slider controls the beginning speed, while the Ease-Out slider controls the ending speed. A high Ease-In percentage increases the time it takes for a sprite to speed up, whereas a high Ease-Out percentage increases the time it takes to slow down. If the speed changes in a path are too abrupt, you can insert more frames between the keyframes and select the Smooth Changes option button in the Sprite Tweening dialog box. The Smooth Changes option adjusts the sprite's speed gradually as it moves between keyframes. Conversely, the Sharp Changes option moves the sprite between keyframe locations without adjusting the speed.

FIGURE F-6

Sprite Tweening dialog box with curvature preview

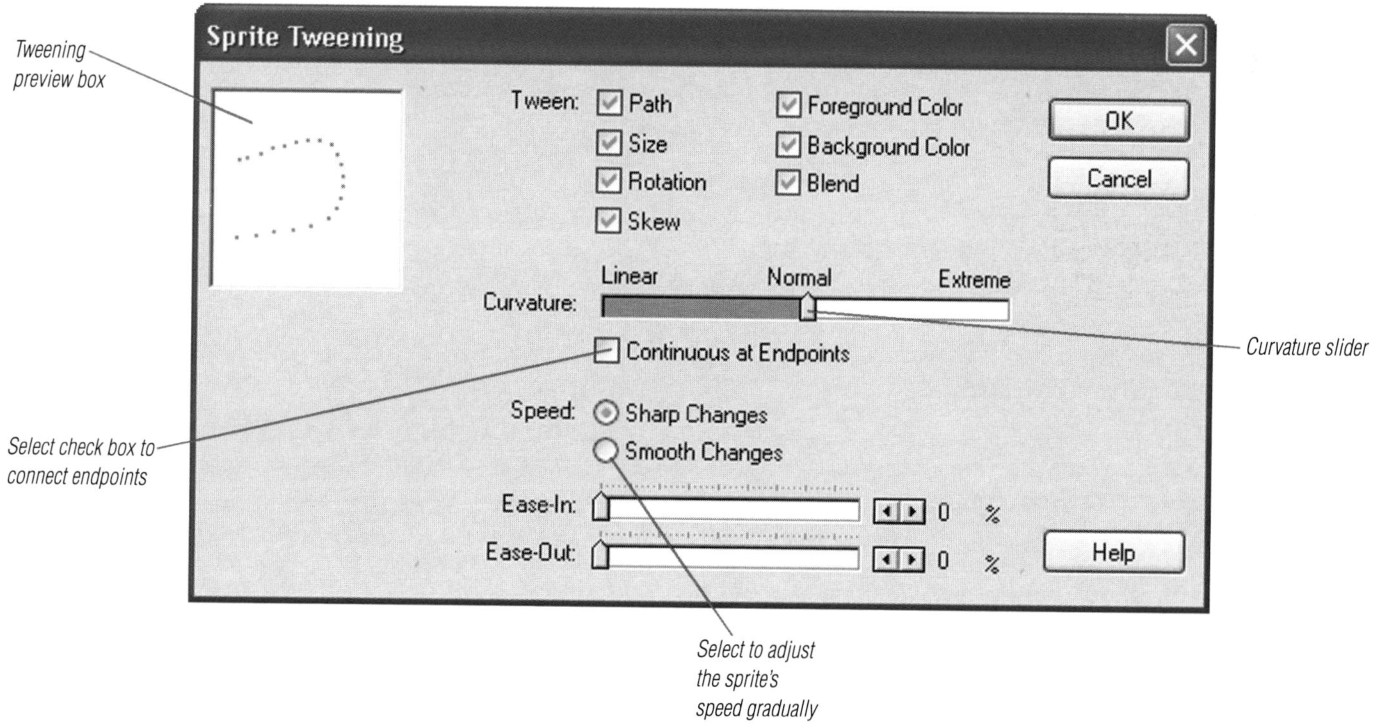

Tweening preview box

Curvature slider

Select check box to connect endpoints

Select to adjust the sprite's speed gradually

Create a circular animation

1. Click frame 7 in channel 2, click Insert on the menu bar, click Keyframe, then on the Stage, drag the Earth 01 sprite to point A, as shown in Figure F-7.

   TIP If the path is not displayed, click View on the menu bar, point to Sprite Overlay, then click Show Paths.

2. Click frame 14 in channel 2, click Insert on the menu bar, click Keyframe, then on the Stage, drag the Earth 01 sprite to point B, as shown in Figure F-7.

3. Click frame 21 in channel 2, click Insert on the menu bar, click Keyframe, then on the Stage, drag the Earth 01 sprite to point C, as shown in Figure F-7.

4. Click Modify on the menu bar, point to Sprite, then click Tweening to open the Sprite Tweening dialog box.

5. Select the Continuous at Endpoints check box, then drag the Curvature slider a little to the right of "Normal" (approximately ¼") to change the curvature of the animation path.

(continued)

Creating circular animation

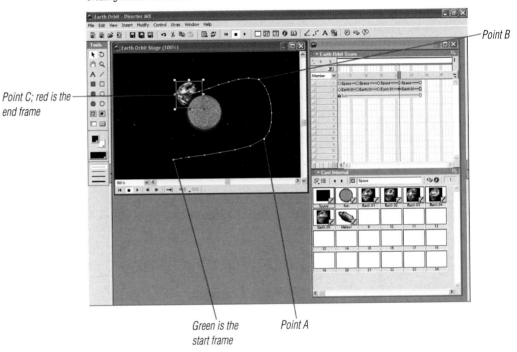

Point B

Point C; red is the end frame

Green is the start frame

Point A

Creating Animation   Unit F

A preview of the curvature change appears in the preview box in the upper-left corner of the dialog box.

6. Drag the Ease-Out slider to 50% to slow down the sprite and to add the illusion of perspective to an orbit.

7. Click OK.

8. Drag the keyframes (the larger circles) within the sprite on the Stage to fine-tune the elliptical path, as shown in Figure F-8.

   TIP If you click or drag a tweening point (the smaller circles) in the path instead of a keyframe, the sprite is deselected. To reselect the sprite, click the sprite again in the Score or on the Stage. To make the sprite's path curve between more points, hold down [Alt] (Win) or [option] (Mac) and drag a tweening point on the Stage to create a keyframe.

9. Rewind and play the movie, then save your work.

You created a circular animation.

FIGURE F-8
Circular animation path

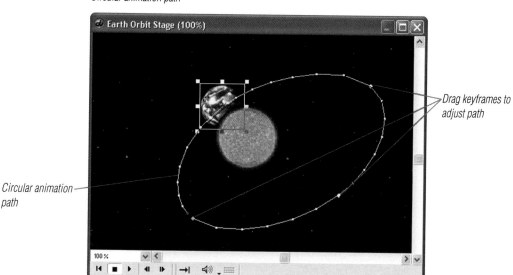

Drag keyframes to adjust path

Circular animation path

Lesson 2   Create a Circular Animation

RECORD ANIMATION

What You'll Do

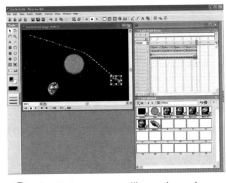

▶ *In this lesson, you will record an animation using step and real-time recording.*

Creating Animation Using Step Recording

Unlike tweening, in which Director creates animation frames for you, step recording is an animation technique in which you manually animate a sprite one frame at a time. You record the position of a sprite in a frame, step forward to the next frame, move the sprite to its new position or change sprite properties, step forward to the next frame, and so on, until you've completed the animation, as shown in Figure F-9. Step recording is especially useful for creating complex animation in which you need precise, frame-by-frame control of the sprite animation. You can also use step recording to redefine a tweened sprite animation.

Creating Animation Using Real-Time Recording

You can create animation by recording the movement of a sprite in real time as you drag it across the Stage, as shown in

Extending an animation using Paste Relative

If you want to extend the length of an existing animation, you can use the different animation techniques to add to the animation, but Director provides an easier way to accomplish the same task. You can use the Paste Relative command to align the start position of one sprite on the Stage with the end position of the preceding sprite. The Paste Relative command treats the end of the preceding sprite as a keyframe for the start position of the next sprite. To extend an animation using Paste Relative, select the animated sprite in the Score, click Edit on the menu bar, click Copy Sprites, click the frame immediately after the last frame of the selected sprite, click Edit on the menu bar, point to Paste Special, then click Relative. Director copies the animation on the Stage beginning where the previous animation ends. If you use Paste instead of Paste Relative, the pasted sprite will not synchronize with the preceding sprite.

Figure F-10. The real-time recording technique is especially useful for simulating the movement of a pointer or for quickly creating a complex motion for later refinement. The disadvantage of real-time recording is controlling the movement of the mouse for intricate animation. If real-time recording seems to be too sensitive for your mouse or too fast to complete within the time frame, you can slow the recording tempo to fix the problem. In the Control Panel, select the tempo setting in the Tempo text box, then type a slower tempo rate. Start the real-time recording, drag selected sprites on the Stage, then release the mouse button to stop recording. In the Control Panel, reset the tempo to a higher rate to play back the animation.

FIGURE F-9

Recording an animation step by step

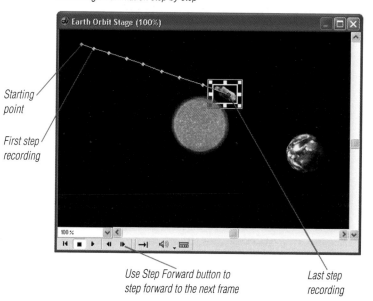

Starting point

First step recording

Use Step Forward button to step forward to the next frame

Last step recording

FIGURE F-10

Recording an animation in real time

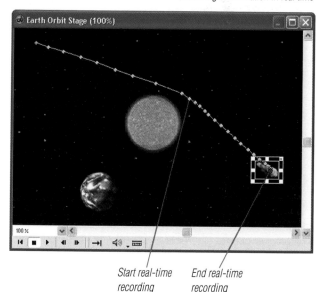

Start real-time recording

End real-time recording

Create animation using step recording

1. Click frame 1 in channel 4 in the Score, then drag the Meteor cast member in the Cast window to the upper-left corner of the Stage.

   TIP You can select more than one sprite for step recording. When you do, the sprites animate together.

2. Click the Score, display the Sprite toolbar, click the Ink list arrow on the Sprite toolbar, click Background Transparent, then hide the Sprite toolbar.

3. Click Control on the menu bar, then click Step Recording.

   An indicator appears next to the selected sprite in the Score, as shown in Figure F-11.

4. Click the Step Forward button in the Control Panel. ▐▶

   Director records the previous frame in the Score and advances to the next frame. The Earth 01 sprite also moves step by step along its elliptical path.

   (continued)

FIGURE F-11
Step recording an animation

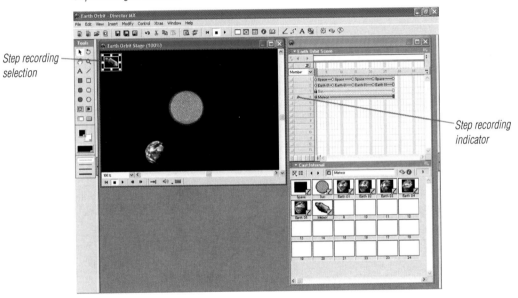

Step recording selection

Step recording indicator

Creating Animation   Unit F

FIGURE F-12

Completed step recording

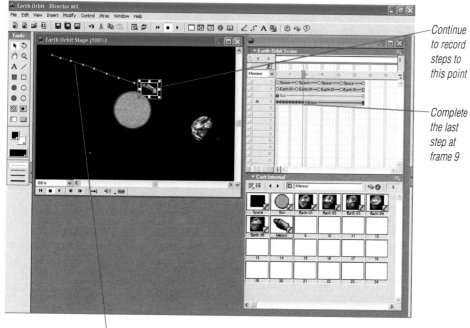

Continue to record steps to this point

Complete the last step at frame 9

Your path might look different

5. Drag the Meteor sprite (not the colored dot in the center) slightly down and to the right.

6. Click the Step Forward button in the Control Panel. ▮▶

   TIP To delete a step recording point, click the keyframe in the Score, then press [Delete].

7. Drag the Meteor sprite to the next point on the Stage, continuing to step record until you match the positions shown in Figure F-12. The last step is at frame 9.

   TIP If necessary, you can drag keyframes on the Stage to adjust the animation path.

8. Click Control on the menu bar, then click Step Recording.

   TIP To move the entire animation path, drag the cast member on the Stage associated with the sprite animation.

9. Rewind and play the movie.

You created animation using step recording.

Create animation using real-time recording

1. Click frame 10 in the Meteor sprite in the Score.

2. Click the Selected Frames Only button in the Control Panel. ⊏▬▬◻

   The Selected Frames Only option prevents the real-time recording from extending beyond the selected sprite. A green dotted line appears in the Score at the bottom of the Frame channel to indicate the selected frames.

3. Click Control on the menu bar, then click Real-Time Recording.

   An indicator appears next to the selected sprite in the Score, and a red selection rectangle appears on the Stage, as shown in Figure F-13.

   (continued)

FIGURE F-13

Real-time recording an animation

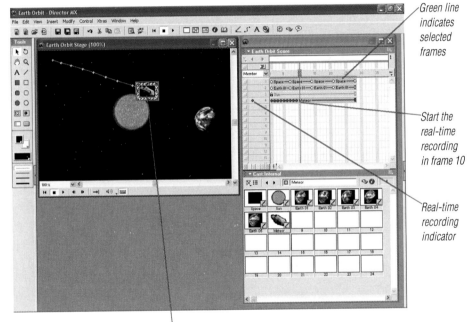

Green line indicates selected frames

Start the real-time recording in frame 10

Real-time recording indicator

Real-time recording selection

FIGURE F-14

Completed real-time recording

Your path might
look different

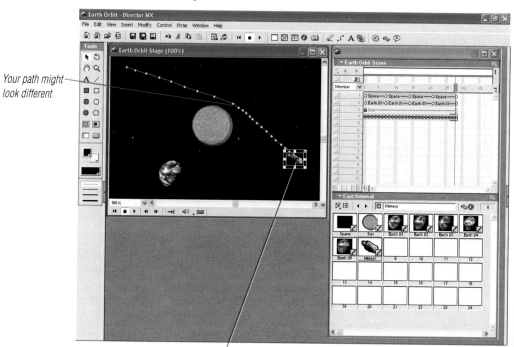

Drag the cast
member here

4. Drag the Meteor sprite to the point on the Stage shown in Figure F-14, then release the mouse to stop recording.

5. Click the Selected Frames Only button in the Control Panel to deselect it.

   TIP If you record beyond the last frame of a sprite, Director extends the sprite through the Score until you stop recording or until the sprite reaches another sprite.

6. Rewind and play the movie.

   TIP If the speed is too fast, adjust the tempo in the Control Panel.

7. Drag any keyframe (the larger circles) on the Stage that is not in a line, to refine the animation path.

   TIP If you have problems adjusting keyframes, make sure the Snap To check boxes on the Guides tab in the Property inspector are deselected.

8. Rewind and play the movie, then save your work.

You created animation using real-time recording.

ANIMATE WITH A SERIES OF CAST MEMBERS

What You'll Do

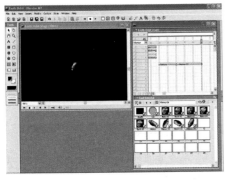

In this lesson, you will create an animation using a series of cast members.

Using Onion Skinning

You can use onion skinning to create a series of cast members that you can use to create animated sequences. Onion skinning allows you to create a new cast member in the Paint window while viewing one or more existing cast members as reference images. The reference images appear dimmed in the background with decreasing levels of brightness, as though you placed tracing paper over them, as shown in Figure F-15. You can draw on top of the reference images, copying the parts of their features that you need for the new cast member. The cast members used as references are not altered in the process. Onion skinning uses registration points to align the current cast member with the

Converting sprites to an animated sequence

When you create an animated sequence, sometimes it is helpful to place each of the cast members in one frame in sequential channels in the Score so that you can view them all at the same time and check positioning. You can use the Space to Time command to convert all the one-frame sprites in sequential channels to a single sprite, which will form an animated sequence. To convert one-frame sprites in sequential channels to an animated sequence, you select a frame in the Score as the start location. Drag the cast members to the Stage in the correct order. Director places the cast members in sequential channels in the Score. Arrange the sprites on the Stage as you want them to appear in the animated sequence. Select the sprites in the Score, and change the duration to one frame. Click Modify on the menu bar, click Space to Time, type a Separation value in the Space to Time dialog box to indicate how many frames you want to use to separate the sprites within the combined sprite animation, then click OK.

previous reference images, so you should be careful not to move registration points for cast members after onion skinning.

Animating with a Series of Cast Members

Until now, you have worked with sprites that display only one cast member, but Director allows you to create a sprite that displays multiple cast members. You can use frame animation to create an animated sequence that consists of a series of cast members. You can achieve this by using multiple cast members in the span of a sprite to create an animation. For example, you can display one cast member for the first 10 frames of a sprite, exchange it for another cast member, display the exchanged cast member for the next 10 frames, and continue in the same way to create an animation using a series of cast members, as shown in Figure F-16. If you want to create an animated sequence that displays cast members with different durations, use the Exchange Cast Members command. If you want a consistent duration, an easy way to create an animated sequence is to use the Cast to Time command.

FIGURE F-15

Creating cast members with onion skinning

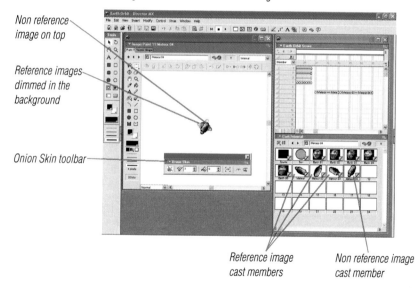

Non reference image on top

Reference images dimmed in the background

Onion Skin toolbar

Reference image cast members

Non reference image cast member

FIGURE F-16

Animating with a series of cast members

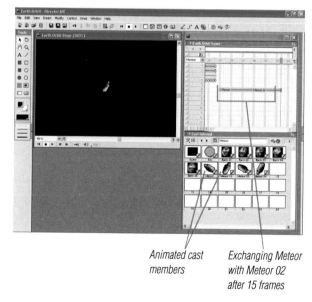

Animated cast members

Exchanging Meteor with Meteor 02 after 15 frames

Use onion skinning

1. Double-click the Meteor cast member in the Cast window.

   TIP If the Meteor image is not centered in the Paint window, scroll to center the image.

2. Click and hold the Marquee tool ⌐-¬ in the Paint window, click No Shrink, select the cast member in the Paint window, then click the Copy button on the toolbar. 🖺

3. Click View on the menu bar, click Onion Skin to display the Onion Skin toolbar, then click the Toggle Onion Skinning button on the Onion Skin toolbar (if necessary) as shown in Figure F-17. ✕

   TIP If the Preceding Cast Members text box and the Following Cast Members text box on the Onion Skin toolbar are not set to zero, you might see dimmed images from the preceding or following positions in the Cast window. To avoid this, click the up or down arrows to set the text boxes to zero.

4. Click the Set Background button 🖾 on the Onion Skin toolbar to set the image to appear in the background as an overlay, then click the Show Background button on the Onion Skin toolbar to display cast members that have the background set as an overlay. ⌇

   (continued)

FIGURE F-17
Enable onion skinning

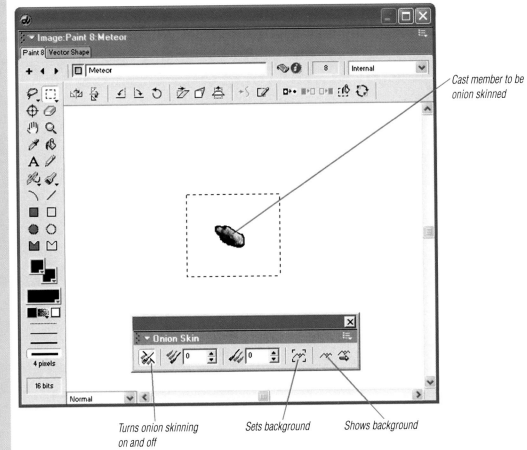

Cast member to be onion skinned

Turns onion skinning on and off

Sets background

Shows background

FIGURE F-18
Onion skinning

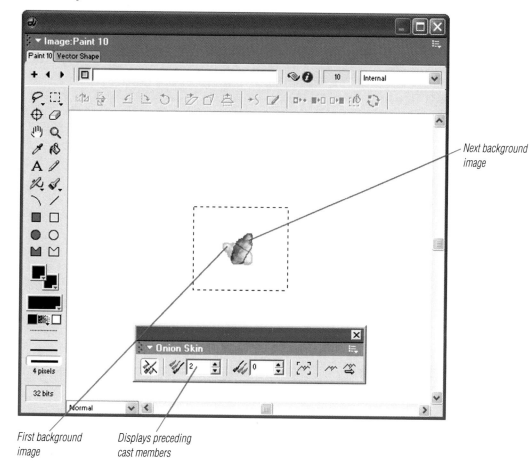

Next background
image

First background
image

Displays preceding
cast members

5. Click the New Cast Member button ✚ in the Paint window, name the cast member **Meteor 02**, click the Paste button 📋 on the toolbar, click the Rotate Right button ↘ in the Paint window, then click the Set Background button. 〰

6. Create a new cast member called **Meteor 03** in the Paint window, then click the Preceding Cast Members up arrow twice on the Onion Skin toolbar to display two reference images from preceding positions in the Cast window, as shown in Figure F-18.

7. Click the Paste button 📋, click the Rotate Right button ↘ twice, then click the Set Background button. 〰

8. Create a new cast member called **Meteor 04** in the Paint window, click the Paste button 📋, click the Rotate Left button ↙, then click the Set Background button. 〰

> **TIP** To use a series of images as a background while painting a series of foreground images, click the Track Background button on the Onion Skin toolbar.

9. Click the Toggle Onion Skinning button on the Onion Skin toolbar, then close the Onion Skin toolbar and the Paint window. ✖

You created a series of cast members using onion skinning.

Lesson 4   Animate with a Series of Cast Members

Animate with a series of cast members

1. Drag the Meteor cast member into the Score at frame 30 in channel 6, click the Meteor sprite in the Score (if necessary), then change the ink to Background Transparent using the Sprite toolbar.

   TIP To select parts of a sprite, press [Alt], click the first frame that you want to select, press [Ctrl] [Alt] (Win) or [⌘] [alt] (Mac), then click each additional frame that you want to select.

2. Click Edit on the menu bar, click Edit Sprite Frames, click frame 45 in the Meteor sprite in channel 6, hold down [Shift], then click frame 57 in the Meteor sprite.

3. Click the Meteor 02 cast member in the Cast window, click Edit on the menu bar, then click Exchange Cast Members to switch from the Meteor cast member to the Meteor 02 cast member in the selected frames.

4. Click any frame in the Meteor sprite in channel 6, click View on the menu bar, point to Sprite Labels, then click Changes Only (if necessary) to show the name of each sprite's cast member in the Score when it changes to a different cast member.

   TIP You might want to zoom the Score to 800% to display the information.

5. Click any frame in the combined Meteor and Meteor 02 sprite in channel 6 (if necessary), click Edit on the menu bar, then click Edit Entire Sprite to select the entire sprite, as shown in Figure F-19.

(continued)

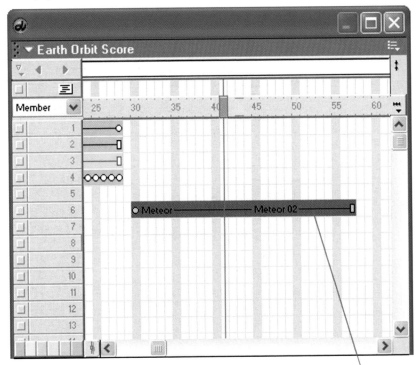

Exchanging Meteor
with Meteor 02 at
the end of the sprite

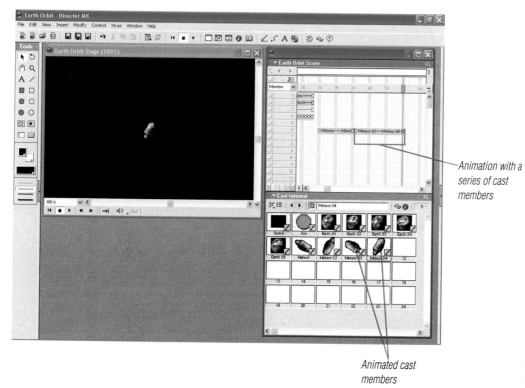

Animation with a
series of cast
members

Animated cast
members

6. Drag the end of the combined Meteor and Meteor 02 sprite to frame 40 so the sprite duration is 10 frames, then click frame 41 in channel 6.

7. Click the Meteor 03 cast member in the Cast window, hold down [Shift], then click the Meteor 04 cast member to select the cast members.

8. Click Modify on the menu bar, click Cast to Time to combine the cast members into one sprite two frames long as an animated sequence, then change the ink to Background Transparent using the Sprite toolbar.

> TIP To reverse an animated sequence, select the sprite animation, click Modify on the menu bar, then click Reverse Sequence.

9. Drag the end of the newly combined sprite in channel 6 to frame 55, click frame 30 to set the playback head to 30, play the movie, as shown in Figure F-20, then save your work.

You created an animation with a series of cast members.

CREATE A FILM LOOP

What You'll Do

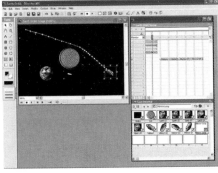

In this lesson, you will create a film loop.

Creating a Film Loop

A film loop combines many sprites and effects over a range of frames into a single cast member. Film loops make it easier to develop and work with large and complex animations by combining them into a single cast member. You can also create a film loop using other film loops. After you create a film loop, a new cast member appears in the Cast window. When you create a film loop, don't delete or modify the cast members from which you created it, because Director needs them to play the film loop. Film loop cast members work a little differently than other cast members; film loop cast members animate only when you play the movie. You can't see the animation if you step through the frames or drag the playback head across the frames. If you change the size of a sprite that contains a film loop, you will change the number of times the film loops. If you want to apply ink effects to a film loop, you need to apply the ink effects to the individual sprites before they become part of the film loop. Also, a film loop sprite cannot be rotated and its registration point cannot be moved from the middle.

FIGURE F-21

Creating a film loop

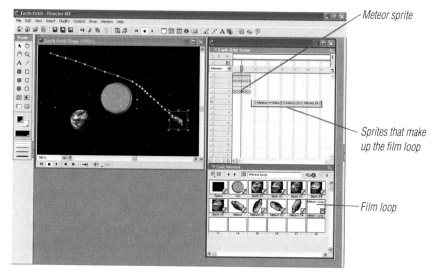

Meteor sprite

Sprites that make up the film loop

Film loop

Animating cursors

An animated cursor is simply an animated sequence of bitmapped cast members. You can display an animated cursor (such as an hourglass) during a long task, to communicate to your users that an action is in progress. Before you create an animated cursor, make sure the cast members you want to animate are 8-bit color bitmapped images, the standard color depth for cursors. To create an animated cursor, click Insert on the menu bar, point to Media Element, then click Cursor. In the Cursor Properties Editor dialog box, click the Cast list arrow, click a Cast window, click the arrows to browse the 8-bit cast members, then click Add to include cast members in the animation. In the Interval text box, enter a value (in milliseconds) to set the time delay between frames of the cursor. In the Hotspot position text boxes, type x and y values to define the cursor position that will activate the sequence when the user clicks there (0,0 marks the top-left corner). Choose a size option button to select the maximum size of the cursor, select the Automask check box to make white pixels in the cursor transparent, click Preview to see the cursor animation, then click OK.

Create a film loop

1. Click the Meteor sprite in channel 6 starting at frame 30 in the Score, hold down [Shift], then click the Meteor 03 sprite starting at frame 41 in the Score.

2. Click Insert on the menu bar, then click Film Loop to open the Create Film Loop dialog box.

3. Type **Meteor Loop**, then click OK.

   The film loop with the two animated sprites appears in the Cast window as a cast member.

4. Select the entire Meteor sprite in channel 4, then click the Meteor Loop cast member in the Cast window to select both items, as shown in Figure F-21.

5. Click Edit on the menu bar, then click Exchange Cast Members to exchange the Meteor cast member (which doesn't rotate) with the Meteor Loop cast member (which rotates) to animate it as it moves along the Meteor sprite's animation path.

6. Click the light gray button to the left of channel 6 in the Score to hide the channel for playback.

7. Rewind and play the movie.

   TIP If the animation plays too fast, double-click frame 1 in the Tempo channel, then reduce the tempo setting in fps.

8. Open the docking channel (Win) or grouped panel (Mac) with the Property inspector.

9. Save your work, then exit Director.

You created a film loop.

Create animation using tweening.

1. Start Director, open the file MD F-2.dir from where your Unit F data files are stored, and save it as **Sports**.
2. Open sprite preferences and make sure Tweening is turned on.
3. Select the Football sprite on the Stage, then drag the red handle in the middle up and to the right to move the football to the top-right corner of the Stage.
4. Insert keyframes at frames 10, 20, 30, and 40 in channel 2.
5. Display the Sprite tab in the Property inspector for the Football sprite.
6. Change the rotation angle to 60 degrees at frame 10 in channel 2; 120 degrees at frame 20 in channel 2; 180 degrees at frame 30 in channel 2; and 240 degrees at frame 40 in channel 2.
7. Rewind and play the animation.

Create a circular animation.

1. Insert a keyframe at frame 15 in channel 3, then drag the Basketball sprite down diagonally to the left to the bottom of the Stage.
2. Insert a keyframe at frame 25 in channel 3, then drag the Basketball sprite up to the left almost to the middle of the Stage.
3. Insert a keyframe at frame 35 in channel 3, then drag the Basketball sprite down diagonally to the left to the bottom of the Stage.

4. Insert a keyframe at frame 40 in channel 3, then drag the Basketball sprite straight left along the bottom of the Stage.
5. Adjust the curvature of the animation to be more linear (less curved at the keyframes).
6. Change the Ease-Out setting to 90%.
7. Rewind and play the animation.
8. Adjust the animation path on the Stage as necessary to create a smooth animation, then rewind and play the animation again.

Record an animation.

1. Select the Baseball sprite at frame 1.
2. Start step recording, then step forward in the Control Panel.
3. Drag the Baseball sprite on the Stage to the right and down a bit.
4. Continue to step forward and drag the Baseball sprite until you reach the bottom of the Stage at frame 15. (*Hint*: Avoid hitting the other balls as you move the sprite across the Stage.)
5. End step recording, then rewind and play the animation.
6. Click frame 16 in the Baseball sprite in the Score.
7. Turn on Selected Frames Only, then start real-time recording.
8. Drag the Baseball sprite to create small bounces at the bottom of the Stage.
9. Turn off Selected Frames Only, then adjust the animation path to fine-tune it.
10. Rewind and play the animation.

Animate with a series of cast members.

1. Open the Basketball cast member.
2. Select the basketball image with no shrink, then copy the image.
3. View the Onion Skin toolbar, then turn on onion skinning.
4. Set the background, then show the background.
5. Create a new cast member, then paste a copy of the basketball image in the Paint window.
6. Rotate the image to the right, then set the background.
7. Repeat Steps 5 and 6 two more times to create two more versions of the basketball. (*Hint*: For Step 6, rotate one image right twice and rotate the other image left.)
8. Set the Preceding Cast Members text box to display the preceding four cast members.
9. Toggle Onion Skinning off, then close the Onion Skin toolbar and the Paint window.
10. Click frame 45 in channel 6.
11. Select the four versions of the Basketball sprite in the Cast window.
12. Create an animation with a series of cast members, using Cast to Time.
13. Extend the sprite to frame 90 in channel 6.

Create a film loop.

1. Select the sprite starting in frame 45 in channel 6.
2. Create a film loop called **Sports Loop**.

3. Select the Basketball sprite in channel 3, then select the Sports Loop cast member in the Cast window.
4. Exchange the cast members.
5. Hide channel 6, rewind and play the animation, then compare your screen to Figure F-22.
6. Save the movie, then exit Director.

FIGURE F-22
Completed Skills Review

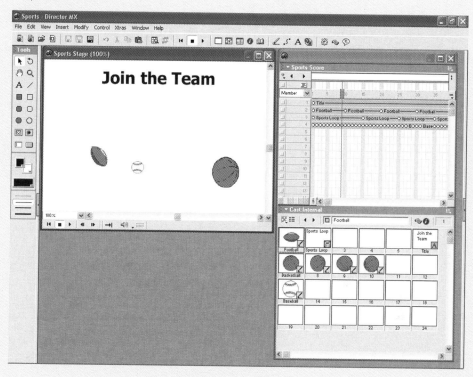

You are the marketing manager for On Target Enterprises, a health and fitness company. The company produces a line of natural health products that includes energy bars and drinks, protein powders, and daily supplements. You want to create an animation for a marketing presentation that depicts hitting a target. You use Director to create an animation of an arrow hitting a target.

1. Download an image of an arrow and a target. Use images from the Web that are free for both personal and commercial use (check the copyright information for any image before downloading it).
2. Start Director and save the movie as **On Target**.
3. Create a text cast member with the text **On Target Health and Fitness**, and drag it to the top of the Stage.
4. Import the images into Director, then add the arrow and target cast members to the Stage.
5. Animate the arrow to hit the target.
6. Compare your screen to Figure F-23.
7. Play and save the movie, then exit Director.

FIGURE F-23
Completed Project Builder 1

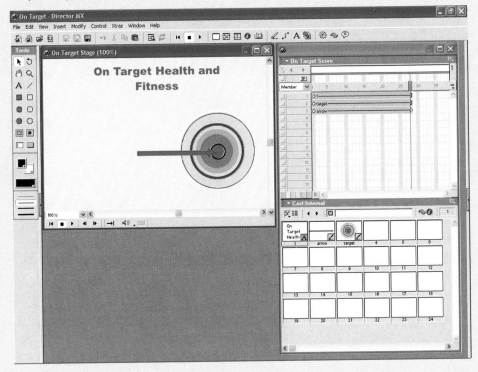

You are the director of Coin Collectors, Inc., an international coin collecting and appraisal company. Coin Collectors is the leading provider of grading and authentication services, in-depth price guides, news, and information, offering more expertise than any other collectibles company. You want to create a presentation for an upcoming coin collecting convention. You use Director to create an animation of coins rolling across the Stage.

1. Download a photograph of a coin. Use an image from the Web that is free for both personal and commercial use (check the copyright information for any image before downloading it).

2. Start Director and save the movie as **Coin Collectors**.

3. Create a text cast member with the text **Coin Collectors, Inc.** and drag it to the top of the Stage.

4. Import the photograph of the coin into Director, then add the coin cast member to the Stage.

5. Animate the coin across the Stage.

6. Change the position of the coin as it moves across the Stage. (*Hint*: Change the rotation value on the Sprite tab in the Property inspector in small increments for each keyframe.)

7. Compare your screen to Figure F-24.

8. Play and save the movie, then exit Director.

FIGURE F-24
Completed Project Builder 2

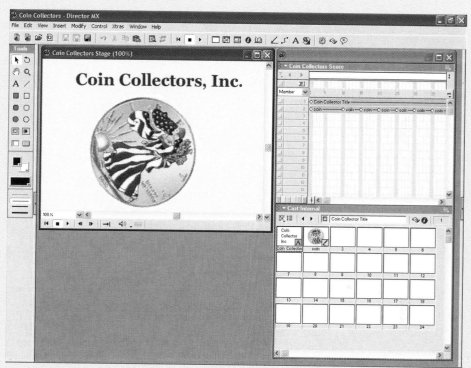

You are the Web site designer for Bug Be Gone, a termite and pest control company. Bug Be Gone employs the most technologically advanced methods for securing buildings against pests such as termites, mice, roaches, ants, and fleas. You want to create an animation of different pests for the Web site. You use Director to create an animation of different pests appearing on the page.

1. Download photographs of at least two pests. Use images from the Web that are free for both personal and commercial use (check the copyright information for any image before downloading it).
2. Start Director and save the movie as **Bug Be Gone**.
3. Create a text cast member with the text **bug be gone** and **we guarantee it** and drag it to the top of the Stage.
4. Import the photographs of pests into Director.
5. Add the pest cast members to the Stage.
6. Create a step recording across the Stage with one pest cast member.
7. Create a real-time recording across the Stage with the other pest cast member.
8. Select the two animations, then create a film loop as **Bug Loop**.
9. Drag the Bug Loop cast member to frame 1 in channel 4 in the Score to create a second set of bugs, then move the Bug Loop sprite

on the Stage to position the bugs next to each other.
10. Compare your screen to Figure F-25.

11. Play and save the movie, then exit Director.
12. Put a copy of this movie in your portfolio.

FIGURE F-25
Completed Design Project

Your group can assign elements of the project to individual members, or work collectively to create the finished product.

You are a member of the graphics design team at Nature Designs, Inc. All Butterflies, Inc., a habitat for exotic butterflies, performs research on all species of butterflies and provides tours of the facilities for schools and the public. The director of All Butterfiles, Inc., asks you to create a butterfly presentation for the tour. You use Director to create an animation of a butterfly moving across the sky.

1. Assign each member of the group to research butterflies on the Web for layout ideas, and to obtain butterfly photos for the project. Use images from the Web that are free for both personal and commercial use (check the copyright information for any image before downloading it).
2. Start Director and save the movie as **All Butterflies**.
3. Create a text cast member with the text **all butterflies tour** and drag it to the top of the Stage, then change the Stage background to light blue.
4. Import the butterfly image into Director.
5. Open the butterfly cast member, then view and toggle on onion skinning.
6. Copy the butterfly, set the background, then show the background.

7. Create a new cast member, paste the butterfly, rotate it 45 degrees right, set the background, then show the background.
8. Repeat Steps 6 and 7 to create six more versions of the butterfly continuing at 45 degree angles to complete an entire range of butterflies.
9. Toggle off onion skinning, then close the Onion Skin toolbar and the Paint window.
10. Select a series of butterfly cast members that creates the illusion of flying, then create an animation sequence. Create several different animation sequences. (*Hint*: Use the Cast to Time command and move cast

members around in the Cast window to select them in different order.)
11. Place the animated sequences in the Score consecutively starting in frame 1 in channel 2, select them, then create a film loop.
12. Create a circular animation using the film loop starting in frame 1 in channel 3, hide the channel with the consecutive animated sequences, then play the movie.
13. Show the channel, then compare your screen to Figure F-26.
14. Play and save the movie, then exit Director.

FIGURE F-26
Completed Group Project

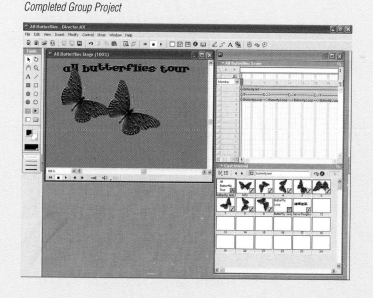

ADDING NAVIGATION
AND USER INTERACTION

1. Change tempo.

2. Add a wait time.

3. Create navigation with behaviors.

4. Create navigation with markers.

5. Add rollover and transition effects.

Adding Navigation and User Interaction

Adding navigation and user interaction to your movies lets you involve your audience in the movie. You can use these features to jump to different parts of movies during authoring or in the completed movie, or to allow users to perform functions such as clicking buttons and downloading files from the Internet. This unit introduces you to basic skills for changing the tempo, or speed, of a movie, adding a wait time, creating navigation controls and markers, and adding transitions between movie scenes.

Types of Navigation and User Interaction

Director provides you with several types of navigation and user interaction controls, which include tempo settings, Library behaviors, Lingo scripts, and transition settings. The tempo settings enable you to set the speed of the movie and to pause the movie at a specific frame, such as when a user clicks or presses a key, or when a specific cue point occurs in a sound or video. The Library behaviors enable you to add navigation controls and interaction to a movie using a built-in behavior from the Library palette that contains a prewritten Lingo script. Lingo enables you to create simple scripts that you can attach to sprites or frames to navigate to a specific location in a movie. The transition settings enable you to select a transition effect that you can use to move smoothly from one scene to another. You can also set the duration and smoothness of a transition.

Tools You'll Use

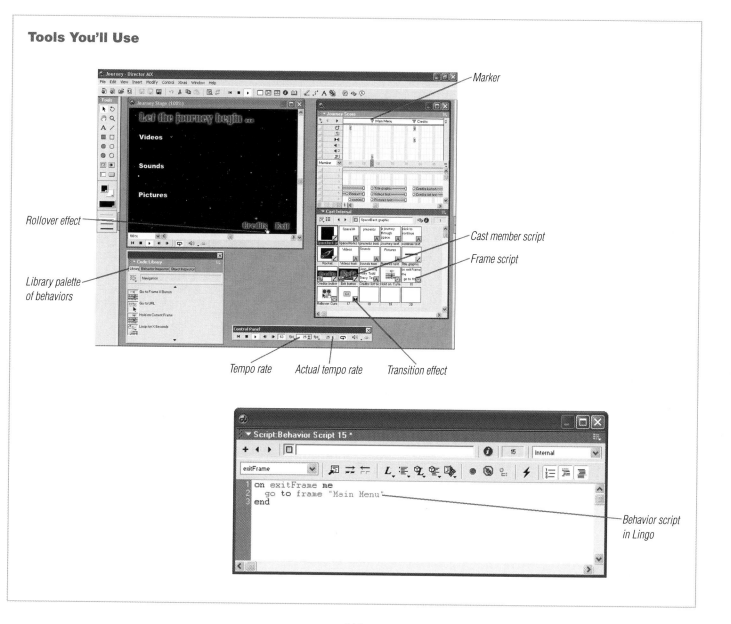

Marker

Rollover effect

Library palette
of behaviors

Cast member script

Frame script

Tempo rate   Actual tempo rate   Transition effect

Behavior script
in Lingo

```
on exitFrame me
    go to frame "Main Menu"
end
```

CHANGE TEMPO

What You'll Do

In this lesson, you will change tempo settings and compare tempo performance.

Changing the Tempo

Director plays a movie at a particular **tempo**, or speed. You can set the tempo to control the maximum speed at which the movie plays from frame to frame. The tempo is measured in frames per second (fps). The higher the tempo, the faster Director plays back animation. You can make animated sprites fly across the Stage to create a high-speed effect, or crawl across the Stage to create a slow-motion effect. You can set the tempo for the entire movie or selected frames. You use the tempo channel in the Score to set the tempo, as shown in Figure G-1. It's a good idea to set the tempo for a movie in the first

Understanding tempo on different computers

Director always attempts to play a movie at the specified tempo, but the computer running the movie might not be fast enough to play it at the desired tempo. If you want your movie to play on a variety of computer systems, you need to test your movie on low-end computers, and set a tempo that allows low-end computers (low CPU speed and small amount of RAM; see Director Help for system requirements) to play the movie at the desired tempo. If you have complex animations and transitions or large cast members in the movie that might cause slower playback, you might need to redesign parts of the movie so that the movie can play at a slower tempo. Otherwise, low-end computer users might be disappointed with the playback performance. To make movies play at the same tempo on all types of computers, you can select the Lock Frame Durations check box in the Movie Playback Properties dialog box. The Lock Frame Durations option prevents a movie from playing too fast on a fast computer. However, it cannot prevent a movie from playing slowly on a slow computer frame. Otherwise, the playback speed will be determined by the frame-by-frame settings in the Control Panel, which can be inconsistent. When you set the tempo in the tempo channel, Director uses the tempo from the selected frame until it reaches the next different tempo setting. You can set the tempo from 1 to 999 frames per second. The tempo doesn't affect the playback rate of sounds and video or the duration of transitions.

Comparing Tempo Performance
Director tries to play the movie at the tempo you set in the tempo channel. However, the actual playback speed might be different, because computers run at different speeds and include different hardware, which can slow down the performance of a movie.

When you play a movie, Director records the actual speed of each frame in the movie for comparison with the desired tempo.

The Control Panel includes the tempo you set in the tempo channel and the actual speed of the movie, as shown in Figure G-2. If you haven't recorded the actual speed of a movie in a frame, the Actual Tempo box on the Control Panel displays two dashes (--). While you play the movie, you can compare the tempo, also known as the target tempo, with the actual tempo. If you need to adjust the tempo after making a comparison (for example, the actual tempo is significantly slower than the target tempo), you can change tempo settings in the tempo channel or use the Tempo up and down arrows

in the Control Panel to adjust the tempo for specific frames. However, the tempo you set in the tempo channel overrides any value you set in the Control Panel.

Tracking Total Movie Time
While Director calculates the actual speed of the movie, it also tracks the running and estimated total elapsed time in seconds from the start of the movie to the current frame. Estimated total is similar to running total, but is more accurate because it includes palette changes and transitions in its calculations of the frame's length. The drawback of estimated total is that the movie might play back at a reduced speed due to its more intensive calculations.

FIGURE G-1
Effects channels in the Score

Tempo channel
Color channel
Transition channel
Behavior channel

Hides and shows
the effects channels

Sound channels

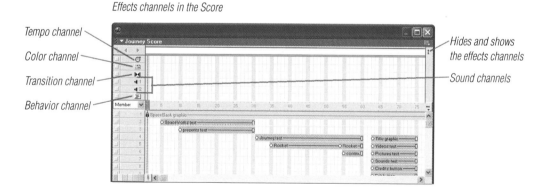

FIGURE G-2
Control Panel with tempo settings

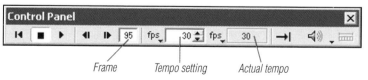

Frame   Tempo setting   Actual tempo

Change the movie tempo

1. Start Director, open the file MD G-1.dir from where your Unit G data files are stored, save it as **Journey**, then resize the Stage to display the gray area around the Stage.

2. Play the movie.

   Notice that the movie's tempo is too fast.

   > TIP If the movie loops, click the Loop Playback button on the Control Panel to turn it off.

3. Click the Hide/Show Effects Channels button in the Score to display the Effects channels, then click frame 1 in the tempo channel. ↕

4. Click Modify on the menu bar, point to Frame, then click Tempo to open the Frame Properties: Tempo dialog box, as shown in Figure G-3.

5. Click the Tempo option button (if necessary), click the Tempo arrow buttons until the setting reaches 25 fps (or as close as possible) to slow down the movie speed, then click OK.

   > TIP To zoom in on the Score, click the Zoom Menu button at the right edge of the frame channel in the Score, then click a percentage.

   (continued)

FIGURE G-3

Frame Properties: Tempo dialog box

Use arrow buttons or drag the slider to set tempo

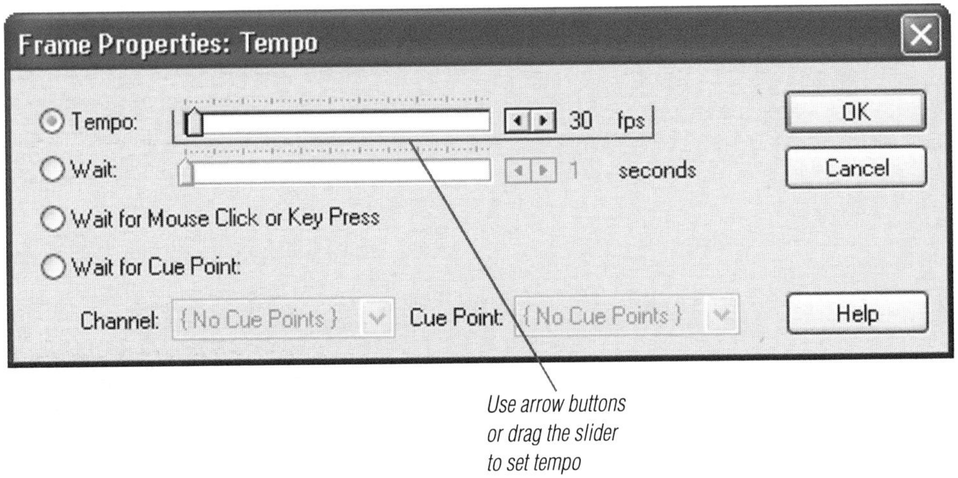

FIGURE G-4

Tooltip of tempo setting in the tempo channel

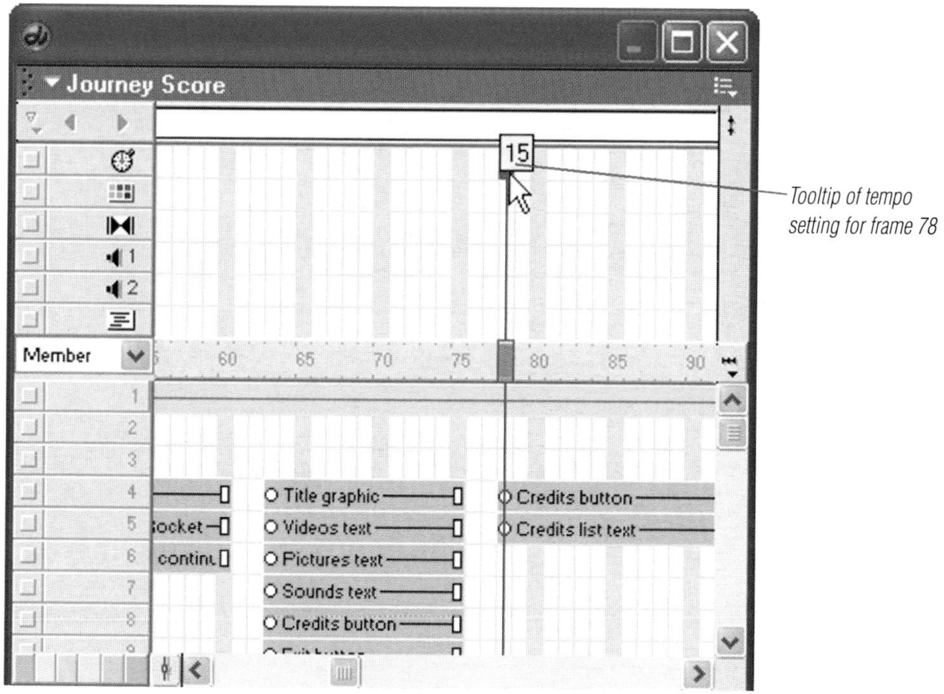

Tooltip of tempo
setting for frame 78

6. Scroll to frame 78, then double-click frame 78 in the tempo channel to open the Frame Properties: Tempo dialog box.

7. Click the Tempo option button (if necessary), click the Tempo arrow buttons until the setting reaches 15 fps (or as close as possible) to slow down the movie speed at frame 78, then click OK.

8. Point to frame 78 in the Tempo channel to display a tooltip with the tempo, as shown in Figure G-4, then rewind and play the movie.

   TIP The tempo also appears in the frame in the tempo channel; however, because the frame size is typically small, you need to zoom in on the Score to view it fully.

You changed the movie tempo.

Compare tempo performance

1. Click Window on the menu bar, click Control Panel (if necessary), then click frame 75 in the frame channel in the Score.

   The Control Panel shows the tempo settings.

2. Click the Step Forward button on the Control Panel until you reach the end of the movie, frame 95, then compare the tempo setting with the actual tempo on the Control Panel. ▌▶

3. Click the Actual Tempo Mode button on the Control Panel, then click Running Total to display the movie's total elapsed time, as shown in Figure G-5. fps▾

4. Click the Actual Tempo Mode button on the Control Panel, then click Frames Per Second. tot▾

5. Rewind and play the movie.

   As the movie plays, depending on the speed of your computer, you may notice a difference between the target tempo and the actual tempo in the Control Panel.

   > TIP If the movie jumps to other parts, make sure you play through all of these parts to record the actual speed at which to store these values in the Actual Tempo box.

   (continued)

FIGURE G-5
Control Panel with total running time

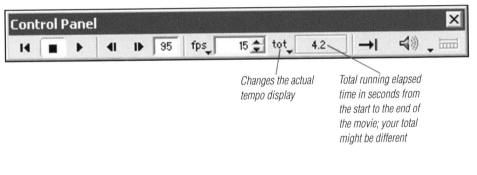

Changes the actual
tempo display

Total running elapsed
time in seconds from
the start to the end of
the movie; your total
might be different

FIGURE G-6

Movie Playback Properties dialog box

Locks the movie
playback speed

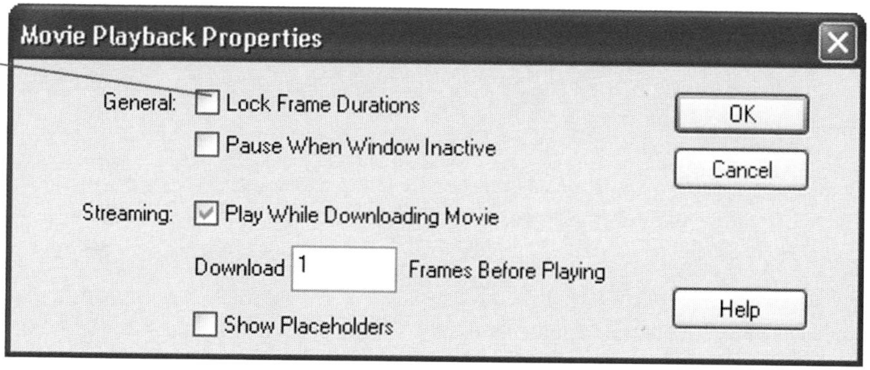

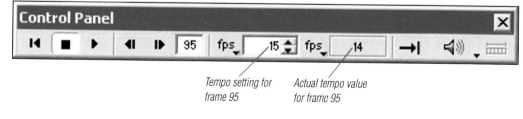

6. Click Modify on the menu bar, point to Movie, then click Playback to open the Movie Playback Properties dialog box, as shown in Figure G-6.

7. Select the Lock Frame Durations check box, then click OK to lock each frame at the actual tempo recorded.

8. Rewind and play the movie to display the Control Panel with roughly the same target and actual tempo settings, as shown in Figure G-7, then close the Control Panel.

9. Click Modify on the menu bar, point to Movie, click Playback, deselect the Lock Frame Durations check box, click OK to reset initial properties, then save your work.

You compared tempo performance and changed movie playback properties.

FIGURE G-7

Control Panel with tempo settings

Tempo setting for
frame 95

Actual tempo value
for frame 95

ADD A WAIT TIME

What You'll Do

In this lesson, you will add a wait time to a movie.

Adding a Wait Time

You can use the tempo channel and the Frame Properties: Tempo dialog box to add a wait time in the playback of a movie. Wait times allow users to read important information on the screen or perform an action. You can set a movie to wait at a frame for a specified number of seconds or until a specific event occurs, such as a mouse click, key press, or a specific cue point in a sound or video. A **cue point** is a marker in a sound or video that you can use to trigger an event in Director. For example, you can use cue points to synchronize an animation with narration. A common use for cue points is to wait for the end of a sound or video to occur before Director starts the next frame in a movie.

Inserting cue points in sound and video files

Inserting cue points in Director with the tempo channel or Lingo pauses the playback head at defined points in a sound or video. Before you import a sound or video file into Director, you need to use a third-party program to place or define cue points in the sound or video file that correspond to the times when you want to trigger an event, such as displaying text or starting an animation in Director. In Windows, use Sound Forge 4.0 or later, or Cool Edit 96 or later, to insert cue points (called markers or regions within these programs). Cue points are not supported in AVI video. On the Macintosh, use Peak LE 2 or later, or another sound edit program to insert cue points in AIFF and Shockwave Audio sounds, and in QuickTime videos. In Director, you use the Wait for Cue Point option in the Frame Properties: Tempo dialog box to determine when you want the playback to pause at a cue point in a sound or video. The Wait for Cue Point option enables you to select the End or Next cue point or any named or numbered cue point in a sound or video. In addition to using the Frame Properties: Tempo dialog box, you can also use Lingo to work with cue points.

Sets the frame to wait for a specified number of seconds

Sets the frame to wait for a mouse click or key press

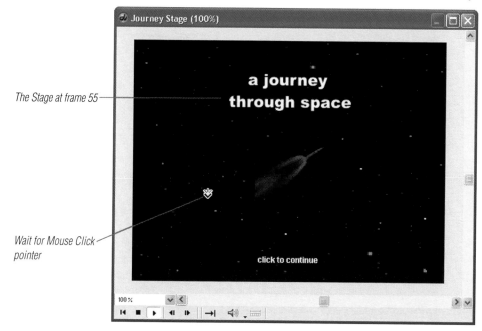

Add a wait time

1. Scroll to frame 55 in the Score, then double-click frame 55 in the tempo channel to open the Frame Properties: Tempo dialog box, as shown in Figure G-8.

2. Click the Wait for Mouse Click or Key Press option button, then click OK.

3. Scroll to frame 95, then double-click frame 95 in the tempo channel.

4. Click the Wait option button, then drag the Wait slider or click the Wait arrow buttons until the number reaches 4 seconds (or as close as possible) to pause the movie at frame 95, then click OK.

   TIP To delete a tempo, select the frame with the tempo setting, then press [Delete].

5. Rewind and play the movie.

6. When the movie stops at frame 55, position the pointer on the Stage, as shown in Figure G-9, then click anywhere on the Stage to continue playing the movie.

   The movie pauses for 4 seconds at frame 95, then ends. In Lesson 4, the pause will be followed by the display of a new scene.

   TIP The wait time number you set in the Frame Properties: Tempo dialog box is displayed in the tempo channel. However, you might need to increase the view size of the Score with the Zoom Menu button to read the number.

7. Save your work.

You added a wait time to a movie.

FIGURE G-9

Wait for Mouse Click on the Stage

The Stage at frame 55 —

Wait for Mouse Click pointer

a journey
through space

click to continue

CREATE NAVIGATION WITH BEHAVIORS

What You'll Do

In this lesson, you will create navigation with a behavior.

Creating Navigation with Behaviors

You can add navigation controls and interaction to a movie without having to understand and write Lingo. You can use a behavior with a prewritten Lingo script to add interactivity to a movie. Director provides a Library palette of useful built-in behaviors on the Library tab in the Code panel that you can drag onto sprites and frames in the Score and on the Stage. The Library palette of built-in behaviors is grouped by category, such as animation, controls, Internet, navigation, and text, and comes with a tooltip description of each behavior, which helps you find the behavior you need. You can attach the same behavior to multiple sprites and frames. You can attach multiple behaviors to an individual sprite, but only one to a frame. If you want a behavior to affect the entire movie, such as Hold on Current Frame, you attach the behavior to a frame. Director attaches a behavior by copying the behavior from the Library palette to a cast member in the Cast window.

QUICKTIP

When you attach a behavior to a sprite or frame, the Parameters dialog box might open, asking you for specific settings.

Getting information about behaviors

Some behaviors have long descriptions and instructions, which you cannot view using the tooltip description in the Library palette. To view a complete description and a set of instructions provided by the behavior's author for a behavior already attached to a sprite or frame, you can use the Behavior Inspector. To display more information about a behavior in the Behavior Inspector, attach a behavior to a sprite or frame, click Window on the menu bar, then click Behavior Inspector. The behavior information appears on the Behavior Inspector tab in the Code panel in a scrolling pane at the bottom.

FIGURE G-10
Library palette with built-in behaviors

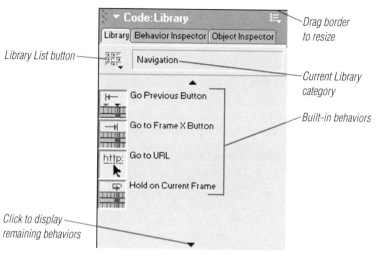

Drag border to resize

Library List button

Current Library category

Built-in behaviors

Click to display remaining behaviors

FIGURE G-11
New behavior in the Cast window

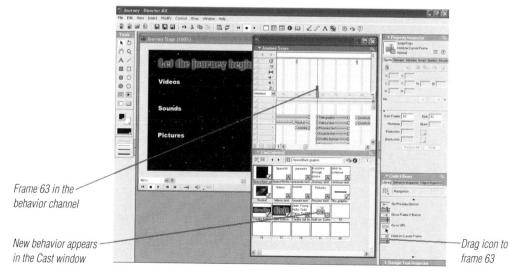

Frame 63 in the behavior channel

New behavior appears in the Cast window

Drag icon to frame 63

Create navigation with behaviors

1. Scroll to display frame 63 in the Score, click Window on the menu bar, then click Library Palette to display the Library tab in the Code panel.

2. Click the Library List button, then click Navigation.

   TIP To hide/show the names of the behaviors in the Library palette, click the Library List button, then click Show Names.

3. Click the down arrow at the bottom of the Library palette until the Hold on Current Frame behavior icon appears, as shown in Figure G-10.

4. Position the Hand pointer on the Hold on Current Frame behavior icon in the Library palette.

5. Drag the Hold on Current Frame behavior icon in the Library palette to frame 63 in the behavior channel, as shown in Figure G-11.

   TIP To attach the same behavior to several sprites at once using the Library palette, select the sprites on the Stage or in the Score, then drag a behavior to any one of them. You cannot apply every behavior to every sprite.

6. Rewind and play the movie, then when the movie stops at frame 55, click the Stage to continue playing the movie.

7. When the movie holds on frame 63, stop the movie, then save your work.

You created navigation with a behavior.

CREATE NAVIGATION WITH MARKERS

What You'll Do

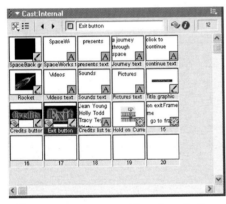

▶ *In this lesson, you will create navigation with markers.*

Adding and Naming Markers

While creating a movie, you might want to move to a specific **scene**, or location in a movie. Markers make it easy to identify and navigate to a specific scene or frame in a movie. You can use the markers channel at the top of the Score, as shown in Figure G-12, to add, name, and move markers. After you add and name a marker, you can use the marker name in behaviors or scripts to move the playback head to the specified marker frame in the Score. Marker names are more reliable to use during authoring than frame numbers. Frame numbers can change if you insert or delete frames in the Score, whereas, unless you move them, markers are static. You can use the Markers window to write comments for individual markers, rename markers, and move the playback head to a particular marker in the Score.

Creating Navigation with Markers

Sometimes it is easier to create a simple Lingo script in a movie than it is to find and use a built-in behavior in the Library palette. After you add a marker to a frame, you can use that marker name to write a Lingo script that will jump to a specific frame in a movie. A Lingo script is a set of one or more instructions, such as `go to frame "Menu"`, that tells Director how to respond to specific events in a movie. A Lingo script is composed of one or more **handlers**, which respond to messages triggered by a specific event during the movie's playback. A handler starts with the word `on` followed by the name of a trigger message for the event, such as `mouseUp`. The handler waits for the specific movie event to occur (such as the user clicking the mouse button), and then carries out the next Lingo instruction in the script, such as quit. A handler stops when it comes to the word end in the script, as shown in the Behavior Script window in Figure G-13. As you can see, the script is color-coded to make it easier to identify different script elements. If the specific movie event associated with a handler doesn't occur in the duration of a sprite or frame, Director continues to play the movie.

QUICK**TIP**

You don't have to remember all of the Lingo instructions; Director provides a list of instructions by category in a pop-up menu. You can also get help and copy Lingo examples from the Lingo Dictionary and paste them into scripts. To open the Lingo Dictionary, click Help on the menu bar, then click Lingo Dictionary.

When you create scripts in Director (in this case, navigation scripts), you attach a script to either a frame or a sprite in the Score (known as a frame behavior or sprite behavior), or a cast member in the Cast window. The frame or sprite behavior script is attached to individual frames or sprites in the Score. When you attach a script to a frame or sprite in the Score, the script is only executed when the playback head reaches the frame or displays the sprite. The cast member script is attached directly to the cast member in the Cast window, independent of the Score. When you attach a script to a cast member in the Cast window, the script is only executed when the cast member is assigned to a sprite and the playback head displays the sprite.

FIGURE G-12
Creating a new marker

FIGURE G-13
Behavior Script window with a handler

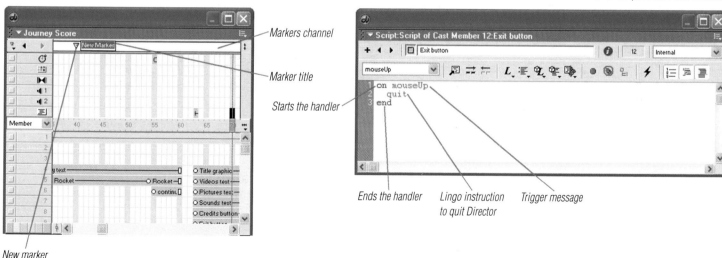

Markers channel
Marker title
Starts the handler
New marker

Ends the handler
Lingo instruction to quit Director
Trigger message

Add and name markers

1. Click the markers channel above frame 40 to create a new marker with the title highlighted.

2. Type **Menu**, then press [Enter] (Win) or [return] (Mac).

3. Position the Hand pointer over the Menu marker, then drag the marker to frame 63, as shown in Figure G-14. 🖑

   | TIP To delete a marker, drag the marker up or down out of the markers channel.

4. Click the markers channel above frame 78, type **Credits**, then press [Enter] (Win) or [return] (Mac).

5. Rewind the movie, then click the Next Marker button on the left side of the markers channel to move the playback head to the Menu marker. ▶

6. Click the Next Marker button to move the playback head to the Credits marker. ▶

7. Click the Markers Menu button, then click Markers to open the Markers window, as shown in Figure G-15. ▽

   | TIP To jump to a specific marker, click the Markers Menu button, then click a marker name in the list.

8. Click Menu in the left box, type **Main Menu**, then press [Enter] (Win) or [return] (Mac) to change the marker name.

9. Close the Markers window.

   | TIP You can also rename a marker in the markers channel. Simply click the marker name to select it, then rename it.

You added and named markers, and moved and renamed a marker.

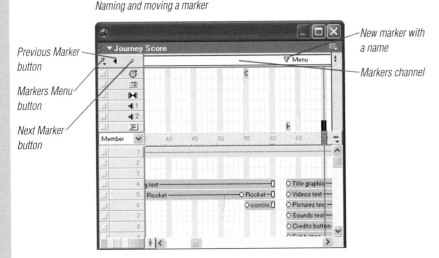

FIGURE G-14
Naming and moving a marker

Previous Marker button

Markers Menu button

Next Marker button

New marker with a name

Markers channel

FIGURE G-15
Markers window

Markers

Marker name

FIGURE G-16

Behavior Script window with Lingo instructions

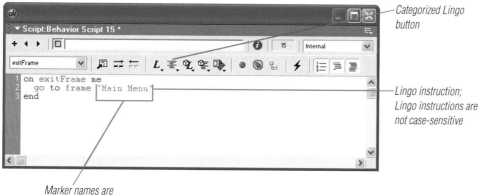

Categorized Lingo button

Lingo instruction; Lingo instructions are not case-sensitive

Marker names are case-sensitive

FIGURE G-17

Cast members with a script

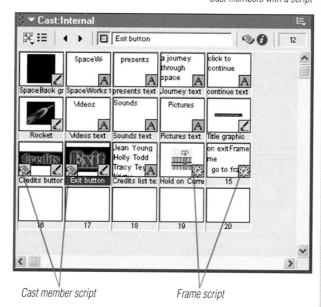

Cast member script

Frame script

Create navigation with markers

1. Scroll to frame 95 in the Score, then double-click frame 95 in the behavior channel to open the Behavior Script window.

2. Click the Categorized Lingo button on the toolbar, point to Navigation, then click go to frame. ⁝≣⌄

3. Type **"Main Menu"** to specify a marker (quotations marks are needed) in the *go to frame* Lingo instruction, as shown in Figure G-16.

4. Close the Behavior Script window to create a frame script.

5. Click the Credits button cast member in the Cast window, then click the Cast Member Script button in the Cast window.

6. Type **go to frame "Credits"**, then close the Behavior Script window.

7. Click the Exit button cast member in the Cast window, click the Cast Member Script button in the Cast window, type **quit**, then close the Behavior Script window to create a cast member script to exit Director and display the Cast window, as shown in Figure G-17.

8. Rewind and play the movie, click the Stage when the movie stops at frame 55, then click Credits on the Stage when the movie stops at the Main Menu marker, frame 63.

   At frame 95, the movie pauses using the 4-second wait time you added in Lesson 2, then returns to the marker using the script.

9. Save your work.

   Clicking Exit on the Stage closes Director.

You created navigation with markers.

ADD ROLLOVER AND TRANSITION EFFECTS

What You'll Do

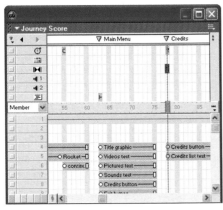

In this lesson, you will add rollover and transition effects.

Adding Rollover Effects

Rollover effects allow you to change the appearance of sprites when a pointer passes over them. Rollover effects make it possible for you to give instructional help and feedback to the user. For example, you can add a rollover effect to text that will change the pointer into a pointing hand when it passes over the text, as shown in Figure G-18. This serves as a visual cue that tells the user to click the text. The Library palette comes with two built-in behaviors to create rollover effects: Rollover Cursor Change and Rollover Member Change. The Rollover Cursor Change behavior allows you to modify a cursor when the pointer rolls over a sprite. The Rollover Member Change behavior allows you to swap a sprite's cast member when the pointer rolls over it, which is ideal for displaying a depressed or high-lighted button to provide additional user feedback.

Adding Xtra transitions to Director

If you don't find exactly the transitions you want within Director, you can add new transitions by installing them as Xtras. An Xtra is a software module developed by a third party that you can add to Director. To add Xtra transitions to Director, exit Director and follow the instructions provided by the Xtra developer. Start Director, double-click a frame in the transition channel for the transition, select the Xtra transition, then click OK. Some Xtra transitions include additional options provided by the software developer. If the Options button is available when you select the Xtra transition, you can use it to add more transition effects. To see which Xtras are installed, click Modify on the menu bar, point to Movie, then click Xtras.

Adding Transition Effects

Director provides special effects called transitions that you can use to move smoothly from one scene to another. A transition occurs between the end of the current scene and the beginning of the next scene. For example, you can use a transition to cover, wipe, or dissolve the screen from one scene to another with different patterns, or you can switch from one scene to another using a transition that resembles a checkerboard or Venetian blinds. You use the transition channel in the Score to add a transition to a frame. To create a transition between two scenes, you set the transition at the first frame of the second scene. The transition begins between the frame you select and the frame that precedes it. You can select a transition effect and set other related settings by double-clicking a frame in the transition channel to open the Frame Properties: Transition dialog box. You can select a transition effect and adjust sliders to change the duration and smoothness of the transition as the movie plays, as shown in Figure G-19. In addition, you can also select whether the transition will affect the entire Stage or just the area that changes in the switch between scenes. After you add a transition in the Score, a transition cast member appears in the Cast window. You can quickly use the same transition again by dragging the transition cast member into the transition channel.

QUICKTIP

In addition to transition effects you can set in the transition channel, Director also comes with a built-in set of sprite transitions, such as Barn Door, Pixelate, and Stretch. You can access these transitions in the Library palette under Animation, which you can attach to one or more sprites.

FIGURE G-18

Rollover effect on the Stage

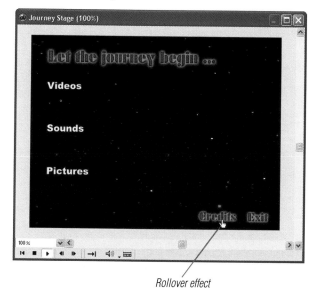

Rollover effect

FIGURE G-19

Selecting a transition effect

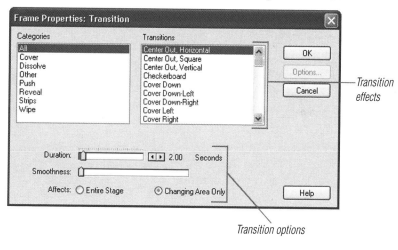

Transition effects

Transition options

Add a rollover effect

1. Click Window on the menu bar, then click Library Palette (if necessary) to display the Library tab in the Code panel.

2. Click the Library List button, point to Animation, then click Interactive.

3. Click the down arrow at the bottom of the Library palette until the Rollover Cursor Change behavior appears, as shown in Figure G-20.

4. Position the Hand pointer on the Rollover Cursor Change behavior icon in the Library palette to display a brief description.

5. Drag the Rollover Cursor Change icon in the Library palette to the Credits cast member on the Stage (a gray rectangle appears around the sprite, indicating where the behavior will be attached).

   The Parameters for "Rollover Cursor Change" dialog box opens, asking which cursor you want to use.

   > TIP To attach the same behavior to several sprites at once using the Library palette, select the sprites on the Stage or in the Score, then drag a behavior to any one of them.

   (continued)

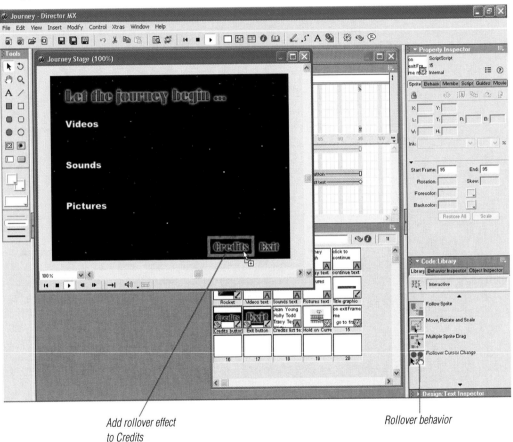

Add rollover effect
to Credits

Rollover behavior

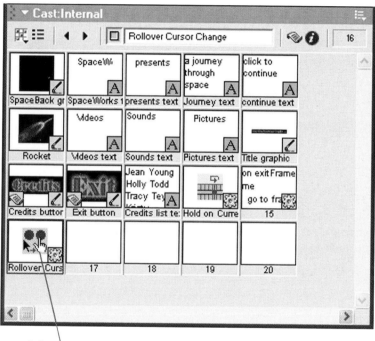

Rollover effect in
Cast window

6. Verify that the cursor for this behavior is the Finger, then click OK.

   The behavior is saved in the Cast window, as shown in Figure G-21.

7. Drag the Rollover Cursor Change cast member in the Cast window to the Exit cast member on the Stage, then click OK.

   > TIP To delete a behavior in the Cast window, select the behavior in the Cast window, then press [Delete].

8. Rewind and play the movie, then click the Stage when the movie stops at frame 55.

9. When the movie stops at frame 63, position the Finger pointer over Credits and Exit on the Stage to show the rollover effect, stop the movie, click a gray area of the Stage, then save your work.

You added a rollover effect.

Add a transition effect

1. Click frame 78 in the transition channel in the Score to select the location where you want to add a transition effect.

   TIP To play a sound while a transition occurs, place the sound in the frame immediately before the transition.

2. Click Modify on the menu bar, point to Frame, then click Transition to open the Frame Properties: Transition dialog box.

   TIP To open the Frame Properties: Transition dialog box quickly, double-click a frame in the transition channel.

3. In the Categories box, click Other.

4. In the Transitions box, click Zoom Close.

5. Drag the Duration slider or click the Duration arrow buttons until the number reaches 2.30 (or as close as possible), as shown in Figure G-22, then click OK.

   (continued)

FIGURE G-22

Frame Properties: Transition dialog box

Transitions in the selected category

Transition length

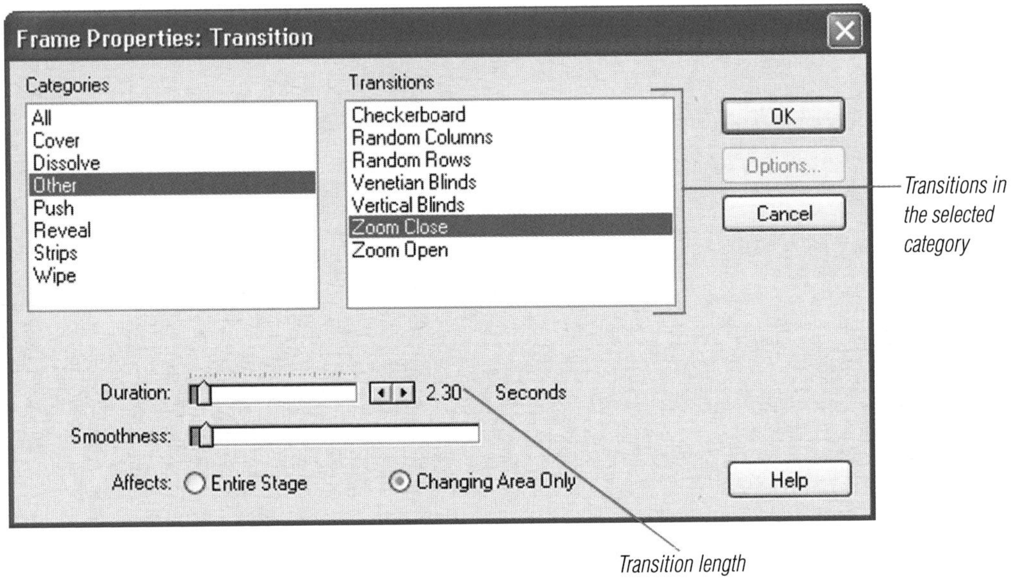

Transition applied to frame in the transition channel

Frame 78 in the
transition channel

The Zoom Close transition with a duration of 2.3 seconds is applied to frame 78, as shown in Figure G-23.

| TIP To delete a transition, select the frame with the transition effect, then press [Delete].

6. Save your work.

7. Rewind and play the movie, then click the Stage when the movie stops at frame 55.

8. When the movie stops at frame 63, click Credits on the Stage, wait for the menu to appear, then click Exit on the Stage.

You added a transition effect.

Change tempo.

1. Start Director, open the file MD G-2.dir from where your Unit G data files are stored, save it as **Nature's Gold**, then resize the Stage to display the gray area around the Stage.
2. Play the movie and show the Effects channels if necessary.
3. Change the tempo to 15 fps (or as close as possible) in frame 1.
4. Change the tempo to 25 fps (or as close as possible) in frame 46.
5. Open the Control Panel if necessary.
6. Rewind and play the movie.
7. Compare the actual tempo to the tempo settings, and write down the results.
8. Close the Control Panel.

Add a wait time.

1. Add a wait for mouse click in frame 26.
2. Add a two-second (or as close as possible) wait time in frame 45.

Create navigation with behaviors.

1. Attach the Hold on Current Frame behavior to frames 47, 66, 86, and 106.

Create navigation with markers.

1. Add and name a marker "Main menu" at frame 46.
2. Add and name a marker "Fruits" at frame 65.
3. Add and name a marker "Vegetables" at frame 85.
4. Add and name a marker "Treats" at frame 105.
5. Attach the navigation script `go to frame "Fruits"` to the text cast member Fruits text.
6. Attach the navigation script `go to frame "Vegetables"` to the text cast member Vegetables text.
7. Attach the navigation script `go to frame "Treats"` to the text cast member Treats text.
8. Attach the navigation script `quit` to the cast member Exit button.
9. Attach the navigation script `go to frame "Main menu"` to the cast member Menu button.

Add rollover and transition effects.

1. Add a rollover cursor change with the Finger cursor to the cast members Exit button, Menu button, Fruits text, Vegetables text, and Treats text.
2. Add the transition effect Dissolve, Pixels Fast with the Changing Area Only option to frame 46.
3. Add the transition effect Wipe Right to frames 65, 85, and 105.
4. Play the movie, then compare your screen to Figure G-24.
5. Save the movie, then exit Director.

FIGURE G-24

Completed Skills Review

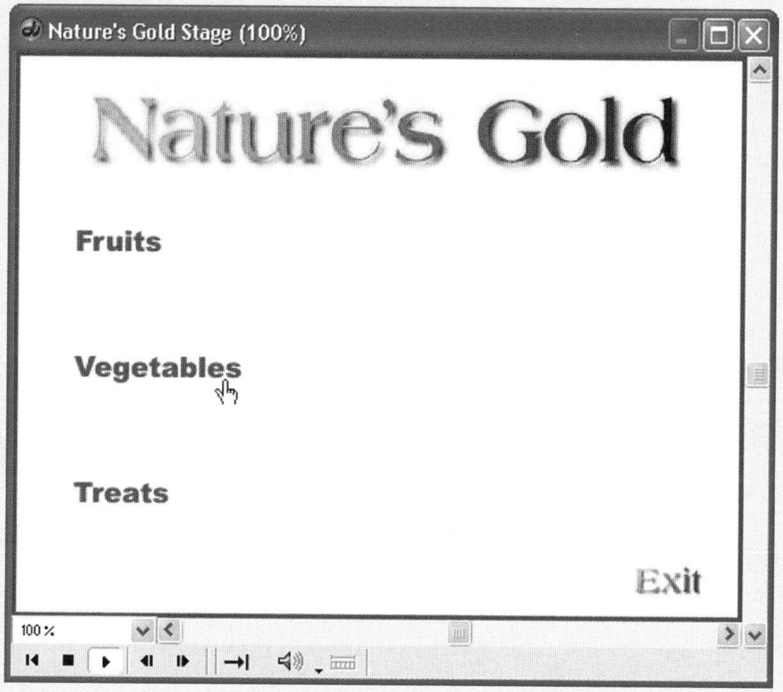

You are a multimedia Web designer at *Astronomy* magazine. In next month's issue, the feature article is about the increasing number of shooting stars. The magazine's editor asks you to create a shooting star animation for the magazine's Web site. You use Director's Paint tool to create a star and animation to move the star across a nighttime scene. You also change the tempo of the animation and compare it to the actual speed.

1. Start Director and save the movie as **Shooting Star**.
2. Open the Paint window, then create a bright orange shooting star.
3. Change the background of the Stage to black.
4. Create a text cast member with the text **Shooting Star**, and drag it to the top of the Stage.
5. Animate the star across the Stage in frames 1 to 30.
6. Set the tempo to 10 frames per second (fps) in the first frame.
7. Change the tempo to 20 fps in frame 10, then change the tempo to 30 fps in frame 20.
8. Play the entire movie to record the tempo settings.

9. Play the movie again, compare the tempo settings to the actual speed using the Control Panel, then write down your observations.
10. Compare your screen to Figure G-25.
11. Print the Stage, save the movie, then exit Director.

FIGURE G-25
Completed Project Builder 1

You work as a multimedia designer at Adventures in Reading. The company is coming out with a new line of books called *Follow the Bouncing Ball*. Your boss asks you to create a bouncing animation to promote the new series on the company's Web site. You use Director's Paint tool to create a ball, the Cast window to make copies and modify colors, and animation tools to bounce the ball with different colors and waiting times.

1. Start Director and save the movie as **Bouncing Ball**.
2. Create and name a Paint cast member of a ball with a filled color.
3. Make three copies of the ball cast member and change the fill color in each.
4. Create a text cast member with the text **Follow the Bouncing Ball**, and drag it to the top of the Stage.
5. Animate the first ball to bounce up and down on the Stage in frames 1 to 15. (*Hint*: Create a straight line angled animation from the bottom to the top and back down again.)
6. Animate the second ball to bounce up and down on the Stage in frames 15 to 30.
7. Pause the second ball in frame 15, before it bounces, for one second.
8. Animate the third ball to bounce up and down on the Stage in frames 30 to 45.
9. Animate the fourth ball to bounce down and up on the Stage in frames 45 to 60.
10. Pause the fourth ball in frame 45 (before it bounces) until a mouse click.
11. Play the movie, then compare your screen to Figure G-26.
12. Print the Stage, save the movie, then exit Director.

FIGURE G-26
Completed Project Builder 2

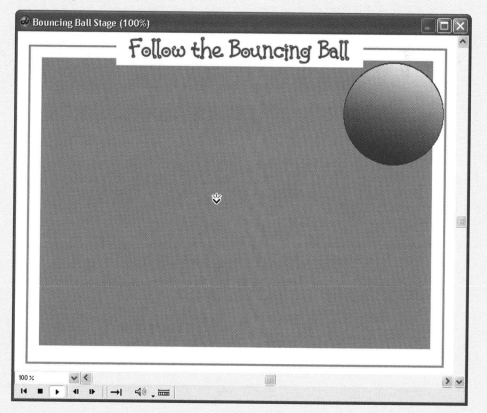

Unit G   Adding Navigation and User Interaction

You are an instructional and multimedia design student at Diablo Valley University, where you are working on your teaching credential. For one of your classes, you are working as an intern at Happiness Hill Preschool. As part of a teaching lesson, you want to create an animated smiley face for the kids. You use Director's Paint tool to create a smiley face, and a built-in behavior to animate the eyes.

1. Start Director and save the movie as **Smiley Face**.
2. Create and name a Paint cast member that has a yellow circle and a black smiling mouth.
3. Create and name a Paint cast member that has a small circle with a black dot on the right side to create an eye.
4. Drag the yellow circle on the Stage and the small circle in the yellow circle twice, to create two eyes.
5. Create a text cast member with the text **Smiley Face**, and drag it to the top of the Stage.
6. Open the Library palette and display the Interactive list of behaviors.
7. Drag the Turn Towards Mouse behavior onto the small circles (eyes of the smiley face) on the Stage, then set the behavior to always turn.
8. Create a text cast member with the text **Exit**, and drag it to the bottom-right corner of the Stage.
9. Add the Rollover effect to the Exit text on the Stage.
10. Add a navigational behavior to the Exit text on the Stage to quit when the text is clicked.
11. Play the movie and move the mouse around to move the eyes, then compare your screen to Figure G-27.

12. Print the Stage, save the movie, then exit Director.
13. Put a copy of this movie in your portfolio.

FIGURE G-27
Completed Design Project

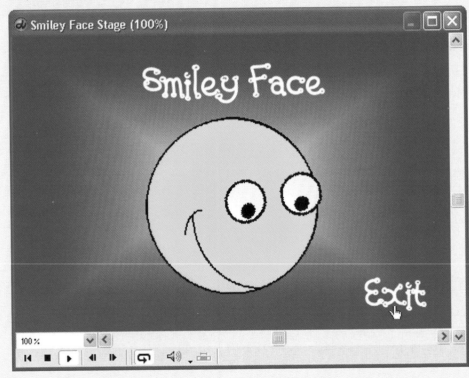

Your group can assign elements of the project to individual members, or work collectively to create the finished product.

You are a member of the graphics design team at WOW! Designs, Inc. The owner of Last Chance Nursery, a small family-operated business, asks you to add a small catalog of products to their Web site. You use Director's navigation and user interaction capabilities to create a main menu with plant categories, and behaviors to link to the different plant categories.

1. Assign each member of the group to research nursery companies on the Web for layout ideas and product descriptions, and to obtain three different food photos and three different flower photos for the project. Use images from the Web that are free for both personal and commercial use (check the copyright information for any image before downloading it).
2. Start Director and save the movie as **Last Chance**.
3. Change the background of the Stage to green.
4. Create a text cast member with the text **Last Chance Nursery**, and drag it to the top of the Stage.
5. Create and name separate text cast members with the text **Main Menu**, **Flowers**, **Food**, and **Exit**, and drag them on the Stage to create a main menu scene.

6. Set the Hold on Current Frame behavior for the main menu scene.
7. Create a separate scene for Flowers, and drag a Flowers title text cast member and flower photographs on the Stage. You can also add other descriptive text.
8. Create a separate scene for Food, and drag a Food title text cast member and food photographs on the Stage. You can also add other descriptive text.
9. Set markers for main menu, Flowers, and Food in associated areas of the Score.

10. Set the Flowers and Food text cast members on the main menu to have a rollover cursor effect, and add scripts so that the text cast members jump to their associated markers, and return to the main menu.
11. Add a quit script to the cast member Exit button.
12. Play the movie and jump to the Flowers and Food scenes, then compare your screen to Figure G-28.
13. Print the Stage, save the movie, then exit Director.

FIGURE G-28
Completed Group Project

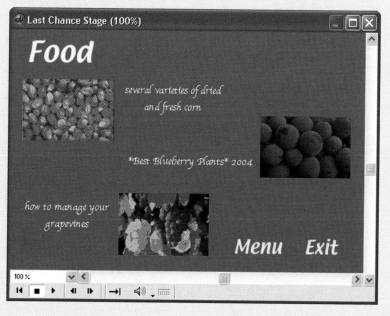

ADDING AUDIO, VIDEO, AND OTHER MEDIA

1. Import media.

2. Control audio in the Score.

3. Stream Shockwave Audio.

4. Control video in the Score.

5. Play and modify video on the Stage.

6. Synchronize media.

7. Export a movie.

Adding Media to a Movie

Director allows you to import audio, video, and other media into a movie and combine the cast members with text, animation, and other effects to create multimedia movies. Unlike other multimedia programs, you can import and play several types of media files in Director by using various options and techniques, and control and synchronize the media to make sure everything works together smoothly. When you complete a movie in Director, you can export it to video for easy distribution.

Playing Media in a Movie

You can import several types of popular video formats, such as QuickTime, RealMedia (Win), and AVI (Win), into Director as cast members. If you import and play Director movies with AVI video on the Macintosh, Director will convert the AVI video to QuickTime. Before you can play QuickTime or RealMedia videos in a Director movie, you need to install a separate player on your computer. The QuickTime player is a software product created by Apple Computer, Inc. for Macintosh and Windows computers. Director supports QuickTime version 2 or later, but recommends version 6. The QuickTime software comes in two versions: QuickTime player, a basic movie player, and QuickTime Pro, a movie creator, editor, and player. You can download the latest version of the QuickTime player for free and QuickTime Pro for a price, from the Apple Computer Web site at *www.apple.com*. The RealMedia player is a software product created by Real Networks, Inc. for Macintosh and Windows computers. The RealMedia player comes in two versions: RealPlayer 8 and RealOne Player. Director supports RealPlayer 8 or RealOne Player for Windows. You can download the latest version of the RealOne Player for free from the Real Networks Web site at *www.real.com*.

Tools You'll Use

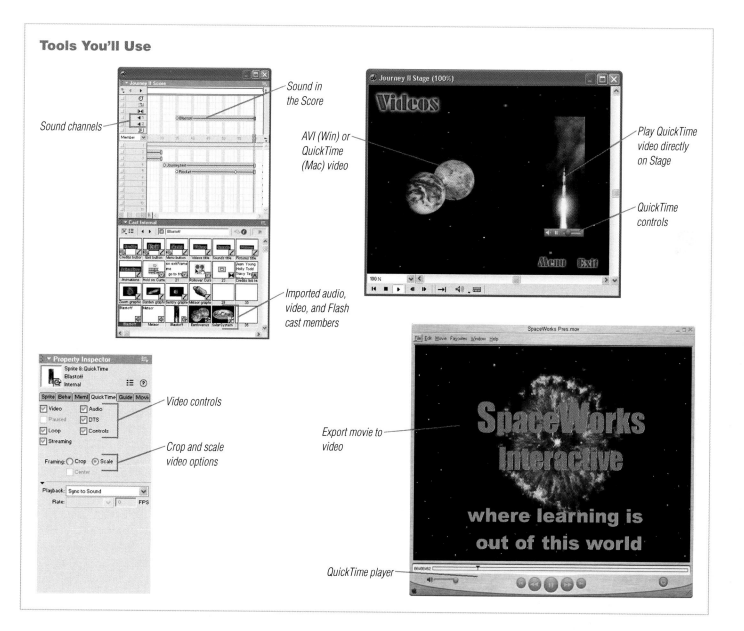

Sound channels

Sound in the Score

AVI (Win) or QuickTime (Mac) video

Play QuickTime video directly on Stage

QuickTime controls

Imported audio, video, and Flash cast members

Video controls

Crop and scale video options

Export movie to video

QuickTime player

IMPORT MEDIA

What You'll Do

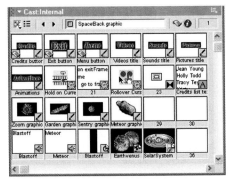

In this lesson, you will import audio, video, and Flash media into a movie.

Importing Audio and Video Media into a Movie

If you've already created digital audio or video in other programs, you can import these media elements into the active Cast window. You can import a variety of sound formats, including AIFF (Audio Interchange File Format), WAV (either compressed or uncompressed), Shockwave Audio, AU (Sun audio), and MP3. You can import a sound into Director as an internal cast member, which is ideal for short sounds such as beeps or clicks, or as an externally linked cast member, which is good for longer sounds such as a voice narration or instruction. When you play a movie, Director loads all internal sounds into RAM first. This allows Director to play the movie at any time without any delays. When the playback head reaches an externally linked sound, Director must load the sound into RAM and then start to play the sound, which can cause an initial delay. To reduce the delay, Director streams externally linked sounds. Streaming allows Director to load a small portion of the

sound file and then play the sound while it continuously loads the rest of the file.

You can import QuickTime, RealMedia, and AVI videos as cast members in Director. You can also import other video formats, such as MPEG, but you need to install an Xtra to run the video. When Director imports video, it creates and maintains a link to the external video file. If you change the video in Director or in the external video file, the corresponding external video file or video in Director becomes automatically updated. If you move the Director movie to another location on your hard disk or computer, you need to move the external sound and video files to that location as well. Otherwise, the sound and video will not play.

QUICKTIP

To record a simple sound in Director (Mac), attach a microphone to your computer, click Insert on the menu bar, click Media Element, click Sound, click Record to begin, then click Stop to end. When you finish, click Save, then name the sound to store it in the Cast window.

Importing Macromedia Flash Media

Flash movies are vector-based animations and media that you can scale, rotate, and modify without losing any degree of sharpness or quality. Flash movies are especially suited for playback over the Web, because they have a small file size, which loads and plays quickly. You can import Flash movies into Director and save them as Shockwave movies for use on the Web. For example, you can insert a Flash movie as an intro that loads and plays quickly while the rest of the Shockwave movie streams into memory from the Web.

Director can import Flash files, version 2 or later, saved in the Flash format (.swf). As you insert a Flash movie, Director allows you to set options to link the movie to an external file on your hard disk or network drive, or to a URL; preload the movie into memory before playing; control movie playback in Director, a projector, or a Shockwave movie; specify a quality rating for anti-aliasing; specify a scale mode for the size of the movie; and specify the tempo to play the Flash movie at a rate that is consistent with the Director movie. Table H-1 describes the Flash movie import options in more detail. When you insert a Flash movie, Director creates a relative link to the file, so the Flash movie must maintain the same location relative to the Director file, or the link will become invalid.

TABLE H-1: Flash Movie Import Options

option	description
Media	Linked leaves the actual media of the Flash movie stored in an external file; Preload requires Director to load the entire Flash movie into memory before playing the movie's first frame
Playback	Image displays the image of the Flash movie when it plays; Sound enables any sound in the Flash movie to play; Direct to Stage displays the movie when it appears on the Stage with the fastest, smoothest playback; Paused displays only the first frame of the movie without playing the movie; Loop makes the movie play again from frame 1 after it finishes
Quality	Auto-High turns on anti-aliasing if tempo stays at the required rate; Auto-Low turns off anti-aliasing if tempo can't stay at the required rate; High turns on anti-aliasing, which slows down performance; Low turns off anti-aliasing, which speeds up performance
Scale Mode	Show All maintains the movie's aspect ratio and fills the gaps with the background color; No Border maintains the movie's aspect ratio by cropping as necessary without a border; Exact Fit stretches the movie to fit the sprite, disregarding the aspect ratio; Auto-Size adjusts the sprite's bounding rectangle to fit the movie when rotated, skewed, or flipped; No Scale places the movie on the Stage with no scaling
Rate	Normal plays the Flash movie at the tempo stored in the Flash movie; Fixed plays the movie at a rate you specify by typing a value in the fps text box; Lock-Step plays a frame of the Flash movie for each Director frame
Scale	Scales the size of the Flash movie by the percentage you specify

Import audio and video media

1. If necessary, connect to the Internet, display the Apple Computer Web site at *www.apple.com*, then search for and install the latest QuickTime software.

2. Start Director, open the file MD H-1.dir from where your Unit H data files are stored, then save it as **Journey II**.

3. Minimize the docking channel (Win) or close the grouped panel (Mac) with the Property inspector.

4. Click the down scroll arrow in the Cast window to display cast member 31, then click cast member 31 (blank).

5. Click the Import button on the toolbar to open the Import Files into "Internal" dialog box, navigate to where your Unit H data files are stored, then double-click the Media folder.

6. Click the Files of type list arrow (Win) or Show list arrow (Mac), then click Sound, as shown in Figure H-1.

   > TIP To link an external sound file to a movie, click the Import button on the toolbar, click the Media list arrow, then click Link to External File.

7. Click the file Blastoff.wav, click Add, click the file Meteor.wav, click Add, then click Import to insert the sound files as cast members in the Cast window.

8. Click the Import button on the toolbar, verify that the Media folder is selected, click the Files of type list arrow (Win) or Show list arrow (Mac), then click All Files.

(continued)

FIGURE H-1
Import Files into "Internal" dialog box

Your sound icon might vary depending on your default sound program

Sounds in Media folder

Displays file types

Displays import methods

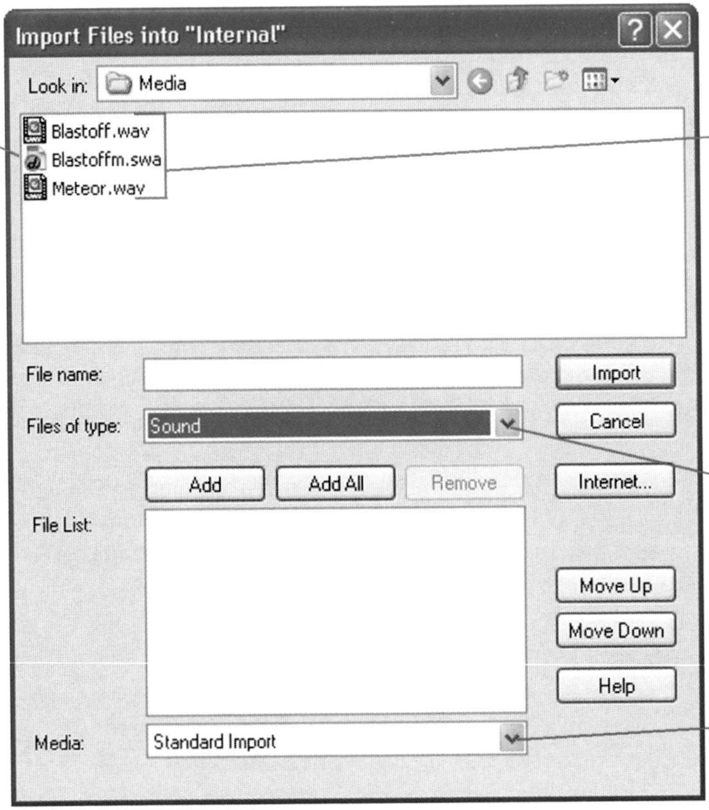

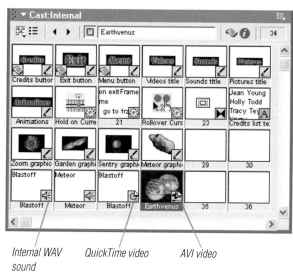

Internal WAV sound   *QuickTime video*   *AVI video*

Flash movie preview

9. Click the file Blastoff.mov, click Add, click the file Earthvenus.avi, click Add, click Import, click AVI, then click OK to insert the videos as cast members in the Cast window (Win), as shown in Figure H-2.

> TIP The Macintosh converts AVI files to QuickTime files. The Select Format dialog box doesn't appear on the Macintosh.

10. If Director asks you to install additional software, follow the instructions.

You imported audio and video media.

Import Flash media

1. Click Insert on the menu bar, point to Media Element, then click Flash Movie to open the Flash Asset Properties dialog box.

2. Click Browse to open the Open Shockwave Flash Movie dialog box (Win) or Open dialog box (Mac), then open the file SolarSystem.swf from the Media folder where your Unit H data files are stored.

3. Click Play to preview the movie in the Flash Asset Properties dialog box, as shown in Figure H-3.

4. Click Stop to discontinue the preview.

5. Select the Direct to Stage check box to display the movie when it appears on the Stage with the fastest, smoothest playback.

6. Click OK to insert the Flash movie as a cast member in the Cast window.

7. Save your work.

You imported a Flash movie.

CONTROL AUDIO IN THE SCORE

What You'll Do

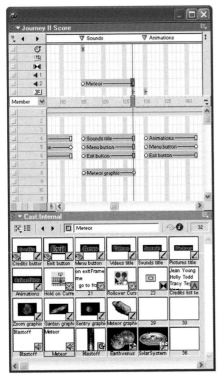

In this lesson, you will control audio in the Score.

Playing Audio

After you import a sound into the Cast window, you can quickly play the sound by selecting the sound cast member in the Cast window or placing and selecting the sound in either of the two sound channels in the Score, as shown in Figure H-4, and using the Sound tab in the Property

Understanding sound

When you record or modify a sound, you should consider four factors that affect the performance and quality of a sound file. The first factor is the sampling rate of the sound. The **sampling rate** (measured in kilohertz, or kHz) is the frequency with which recordings are taken per second. For example, a sound sampled at 22.050 kHz records the audio value 22,050 times per second. The higher the sampling rate, the higher the sound quality. Common sampling rates include 5.5125 kHz (standard telephone call), 11.025 kHz (broadcast television audio), 22.050 kHz (FM radio), 44.100 kHz (compact disc), and 48.000 kHz (digital audio tape). The second factor is the bit depth at which the sound is recorded. The **bit depth** is a measure of how much data space is available to store a given moment of sound. The sounds you import into a movie can have different bit depths. The two most common are 8 bits and 16 bits. The higher the bit depth, the higher the sound quality. The third factor is the channel type: stereo or mono encoding, which are two types of sound quality. Stereo encoding produces high-quality sound, but the file size associated with a stereo sound is twice the size of a mono sound. The final factor is the compression ratio of the sound file. **Compression** reduces the size of a file. Different compression standards and ratios can produce a wide range of sound quality. The higher the compression ratio, the smaller the file size. However, the reduction in size might result in lower quality inspector. A sound plays in Director at the rate and duration in which it was recorded; Director's tempo settings do not affect the sound's playback speed. Audio and video files are time-based media, which means that files play according to a timeline with a start time and an end time. Director, on the other hand, is a frame-based medium, which means that movies play according to a set number of frames.

Controlling Audio in the Score

When you place an audio or video cast member in the Score, you need to assign it a sufficient number of frames or change the tempo setting so that the file plays completely. Otherwise, the audio or video file will cut off abruptly when you play the movie. If a sound stops prematurely, you can set the sound to loop, or repeat. If you want to match a sound with an animation,

you need to place the sound in the Score to match the frame with the action.

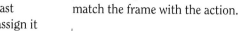

You can also play and control audio using Lingo regardless of the settings in the Score. You can use Lingo to play one or more sounds consecutively and control when sounds start and stop.

FIGURE H-4
Sound channels in the Score

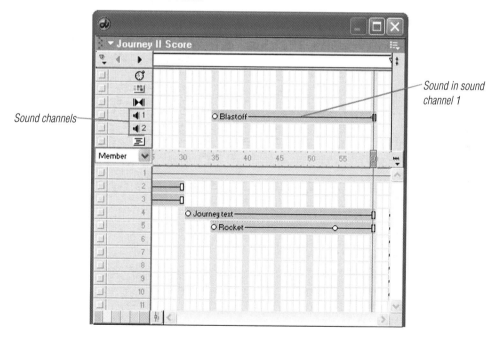

Sound channels

Sound in sound channel 1

Play audio in a movie

1. Scroll down the Cast window (if necessary), then click the Blastoff sound cast member to select it.

2. Open the docking channel (Win) or grouped panel (Mac) with the Property inspector.

3. Click the Sound tab in the Property inspector.

4. Click the Play button on the Sound tab in the Property inspector, as shown in Figure H-5, to play the audio. ▶

   TIP Although you can't set a volume for a specific sound, you can use the Volume button in the Control Panel to set the volume for the entire movie.

5. Click the Meteor sound cast member in the Cast window to select it.

6. Select the Loop check box, then click the Play button on the Sound tab of the Property inspector. ▶

   TIP You can also select a sound in a sound channel in the Score and play it using the Sound tab in the Property inspector.

7. Click the Stop button, then deselect the Loop check box. ■

8. Minimize the docking channel (Win) or close the grouped panel (Mac) with the Property inspector.

You played audio in a movie.

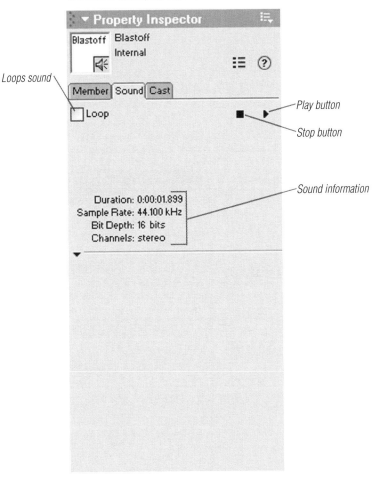

FIGURE H-5
Sound tab in the Property inspector

Loops sound

Play button

Stop button

Sound information

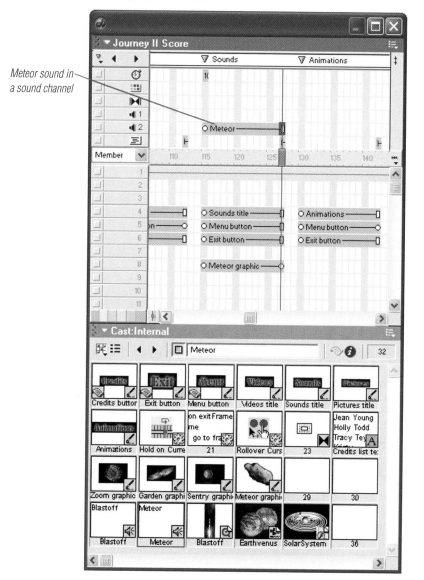

FIGURE H-6

Controlling audio in the Score

Meteor sound in a sound channel

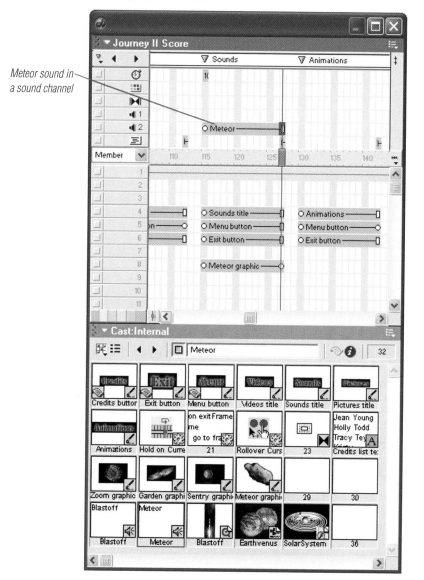

Control audio in the Score

1. Click the Hide/Show Effects Channels button in the Score to display the Effects channels if necessary, then scroll in the Score to display frame 35.

2. Drag the Blastoff sound cast member to frame 35 in sound channel 1, then drag the end of the sprite to frame 60.

3. Rewind and play the movie, then stop it after the playback head stops at frame 63.

4. Scroll in the Score to display frame 115, drag the Meteor sound cast member to frame 115 in sound channel 2, then drag the end of the sprite to frame 127, as shown in Figure H-6.

   TIP To play a sound in the Score, double-click a sound, select a sound in the Frame Properties: Sound dialog box, then click Play

5. Rewind and play the movie, click Sounds on the Stage, then stop the movie when the playback head stops at frame 127.

6. Save your work.

You controlled audio in the Score.

STREAM SHOCKWAVE AUDIO

What You'll Do

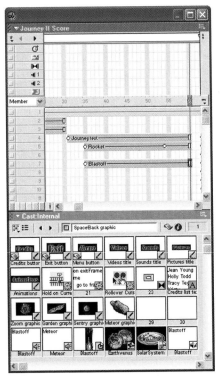

In this lesson, you will stream Shockwave Audio.

Streaming Shockwave Audio

Shockwave Audio is a technology that compresses (reduces the size of) and streams sound files to provide fast playback of high-quality audio. You can use Shockwave Audio to compress the size of sounds by a ratio as high as 176 to 1. Director compresses and streams Shockwave Audio and MP3 sound files to reduce the delay time in playing a sound from a hard disk or from the Internet, even if you have a slow modem connection. When Director

Compressing internal sounds with Shockwave Audio

You can store and compress a sound internally in Director, using Shockwave Audio. Compressing sounds decreases the size of the movie file, shortens the download time from the Internet, and reduces the preload time required to play a sound without a delay. You can use Shockwave Audio settings to compress internal sound cast members, but the compression takes place only when you package a Director movie. You can compress a movie using several commands, including Create Projector (creates a stand-alone movie) and Publish (creates a Shockwave movie) on the File menu, and Update Movies (converts a movie from Director 7 or later) on the Xtras menu. To set the Shockwave Audio compression options for all internal sound cast members, click File on the menu bar, click Publish Settings, click the Compression tab, select the Compression Enabled check box, select a bit rate setting from the kBits/second list (the bit rate refers to the number of samples per second, so lower values produce smaller and faster files with lower quality; 32 kBits/second is fine for most sounds), select the Convert Stereo to Mono check box if necessary, then click OK. You should try several different bit rates to see how the sounds change.

streams a sound, it doesn't have to load the entire sound file into RAM before it begins to play the sound. Director loads and plays the beginning of the sound as the rest of the sound continues to load. Before you can stream a Shockwave Audio cast member, you need to create a Shockwave Audio or MP3 sound file. You can use Peak LE 2 or later audio editing and processing software created by Bias, Inc. (Mac) or the Convert WAV to SWA command in Director (Win) to convert a sound to the Shockwave Audio format. In the Convert .WAV Files to .SWA Files dialog box, you set the **bit rate**, or degree of compression. The default bit rate is 16 kbps (kilobytes per second). A higher bit rate provides better quality sound, but the file size and streaming time increases dramatically. If you are creating movies for desktop use, you should use 23 to 56 kbps for the best results. If you are creating movies for the Web, you should use 16 to 24 kbps for the best results. The Accuracy setting in the Convert .WAV Files to .SWA Files dialog box, as shown in Figure H-7, can be either High or Normal. The High setting takes longer to perform, but provides higher quality than the Normal setting. The file size is the same for both, so you should use the High setting. When you insert a Shockwave Audio or MP3 file either from a local hard disk, network drive, or Web address, the sound is imported as an externally linked cast member.

FIGURE H-7
Convert .WAV Files to .SWA Files dialog box

Convert .WAV Files to .SWA Files

Files to Convert:

Blastoff.wav

Compression Settings

Bit Rate: 16

Accuracy: ○ Normal ⊙ High

☑ Convert Stereo To Mono

☑ Prompt before overwriting files

Copyright Info: © 2002 Macromedia Inc.

Folder for Converted Files: [Select New Folder...]

C:\Documents and Settings\Steve Johnson\My Documents\

[Add Files...] [Remove] [Convert] [Close]

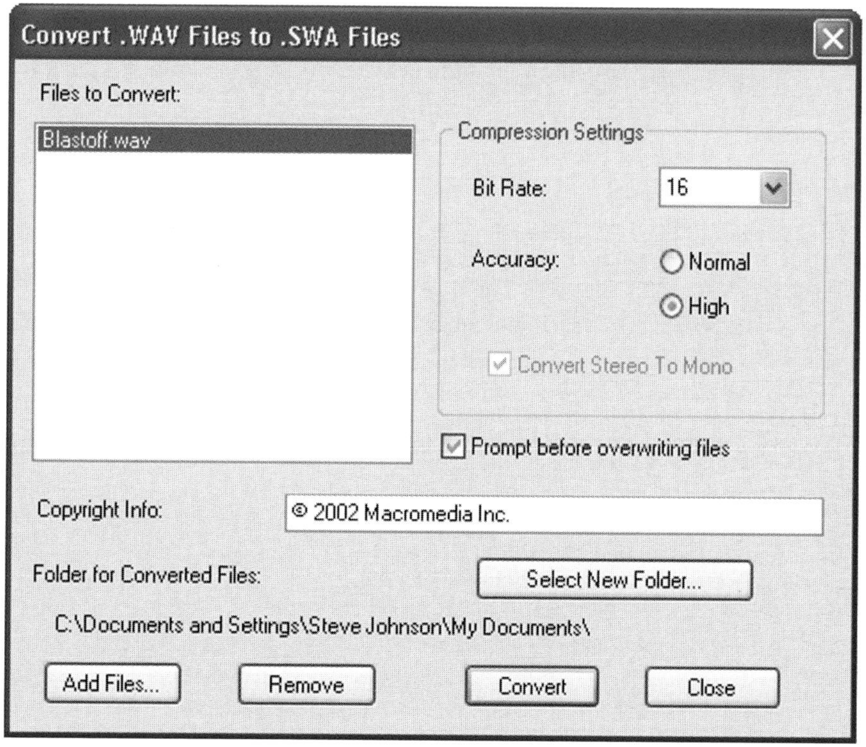

Stream Shockwave Audio

1. Click Xtras on the menu bar, click Convert WAV to SWA (Win) to open the Convert .WAV Files to .SWA Files dialog box, or skip to Step 4 (Mac).

2. Verify that the Bit Rate option is set to 16, click Add Files, navigate to where your Unit H data files are stored, double-click the Media folder, then double-click the file Blastoff.wav.

3. Click Select New Folder, navigate to where your Unit H data files are stored, click Select Folder to redisplay the Convert .WAV Files to .SWA Files dialog box, click Convert, then click Close to complete the conversion.

4. Scroll to frame 35, click the Blastoff sound in sound channel 1, then press [Delete].

5. Click Insert on the menu bar, point to Media Element, then click Shockwave Audio to open the SWA Cast Member Properties dialog box.

6. Click Browse, navigate to where your Unit H data files are stored, then double-click the Blastoff.swa file (Win), or the Blastoffm.swa file (Mac).

   TIP To adjust the initial download time of an SWA sound, click the Preload Time list arrow in the SWA Cast Member Properties dialog box, then click a preload time.

7. Drag the Volume slider to the fifth mark from the right, click Play, as shown in Figure H-8, then click OK.

(continued)

FIGURE H-8

SWA Cast Member Properties dialog box

Displays the files on your computer

Plays sound and displays sound information

Location of the SWA file; your location might differ

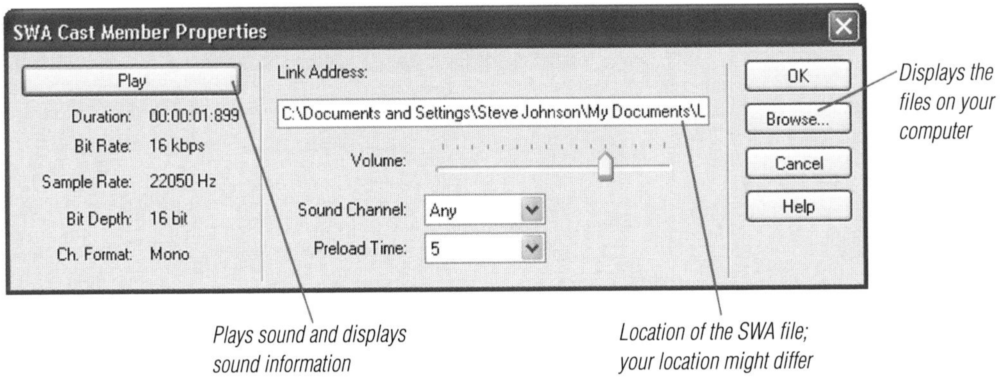

FIGURE H-9

Shockwave Audio in the Score

Shockwave Audio

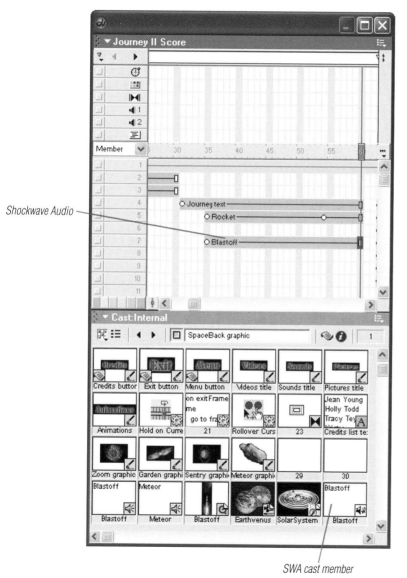

SWA cast member

8. Drag the SWA cast member with the Blastoff sound to frame 35 in channel 7, then drag the end of the sprite to frame 60, as shown in Figure H-9.

   TIP To change SWA sound settings, click the SWA cast member, click the SWA tab in the Property inspector, then modify settings.

9. Rewind and play the movie, stop the movie when the playback head stops at frame 63, then save your work.

You streamed Shockwave Audio.

CONTROL VIDEO IN THE SCORE

What You'll Do

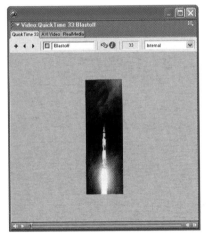

In this lesson, you will control video in the Score.

Controlling Video in the Score

After you import a digital video into the Cast window, you can place it into any frame channel in the Score, just as you would any other sprite, and preview it in the Video window, which includes different versions for QuickTime, RealMedia, and AVI movies. Digital videos begin to play when the playback head reaches the sprite containing the video sprite. A digital video, like a sound, plays for the duration of the sprite. If you do not assign enough frames to play the video completely, it will cut off abruptly when you play the movie. You can extend the video to occupy enough frames in the Score to play completely. You can also use the QuickTime or AVI tab in the Property inspector to make the video loop or pause.

Using QuickTime and AVI in Director

Director supports Apple's QuickTime 2 or later for Macintosh and Windows. If you want to play or author Director movies that use QuickTime cast members, you must have QuickTime installed on your computer. In Windows, you can play AVI movies with no additional software requirements.

Controlling an animated GIF

Many Web sites include animated GIF (Graphics Interchange Format) files that you can use in a Director movie. You can import an animated GIF in the same way you import a video. Director supports the GIF89a and GIF87 formats with a global color table. After you import an animated GIF, you can set options to change the link to the GIF file on your hard disk or a URL, play the GIF directly on the Stage at the fastest possible playback rate, or change the tempo to play the GIF at a rate consistent with the movie. To preview the GIF animation, double-click the GIF cast member in the Cast window, then click Play.

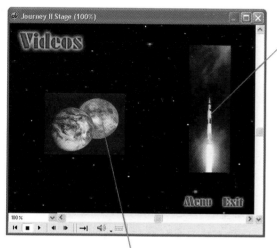

QuickTime video

AVI video

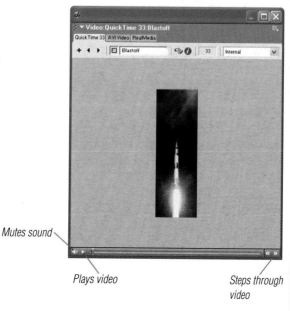

Mutes sound

Plays video

Steps through
video

Control video in the Score

1. Drag the Blastoff video cast member to frame 100 in channel 8 in the Score, drag the end of the sprite to frame 112, select the Blastoff sprite in the Score, then drag the Blastoff video above the Menu and Exit text on the Stage.

2. Drag the Earthvenus video cast member to frame 100 in channel 9 in the Score, drag the end of the sprite to frame 112, select the Earthvenus sprite in the Score, drag the Earthvenus video to the left side of the Stage, then click an empty area of the Stage to deselect the sprites, as shown in Figure H-10.

3. Double-click the Blastoff video sprite in the Score to open the Video window, as shown in Figure H-11.

4. Click the Play button in the Video window, watch the video, then close the window.

5. Click the Earthvenus video sprite in the Score, then open the docking channel (Win) or grouped panel (Mac) with the Property inspector.

6. Click the AVI tab (Win) or the QuickTime tab (Mac) in the Property inspector, select the Loop check box if necessary, then minimize the docking channel (Win) or close the grouped panel (Mac) with the Property inspector.

7. Double-click the Earthvenus video sprite in the Score to open the Video window.

8. Double-click the image in the Video window to play the video (Win) or click the Play button in the QuickTime window (Mac).

9. After the video loops, click the image in the Video window to stop it, close the Video window, then save your work.

You controlled video in the Score.

PLAY AND MODIFY VIDEO ON THE STAGE

What You'll Do

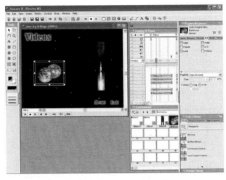

In this lesson, you will play and modify video on the Stage.

Playing Video Directly on the Stage

The performance of a video can vary when it plays in Director. The DTS (Direct to Stage) option provides the best performance for playing Flash, QuickTime, or AVI videos in a Director movie. When you select the DTS option on the Flash, QuickTime, or AVI tab in the Property inspector, as shown in Figure H-12, Director allows Flash, QuickTime, or AVI software installed on your computer to control the video playback completely. The DTS option provides optimal performance in video playback, but it also limits where you can locate the video on the Stage in relation to other sprites; for example, the video will always appear in front of all other sprites on the Stage, no matter which channel contains the video sprite. The DTS option also prohibits applying ink effects to a video. When you select the DTS option, you can also choose the

Editing a QuickTime video

Director allows you to perform simple editing tasks, such as deleting or reordering a sequence of video frames, in a QuickTime video. Before you can edit a QuickTime video, you need first to open the video in the QuickTime video window of Director. To open the video in Director, double-click the QuickTime video sprite in the Score, or the cast member in the Cast window. After you open the QuickTime video, you can select a single video frame or a range of frames, and then use the Cut command on the Edit menu to delete the selected video frames, or the Cut, Copy, and Paste commands on the Edit menu to reorder the selected video frames. To select a range of video frames, drag the slider to the frame at which you want to start, hold down [Shift], and drag the slider until you reach the last video frame you want to select. The selected range of video frames appears in a dark shade of gray.

Sync to Sound playback option to play the video in synchronization with the audio soundtrack, or the Play Every Frame (No Sound) playback option to play every frame of the video at a normal, maximum, or fixed speed without the soundtrack. For Quick-Time videos, you can also select the Controls check box to display a **controller bar**, which has DVD-type buttons to start, stop, and step through a QuickTime video on the Stage.

Cropping and Scaling a Video

When you place a video on the Stage, the shape and size of the video might not look the way you want. In Director, you can crop, or trim, any unwanted areas around the edge of the video, or resize the video to fit the Stage better. When you crop a video, the edges you trim are not removed from the video; they are just hidden, as shown in Figure H-13. You can restore the cropped

area of a video at any time. You can also use the Scale option to change the size or dimension of a video, as shown in Figure H-13. When you scale a video, you need to hold down [Shift] as you drag a sizing handle so that the video can be resized proportionally larger or smaller, which avoids a distorted display. Large-scale changes can dramatically reduce the quality of the video display.

FIGURE H-12
DTS option on the Flash tab in the Property inspector

FIGURE H-13
Cropping and scaling a video

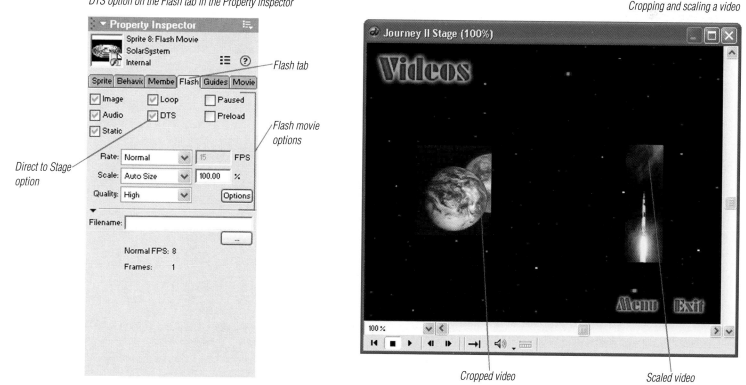

Cropped video   *Scaled video*

Play video directly on the Stage

1. Scroll to frame 130 in the Score, drag the SolarSystem cast member to frame 130 in channel 8, drag the end of the sprite to frame 142, then resize the Flash movie to fit on the Stage without covering the existing text.

2. Open the docking channel (Win) or grouped panel (Mac) with the Property inspector, click the Flash tab in the Property inspector, then select the DTS check box if necessary.

3. Rewind and play the movie, click Animations on the Stage to display the Flash movie, as shown in Figure H-14, then stop the movie.

4. Scroll to frame 100 in the Score, click the Blastoff video sprite in the Score to select it, click the QuickTime tab in the Property inspector, then select the DTS check box if necessary.

5. Select the Loop check box on the QuickTime tab of the Property inspector, rewind and play the movie, then click Videos on the Stage.

6. While the video plays, select the Controls check box on the QuickTime tab in the Property inspector to display volume and playback controls, as shown in Figure H-15, then deselect the Audio check box to disable audio playback.

   TIP If the video delivery speed is slow, the controller bar might flicker.

7. Select the Audio check box in the QuickTime tab of the Property inspector (if necessary), deselect the Controls check box, then deselect the Loop check box to restore settings.

   (continued)

Playing a Flash movie directly on the Stage

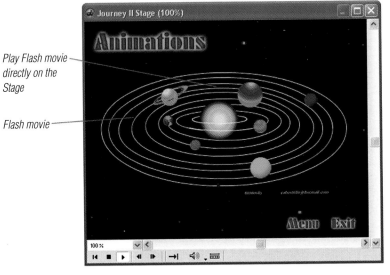

Play Flash movie directly on the Stage

Flash movie

FIGURE H-15
Playing a video directly on the Stage

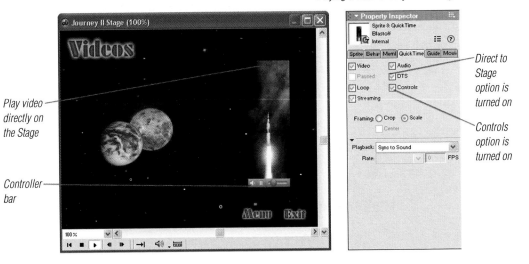

Play video directly on the Stage

Controller bar

Direct to Stage option is turned on

Controls option is turned on

FIGURE H-16
Cropping a video

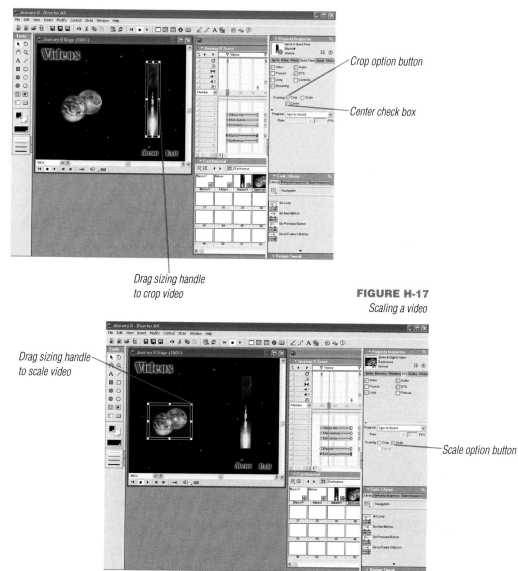

Crop option button

Center check box

*Drag sizing handle
to crop video*

FIGURE H-17
Scaling a video

*Drag sizing handle
to scale video*

Scale option button

8. When the Blastoff video ends, stop the movie, then save your work.

You played a video directly on the Stage and modified control settings.

Crop and scale a video

1. Click the Blastoff video sprite in the Score if necessary.

2. Click the Crop option button on the QuickTime tab of the Property inspector, then select the Center check box.

3. Drag the right-middle sizing handle of the Blastoff video sprite on the Stage to the left (which crops both sides) to match Figure H-16.

   TIP To undo the action you just performed, click the Undo button on the toolbar

4. Click the Earthvenus video sprite on the Stage, then click the AVI tab (Win) or QuickTime tab (Mac) in the Property inspector if necessary.

5. Click the Scale option button in the AVI tab (Win) or QuickTime tab (Mac) of the Property inspector if necessary.

6. Press and hold [Shift], then drag the sizing handle in the upper-right corner of the Earthvenus video sprite inward slightly to match Figure H-17.

7. Rewind and play the movie, click Videos on the Stage, then stop the movie when the Blastoff video ends.

8. Save your work.

You cropped and scaled a video.

SYNCHRONIZE MEDIA

What You'll Do

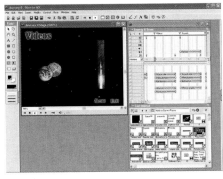

In this lesson, you will synchronize media.

Synchronizing Media

You can synchronize, or match, sounds and videos with other actions in a Director movie. For example, you can synchronize points in a sound file to make text appear in time with the narration. You can use the Wait for Cue Point option to synchronize points in a sound or video file with specific frames in a Director movie. A common use for the Wait for Cue Point option with sound and video files is to wait for the end of the sound or video before you continue to the next frame, as shown in Figure H-18. If you want Director to identify the cue points anywhere inside a sound or video

file, you need to insert the points in the actual sound or video file using a more advanced media editing program, such as QuickTime Pro or SoundEdit.

To help eliminate delays in loading video files during the playback of a Director movie, you can preload the video into RAM at the beginning of the movie, so it's ready to play at any time, instead of waiting to load and play it from your hard disk, CD-ROM, or the Web when needed. For small videos, you may not notice the difference, but for larger videos or computers with small RAM, the delays can be significant.

FIGURE H-18
Wait for Cue Point option

Wait for Cue Point option

Channel number and cast member name

Cue point

Frame Properties: Tempo

- ○ Tempo: 20 fps
- ○ Wait: 1 seconds
- ○ Wait for Mouse Click or Key Press
- ● Wait for Cue Point:

Channel: 8: Blastoff   Cue Point: {End}

OK   Cancel   Help

FIGURE H-19
AVI tab in the Property inspector (Windows)

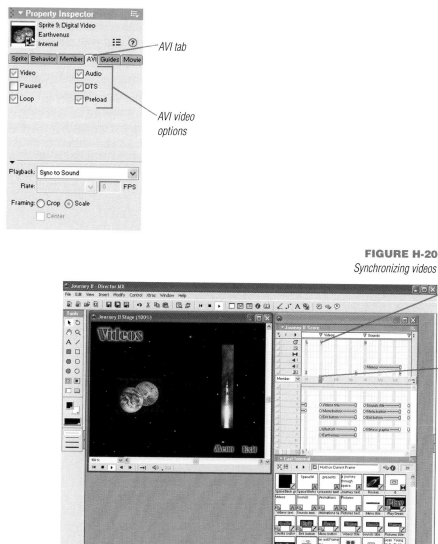

AVI tab

AVI video options

FIGURE H-20
Synchronizing videos

Wait for Cue Point option set for the end

Waits here until the end of the video

1. Click the Earthvenus video sprite in the Score, then click the AVI tab (Win) or QuickTime tab (Mac) in the Property inspector if necessary.

2. Select the Preload check box on the AVI tab (Win) or the Streaming check box on the QuickTime tab (Mac) in the Property inspector, as shown in Figure H-19, to set the option to start loading the Earthvenus video at the start of the movie.

3. Minimize the docking channel (Win) or close the grouped panel (Mac) with the Property inspector.

4. Click the Blastoff video sprite on the Stage.

5. Double-click frame 100 in the tempo channel to open the Frame Properties: Tempo dialog box.

6. Click the Wait for Cue Point option button, click the Cue Point list arrow, click {End}, then click OK.

7. Rewind and play the movie, then click Videos on the Stage to display the synchronized videos, as shown in Figure H-20.

   Notice that the playback head stops at frame 100, and then it moves to frame 112 after the Blastoff video ends.

8. Stop the movie when the Blastoff video ends.

9. Save your work.

You synchronized media.

EXPORT A MOVIE

What You'll Do

In this lesson, you will export a movie.

Exporting a Movie

You can export all or part of a movie as a digital video or a series of frame-by-frame bitmaps. You can use the movie in other applications or import it back into Director. Exporting a movie to digital video is recommended only for straightforward linear animations or presentations. When Director exports any interactivity, such as button scripts and frame scripts, the Lingo programming information is not included after the exporting process.

When Director exports animation as a digital video, it takes snapshots of the entire Stage moment by moment and turns each snapshot into a single frame in the video. Director allows you to export a movie as an AVI (Win) or QuickTime (Mac) video, or as a BMP (Win), PICT (Mac), Scrapbook (Mac), or PICS (Mac) graphic. Before you can export a movie as a QuickTime digital video, QuickTime must be installed on your computer. Some of the export formats enable you to set additional parameters specific to the format. For example, QuickTime enables you to set a frame rate to the tempo setting in Director or to real time. QuickTime also enables you to select a Compressor option, which is optimized for cross-platform use and 16-bit and 24-bit color images. The average compression ratio is about 5 to 1 (the compressed video is 5 times smaller than the original). See Table H-2 for a description of the Compressor options; different options appear in the list depending on the video hardware and software on your computer.

TABLE H-2: Compressor Options

option	description
Animation	Optimized for simple sprite motions, minimal transitions, and sound play instructions
Cinepak	A standard for high-quality video; recommended for transferring the digital video to traditional video tape; the compression ratio is 10 to 1
Component Video	Optimized for capturing raw video footage; the compression ratio is 2 to 1
Graphics	Optimized for 8-bit color; the compression ratio is 11 to 1; files take longer to decompress
None	No compression
Photo-JPEG	A standard for digitized images, such as scanned photographs; the compression ratio is between 10 to 1 and 20 to 1
Video	A standard for QuickTime video; optimized for cross-platform use and 16-bit and 24-bit color images; the compression ratio is 5 to 1
Intel Indeo Video	Optimized for the Intel Indeo video chip

Export a movie

1. Open the file SpaceWorks Pres.dir from where your Unit H data files are stored, and don't save any changes to the previous file if asked.

2. Click File on the menu bar, then click Export to open the Export dialog box.

3. Click the All Frames option button, click the Format list arrow, then click Quicktime Movie (.MOV), as shown in Figure H-21.

4. Click Options to open the QuickTime Options dialog box.

   > TIP For an export to AVI, the Options dialog box only contains an option to set the export rate in frames per second. In addition, when you export to AVI, sounds in the movie are not included.

   (continued)

(continued)

FIGURE H-21
Export dialog box

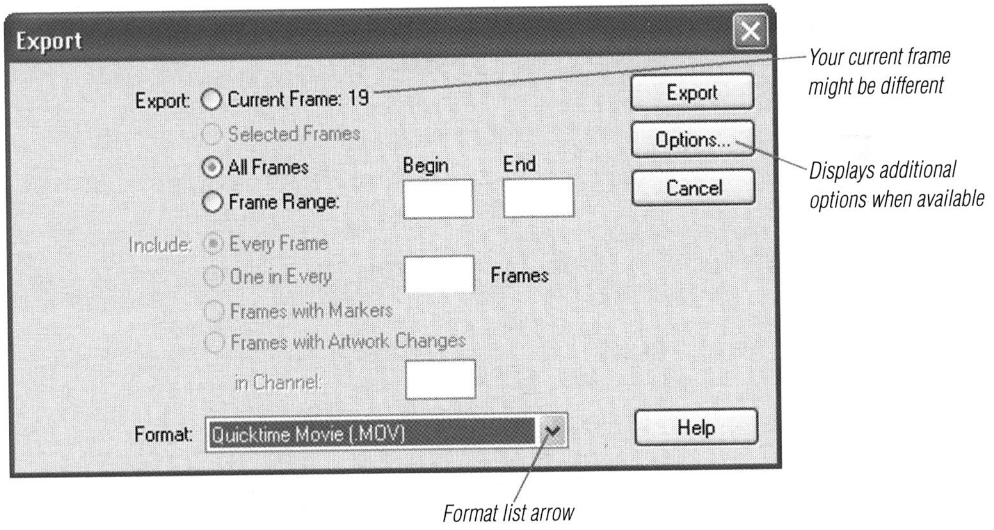

Your current frame might be different

Displays additional options when available

Format list arrow

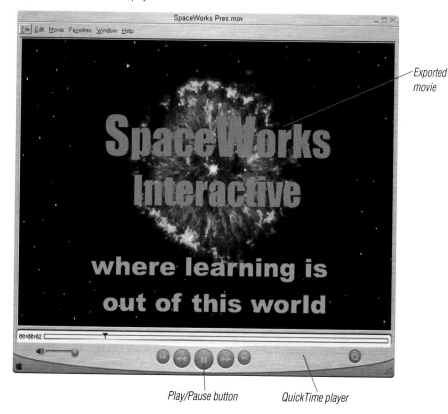

Exported movie

Play/Pause button   QuickTime player

5. Click the Tempo Settings option button (if necessary), click the Compressor list arrow, then click Video (scroll as necessary).

6. Click OK, then click Export (if a Ready to Export dialog box opens, follow the instructions), navigate to where your Unit H data files are stored, click Save, then click OK.

   While Director exports the movie, your screen might change in appearance. Wait until the Director window appears before you continue; changes in the screen might get recorded in the QuickTime movie.

7. Exit Director, and don't save any changes to the previous file if asked.

8. Using My Computer (Win) or Finder (Mac), navigate to where your Unit H data files are stored, double-click the file SpaceWorks Pres.mov to open the QuickTime player, as shown in Figure H-22, click the Play button, watch the movie, then close the QuickTime player.

You exported a movie.

Import media.

1. Start Director, open the file MD H-2.dir from where your Unit H data files are stored, then save it as **Animal Life**.
2. Select cast member 20.
3. Import all the sound files, except Eagle.wav and Lion.au, from the Media2 folder. For Windows, exclude Birdsm.swa; for the Macintosh, exclude Birds.wav.
4. Select cast member 26, then import all the video files (AVIs and MOVs) from the Media2 folder.
5. If the Select Format dialog box opens, import AVI files in the AVI format.
6. Select cast member 31, then import the Flash file Dolphin .swf from the Media2 folder.

Control audio in the Score.

1. Add the Birds sound to frames 26 through 45 in sound channel 1, then play and loop the sound using the Sound tab in the Property inspector.
2. Add the Dog sound to frames 106 through 120 in sound channel 1, and the Dog video to frames 105 through 120 in channel 8.
3. Add the Monkey sound to frames 66 through 80 in sound channel 1, and the Monkey video to frames 65 through 80 in channel 8.
4. Add the Tiger sound to frames 146 through 160 in sound channel 1, and the Tiger video to frames 145 through 160 in channel 8.

5. Add the Wolf sound to frames 126 through 140 in sound channel 1, and the Wolf video to frames 125 through 140 in channel 8.
6. Add the Zebra sound to frames 86 through 100 in sound channel 1, and the Zebra video to frames 85 through 100 in channel 8.

Stream Shockwave Audio.

1. Convert the Birds sound to SWA (Win).
2. Insert the Birds.swa (Win) or Birdsm.swa (Mac) SWA sound in the Cast window.
3. Add the Birds SWA sound to frames 46 through 60 in channel 12.
4. Play the Birds SWA sound.

Control video in the Score.

1. Loop the Wolf video.
2. Play the Wolf video.

Play and modify video on the Stage.

1. Add the Dolphin Flash movie to frames 165 through 180 in channel 8.
2. Set the Flash movie to DTS, then play the Flash movie.
3. Verify that all the videos are set to Direct to Stage.
4. Show the controller bar on the Monkey video.
5. Play the Monkey video.
6. Crop the edges of the Tiger video.
7. Scale the Zebra video slightly larger.
8. Play the Tiger video and the Zebra video.

Synchronize media.

1. Select the Preload check box for the Tiger video.
2. Set the Wait for Cue Point option at frame 46 for the end of the Birds sound (WAV) in the sound channel.
3. Save the movie.

Export a movie.

1. Open the file Animal Pres.dir from where your Unit H data files are stored, and don't save any changes to the previous file if asked.
2. Export all the frames using the QuickTime Movie format, the real time frame rate, and the Video compressor option.
3. Save the file as **Animal Pres**.
4. Exit Director, and don't save any changes to the previous file if asked.
5. Open and play the movie file Animal Pres.mov in the QuickTime player.
6. Compare your screen to Figure H-23.
7. Exit the QuickTime player.

FIGURE H-23
Completed Skills Review

You are the owner of World Travelers, Inc., an international travel tours company. You package and promote customized tours to unique destinations around the world. A client wants to book a travel tour to Israel. The client developed a promotional presentation, but you need the presentation in digital video. You use Director to export the movie to a digital video.

1. Start Director, then open the file World Travelers.dir from where your Unit H data files are stored.
2. Export the movie to video.
3. Export all the frames, using the QuickTime Movie format, the Tempo Settings option, and the Video compressor.
4. Save the file as **World Travelers**.
5. Exit Director without saving the movie.
6. Open and play the file World Travelers.mov in the QuickTime player.
7. Compare your screen to Figure H-24.
8. Exit the QuickTime player.

FIGURE H-24
Completed Project Builder 1

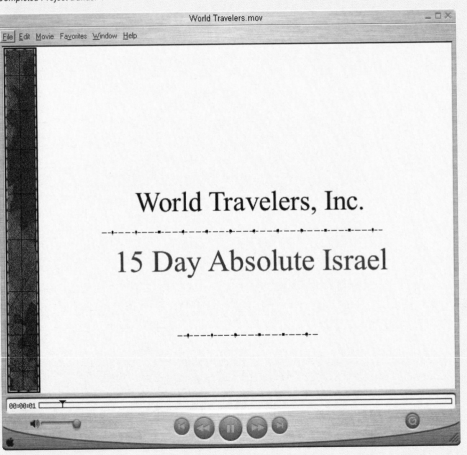

You are a sound effects engineer at True 2 Life Studios, a movie sound development company. You have developed a library of custom sound effects. Your boss asks you to create a simple sound player that customers can use to play sounds. You use Director to import a variety of sounds and create a main menu where you click the name of each sound to play it.

1. Download three or four sounds, including at least one WAV file, and an image of speakers. (*Hint*: Right-click a sound, click Save Target As, navigate to where your Unit H data files are stored, then click Save.) Use media from the Web that are free for both personal and commercial use (check the copyright information for any such media before downloading the media).

2. Start Director and save the movie as **True 2 Life**.

3. Create a text cast member with the text **True 2 Life Sound Effects**, and drag it to the top of the Stage.

4. Import the sounds and image into Director.

5. Convert a WAV sound to Shockwave Audio.

6. Add a background color to the Stage.

7. Create a main menu with the names of the sounds.

8. Add the speaker image to the main menu on the Stage.

9. Add the sounds to the Score.

10. Add markers to the frames with each sound, and create scripts to jump to each marker from the Main menu.

11. Compare your screen to Figure H-25.

12. Play each sound, save the movie, then exit Director.

FIGURE H-25
Completed Project Builder 2

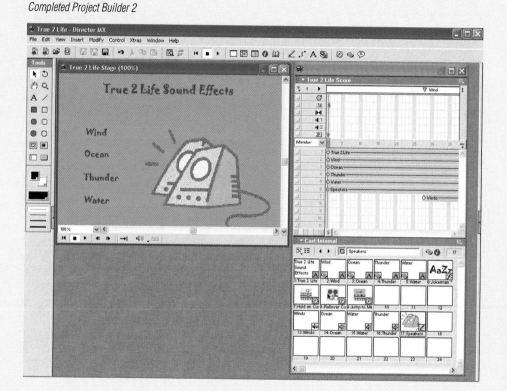

You are a media designer at Play It Again Media, a sound and video development company. A chemistry professor at a local university asks you to create a simple video player with controls to start, stop, and replay video tutorials for students to view during lab time. You use Director to import a variety of videos, create a main menu where you click the name of each video to play it, and display controls to start, stop, and replay the videos.

1. Download at least three QuickTime tutorial-related videos. Use videos from the Web that are free for both personal and commercial use (check the copyright information for any video before downloading it).
2. Start Director and save the movie as **Chem101**.
3. Create a text cast member with the text **Chemistry 101**, and drag it to the top of the Stage.
4. Import the videos into Director.
5. Add a background color to the Stage.
6. Create a main menu with the names of the videos.
7. Add the videos to the Stage.
8. Add markers to the frames with each video, and create scripts to jump to each marker from the main menu.
9. Play the videos directly to the Stage and show controls for each video.
10. Compare your screen to Figure H-26.

11. Play each video, save the movie, then exit Director.

12. Put a copy of this movie in your portfolio.

FIGURE H-26
Completed Design Project

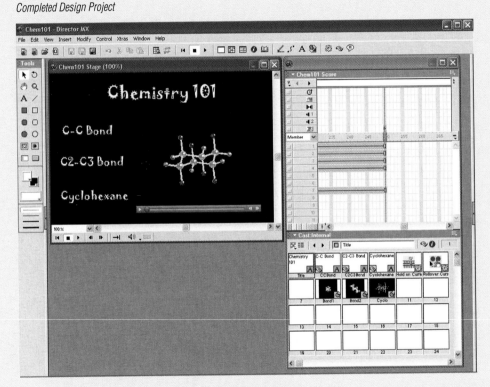

Your group can assign elements of the project to individual members, or work collectively to create the finished product.

You are a member of the graphics design team at Wild Designs, Inc. The publisher of Animal Fun, an online Web magazine for kids, asks you to create a fun story about an animal that includes sound and video. You use Director to insert an animal sound and video and control the playback of the media.

1. Assign each member of the group to view wildlife on the Web for layout ideas, and to obtain a sound and video for an animal for the project. Use media from the Web that are free for both personal and commercial use (check the copyright information for any such media before downloading the media).

2. Start Director, then save the movie as **Animal Fun**.

3. Change the background of the Stage to a color appropriate for the colors in the video.

4. Create a text cast member with the text **Animal Fun**, and drag it to the top of the Stage.

5. Create a text cast member with text for the story title and drag it to the top of the Stage.

6. Create a text cast member with text for the body of the story and drag it below the story title.

7. Drag the animal sound and video on the Stage.

8. Set the video and sound to play when you click the story title. (*Hint*: Set the Hold on Current Frame behavior for the animal sound and video.)

9. Set a rollover cursor effect for the story title.

10. Compare your screen to Figure H-27.

11. Play and save the movie, then exit Director.

FIGURE H-27
Completed Group Project

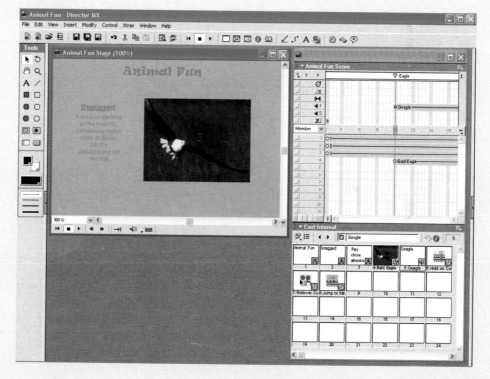

UNIT I

MANAGING COLOR

1. Work with color in Director.

2. Change movie color depth.

3. Change a color palette.

4. Import a color palette.

5. Edit favorite colors in a color palette.

6. Change color palettes during a movie.

7. Create a custom color palette.

Managing Color

Color is a resource in Director. Like any resource, color needs to be managed to achieve the best look and functionality for the movie. Managing color is a balance between achieving the best color display and minimizing the amount of memory, disk space, and the time images take to load. Director manages colors as sets of colors, or palettes. Director allows you to have multiple color palettes (one associated with the movie and others associated with cast members) in a movie and switch between them to display images and other content on the Stage in the color detail you want. You need to plan the use of each palette, because you can only use one palette at a time. You need to take into consideration all the colors on the Stage and in the cast members, and use colors that are available in the current color palette. The colors that can appear in any single frame of a movie must be in the current color palette.

Tools You'll Use

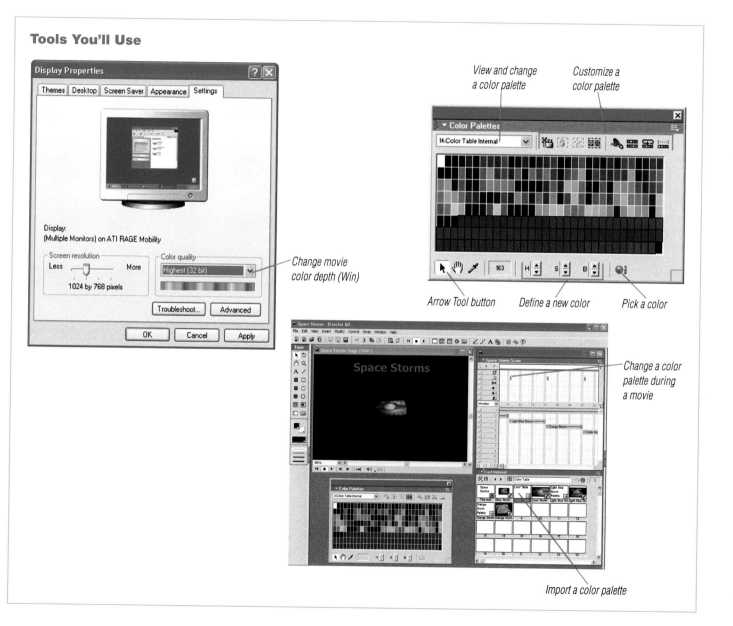

View and change a color palette

Customize a color palette

Change movie color depth (Win)

Arrow Tool button

Define a new color

Pick a color

Change a color palette during a movie

Import a color palette

277

WORK WITH COLOR IN DIRECTOR

What You'll Do

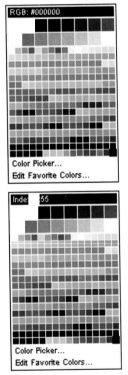

Color Picker...
Edit Favorite Colors...

Color Picker...
Edit Favorite Colors...

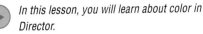

In this lesson, you will learn about color in Director.

Understanding Color Depth

Color depth, or bit depth, is the measure of the number of colors that an image can contain. The maximum number of colors is limited by the number of bits a computer can store for each dot, or pixel, on the screen. For 8-bit color depth, a computer stores 8 bits of color information for each pixel on the screen, which can yield 256 possible color combinations. The higher the number of bits a computer stores for each pixel, the greater the number of different colors that can be displayed on the screen, (16-bit yields 32,768 colors and 32-bit yields 16.7 million colors) which necessitates greater system memory.

If you are developing a movie for the Web, typically a color depth of 8 bits, or 256 colors, offers the best balance between quality color and the time it takes to download from the Web. If you are developing a movie for a computer display, such as a kiosk, a color depth of 16 or 32 bits offers higher quality color. Since downloading from the Web is unnecessary, you can take advantage of the increased number of colors available with 16 and 32 bits and reduce the need for multiple color palettes.

Understanding Color Modes

Director offers a choice of two basic **color modes**: RGB (red, green, blue) and Index, also known as palette index, as shown in Figure I-1. The RGB color mode identifies a color by a set of hexadecimal numbers, an internal computer numbering scheme that specifies the amounts of red, green, and blue needed to create the color. The RGB color mode works best with 16-bit or 32-bit color depth and offers the most accurate way of specifying colors. (For 8-bit color depth, Director uses the color in the color palette that is closest to the RGB color.) The palette index color mode identifies a color by the number (0 through 255) of its position in a color palette and works best with 8-bit (or less) color depth. If you switch color palettes within a movie, the colors of an image in one palette need to match the colors of the other palette, by position number, to ensure that the image colors are displayed correctly.

Understanding Color on Different Platforms

Color is managed differently on the Macintosh than it is in Windows. If you are creating movies for both platforms, you need to be aware of the differences. The Macintosh displays 8-bit color using a constant set of 256 colors, unless a program uses a custom palette. These colors are the Macintosh system palette. For movies created on the Macintosh, you can use Director's System—Mac color palette, a custom color palette based on the Macintosh system palette designed to work specifically for Macintosh computers.

Windows, in contrast, lets the program define all but 16 colors, which Windows reserves for its interface elements in the 256-color palette. This use of a changeable color palette is called **dynamic color management**. Most Windows programs use a 256-color system palette that includes a sampling of RGB colors and a broad range of colors designed for optimal display of graphics and text. These colors are the Windows system palette. For movies created in Windows, you can use Director's System—Win color palette, a custom color palette based on a 256-color system palette designed to work specifically on Windows computers. For cross-platform movies, you need to create a custom color palette that includes the colors reserved for the Windows system palette, in addition to the common colors used from the System—Mac, System—Win, or custom palettes. If you use any Windows interface elements, such as menus or dialog boxes, in your movie, you should modify your color palette to include the reserved colors in the Windows system palette. The colors reserved for the Windows system palette are the first 10 colors and the last 10 colors (positions 1 through 10 and 246 through 255) in the Windows system palette. Including these colors ensures that your Windows interface elements will have the correct operating system colors.

FIGURE I-1
RGB and palette index modes

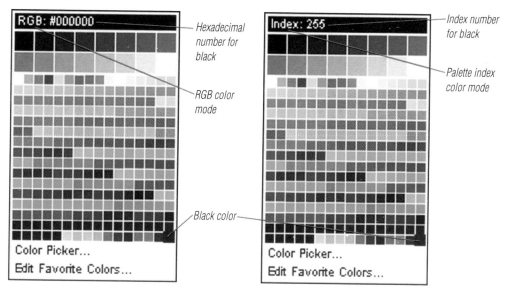

Hexadecimal number for black

RGB color mode

Black color

Index number for black

Palette index color mode

CHANGE MOVIE COLOR DEPTH

What You'll Do

In this lesson, you will change movie color depth.

Changing Movie Color Depth

When you specify the color depth for a movie, you set the maximum number of colors for all the images it contains. For example, a movie set to 8-bit color depth displays all 16-bit or 32-bit graphic cast members in 8-bit color, substituting the closest colors available out of the 256 colors. The color depth for a cast member can differ from the movie color depth. However, the movie color depth setting must be at least as high as the cast member color depth to display the cast member's full range of colors. The greater a cast member's color depth, the more memory it requires and the more time it takes to load. Changing the movie color depth during the development of the movie may produce images at nonsupported color depths, which may create incorrect color results, so it is a good idea to decide on the maximum color depth at the start of the project, and import graphics at a consistent color depth. The maximum color depth for a movie is limited to the color depth of the computer on which you create your movie. Your computer's monitor and display adapter, a hardware device that processes signals from the monitor to the computer, determine the maximum color depth of the computer, which you can change using your operating system's Control Panel (Win) or System Preferences (Mac). By default, Director uses the maximum color depth of the monitor and display adapter for the current movie.

Checking the movie color depth

After you set the movie color depth in Windows or Macintosh, you can check to make sure the color depth is set correctly in Director. To check the movie color depth in Director, click the Paint Window button on the toolbar to open the Paint window, then look at the bottom of the Tool palette in the lower-left corner of the window for the movie's current color depth.

FIGURE I-2

Changing movie color depth for Windows

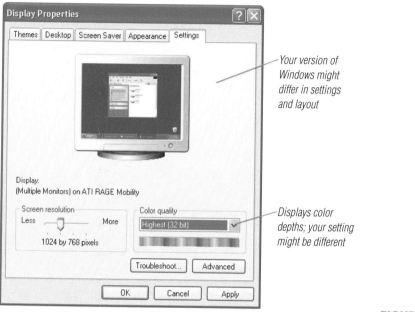

*Your version of
Windows might
differ in settings
and layout*

*Displays color
depths; your setting
might be different*

FIGURE I-3

Changing movie color depth for Macintosh

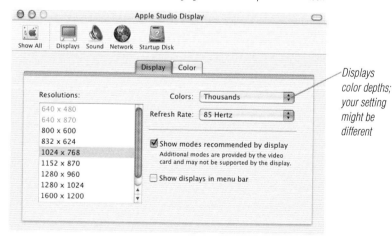

*Displays
color depths;
your setting
might be
different*

Change movie color depth for Windows

1. Click the Start button on the taskbar, point to Settings (if necessary) then click Control Panel.

2. Click Switch to Classic View (if necessary), double-click the Display icon to open the Display Properties dialog box, then click the Settings tab, as shown in Figure I-2.

3. Click the Color quality list arrow or the Colors list arrow, click the 16-bit setting, then click Yes to keep the changed setting if necessary.

4. Close the Control Panel.

You changed movie color depth for Windows.

Change movie color depth for Macintosh

1. Click Apple on the menu bar, then click System Preferences to open the System Preferences window.

2. Double-click the Displays icon to view the Display tab with color and resolution settings, as shown in Figure I-3.

   TIP To change the monitor's color depth setting to match the current movie, click Director on the menu bar, point to Preferences, click General, select the Reset Monitor to Movie's Color Depth check box, then click OK.

3. Click the Colors pop-up menu, then click Thousands, if available; otherwise click 256.

4. Close the System Preferences window.

You changed movie color depth for Macintosh.

CHANGE A COLOR PALETTE

What You'll Do

In this lesson, you will change a color palette.

Accessing Color Palettes

Director comes with two color palette displays: the Color Palettes window and a pop-up color palette. The Color Palettes window provides you with the ability to switch, organize, or create a color palette, define new colors, or change colors. You can access the Color Palettes window by double-clicking any color box. The pop-up color palette provides quick access to select colors in the color palette. You can access the pop-up color palette by clicking and holding any color box. When you open the pop-up color palette, you can view the current color mode, either palette index or RGB, at the top of the menu.

Changing a Color Palette

Although Director displays the Windows and Macintosh system palettes by default, Director comes with several color palettes from which you can choose, or you can create your own color palettes. You can set the color palette for the entire movie or individual bitmap cast members. When you set the color palette for the movie, the color palette is used in all frames until you change it to a different one in the palette channel, which is one of the Effects channels in the Score. If you want to maintain the current movie palette, yet change the color palette for a specific bitmap cast member (to correct a color problem, for example), you can select the bitmap and then choose a new color palette on the Bitmap tab in the Property inspector.

FIGURE I-4

Bitmap tab in the Property inspector

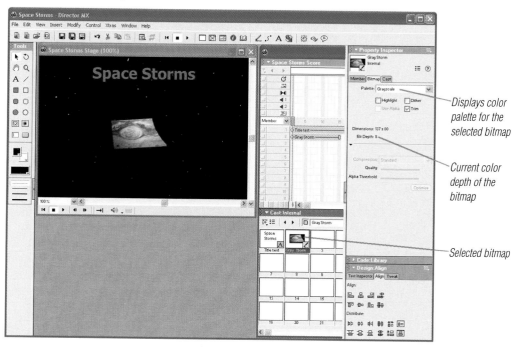

Displays color palette for the selected bitmap

Current color depth of the bitmap

Selected bitmap

Change a color palette

1. Start Director, open the file MD I-1.dir from where your Unit I data files are stored, then save it as **Space Storms**.

2. Click the Stage, display the Property inspector (if necessary), then click the Movie tab in the Property inspector.

3. Click the Palette list arrow, then click Web 216 (if necessary), to change the movie color palette to a set of Web-safe colors.

4. Click the Index option button to change the color palette from RGB to palette index.

5. Click and hold the color box to display the pop-up color palette with the palette index.

   | TIP To open the pop-up color palette in the opposite mode, hold down [Alt] (Win) or [option] (Mac), then click the color box.

6. Click the Stage to deselect the color palette.

7. Click the Gray Storm cast member in the Cast window, then click the Bitmap tab in the Property inspector if necessary.

8. Click the Palette list arrow, then click Grayscale to change the cast member color palette to grayscale, as shown in Figure I-4.

9. Minimize the docking channel (Win) or close the grouped panel (Mac) with the Property inspector, then save your work.

You changed a color palette.

Choosing a color palette for the Web

If you are developing movies for the Web, you should use the Web 216 color palette for the entire movie and all cast members. The Web 216 color palette contains the set of colors used by both Netscape and Internet Explorer on Windows and Macintosh. When you select this color palette, the browser, not the Director movie, controls the palette. The settings in the palette channel have no effect on a movie playing in a browser. To avoid color problems for bitmaps displayed on the Web, you should remap the colors in all bitmaps to the Web 216 color palette, which reassigns the original bitmap colors to positions in the Web 216 color palette that best match the original colors. To remap colors in a bitmap to the Web 216 color palette, you select the bitmap, use the Transform Bitmap command on the Modify menu, and choose the Web 216 palette and Remap Colors option.

IMPORT A COLOR PALETTE

What You'll Do

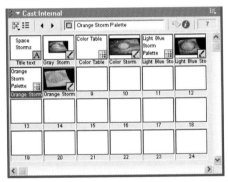

In this lesson, you will import color palettes.

Importing a Color Palette

You can import a color palette as a file from another program, or you can import a color palette along with an image. If you create custom images in a graphics program, such as Adobe Photoshop or Corel Draw, with a custom set of colors, you can export the color palette from the graphics program, and import it into Director (When you import an image, you also import the color palette that the image uses.) During the importing process, you can change the color depth of the image and remap the image to a different color palette. If you remap the color palette of an image, Director examines the cast member's original colors and then reassigns the colors to positions in the new color palette that best match the original colors. Remember that the look of the image could change slightly or dramatically depending on the color depth and colors in the color palette. The original image does not change, just the copy you imported into Director.

Remapping the Colors of a Cast Member to a Different Color Palette

After you import or create a cast member, you can remap the cast member color palette to a different palette to match the cast member colors to the rest of the movie or create a color effect. You can permanently or temporarily remap the colors of a cast member. Before you permanently remap the colors of a cast member, it is a good idea to make a copy of it, because you cannot reverse the action. To remap the colors of a cast member permanently to a different color palette, you use the Transform Bitmap command on the Modify menu, while to remap the colors of a cast member temporarily to a different color palette, you use the Bitmap tab in the Property inspector for the cast member

FIGURE I-5
Imported color palette and images

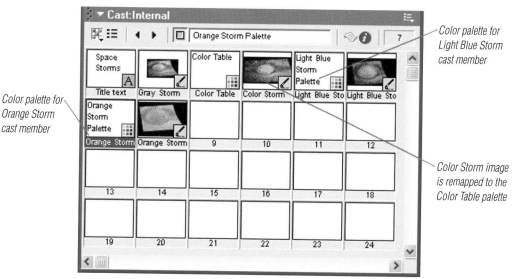

Color palette for
Orange Storm
cast member

Color palette for
Light Blue Storm
cast member

Color Storm image
is remapped to the
Color Table palette

Import a color palette

1. Click the Import button on the toolbar to open the Import Files dialog box, navigate to where your Unit I data files are stored, then double-click the Media folder.

2. Click the Files (Win) or Show (Mac) of type list arrow, then click Palette.

3. Click the file Color Table.act (Win) or Color Tablem.act (Mac), click Add, then click Import to import the Photoshop color palette file as a new cast member in the Cast window.

4. Click the Import button on the toolbar, verify that the Media folder is selected, click the Files of type (Win) or Show (Mac) list arrow, then click All Files.

5. Click the Color Storm.gif file, click Add, click the Light Blue Storm.gif file, click Add, click the Orange Storm.gif file, click Add, then click Import to open the Select Format dialog box.

6. Click Bitmap Image, select the Same Format for Remaining Files check box, then click OK to select the image format and open the Image Options dialog box for the Color Storm image.

7. In the Palette section, click the Remap to option button, click the Palette list arrow, click 3:Color Table Internal (Win) or 3:Color Tablem Internal (Mac) (if necessary), then click OK to remap the image color palette and open the Image Options dialog box for the Light Blue Storm image.

8. In the Palette section, click the Import option button, select the Same Settings for Remaining Images check box, then click OK to import the color palettes shown in Figure I-5.

9. Save your work.

You imported color palettes.

Dithering a sprite to a different color palette

If you have a cast member on the Stage that uses a color palette different from the current palette, you can dither the colors in the cast member to the current color palette without transforming it, which only affects the sprite appearance on the Stage, not the cast member itself. **Dithering** simulates a color not available in the color palette by blending pixels from two available colors. Dithering is often used when a high-quality image (16 bits) is converted to a lower-quality image (8 bits). To dither a sprite on the Stage, select the sprite, click the Bitmap tab in the Property inspector, choose a color palette, then select the dither check box. To dither a cast member permanently to a different color palette, select the cast member, click Modify on the menu bar, click Transform Bitmap, click Continue, if necessary, to change a cast member, click the Palette list arrow, click a color palette, click the Dither option button if necessary, then click Transform.

EDIT FAVORITE COLORS IN A COLOR PALETTE

What You'll Do

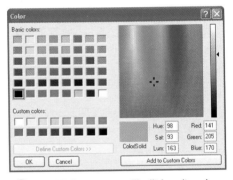

▶ *In this lesson, you will edit favorite colors in a color palette.*

Editing Favorite Colors in the Color Palette

In the pop-up color palette, 16 large color square spots appear underneath the color mode indicator. These spots are reserved to store your favorite colors. You can edit one of the default favorite colors to specify a new favorite color. The favorite colors remain the same even if you change the color palette. You can use any of the 16 color spots to store colors, such as a corporate logo color or a favorite color scheme. The 16 favorite colors only appear on the pop-up color palette; they do not appear in the Color Palettes window.

Selecting a Color

In Windows, you can use the Color dialog box, which displays basic and custom color squares and a color matrix with the full range of colors in the color spectrum, to help you select a color. You can enter RGB values or hue, saturation, and luminosity (also known as brightness) values to specify a color. **Hue** is the color created by mixing primary colors (Red, Blue, and Yellow).

Saturation is a measure of how much white is mixed in with the color. A fully saturated color is vivid; a less saturated color is washed-out pastel. **Luminosity** is a measure of how much black is mixed with the color. A very bright color contains little or no black. You can also change the hue by moving the pointer in the color matrix box horizontally, the saturation by moving the pointer vertically, and the luminosity by adjusting the slider to the right of the color matrix box. On the Macintosh, you click one of the color modes and select a color using its controls. You can select RGB values by selecting the color sliders at the top of the dialog box; by choosing RGB Sliders from the pop-up menu, then dragging Red, Green, and Blue sliders; or by entering values to select a color. You can select hue, saturation, and brightness (or luminosity) values by selecting Color Sliders, choosing HSB Sliders, then dragging sliders or entering values. The Macintosh also has other choices for selecting a color, including a box of crayons, a color wheel, and built-in color palettes.

FIGURE I-6
Edit Favorite Colors dialog box

Color identification number

Color box

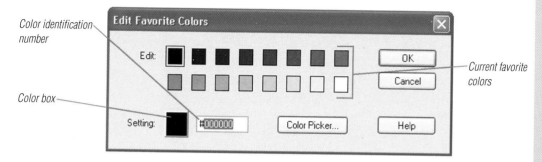

Current favorite colors

Edit favorite colors in a color palette

1. Click and hold the Foreground Color box on the Tool palette.

2. Click Edit Favorite Colors at the bottom of the pop-up color palette to open the Edit Favorite Colors dialog box, as shown in Figure I-6.

3. Click the first color square in the first row (if necessary) to display the black color with the color value of #000000, the hexidecimal number for black.

    TIP To select a color quickly from the color palette, click the Setting color box, then click a color square.

4. Click Color Picker to open the Color (Win) or Colors (Mac) dialog box, then click the Image Palettes button (Mac) at the top of the dialog box.

5. Click a color in the color matrix box, then drag the color slider to adjust it and specify the color you want in the Color|Solid (Win) or Color (Mac) box, as shown in Figure I-7.

6. Click OK to close the Color (Win) or Colors (Mac) dialog box, then click OK in the Edit Favorite Colors dialog box to store the new favorite color in the first color square on the color palette.

7. Click and hold the Foreground Color box on the Tool palette to display the color palette with the new first color, then click the Stage to close the color palette.

8. Save your work.

You edited favorite colors in a color palette.

FIGURE I-7
Color(s) dialog box

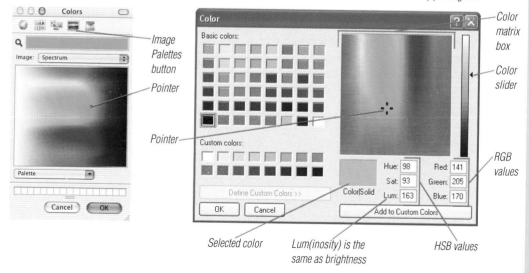

Image Palettes button

Pointer

Pointer

Color matrix box

Color slider

RGB values

HSB values

Selected color

Lum(inosity) is the same as brightness

Lesson 5   Edit Favorite Colors in a Color Palette

CHANGE COLOR PALETTES DURING A MOVIE

What You'll Do

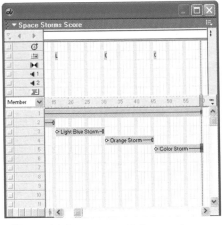

In this lesson, you will change color palettes during a movie.

Changing Color Palettes during a Movie

If you use many images in a movie, the range of colors displayed by the images may not be available in a single color palette. You can remap the colors in the images to a common color palette, which may alter the look of the images, or you can change color palettes during the movie by displaying each image with its own color palette. The color palette is initially set on the Movie tab of the Property inspector, but the palette channel in the Score determines which palette is active for a particular frame in a movie. The palette channel settings override the palette selection in the Color Palettes window. The

palette channel works similarly to the tempo channel. Director uses the current color palette set in the palette channel until a new color palette is set.

When you change from one color palette to another in the palette channel, the change can be abrupt. Sometimes the colors change before the images on the Stage change. To smooth the transition between the two color palettes, you use the Frame Properties: Palette dialog box to add a fade transition, either Fade to Black or Fade to White, between color palettes and to control the speed at which the colors change. You can set a smooth palette transition in one frame or make a gradual transition over a series of frames.

FIGURE I-8
Frame Properties: Palette dialog box

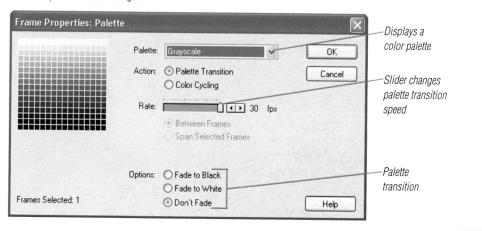

Displays a color palette

Slider changes palette transition speed

Palette transition

Change color palettes during a movie

1. Click the Hide/Show Effects Channels button in the Score (if necessary) to display the Effects channels, then click frame 1 in the palette channel in the Score. ↕

2. Click Modify on the menu bar, point to Frame, then click Palette to open the Frame Properties: Palette dialog box.

3. Click the Palette list arrow, then click Grayscale, as shown in Figure I-8.

4. Click OK to change the color palette in the palette channel in frame 1.

   The Stage colors change shades of gray based on color position or the index palette.

5. Using Figure I-9 as a guide, drag the cast members (Light Blue Storm, Orange Storm, and Color Storm) to the Score and adjust the sprite duration.

   Director places cast member color palettes in the palette channel.

6. Double-click frame 16 in the palette channel in the Score to open the Frame Properties: Palette dialog box.

7. Drag the Rate slider to 20 fps, click the Fade to Black option button to set the palette transition with a subtle fade, then click OK.

8. Double-click frame 31 in the palette channel, drag the Rate slider to 20 fps, click the Fade to Black option button, then click OK.

9. Rewind and play the movie, then save your work.

You changed color palettes during a movie.

FIGURE I-9
Score with color palettes

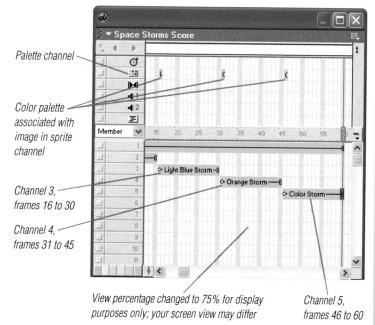

Palette channel

Color palette associated with image in sprite channel

Channel 3, frames 16 to 30

Channel 4, frames 31 to 45

View percentage changed to 75% for display purposes only; your screen view may differ

Channel 5, frames 46 to 60

CREATE A CUSTOM COLOR PALETTE

What You'll Do

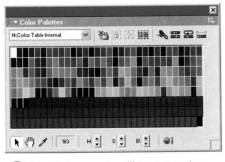

In this lesson, you will create a custom color palette.

Creating a Custom Color Palette

A custom color palette is a set of colors that you create, select, and arrange to meet the color requirements of your movie. You can create a custom color palette by editing one of Director's standard color palettes or editing an imported color palette. To create a color palette or select an imported one, you need to use the Color Palettes window. In the Color Palettes window, you can change colors, move colors from one palette to another, blend colors to create a gradient, match colors in sprites, reverse the order of colors in a palette, and sort colors in a palette. When you modify a color palette, all the cast members that use the palette change too. Remember that changing the position of colors in a movie using the index palette and 8-bit color depth or less may change the coloring of cast members that are based on that particular palette.

Matching colors in sprites and cast members

You can use the Eyedropper Tool button to find a color square that matches any color in any sprite on the Stage. To match a color in a sprite, display the sprite on the Stage, open the Color Palettes window and display the color palette, click the Eyedropper Tool button, then drag any palette color square to the color on the Stage that you want to pick up. When you release the mouse button, Director selects the color in the color palette that is closest to the one you picked up. You can also find the colors used by a cast member in a color palette. To select the colors in the color palette used by a cast member, select the cast member in the Cast window, open the Color Palettes window and display the color palette, click the Select Used Color button, then click Select. To select all colors not currently selected, click the Invert Selection button in the Color Palettes window.

FIGURE I-10

Color Palettes window with sorted colors

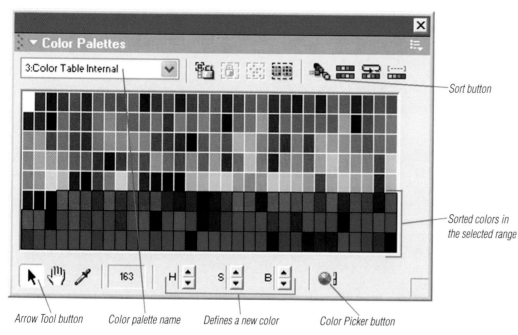

Sort button

Sorted colors in the selected range

Arrow Tool button   *Color palette name*   *Defines a new color*   *Color Picker button*

FIGURE I-11

Color Palettes window and Stage with blended and reversed colors

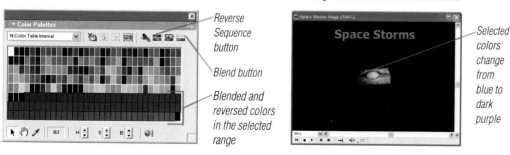

Reverse Sequence button

Blend button

Blended and reversed colors in the selected range

Selected colors change from blue to dark purple

Create a custom color palette

1. Click Window on the menu bar, then click Color Palettes to open the Color Palettes window.

2. Click the Palette list arrow, then click 3:Color Table Internal (Win) or 3:Color Tablem Internal (Mac) if necessary.

3. Click the Arrow Tool button (if necessary), click the fourth color square in the sixth row, press and hold [Shift], then click the second to last color square in the eighth row to select the colors you want to customize.

   > TIP To change a color, select the color square, click Color Picker, select a color, then click OK.

4. Click the Sort button in the Color Palettes window to open the Sort Colors dialog box with options to sort the selected range of colors by hue, saturation, or brightness.

5. Click the Hue option button (if necessary), then click Sort to sort the selected range of colors, as shown in Figure I-10.

6. Click the Blend button in the Color Palettes window to blend the palette colors from the first selected color to the last color.

7. Click the Reverse Sequence button in the Color Palettes window to reverse the color order of the selected range of colors, as shown in Figure I-11.

8. Close the Color Palettes window, then rewind and play the movie.

9. Save your work, exit Director, then change the movie color depth back to its original state in the Control Panel (Win) or System Preferences (Mac).

You created a custom color palette.

Lesson 7   Create a Custom Color Palette

Work with color in Director.

1. Define and describe color depth.
2. List and describe the two basic color modes.
3. List and describe the color differences between Macintosh and Windows.

Change movie color depth.

1. Open the Control Panel (Win) or System Preferences (Mac) on the computer.
2. Change the color setting to 16-bit (Win) or Thousands (Mac).
3. Close the Control Panel (Win) or System Preferences (Mac).

Change a color palette.

1. Start Director, open the file MD I-2.dir from where your Unit I data files are stored, then save it as **Color Meter**.
2. Change the color palette for the movie to Web 216 on the Movie tab of the Property inspector.
3. Change the color mode to Index.

Import a color palette.

1. Import the Color Meter Table.act (Win) or Color Meter Tablem.act (Mac) color palette file from the Media2 folder.

2. Import the Color Meter.gif image file from the Media2 folder, using the Bitmap Image format, and remap the image's colors to the colors in the Color Meter Table (Win) or Color Meter Tablem (Mac) color palette.
3. Make three copies of the Color Meter cast member, paste them in positions 4 through 6 in the Cast window, and change all four names to Color Meter 1, Color Meter 2, etc. (*Hint*: Use the Copy Cast Members and Paste commands on the Edit menu.)
4. Move cast member 3 (Color Meter 1) to channel 2 in frames 1 to 15; move cast member 4 (Color Meter 2) to channel 3 in frames 16 to 30; move cast member 5 (Color Meter 3) to channel 4 in frames 31 to 45; and move cast member 6 (Color Meter 4) to channel 5 in frames 46 to 60.
5. Change the color palette for Color Meter 2 to Rainbow; change the color palette for Color Meter 3 to Vivid; and change the color palette for Color Meter 4 to Web 216. (*Hint*: Use the Bitmap tab in the Property inspector to change color palettes.)

Edit favorite colors in a color palette.

1. Open the Edit Favorite Colors dialog box and select the second color position.
2. Select a new color from the Color dialog box.

Change color palettes during a movie.

1. Add the Rainbow color palette to frame 16; add the Vivid color palette to frame 31; and add the Web 216 color palette to frame 46.
2. Add the palette transition duration of 20 frames per second and the Fade to Black palette transition to each color palette (except the one in frame 1).

Create a custom color palette.

1. Open the Color Palettes window, then select the Color Meter Table (Win) or Color Meter Tablem (Mac) color palette.
2. Select the color squares in the first two rows.
3. Blend the selected colors, then reverse the selected colors.
4. Cycle the selected colors five positions. (*Hint*: Use the Cycle button five times.)
5. Close the Color Palettes window.
6. Rewind and play the movie.
7. Compare your screen to Figure I-12.
8. Save the movie and exit Director.
9. Change the movie color depth back to its original state.

FIGURE I-12

Completed Skills Review

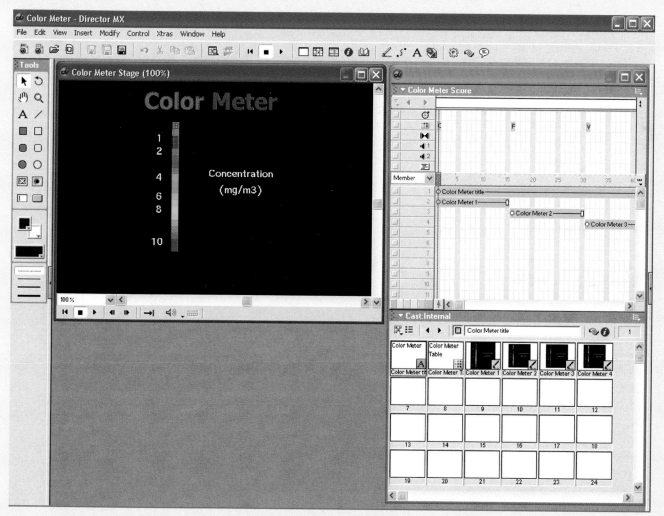

You have found a box of old black and white photographs in the attic. Your family is planning a reunion next year, and you want to create a movie with the photographs for the event. You use Director to create a slide show of the photographs, using a grayscale color palette and transitions.

1. Download three black and white photographs of families. Use images from the Web that are free for both personal and commercial use (check the copyright information for any image before downloading it).

2. Start Director and save the movie as **Family Reunion**.

3. Create a text cast member with the text **Family Reunion**, and drag it to the top of the Stage.

4. Import the black and white photographs into Director and remap the color palettes to grayscale.

5. Add the black and white cast members to the Stage to display them one at a time.

6. Add Fade to Black transitions between each photograph.

7. Compare your screen to Figure I-13.

8. Play and save the movie, then exit Director.

FIGURE I-13
Completed Project Builder 1

You are a kindergarten teacher who is teaching both the letter L and animals this week to your students. You want to create a simple movie that your kids can play on the computer in your classroom during "computer time." You use Director to create a slide show of pictures of animals that begin with the letter L (for example, lion), using the color palettes associated with the pictures.

1. Download three or four pictures of animals that begin with the letter L. Use images from the Web that are free for both personal and commercial use (check the copyright information for any image before downloading it).

2. Start Director and save the movie as **L is for**.

3. Create a text cast member with the text **"L" is for...**, and drag it to the top of the Stage.

4. Import the pictures and their associated color palettes into Director.

5. Add the animal cast members to the Stage to display them one at a time.

6. Add Fade to White transitions between each picture.

7. Compare your screen to Figure I-14.

8. Play and save the movie, then exit Director.

FIGURE I-14
Completed Project Builder 2

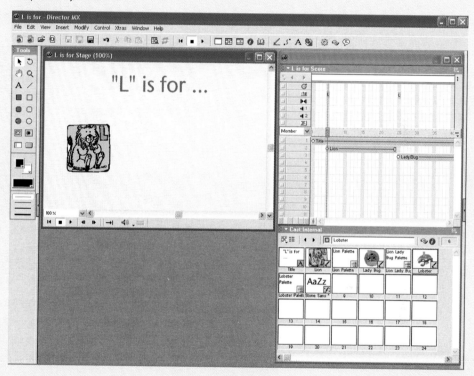

DESIGN PROJECT

You are a media designer at Sojourn Design, Inc., an independent multimedia Web design company. An art dealer at SoHo Art Studios in New York City is holding an open house and asks you to create a presentation of a new talented contemporary artist to promote the event. You use Director to create a slide show of paintings, using the color palettes associated with the paintings.

1. Download two or three photographs of art. Use images from the Web that are free for both personal and commercial use (check the copyright information for any image before downloading it).

2. Start Director, then save the movie as **SoHo Art Studios**.

3. Create a text cast member with the text **SoHo Art Studios**, and animate it so that it ends up near the top of the Stage.

4. Create a text cast member with your name, and animate it so that it ends up near the bottom of the Stage.

5. Import the art photographs and their associated color palettes into Director.

6. Add the art cast members to the Stage to display them one at a time.

7. Customize the color palettes with new colors, blends, cycles, reverses, and sorts to enhance the photographs or add special effects.

8. Compare your screen to Figure I-15.

9. Play and save the movie, then exit Director.

10. Put a copy of this movie in your portfolio.

FIGURE I-15
Completed Design Project

Your group can assign elements of the project to individual members, or work collectively to create the finished product.

You are a member of the graphics design team at You-nique Designs, Inc. The owner of Woodwork Toys, a custom toy company, has been building custom wooden toys for over 25 years and wants you to showcase his work in a Web catalog. You use Director to create a slide show of toys, using the color palettes associated with the toy images. You also create custom color palettes for the movie.

1. Assign each member of the group to research wooden toy companies on the Web for layout ideas and obtain photographs of wooden toys for the project. Use images from the Web that are free for both personal and commercial use (check the copyright information for any image before downloading it).
2. Start Director, then save the movie as **Woodwork Toys**.
3. Create a text cast member with the text **Woodwork Toys**, and drag it to the top of the Stage.
4. Import the wooden toy photographs and their associated color palettes into Director.
5. Add the wooden toy cast members to the Stage to display them one at a time.

6. Customize the color palettes with new colors, blends, cycles, reverses, and sorts to enhance the photographs or add special effects.

7. Compare your screen to Figure I-16.
8. Play and save the movie, then exit Director.

FIGURE I-16
Completed Group Project

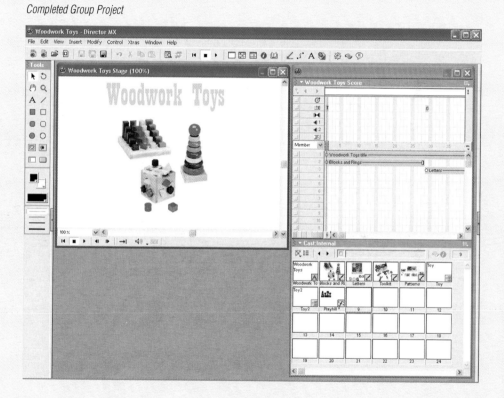

UNIT J
ATTACHING BEHAVIORS

1. Attach built-in behaviors.

2. Create a behavior.

3. Add and modify a behavior.

4. Open a movie with a behavior.

5. Create a dropdown list with a behavior.

6. Add keyboard navigation with a behavior.

7. Change text to speech with a behavior.

UNIT J
ATTACHING BEHAVIORS

Understanding Behaviors

A behavior is a prewritten Lingo script that makes it easy to add interactivity to a movie. You can use built-in behaviors that come with Director, or create your own to add interactive functionality to movies without having to write or understand Lingo. Director provides a Library palette with over 100 built-in behaviors. The built-in behaviors are grouped by category, such as 3D, Accessibility, Animation, Controls, Internet, Media, Navigation, Paintbox, and Text.

The behaviors in the 3D library (Triggers and Actions categories) perform actions on 3D objects based on triggers. The Accessibility library makes movies accessible for the hearing- and visually-impaired using added keyboard navigation, text-to-speech, and captioning. The behaviors in the Animation library (Automatic, Interactive, and Sprite Transitions categories) make sprites move with or without user input in ways that would be difficult or impossible to achieve using conventional Score-based animation. The behaviors in the Controls library allow you to create and control user interface elements, such as push, toggle, and radio buttons, pop-up lists, and tooltips. The behaviors in the Internet library (Forms and Streaming categories) control activities on the Web. The behaviors in the Media library control playback for Flash, QuickTime, RealMedia, and Sound media. The behaviors in the Navigation library allow you to control the movement and location of the playback head. The behaviors in the Paintbox library allow you to create and modify bitmap images, using Director's built-in drawing tools. You can draw shapes, change colors, erase contents, and undo actions. The behaviors in the Text library allow you to format numbers, force uppercase or lowercase characters, and create hypertext. You can also create a calendar, countdown timer, custom scroll bar, or tickertape text.

Tools You'll Use

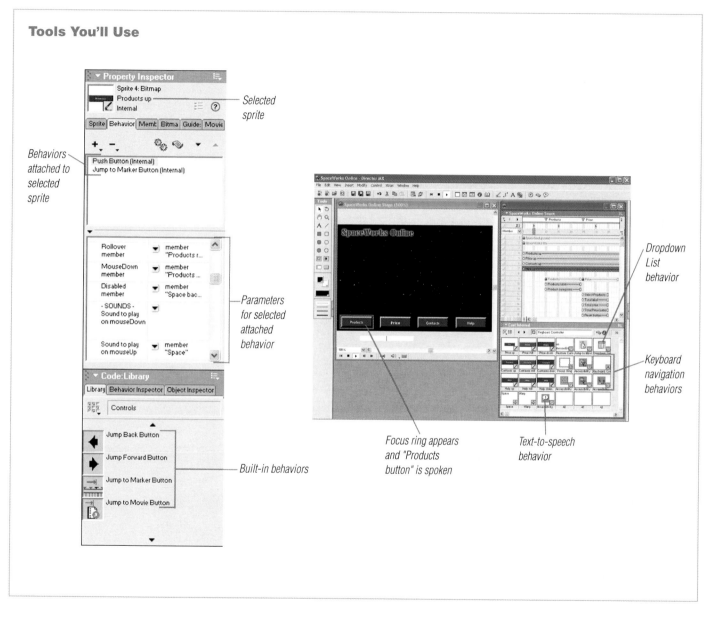

Selected sprite

Behaviors attached to selected sprite

Parameters for selected attached behavior

Built-in behaviors

Focus ring appears and "Products button" is spoken

Text-to-speech behavior

Dropdown List behavior

Keyboard navigation behaviors

ATTACH BUILT-IN BEHAVIORS

What You'll Do

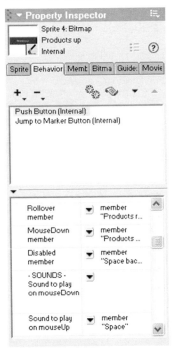

In this lesson, you will attach a built-in behavior and change behavior parameters.

Attaching Built-In Behaviors

With the Library palette of built-in behaviors, shown in Figure J-1, you can quickly and easily drag behaviors onto frames and sprites in the Score and on the Stage. You can attach the same built-in behavior to multiple sprites and frames. If you want a behavior, such as Push Button, to affect a cast member, you attach the behavior to the associated sprite. If you want a behavior, such as Hold on Current Frame, to affect the entire movie, you attach the behavior to a frame. Director copies the behavior from the Library palette to the cast member in the Cast window. If you can't tell what a built-in behavior does based on the name, you can point to a built-in behavior on the Library palette to display a tooltip description quickly. You cannot modify the original behaviors stored in the Library palette.

Changing the order of behaviors

When you attach more than one behavior to a sprite, the behaviors are carried out in the order in which they appear from top to bottom. In some cases the order makes a significant difference, and in other cases it doesn't matter You can use the Shuffle buttons in the Behavior Inspector or on the Behavior tab in the Property inspector to modify the order of behaviors so that actions occur in the proper order To change the order of the behaviors attached to a sprite, click the sprite in the Score or on the Stage, click the Behavior tab in the Property inspector or open the Behavior Inspector select a behavior from the list, then click the Shuffle Up button or Shuffle Down button to move the behavior up or down in the list.

When you attach a behavior to a sprite or frame, a Parameters dialog box might open, asking you for specific settings. For example, when you drag the behavior icon, such as the Push Button icon, onto a button sprite on the Stage, a gray rectangle appears around the object, indicating where the behavior will be attached. The Parameters for "Push Button" dialog box will open, displaying default parameter settings in three areas: Graphics, Sounds, and Interaction. If the cast members associated with the sprite button for the Push Button behavior are placed consecutively in the Cast window, the cast members appear as the default values for the Standard member for sprite, Rollover member, and MouseDown member options in the dialog box. See Table J-1 for a description of the parameter settings for the Push Button behavior.

You can attach multiple behaviors to an individual sprite, but only one to a frame.

After you attach one or more behaviors to a sprite or frame, you may need to change the parameters of a behavior, change the order of the behaviors, or remove one or more attached behaviors. You can use the Behavior Inspector or the Behavior tab in the Property inspector to view, add, modify, and remove behaviors attached to a sprite or frame. On the Behavior tab, you can quickly change parameter settings for a selected behavior.

FIGURE J-1
Library palette in the Code panel

Behaviors

TABLE J-1: Parameters for "Push Button" Dialog Box

parameter	description
Standard member for sprite	Displays the cast member when the mouse is elsewhere (not on the standard cast member)
Rollover member	Displays the cast member when the mouse is positioned on the standard cast member
MouseDown member	Displays the cast member when the mouse button is clicked on the standard cast member
Disabled member	Indicates the cast member when the standard cast member cannot be clicked
Sound to play on mouseDown	Plays a brief sound when the mouse button is clicked on the standard cast member
Sound to play on mouseUp	Plays a brief sound when the mouse button is released from the standard cast member
Button is initially	Sets the initial state of the push button
Sprites which cover the button	Indicates mouse functionality for sprites that cover the push button
Action on mouseUp	Triggers actions to other sprites
Text box with no label	Sends out a custom message on mouse up to a Lingo script

Attach a built-in behavior

1. Start Director, open the file MD J-1.dir from where your Unit J data files are stored, then save it as **SpaceWorks Online**.

2. Play the movie, click the Price button on the Stage (which is unaffected by clicking it), then stop the movie.

3. Click Window on the menu bar, click Library Palette to display the Library tab in the Code panel, click the Library List button, then click Controls. 🖳

4. Scroll down the Library palette until the Push Button behavior appears (if necessary), then position the Hand pointer on the Push Button icon to display a description of the behavior. 🖑

5. Drag the Push Button icon in the Library palette to the Products up sprite (the Products button) on the Stage to open the Parameters for "Push Button" dialog box, as shown in Figure J-2.

6. Click OK to accept the default parameter settings and to place the Push Button cast member in the Cast window.

7. Minimize the docking channel (Win) or close the grouped panel (Mac) with the Property inspector.

(continued)

FIGURE J-2
Parameters for "Push Button" dialog box

Parameters for the Push Button behavior

Cast members 13, 14, and 15; all in consecutive order

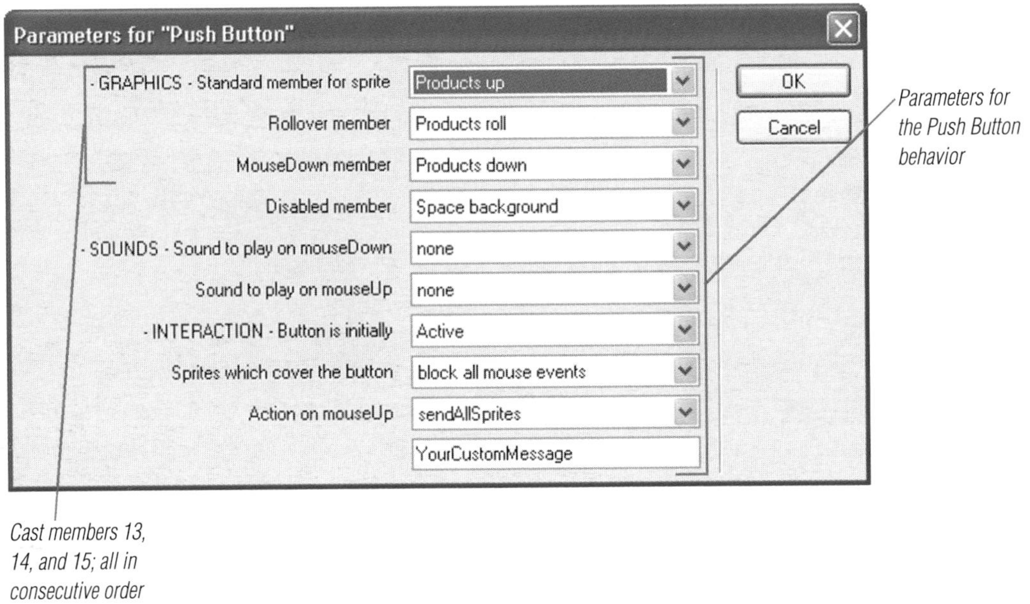

Push Button
behavior in the
Cast window

Push Button
graphics; cast
members 13,
14, and 15

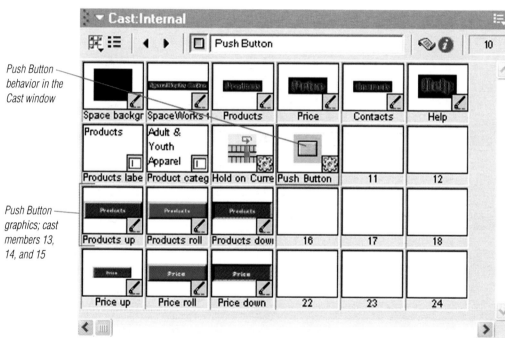

8. Drag the Push Button cast member in the Cast window, as shown in Figure J-3, to the Price up sprite, Contacts up sprite, and Help up sprite (the Price, Contacts, and Help buttons) on the Stage and accept the default settings for each button.

9. Rewind and play the movie, click the Price button on the Stage, click the Contacts button on the Stage, then stop the movie.

Notice that the buttons appear pushed in when you click them.

You attached a built-in behavior.

View and change behavior parameters

1. Click Window on the menu bar, click Library Palette, scroll up or down the Library palette (if necessary), then drag the Jump to Marker Button icon in the Controls library to the Products up sprite (the Products button) on the Stage to open the Parameters for "Jump to Marker Button" dialog box, as shown in Figure J-4.

2. Click the On mouseUp, jump to marker list arrow, click Products, then click OK to accept the settings.

3. Drag the Jump to Marker Button cast member in the Cast window to the Price up, Contacts up, and Help up sprites (the Price, Contacts, and Help buttons) on the Stage and use the On mouseUp, jump to marker list arrow to select the jump to marker that corresponds to the button name.

4. Click the Products up sprite (the Products button) on the Stage, then click the Behavior tab in the Property inspector.

5. Double-click the Push Button (Internal) behavior on the Behavior tab in the Property inspector to open the Parameters for "Push Button" dialog box.

> TIP To delete a behavior, click the behavior on the Behavior tab, click the Clear Behavior button, then click Remove Behavior or Remove All Behaviors.

(continued)

FIGURE J-4
Parameters for "Jump to Marker Button" dialog box

Displays target marker

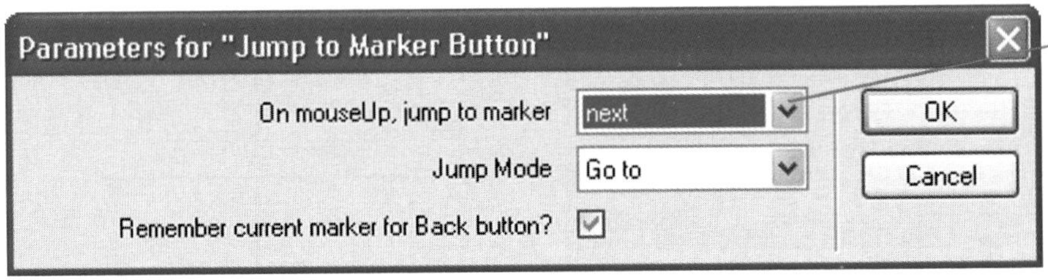

Behavior tab with a selected behavior and parameter settings

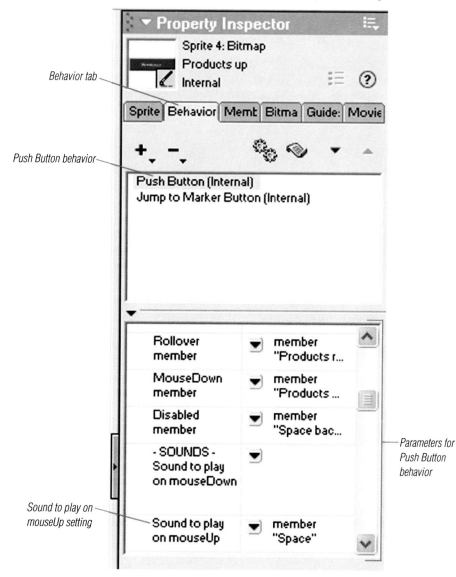

Behavior tab

Push Button behavior

Parameters for Push Button behavior

Sound to play on mouseUp setting

6. Click the Sound to play on mouseUp list arrow, click Space, click OK to accept the new settings, then scroll down the parameter list on the Behavior tab to display the new setting, as shown in Figure J-5.

7. Using Steps 5 and 6 as a guide, change the Sound to play on mouseUp parameter to Space for the Price up, Contacts up, and Help up sprites (the Price, Contacts, and Help buttons) on the Stage.

8. Rewind and play the movie, click the Products button on the Stage, click the Contacts button on the Stage, then stop the movie.

9. Save your work.

You viewed and changed behavior parameters.

CREATE A BEHAVIOR

What You'll Do

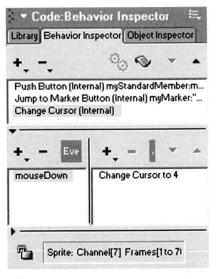

In this lesson, you will create a behavior.

Creating a Behavior

When a built-in behavior doesn't perform the type of action you want, you can create your own behavior. For basic operations, you can use the Behavior Inspector to create simple behaviors. To create complex behaviors, you need to understand and write Lingo scripts. A behavior performs two main functions. The first function is to detect a specified event, such as a mouse click and release (called a MouseDown and MouseUp) or the playback head exits the current frame (called an Exit Frame), associated with a sprite or frame; the second function is to perform one or more actions, such as the playback head jumping to a frame (called a Go to Frame) or the playback head staying at the current frame (called a Wait on Current Frame), in response. The Behavior Inspector lists the most common events and actions used in behaviors. For many of the built-in behaviors, the Behavior Inspector also includes a description and a set of instructions provided by the behavior's author for a behavior already attached to a sprite or frame. The behavior information appears in a scrolling description pane at the bottom of the Behavior Inspector.

Creating a sound behavior

You can add sound behaviors to a movie to give users feedback about an operation, such as the clicking of a button, or provide an interesting effect. You can play a simple beep, or a sound from a cast member or external file, in response to a specific event. To create a sound behavior, open the Behavior Inspector, click the Behavior Popup button, click New Behavior, type a name, click OK, click the Event Popup button, select an event, click the Action Popup button, point to Sound, then click Play Cast Member, Play External File, Beep, or Set Volume. Drag the sound behavior from the Cast window to a sprite in the Score or on the Stage, then play the movie to test the sound.

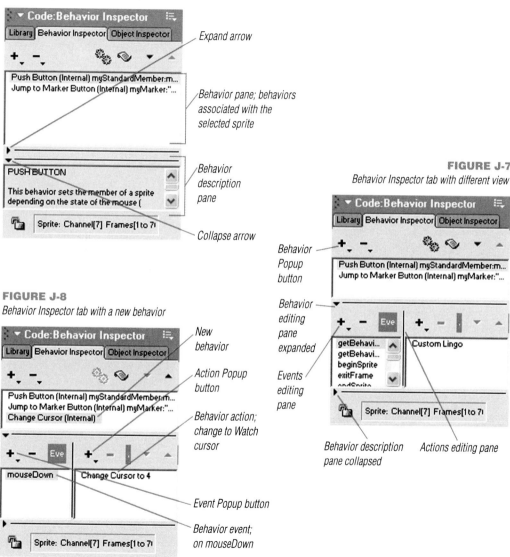

FIGURE J-6
Behavior Inspector tab in the Code panel

Expand arrow

Behavior pane; behaviors associated with the selected sprite

Behavior description pane

Collapse arrow

FIGURE J-7
Behavior Inspector tab with different view

Behavior Popup button

Behavior editing pane expanded

Events editing pane

Behavior description pane collapsed

Actions editing pane

FIGURE J-8
Behavior Inspector tab with a new behavior

New behavior

Action Popup button

Behavior action; change to Watch cursor

Event Popup button

Behavior event; on mouseDown

Create a behavior

1. Click the Help up sprite (the Help button) on the Stage, then click the Behavior Inspector tab in the Code panel, as shown in Figure J-6.

2. Click the Collapse arrow to hide the behavior description pane, click the Expand arrow above it to display the editing pane, then drag the border line to adjust the pane view, as shown in Figure J-7.

3. Click the Behavior Popup button (at the top of the tab) in the Behavior Inspector, then click New Behavior to open the New Behavior dialog box.

4. Type **Change Cursor**, then click OK.

5. Click the Event Popup button in the Events editing pane, then click mouseDown.

6. Click the Action Popup button in the Actions editing pane, point to Cursor, then click Change Cursor to open the Specify Cursor dialog box, which displays the Watch cursor in the Change Cursor to list.

7. Click OK to display the Behavior Inspector tab with the new behavior, as shown in Figure J-8.

8. Rewind and play the movie, click the Help button on the Stage, move the pointer around the Stage to view the Watch cursor, then stop the movie.

9. Save your work.

You created a behavior.

ADD AND MODIFY A BEHAVIOR

What You'll Do

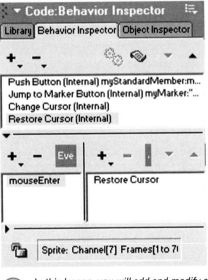

In this lesson, you will add and modify a behavior.

Adding a Behavior

When you create a behavior, you need to consider how Director runs it with the other behaviors attached to a sprite or frame. In many instances, you need to create a set of behaviors to complete a single operation. For example, the Change Cursor behavior and the Restore Cursor behavior are commonly used together to change a cursor temporarily when an event takes place and then redisplay the default cursor when the event is complete.

In the previous lesson, you created a behavior to change the cursor to an hour-glass (Win) or watch (Mac) when you click the Help button on the Stage. Until you change it again, the cursor will remain an hourglass (Win) or watch (Mac). You need to add another behavior to restore the default system cursor. You use the Behavior Inspector tab in the Code panel or the Behavior tab in the Property inspector to add a behavior.

Modifying a Behavior

After you create a behavior and play back the movie to check its performance, you may need to modify behavior settings. Sometimes a behavior doesn't work the way you intended, or the results don't meet your specific needs. You use the Behavior Inspector to modify a behavior. If you want to modify a behavior throughout the entire movie, you double-click the behavior in the Cast window to open the Behavior Inspector and make changes. If you want to modify a behavior for a specific sprite, you select the sprite in the Score or on the Stage, open the Behavior Inspector, select a behavior, and make changes. In the Behavior Inspector, you can add events and actions to an existing behavior, but you cannot directly modify the existing events and actions associated with a behavior. Instead, you remove the events and actions you want to change from the editing panes and create new ones. You can also use the Behavior tab to make changes to a behavior. The Behavior tab includes the same fields for the behavior as those included in the Parameters dialog box.

Creating a hyperlink with a behavior

You can create hyperlinks in a movie to access Web sites on the Internet. You create a hyperlink in two steps. The first step is to create a text cast member and add hyperlink formatting, and the second is to attach the Hyperlink behavior. You use the Text window to create a text cast member, and the Text Inspector to add hyperlink formatting. In the Text Inspector, you can turn any selected range of text into a hyperlink that links to a URL. Director automatically adds standard hyperlink formatting to the selected text so that it initially appears with hyperlink underlining. The URL cannot contain a double quotation mark or the Lingo continuation character (\), which wraps a Lingo statement onto two lines. To complete the first step, select the text you want to define as a hyperlink, click Window on the menu bar then click Text Inspector. In the Hyperlink Data text box, enter the complete URL that you want to link to. The complete URL needs to include one of the following supported URL schemes: http//, https://, mailto:, or ftp://. After you enter the complete URL, press Enter (Win) or return (Mac) to create a text cast member with hyperlink formatting. To complete the second step, click Window on the menu bar, click Library Palette, click the Library List button, click Text, drag the Hypertext - General icon onto the sprite of the text cast member, then click OK. When you play the movie and position the pointer over the hyperlink, the pointer changes to a pointing hand. When you click the hyperlink, Lingo will perform a command (gotoNetPage) to jump to the URL.

Add a behavior

1. Click the Help up sprite (the Help button) on the Stage (if necessary), then click the Behavior Inspector tab in the Code panel if necessary.

   > TIP To adjust the size for the editing and description panes, drag the dark line at the bottom of each section.

2. Click the Behavior Popup button in the Behavior Inspector, then click New Behavior to open the New Behavior dialog box. **+.**

3. Type **Restore Cursor**, then click OK.

4. Click the Event Popup button in the Events editing pane, then click mouseLeave. **+.**

5. Click the Action Popup button in the Actions editing pane, point to Cursor, then click Restore Cursor to add the behavior to the Code panel, as shown in Figure J-9. **+.**

   > TIP To change the sequence of actions in an event or action group, select an event from the Events editing pane, select an action from the Actions editing pane, then click the Shuffle Up button or the Shuffle Down button in the Behavior Inspector.

6. Rewind and play the movie.

7. Click the Help button on the Stage to change the cursor to a Watch cursor.

8. Slowly move the pointer off the button (leave it) to restore the cursor to the arrow, then stop the movie.

You added a behavior.

FIGURE J-9
Restore Cursor behavior

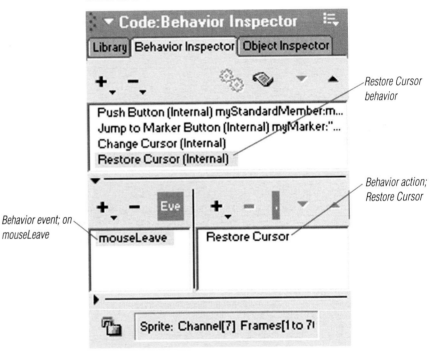

Restore Cursor behavior

Behavior action; Restore Cursor

Behavior event; on mouseLeave

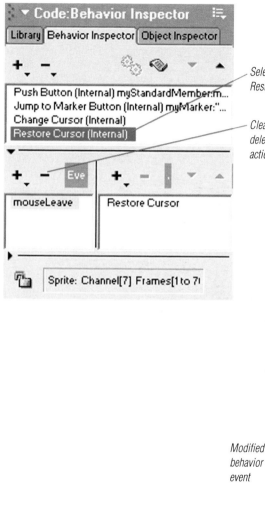

Selected behavior;
Restore Cursor

Clear Event button;
deletes event and
action below

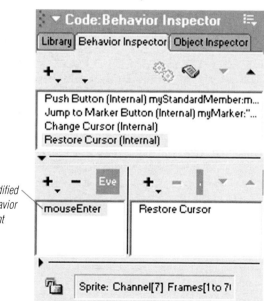

Modified
behavior
event

Modify a behavior

1. Click the Help up sprite (the Help button) on the Stage if necessary.

2. Click the Restore Cursor (Internal) behavior in the Behavior pane of the Behavior Inspector, as shown in Figure J-10.

3. Click the Clear Event button in the Events editing pane to delete the event and action associated with it. $\boxed{-}$

   TIP   To remove an event or action from a behavior, you can also select the event or action, then press [Delete].

4. Click the Event Popup button in the Events editing pane, then click mouseEnter. $\boxed{+}$

5. Click the Action Popup button in the Actions editing pane, point to Cursor, then click Restore Cursor to modify the behavior, as shown in Figure J-11. $\boxed{+}$

6. Minimize the docking channel (Win) or close the grouped panel (Mac) with the Property inspector.

7. Drag the Restore Cursor cast member in the Cast window to the Products, Price, and Contacts button sprites on the Stage.

8. Rewind and play the movie, click the Help button on the Stage to change the cursor to a Watch cursor, move the mouse around the screen, point to a button to restore the cursor, then stop the movie.

9. Save your work.

You modified a behavior.

OPEN A MOVIE WITH A BEHAVIOR

What You'll Do

In this lesson, you will open a movie with a behavior.

Opening a Movie with a Behavior

When you create or modify a large movie, it's difficult to organize and manage all the pieces of the production, and it occupies a lot of RAM when loaded into memory. To help alleviate these problems, you can open a movie from within a movie. When you use this technique, you actually close the current movie and open another. This allows you to organize large sections of a movie into smaller separate movies, which require less RAM. With a multiple-movie structure, you can create movie modules (independent movies) simultaneously to save time and maximize the production effort. When you use a multiple-movie structure, you need to store the movie modules in the same location to play and package the movie. The best place to store movie modules is in the same location as the main movie or in a folder within it. You can quickly and easily use a behavior in the Library palette to open a movie module.

Understanding file path locations

When you open a movie module that resides in a different location from the main movie, you need to refer to it by its full name (in the Parameters for "Jump to Movie Button" dia-log box, for example), to make sure the main movie can find it. The name that appears on the desktop is only part of a file's full name, according to the computer. The full name, or path name, includes specific information about the file's location on a floppy disk, CD-ROM, hard disk, or network. For example, the path name of a movie called Help-that resides on a network drive might be N:\Data Files\Unit J\Help.dir (Win) or DD Network:Data Files:Unit J:Help.dir (Mac). The N is the drive letter of the network for Windows, and DD Network is the name of the network drive for Macintosh. The backslash (\) is a special character used in path names for Windows, which indicates another level down in the file hierarchy. For Macintosh, the colon (:) serves the same purpose.

Parameters for "Jump to Movie Button" dialog box

Parameters for "Jump to Movie Button" ☒

On mouseUp, go to movie | Type the name of your movie here | OK
(Include path if necessary) | | Cancel
Marker in the other movie (optional) |

Jump Mode | Go to ▼

Remember current marker for Back button? ☑

*Type the full path name to
the movie if movie resides
in a different folder from the
main movie*

Open a movie with a behavior

1. Click Window on the menu bar, then click Library Palette to display the Library tab.

2. Scroll down the Library palette (if necessary), then drag the Jump to Movie Button icon in the Controls library to the Help up sprite (the Help button) on the Stage to open the Parameters for "Jump to Movie Button" dialog box, as shown in Figure J-12.

3. In the top text box, type **Help**, then click OK.

4. Click the Jump to Movie Button (Internal) behavior on the Behavior tab in the Property inspector to select it, then click the Shuffle Up button until the Jump to Movie Button (Internal) behavior is above the Jump to Marker Button (Internal) behavior, as shown in Figure J-13. ◢

FIGURE J-13
Behavior position changed on Behavior tab

▼ Property Inspector ☰

Sprite 7: Bitmap
Help up
Internal ☰ ⑦

Sprite | Behavior | Memb | Bitma | Guide | Movie

➕ ➖   ⚙ ◈ ▼ ▲

Push Button (Internal)
Jump to Movie Button (Internal)
Jump to Marker Button (Internal)
Change Cursor (Internal)
Restore Cursor (Internal)

*New behavior
execution order*

On mouseUp, | Help
go to movie
(Include path if
necessary)

Marker in the
other movie
(optional)

Jump Mode | ▼ Go to

Remember | ☑ true
current marker
for Back
button?

5. Save the movie, rewind and play the movie, then click the Help button on the Stage to open the Help movie.

   TIP If the Help movie file isn't located in the data files folder with the SpaceWorks Online movie file, a Where is "Help?" dialog box opens, asking for the location of the file.

6. Stop the movie, then click the Return up sprite (the Return button) on the Stage.

7. Click the Behavior tab in the Property inspector (if necessary), to display the Jump Back behavior that returns you to your previous location, the SpaceWorks Online movie.

8. Minimize the docking channel (Win) or close the grouped panel (Mac) with the Property inspector.

9. Rewind and play the movie, click the Return button on the Stage to open the SpaceWorks Online movie, then stop the movie.

You opened a movie with a behavior.

CREATE A DROPDOWN LIST WITH A BEHAVIOR

What You'll Do

In this lesson, you will create a dropdown list with a behavior.

Creating a Dropdown List with a Behavior

The Library palette comes with a behavior to create a dropdown list from a field text box. This behavior comes in handy when you want a user to select an item in a list. To create a dropdown list, you create a field sprite on the Stage, enter text for each list item, then drag the Dropdown List behavior from the Library palette onto the field sprite. When you drag the Dropdown List behavior icon to a sprite on the Stage, a gray rectangle appears around the object, indicating where the behavior will be attached. The Parameters for "Dropdown List" dialog box opens, asking you to enter a name for the dropdown list and select other settings relevant to dropdown lists.

Using a Dropdown List during a Movie

You can use the dropdown list to allow a user to make a selection or perform a simple command. If you use the dropdown list to perform a simple command, you can run Lingo commands to open a movie or perform a task. The type of command that runs depends on the purpose and contents of the list.

When the user clicks a dropdown list sprite, the dropdown list opens to reveal all its items. If the user immediately releases the mouse button, the list remains open until the next click. When the user selects a list item, the list closes to display the selected item. If the user clicks elsewhere, the list closes to display the currently selected item.

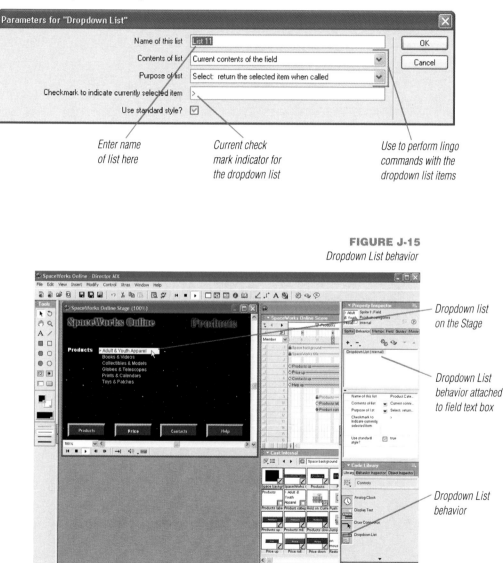

Enter name
of list here

Current check
mark indicator for
the dropdown list

Use to perform lingo
commands with the
dropdown list items

FIGURE J-15

Dropdown List behavior

Dropdown list
on the Stage

Dropdown List
behavior attached
to field text box

Dropdown List
behavior

Create a dropdown list with a behavior

1. Click the Product categories sprite in the Score.

2. Click Window on the menu bar, then click Library Palette (if necessary) to display the Library tab with the Controls library in the Code panel.

3. Scroll up the Library palette, then drag the Dropdown List icon in the Controls library to the Product categories sprite on the Stage to open the Parameters for "Dropdown List" dialog box, as shown in Figure J-14.

   TIP To change the appearance of a dropdown list frame, select the field, click the Field tab in the Property inspector, then change the frame settings at the bottom.

4. In the Name of this list text box, type **Product Categories**.

5. Click OK to change the field text box to a dropdown list, and add a new behavior cast member to the Cast window.

   TIP You can choose any character to act as a check mark to indicate the current selection when the dropdown list is open.

6. Rewind and play the movie.

7. Click the Products button on the Stage, click the Product categories sprite on the Stage to display the dropdown list shown in Figure J-15, then click Prints & Calendars from the dropdown list to select the item.

8. Stop the movie, then save your work.

9. Minimize the docking channel (Win) or close the grouped panel (Mac) with the Property inspector.

You created a dropdown list with a behavior.

ADD KEYBOARD NAVIGATION WITH A BEHAVIOR

What You'll Do

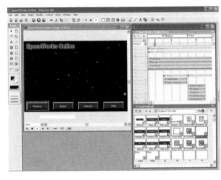

In this lesson, you will add keyboard navigation with a behavior.

Making a Movie Accessible

Director MX includes several new behaviors that let you add accessibility features, such as keyboard navigation, text-to-speech, and captioning, to make your movies more accessible to hearing- and visually-impaired users. These behaviors are available in the Accessibility library on the Library palette, as shown in Figure J-16.

Enabling Keyboard Navigation

The keyboard navigation behaviors let mobility-impaired users select sprites and simulate mouse clicks without using a mouse. For example, if your movie displays several button sprites on the Stage, you can apply keyboard navigation

behaviors that let users select the buttons using the Tab key. As the user selects a button sprite using the Tab key, it's highlighted with a colored rectangle, called a **focus ring**, around its boundaries. When the sprite is selected, the user can press Enter (Win) or return (Mac) to perform the same command as a mouse click. Table J-2 describes the keyboard navigation options.

Setting Up Keyboard Navigation

Most of the accessibility behaviors must be used with other accessibility behaviors. To enable keyboard navigation, you need to use the Accessibility Target, Accessibility Keyboard Controller, Accessibility Item or

Accessibility Text Edit Item, and Accessibility Group Order behaviors together. Because the accessibility behaviors work together and are dependent on each other, the first step you need to take is to create an Accessibility group, which associates all the accessibility behaviors within the group with a specific scene. If you create a different scene, you should use a different group name. The Accessibility Target behavior creates the group and enables the other accessibility behaviors to communicate with each other. The second step is to use the Accessibility Keyboard Controller behavior, which intercepts keystrokes from the keyboard and enables those keyboard events to be used for navigation. You attach the Accessibility Keyboard Controller to an editable sprite that you place off the Stage. The next step is to attach the Accessibility Item behavior to a sprite or sprites or attach the Accessibility Text Edit Item behavior to a text sprite. The last step is to attach the Accessibility Group Order behavior (which enables you to specify the order in which each sprite is selected on the Stage when the user presses the Tab key) to the sprites that have the Accessibility Item or Accessibility Text Edit Item behaviors.

FIGURE J-16
Library palette with Accessibility library

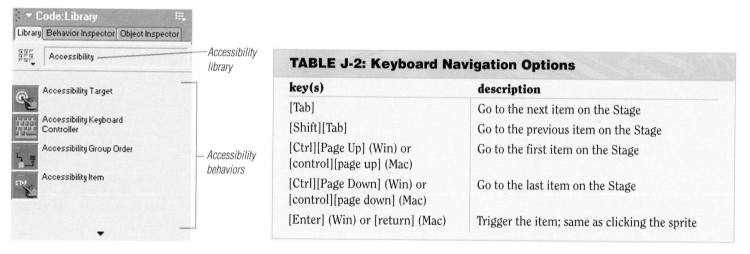

TABLE J-2: Keyboard Navigation Options

key(s)	description
[Tab]	Go to the next item on the Stage
[Shift][Tab]	Go to the previous item on the Stage
[Ctrl][Page Up] (Win) or [control][page up] (Mac)	Go to the first item on the Stage
[Ctrl][Page Down] (Win) or [control][page down] (Mac)	Go to the last item on the Stage
[Enter] (Win) or [return] (Mac)	Trigger the item; same as clicking the sprite

Apply the Accessibility Target behavior

1. Resize the Stage (if necessary) to display the gray area at the bottom, then click frame 1 in channel 20 in the Score.

2. Click the Rectangle tool on the Tool palette, click the Foreground Color box, click the seventh color square (red) in the third row, then click the Three-Pixel Line button on the Tool palette. ☐

3. Drag to create a rectangle in the gray area at the bottom, as shown in Figure J-17, to create a focus ring to highlight other sprites, name the rectangle sprite **Focus Ring**, then extend the sprite to frame 70 in the Score.

4. Click Window on the menu bar, click Library Palette, click the Library List button, then click Accessibility. ▦

5. Click the focus ring off the Stage to select it, then drag the Accessibility Target behavior from the Library palette onto the rectangle sprite off the Stage to open the Parameters for "Accessibility Target" dialog box.

6. In the Name of this Accessibility group? text box, type **Buttons**.

7. Select the Speech initially enabled? check box if necessary.

8. Click OK to attach the behavior to the sprite and place the behavior in the Cast window.

9. Minimize the docking channel (Win) or close the grouped panel (Mac) with the Property inspector.

   The Accessibility Target behavior appears in the Cast window, as shown in Figure J-17.

You applied the Accessibility Target behavior to a shape sprite.

FIGURE J-17
Applying the Accessibility Target behavior

Gray area off Stage

Rectangle sprite

Accessibility Target behavior cast member

Displays the accessibility group

Apply the Accessibility Keyboard Controller behavior

1. Click frame 1 in channel 21 in the Score, click the Text tool on the Tool palette, drag to create a text box in the gray area at the bottom next to the rectangle sprite, as shown in Figure J-19, name the text sprite **Keyboard Controller**, then extend the text sprite to frame 70 in the Score. A

2. Expand the docking channel (Win) or open the grouped panel (Mac) with the Property inspector.

3. Select the Keyboard Controller sprite (if necessary), click the Text tab in the Property inspector, then select the Editable check box.

4. Drag the Accessibility Keyboard Controller behavior from the Library palette onto the text sprite off the Stage to open the Parameters for "Accessibility Keyboard Controller" dialog box.

5. Click the Which Accessibility Group does this belong to? list arrow, then click Buttons (if necessary), as shown in Figure J-18.

6. Click OK to attach the behavior to the sprite and place the behavior in the Cast window.

7. Minimize the docking channel (Win) or close the grouped panel (Mac) with the Property inspector.

   The Accessibility Keyboard Controller behavior appears in the Cast window, as shown in Figure J-19.

8. Save your work.

You applied the Accessibility Keyboard Controller behavior to a text sprite.

FIGURE J-19
Applying the Accessibility Keyboard Controller behavior

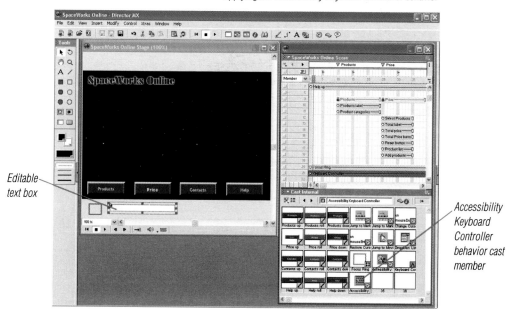

Editable text box

Accessibility Keyboard Controller behavior cast member

Apply the Accessibility Item behavior

1. Click Window on the menu bar, then click Library Palette to display the Library tab.

2. Scroll down the Library palette (if necessary), then drag the Accessibility Item behavior from the Library palette to the Products up sprite (the Products button) on the Stage to open the Parameters for "Accessibility Item" dialog box.

3. Click the Which Accessibility Group does this belong to? list arrow, then click Buttons if necessary.

4. In the Command to execute? text box, select the current text, then type **Go to frame "Products"**, as shown in Figure J-20.

5. Click OK to attach the accessibility item to the sprite and create a cast member in the Cast window.

6. Drag the Accessibility Item behavior from the Library palette onto the Price up sprite, Contacts up sprite, and Help up sprite (the Price, Contacts, and Help buttons) on the Stage then type a command (**Go to frame "Price"**, **Go to frame "Contacts"**, and **Go to frame "Help"**) for each button.

7. Click the Help up sprite (the Help button) on the Stage, click the Behavior tab in the Property inspector, then click the Accessibility Item (Internal) behavior, as shown in Figure J-21.

8. Save your work.

You applied the Accessibility Item behavior to buttons.

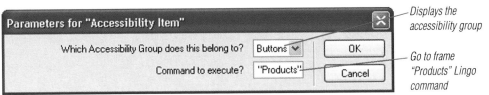

Displays the accessibility group

Go to frame "Products" Lingo command

FIGURE J-21
Applying the Accessibility Item behavior

Accessibility Item behavior

Parameters

FIGURE J-22

Parameters for "Accessibility Group Order" dialog box

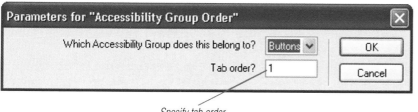

Specify tab order

FIGURE J-23

Using keyboard navigation

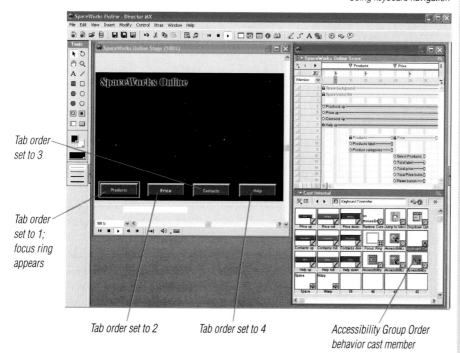

Tab order set to 3

Tab order set to 1; focus ring appears

Tab order set to 2

Tab order set to 4

Accessibility Group Order behavior cast member

Apply the Accessibility Group Order behavior

1. Scroll down the Library palette (if necessary), then drag the Accessibility Group Order behavior from the Library palette to the Products up sprite (the Products button) to open the Parameters for "Accessibility Group Order" dialog box, as shown in Figure J-22.

2. Click the Which Accessibility Group does this belong to? list arrow, then click Buttons if necessary.

3. In the Tab order? text box, select the current number, then type **1** if necessary.

4. Click OK to add the tab order to the sprite and place the behavior in the Cast window.

5. Drag the Accessibility Group Order behavior from the Library palette onto the Price up sprite, Contacts up sprite, and Help up sprite (the Price, Contacts, and Help buttons) on the Stage, then type a tab order number in consecutive order (**2**, **3**, and **4**) for each button.

6. Minimize the docking channel (Win) or close the grouped panel (Mac) with the Property inspector, then scroll through the Cast window to display the Accessibility Group Order cast member if necessary.

7. Save your work, then rewind and play the movie, as shown in Figure J-23.

8. Press [Tab] (or [Shift][Tab]) several times to move the keyboard navigation, press [Enter] (Win) or [return] (Mac) to run the button script, then stop the movie.

You applied the Accessibility Group Order behavior

Lesson 6   Add Keyboard Navigation with a Behavior

323

CHANGE TEXT TO SPEECH WITH A BEHAVIOR

What You'll Do

In this lesson, you will change text to speech with a behavior.

Enabling Text-to-Speech

You can use Accessibility behaviors to help visually-impaired users. You use text-to-speech behaviors to make a text cast member or text in a selected sprite audible. Director comes with three text-to-speech behaviors: Accessibility Speak, Accessibility Speak Member Text, and Accessibility Speak Enable/Disable. The Accessibility Speak behavior lets you specify text to be spoken when a user navigates to a sprite with the Tab key. The Accessibility Speak Member Text behavior lets you specify a text cast member to be spoken when a user navigates to a sprite with the Tab key. The Accessibility Speak Enable/Disable behavior lets you specify a user event that can turn the text-to-speech feature on or off. The text-to-speech features are designed to be used with the keyboard navigation behaviors.

Using the Speech Xtra

If you use text-to-speech in a projector, you need to add the Speech Xtra (Speech.x32) to your movie's Xtra list. Otherwise, Lingo will not be able to run the text-to-speech commands. The Speech Xtra adds special commands to Lingo that enable the text-to-speech capability. The text-to-speech behaviors require the Xtra because they use these Lingo commands. The Speech Xtra supports Microsoft SAPI 4 and 5.1 on Windows. The Xtra supports all versions of text-to-speech on the Macintosh.

To add the Speech Xtra to the movie's Xtra list, click Modify on the menu bar, point to Movie, then click Xtras. In the Movie Xtras dialog box, click Add. In the Add Xtras dialog box, click Speech.x32, then click OK to close the Add Xtras dialog box. Click OK to close the Movie Xtras dialog box, then save your movie.

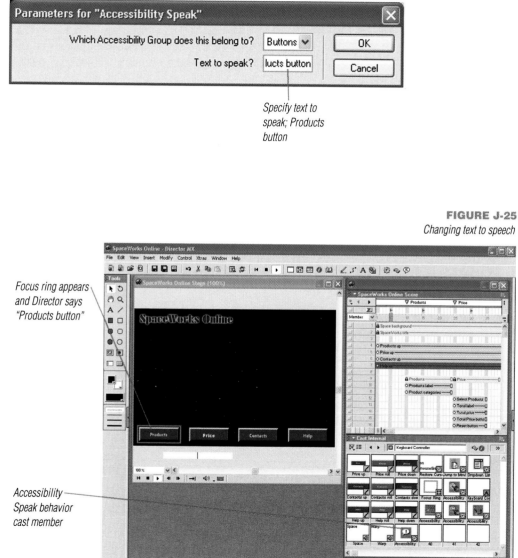

Parameters for "Accessibility Speak"

Which Accessibility Group does this belong to? Buttons ▾   OK

Text to speak? lucts button   Cancel

Specify text to speak; Products button

Focus ring appears and Director says "Products button"

FIGURE J-25

Changing text to speech

Accessibility Speak behavior cast member

Apply the Accessibility Speak behavior

1. Click Window on the menu bar, click Library Palette to open the Library tab in the Code panel, click the Library List button, then click Accessibility if necessary. ▓▓

2. Scroll down the Library palette, then drag the Accessibility Speak behavior from the Library palette onto the Products up sprite (the Products button) to open the Parameters for "Accessibility Speak" dialog box.

   > TIP When the focus ring appears on top of an item on the Stage, you can't attach the Accessibility Speak behavior (the sprite is not selectable), and you need to drag the behavior to the sprite in the Score.

3. Click the Which Accessibility Group does this belong to? list arrow, then click Buttons if necessary.

4. In the Text to speak? text box, select the current text, type **Products button**, as shown in Figure J-24, then click OK.

5. Drag the Accessibility Speak behavior from the Library palette onto the Price up sprite, Contacts up sprite, and Help up sprite (the Price, Contacts, and Help buttons) on the Stage, and type the item name (**Price button**, **Contacts button**, and **Help button**) for each button.

6. Minimize the docking channel (Win) or close the grouped panel (Mac) with the Property inspector.

7. Rewind and play the movie to display the focus ring around the Products button, as shown in Figure J-25, and hear the text.

8. Save your work, then exit Director.

You changed text to speech with a behavior.

Attach built-in behaviors.

1. Start Director, open the file MD J-2.dir from where your Unit J data files are stored, then save it as **Nova**.
2. Open the Library palette and the Controls library.
3. Drag the Push Button behavior to the Loan up sprite on the Stage and accept the default parameter settings.
4. Drag the Push Button cast member to the Calculator up, Contacts up, and Guide up sprites, and accept the default parameter settings.
5. Rewind and play the movie, click the buttons on the Stage, then stop the movie.
6. Attach the Jump to Marker Button behavior to the button sprites on the Stage, and select the corresponding jump to marker.
7. Close the Library palette, select the Loan up sprite, then display the Behavior tab in the Property inspector.
8. Double-click the Push Button behavior on the Behavior tab, then change the mouseUp sound to Chimes.
9. Change the Sound to play on mouseUp parameter to Chimes for the Calculator up, Contacts up, and Guide up sprites on the Stage.
10. Rewind and play the movie, click the buttons on the Stage, then stop the movie.

Create a behavior.

1. Select the Guide up sprite, then open the Behavior Inspector.
2. Create a behavior called **Change Cursor** to change the cursor to the Closed Hand on MouseDown.
3. Close the Behavior Inspector.
4. Rewind and play the movie, click the Guide button on the Stage, move the pointer around the Stage, then stop the movie.

Add and modify a behavior.

1. Select the Guide up sprite (if necessary), then open the Behavior Inspector.
2. Create another behavior called **Restore Cursor** to restore the cursor to the default on MouseLeave.
3. Close the Behavior Inspector.
4. Rewind and play the movie, click the Guide button on the Stage, slowly move the pointer off the Guide button, then stop the movie.
5. Select the Guide up sprite (if necessary), then open the Behavior Inspector.
6. Select the Restore Cursor behavior.
7. Clear the event.
8. Create a new event to restore the cursor to the default on MouseEnter.
9. Close the Behavior Inspector.
10. Drag the Restore Cursor cast member to the Loan up, Calculator up, and Contacts up sprites.

11. Rewind and play the movie, click the Guide button on the Stage, move the pointer around the Stage, point to a button, then stop the movie.

Open a movie with a behavior.

1. Open the Library palette and the Controls library.
2. Drag the Jump to Movie Button behavior to the Guide up sprite on the Stage, and type **Guide** for the movie name in the top text box.
3. Select the Jump to Movie Button behavior on the Behavior tab, then shuffle it up the list, above the Jump to Marker behavior.
4. Close the Library palette and save the movie.
5. Rewind and play the movie, then click the Guide button on the Stage.
6. Play the movie, click the Return button on the Stage, then stop the movie.

Create a dropdown list with a behavior.

1. Open the Library palette and the Controls library.
2. Drag the Dropdown List behavior to the Loan Amount list sprite on the Stage.
3. Type **Loan Amounts**, and accept the default settings.
4. Close the Library palette.
5. Rewind and play the movie, then click the Loan button.
6. Click the Loan Amount list sprite on the Stage, click $175,000, then stop the movie.

Add keyboard navigation with a behavior.

1. Resize the Stage to display the gray area, then click frame 1 in channel 13.
2. Create a rectangle with a 3-pixel, orange border named **Focus Ring** off the Stage, then extend the sprite to frame 70.
3. Create an accessibility group called **Navigate** with speech enabled.
4. Click frame 1 in channel 14, then create an editable text box named **Keyboard Controller** off the Stage, then extend the sprite to frame 70.
5. Attach the Accessibility Keyboard Controller behavior to the Keyboard Controller sprite, then select the Navigate accessibility group.
6. Attach the Accessibility Item behavior to the buttons at the bottom of the Stage, select the Navigate accessibility group, and execute a command (Go to frame "Loan", Go to frame "Calculator", Go to frame "Contacts", and Go to frame "Guide") for each button.
7. Use the Accessibility Group Order behavior to set the tab order to Loan = 1, Calculator = 2, Contacts = 3, and Guide = 4.
8. Rewind and play the movie, press the Tab key several times, then stop the movie.

Change text to speech with a behavior.

1. Attach the Accessibility Speak behavior to the buttons at the bottom of the Stage, select the Navigate accessibility group, and enter the text to speak (Loan button, Calculator button, Contacts button, and Guide button) for each button.

FIGURE J-26
Completed Skills Review

2. Rewind and play the movie, press the Tab key several times, select the Loan button, press Enter (Win) or return (Mac), then click the Loan Amount list.
3. Compare your screen to Figure J-26.
4. Stop the movie, save the movie, then exit Director.

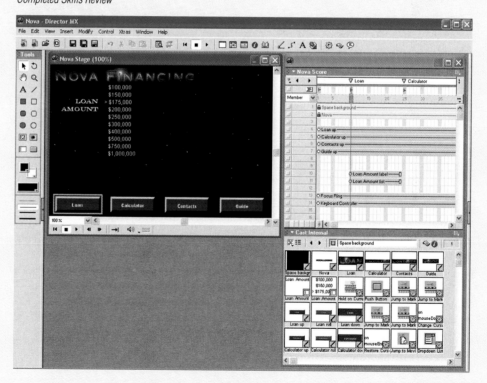

You are a freelance computer programmer and want to create a game in Director that allows the user to zoom in and zoom out of the current scene. You are at the beginning stages of development and want to test the Change Cursor behavior with the two different zoom cursors. You use Director to change the cursor to the Zoom In or Zoom Out cursor.

1. Start Director and save the movie as **Zoom**.
2. Using the Filled Rectangle tool on the Tool palette, draw a filled rectangle the size of the Stage to create a background.
3. Create a text cast member with the text **Zoom Cursor Test** and drag it to the top of the Stage.
4. In the Paint window, create a button cast member with the text **Zoom In**, then add the cast member to the Stage.
5. In the Paint window, create a button cast member with the text **Zoom Out**, then add the cast member to the Stage.
6. Attach a behavior to the Zoom In button on the Stage that changes the cursor to the Zoom In cursor.
7. Attach a behavior to the Zoom Out button on the Stage that changes the cursor to the Zoom Out cursor.

8. Attach a behavior to the filled rectangle on the Stage that restores the cursor.
9. Play the movie, click the Zoom In button, then compare your screen to Figure J-27.

FIGURE J-27
Completed Project Builder 1

10. Click the filled rectangle, click the Zoom Out button, then click the filled rectangle again.
11. Save the movie, then exit Director.

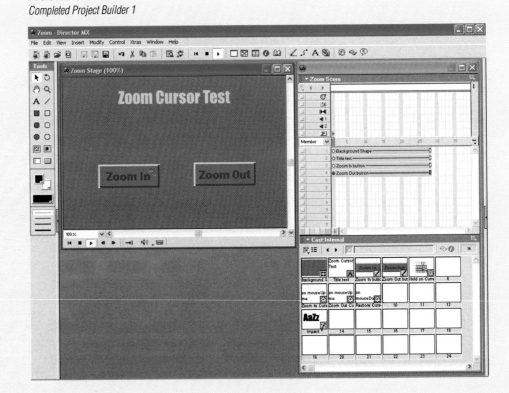

You work in the marketing department at Toy Think, an educational toy company. You are developing a sales and promotion plan for the next six months and want to find out current customer buying trends. You want to create a survey for your company Web site to gather the customer information. You use Director to create dropdown lists from which customers can make recommendations.

1. Start Director and save the movie as **Toy Think**.
2. Create a text cast member with the text **Toy Think Survey** and drag it to the top of the Stage.
3. Create four field text boxes on the Stage, and name them **Boys 3-5**, **Girls 3-5**, **Boys 6-10**, and **Girls 6-10**.
4. Create a text cast member with the text **Boys 3 to 5 years**, and drag it above the Boys 3-5 field text box (as a label) on the Stage.
5. Enter five toy items related to boys 3 to 5 years old in the field text box.
6. Repeat Steps 4 and 5 for the remaining text boxes using the following text: **Girls 3 to 5 years**, **Boys 6 to 10 years**, and **Girls 6 to 10 years**.
7. Attach the Dropdown List behavior to the four field text boxes you created in Step 3,

and use the default parameter dialog box settings.
8. Compare your screen to Figure J-28.

9. Play the movie, then select an item from each dropdown list.
10. Save the movie, then exit Director.

FIGURE J-28
Completed Project Builder 2

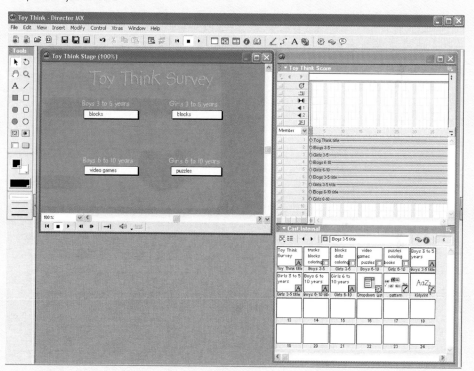

You are the multimedia designer for Digital Magic, a sports game development company. Digital Magic is in final production for an upcoming sports game. You want to create a separate Director movie with the credits, so you can use it in more than one game. You use Director to create a movie with text animation to simulate rolling credits and a Return button, then create another movie with a Credits button to test the process of opening a separate movie.

1. Start Director and save the movie as **Credits**.
2. Create a text cast member with the text **Credits** and drag it to the top of the Stage.
3. Create a text cast member with five to ten names, and then drag it on the Stage.
4. Animate the text cast member with the names to appear from the bottom of the Stage, then move up under the text Credits, like rolling credits in a movie. (*Hint*: See the "Creating Animation Using Keyframes" lesson in Unit B.)
5. In the Paint window, create a button cast member with the text **Return**, add the cast member to the Stage, then attach a behavior to the Return button on the Stage that jumps back to the main movie.
6. Save the movie.
7. Create a new movie and save the movie as **Sports Game**.

8. In the Paint window, create a button cast member with the text **Credits**, add the cast member to the Stage, then attach a behavior to the Credits button on the Stage that opens the Credits movie.
9. Save and play the movie.

FIGURE J-29
Completed Design Project

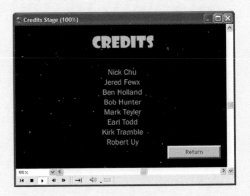

10. Click the Credits button, click the Return button, then compare your screen to Figure J-29.
11. Stop the movie, exit Director, then put a copy of this movie in your portfolio.

Your group can assign elements of the project to individual members, or work collectively to create the finished product.

You are a member of the computer support team at Cornerstone Books, a small book publishing company. You are responsible for helping employees get answers to computer-related problems. You don't have the time to answer every question, so you want to create a movie with hyperlinks to computer support Web sites, to help employees get answers. You use Director to create a movie with hyperlinks to several computer support Web sites.

1. Assign each member of the group to browse computer support Web sites for layout ideas, and to write down three or four URLs for the project.
2. Start Director and save the movie as **Computer Support**.
3. Create a text cast member with the text **Computer Support Web Sites**, then drag it to the top of the Stage.
4. Create text cast members with the name of each computer support Web site, then drag each one on the Stage.
5. Create text cast members with the URL for each site, then drag each one on the Stage beneath the Web site name.
6. Open the Text Inspector.

7. Double-click a URL text sprite to select the URL, then enter the complete URL in the Hyperlink Data text box and press Enter (Win) or return (Mac). Repeat this step for each text sprite.
8. Open the Library palette and display the Text library.
9. Drag the Hypertext - General behavior to the URL text sprites.
10. Add keyboard navigation to the URL text cast members. (When you apply the Accessibility Item behavior, execute the gotonetpage Lingo command for each URL; for example, gotonetpage "http://www.course.com"; include quotation marks.)

11. Add text-to-speech to the URL text cast members.
12. Save your movie.
13. Play the movie, compare your screen to Figure J-30, then tab through each URL.
14. Click a hyperlink, close your browser, then repeat for each hyperlink.
15. Stop the movie, then exit Director.

FIGURE J-30
Completed Group Project

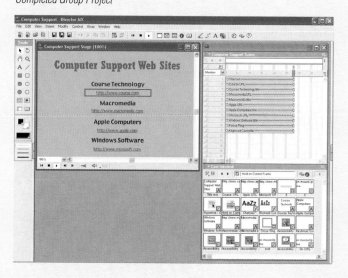

1. Understand scripts.

2. Understand handlers, messages, and events.

3. Examine Lingo elements.

4. Create and run a script.

5. Create cast member and frame scripts.

6. Use variables in a script.

7. Add functions to a script.

8. Use the Debugger window.

9. Open a movie in a window.

UNIT K
WRITING SCRIPTS WITH LINGO

Understanding Lingo

Lingo, Director's scripting language, allows you to add functionality to a movie beyond what is normally possible when you only use the Score. A Lingo script is a set of instructions that tells Director how to respond to specific events in a movie. An event is an action in a movie that generates messages for a script to perform specific actions. Events include mouse and keyboard input from a user (such as clicking the mouse button, typing, or closing a window), or the frame position of the playback head.

Director uses four types of scripts: behavior (sprite and frame), cast member, movie, and parent. The instructions in a script are organized into event handlers. When a movie plays, Director continuously checks for events that trigger messages associated with an event handler. If Director does not find an event handler, nothing happens. An event handler is composed of a combination of Lingo elements, which form statements, such as `go to frame "Main Menu"`.

Troubleshooting Lingo

After you create a script, you can use the Message window and Debugger to help you test and troubleshoot the script. The Message window is a useful tool for executing and testing Lingo commands and scripts within Director. You can use the Message window to execute handlers in a separate window, not related to the movie, which can help isolate any problems. When Director encounters a problem executing part of a script, an alert box appears, telling you what went wrong with the script and giving you the option to debug the script. The Debugger helps you use basic troubleshooting techniques to quickly find and fix Lingo code that isn't doing what you want.

Tools You'll Use

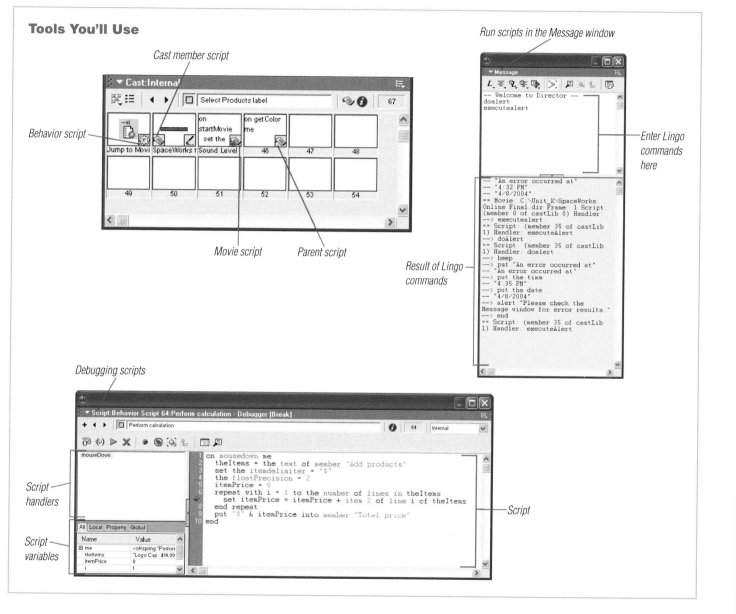

Cast member script

Behavior script

Jump to Movi | SpaceWorks 1 | Sound Level | 46 | 47 | 48

49 | 50 | 51 | 52 | 53 | 54

Movie script

Parent script

Run scripts in the Message window

Enter Lingo commands here

Result of Lingo commands

Debugging scripts

Script handlers

Script variables

Script

UNDERSTAND SCRIPTS

What You'll Do

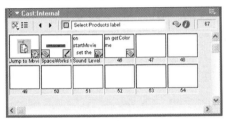

In this lesson, you will learn about scripts.

Understanding Scripts

As mentioned, Director uses four types of scripts: behavior (sprite and frame), cast member, movie, and parent. The behavior, movie, and parent scripts appear as separate cast members in the Cast window, while a cast member script is attached to a cast member and is indicated by a script icon in the lower-right corner of the cast member thumbnail, as shown in Figure K-1. You can attach a script to a sprite, a frame in the behavior channel (also known as the script channel), a cast member, or the movie itself. See Table K-1 for instructions on how to create a script. The object or element to which you attach a script determines when and where its instructions are available for execution. You can view or change a script type on the Script tab in the Property inspector.

Behavior scripts (sprite and frame) are Lingo scripts that make it easy to add interactivity to a movie. Director provides a Library palette with over 100 built-in behaviors that you can drag onto frames and sprites in the Score and on the Stage. You can use a prewritten script from a built-in behavior or create a script in the Behavior Inspector. You can attach multiple behavior scripts to one sprite, but you can attach only one script to a frame. Behavior scripts attached to sprites are helpful for mouse or keyboard input, while behavior scripts attached to frames are helpful for executing a command when the playback head reaches a frame.

Cast member scripts are attached to a specific cast member and cannot be shared. These scripts are independent of the Score. When a cast member script is assigned to a sprite, the cast member's script becomes available for all sprites based on the cast member. A behavior script, unlike a cast member script, may or may not be attached to a particular sprite. Cast member scripts are helpful for creating buttons that always produce the same response. You can attach only one script to a single cast member.

Movie scripts are available during playback of an entire movie; they are not attached to any object, such as a sprite or cast member. The movie scripts are available regardless of which sprite or frame the movie is currently playing. Movie scripts are helpful for controlling events that determine when a movie starts, stops, or pauses. A movie script is available only to its own movie. When a movie module plays in a separate window or as a linked movie, a movie script in the main movie will not be available; only a movie script in the movie module will be available. A movie can contain more than one movie script.

Parent scripts are special scripts that contain Lingo commands used to create child scripts, known as **child objects.** A parent script contains a set of rules that determines when and where to create a child object. When you create a parent script associated with a sprite, it only executes a child object when the conditions of the rule(s) are met. Parent scripts provide a powerful way to customize a movie. Parent scripts are an advanced form of programming and are beyond the scope of this book.

FIGURE K-1
Cast window with different script types

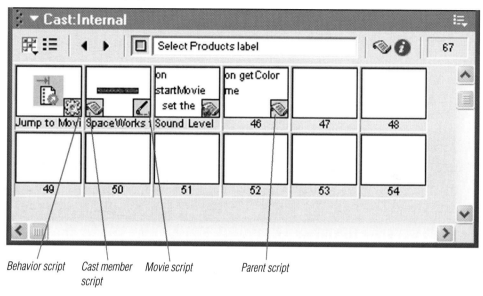

Behavior script   Cast member   Movie script   Parent script
script

TABLE K-1: Creating Scripts in Director

script type	instruction
Behavior (sprite)	In the Score or on the Stage, select a sprite, click Window on the menu bar, click Behavior Inspector, click the Behavior Popup button, then click New Behavior.
Behavior (frame)	Double-click a frame in the script channel.
Cast member	Select a cast member in the Cast window, then click the Cast Member Script button.
Movie	With no sprites or scripts selected in the Cast window, Score, or Stage, click Window on the menu bar, then click Script.
Parent	Create a script, select the script in the Cast window click the Script tab in the Property inspector, click the Type list arrow, then click Parent.

UNDERSTAND HANDLERS, MESSAGES, AND EVENTS

What You'll Do

In this lesson, you will learn about handlers, messages, and events.

Understanding Handlers, Messages, and Events

The instructions in a Lingo script are organized into event handlers, which respond to messages sent by Director that are triggered by a specific event during a movie's playback. An event is an occurrence, such as a mouse click or key press, that Director detects, and to which it responds by sending an internal message. The associated handler responds to the message. Each handler starts with the word on and ends with the word end. The word on is followed by a trigger message, such as mouseUp or keyUp, which is a specific event to which the handler responds. The handler waits for the specific event to occur (for example, the user releases the mouse button), and then carries out Lingo commands, one after another in the script, until it reaches the word end. Lingo scripts are written in a script window, as shown in Figure K-2.

When a movie plays, Director continuously checks for events that trigger messages associated with a handler. Because multiple handlers can respond to the same kind of event, Director uses a structured handler hierarchy to determine the order in which scripts can respond to a handler, as shown in Figure K-3. For example, when you click a sprite, Director sends a mouseUp message and checks each handler (primary event, sprite, cast member, frame, or movie script) in the order shown in the handler hierarchy flowchart in Figure K-3 until it finds a match. When it finds a match, the associated handler executes the Lingo commands in the script. There are some exceptions to this rule (which are listed in the Lingo documentation that comes with Director). If Director does not find an event handler, nothing happens.

Understanding Event Types

Director detects and responds to many types of events by sending a message. The most commonly used event types are user feedback, playback, time, and window.

- **User feedback events** are related to mouse and keyboard actions performed by a user. Examples include `keyDown`, `keyUp`, `mouseDown`, and `mouseUp`.

- **Playback events** are related to what happens when the playback head moves to another frame and when a movie is played. Common playback events include `enterFrame`, `exitFrame`, `prepareMovie`, and `startMovie`.
- **Time events** are related to the operating system and the user when the system is inactive. There are only two time events: `idle` and `timeOut`.
- **Window events** are related to the running of multiple Director movies in multiple windows. Examples include: `activeWindow`, `openWindow`, and `moveWindow`.

Understanding Handler Types

Director has two types of event handlers: system event handlers and custom event handlers. System event handlers are built-in predefined handlers that recognize Director events. Custom event handlers are user-defined handlers that recognize actions defined by the developer.

Primary event handlers are a subset of Director's system event handlers. The primary event handler is the first handler that Director checks when an event message is sent. The primary event handler is an important Lingo element, because you can define, or set up, the handler to meet your specific needs. The primary event handler uses an event handler property that corresponds to the message you want to handle, as shown in Figure K-2. For example, the event handler property `mouseupScript` in Figure K-2 is set to move the playback head to frame 1 when the user clicks and releases the mouse button in a movie.

FIGURE K-3

Handler hierarchy flowchart

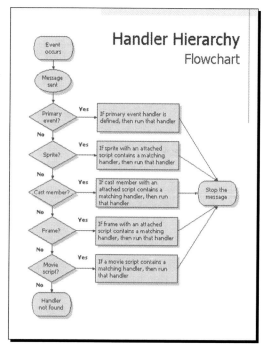

FIGURE K-2

Handler in the Movie Script window

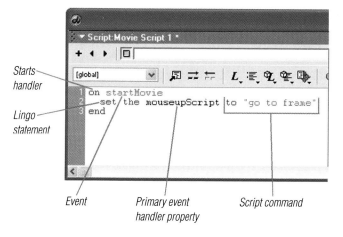

Starts handler

Lingo statement

Event

Primary event handler property

Script command

EXAMINE LINGO ELEMENTS

What You'll Do

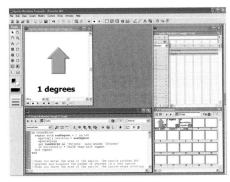

In this lesson, you will learn about Lingo elements and view Lingo elements in a script.

Examining Lingo Elements

A handler is composed of a combination of Lingo elements, which form statements, such as go to frame 1. Statements are complete Lingo instructions that Director executes when the handler is triggered. Director executes a script starting with the first Lingo statement and continues in order until it reaches the last Lingo statement. The order in which Director executes statements affects the order in which you place statements. For example, if you write a statement that requires a calculated value, you need to put in the statement that calculates the value first. Like most programming languages, Lingo has rules about how you can use Lingo elements to produce valid statements. See Table K-2 for a list of some common Lingo rules. Lingo interprets some keyboard commands differently between Windows and Macintosh platforms. See Table K-3 for a list of Lingo elements for cross-platform keys.

Here are some common Lingo elements and some examples of their use:

- **Arguments** are placeholders that let you pass values to scripts. For example, the handler on subtractThem a, b subtracts the value it receives in argument a from the value it receives in argument b.
- **Commands** instruct a movie to do something while the movie plays. Examples include go previous, which moves the playback head to the previous marker, and beep, which produces a beep sound.
- **Comments** are information, such as notes or instructions, that you can add to a script to make it easier for you or someone else to use. Comments are preceded by double hyphens (--). You can place a comment on its own line before or after any statement.
- **Constants** are elements that never change. For example, TRUE and FALSE are constants that always have

TABLE K-2: Lingo Rules

category	rule	example
Parentheses	You need to use parentheses to define a function. You can use parentheses after keywords to refer to the sprite or cast member object. You can use parentheses to establish precedence in math operations.	`sprite(whichSpriteNumber).color` `open window (the application Path & "theMovie")` The expression 10 * 6 – 4 will yield 56, while 10 * (6 – 4) will yield 20
Character spaces	Words within statements and expressions are separated by spaces. Lingo ignores extra spaces.	`play movie "Help"` is the same as `play movie  "Help"`
Uppercase and lowercase letters	You can use uppercase and lowercase letters. However, most strings in quotation marks are case sensitive.	`Go To Frame "Main Menu"` is the same as `go to frame "main menu"`
Abbreviated commands	You can abbreviate some Lingo commands to make them easier to enter.	`go to frame "Main Menu"` is the same as `go "Main Menu"`

TABLE K-3: Lingo Elements for Cross-Platform Keys

Lingo element	Windows key	Macintosh key
Return	[Enter]	[return]
commandDown	[Ctrl]	⌘
optionDown	[Alt]	[option]
controlDown	[Ctrl]	[control]
Enter	[Enter] on the numeric keypad	[enter] on the numeric keypad
Backspace	[Backspace]	[delete]

the values 1 and 0, respectively, and the constants `TAB`, `SPACE`, `EMPTY`, `RETURN`, and `ENTER` always have the same meaning.

- **Variables** are storage places in which you name and assign values. To assign values to variables or change the values, you use the equals (=) sign (called an operator) or the `set` command. For example, typing `price = 0` in a script creates a local variable named *price* and assigns the value 0 to it. Lingo supports both local and global variables. A **local variable** is only available while the handler that contains it is being executed, while a **global variable** is available in any handler.

- **Expressions** are parts of a Lingo statement that generate values. For example, `total = price * .0825` in a script creates a local variable named *total* and uses the expression `price * .0825` to generate the value.

- **Functions** return a value. Examples include `the date`, which returns the current date set in the computer, and `the number of words in`, which returns the number of words in a text cast member.

- **Keywords** are reserved words in Lingo defined to represent a fixed element or concept. Keywords usually exist in the context of other data. In the statement `go to the frame "Menu"`, the keywords are `go`, `to`, and `the`. Other examples include `sprite`, `next`, `field`, `of`, `cast`, `end`, and `me`.

- **Lists** are an effective way to store, track, and update a set of data, such as a series of names or numbers. Examples include `[1, 2, 3, 4]` and `["Bruno", "Thielen", "Teyler"]`.

- **Operators** are terms that change values using arithmetic symbols, compare two values and determine if the comparison is true or false, or combine text strings. Examples include + (plus), − (minus), <> (not equal), < (less than), " (string), & (concatenation), && (concatenation with space), and `not` (a logical operator).

- **Properties** are the various attributes of an object. Examples include `depth`, which retrieves the current color depth of a given graphic cast member or image object, and `cursor`, which determines which cursor appears when the pointer rolls over a given sprite.

Viewing Lingo Elements in a Script

You can view and run Lingo scripts to learn how Lingo works. If you want to view or edit a behavior's Lingo script for all sprites and frames to which the behavior is attached, select the behavior in the Cast window, then use the Script Window button on the toolbar or the Cast Member Script button in the Cast window to open the Script window. If you want to view or edit a behavior's Lingo script for an individual sprite or frame, select the individual sprite or frame, open the Behavior Inspector, select the behavior, then use the Script Window button to open the Script window

FIGURE K-4

Lingo elements in a script

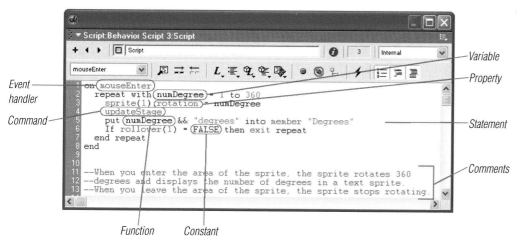

Event handler

Command

Function   Constant

Variable

Property

Statement

Comments

1. Start Director, then open the file Sprite Rotation Example.dir from where your Unit K data files are stored.

2. Minimize the docking channel (Win) or close the grouped panel (Mac) with the Property inspector.

3. Click cast member 3 with the script in the Cast window.

4. Click the Cast Member Script button in the Cast window to open the Script window, as shown in Figure K-4.

5. Read the comments at the bottom of the script in red (scroll down if necessary).

6. Play the movie, then move the pointer over the green arrow on the Stage to activate the event handler (mouseEnter) and run the Lingo commands (change the number of degrees from 1 to 360 and rotate an arrow by the current number of degrees) in the script.

7. Rewind and play the movie, then move the pointer on and off the green arrow to start and stop the script.

8. Close the Script window.

9. Exit Director and don't save changes to the movie.

You viewed Lingo elements in a cast member script.

CREATE AND RUN A SCRIPT

What You'll Do

In this lesson, you will create a script and use the Message window.

Creating a Script

The movie script is one of the four types of scripts you can create in Director. Movie scripts are available during an entire movie, regardless of which sprite or frame the movie is currently playing. Movie scripts are helpful for controlling events that determine when a movie starts, stops, or pauses. To create a movie script, you open the Script window using the Script Window button on the toolbar and compose a script consisting of an event handler and Lingo statements. You don't have to remember all of the Lingo elements; Director provides a list of commands by category and by alphabetical order in pop-up menus. For help with Lingo commands, you can access the Lingo Dictionary from the Help menu. After each line in the Script window, you press

Writing Lingo statements in verbose or dot

When you write a Lingo statement, you can choose between two different styles: verbose and dot. The **verbose** writing style is similar to English, while the **dot** writing style is a more concise, shorter form of verbose. The verbose style is easier to read and understand, which makes it an excellent way to learn to use Lingo. However, the verbose style can become very long and hard to test. The dot style is harder to read and understand, but easier to manage and test. If you are just learning Lingo, it is a good idea to start with the verbose style and then start to use the dot style as you learn more about Lingo. You can use the verbose and dot styles in combination. Almost any Lingo statement can be written in the verbose or dot style. For example, the function for setting the window type can be written in the verbose style as `theMember = the number of the member in sprite1` or in the dot style as `theMember = sprite(1).member`.

[Enter] (Win) or [return] (Mac); after you type end, you press [Enter] (Win) or [return] (Mac) twice. Director will organize the script and indent commands automatically. When you type end, a new script cast member appears in the Cast window. When you create or edit a script, an asterisk appears in the Script window title bar, indicating that the script needs to be recompiled before you can execute it, as shown in Figure K-5. **Recompiling** translates the script written in a high-level programming language into a low-level language. When you recompile all modified scripts, Director automatically checks a script for errors. If any problems exist, a dialog box opens, asking how you want to resolve the error. See the lesson "Debug a Script" later in this unit for details.

Running a Script Using the Message Window

Scripts don't always work the first time you run them. The Message window is a useful tool for executing and testing Lingo commands and scripts within Director. You can use the Message window to execute handlers or to display messages activated by commands. The Message window shows you everything that goes on in the background, from event messages to Lingo commands. The Message window allows you to monitor, or trace, which handlers Director is currently executing. If a script is not working as expected, you can click the Trace button to help you uncover the problem. When a movie is playing, the Trace option posts all script-related activities to the Message window, which also slows down the performance of the movie.

FIGURE K-5
Script before recompiling

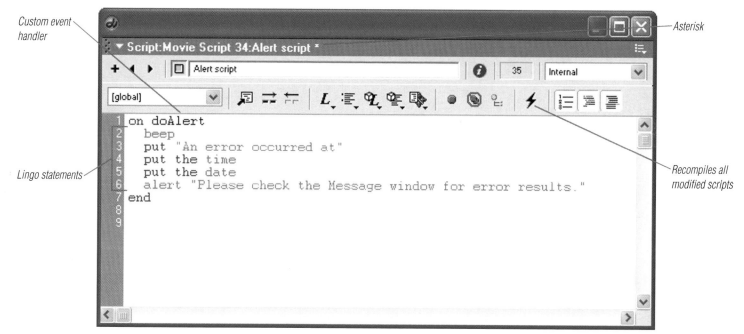

Custom event handler

Lingo statements

Asterisk

Recompiles all modified scripts

Create a movie script

1. Start Director, open the file MD K-1.dir from where your Unit K data files are stored, then save it as **SpaceWorks Online Final**.

2. Click cast member 34 (blank) in the Cast window.

3. Click the Script Window button on the tool-bar to open the Movie Script window. 📞

4. Type the script (include two blank lines at the end by pressing [Enter] (Win) or [return] (Mac)) shown in Figure K-6 with the name **Alert script**.

   Director automatically colors different types of Lingo elements unless you turn off Auto Coloring in the Script Window Preferences dialog box.

   > TIP You can change the default font type, size, and color in the Script window as well as the color of various Lingo elements. To set Script window preferences, click Edit (Win) or Director (Mac), point to Preferences, then click Script.

5. Click the Recompile All Modified Scripts but-ton in the Movie Script window (resize win-dow if necessary) to activate the script. ⚡

6. Expand the docking channel (Win) or open the grouped panel (Mac) with the Property inspector.

7. Click the Script tab in the Property inspector to view that the script type is Movie.

8. Minimize the docking channel (Win) or close the grouped panel (Mac) with the Property inspector.

You created a movie script.

FIGURE K-6
Movie script with a custom handler

Custom handler

Executes a system beep

Recompiles all modified scripts

Displays the text, time, and date in the Message window

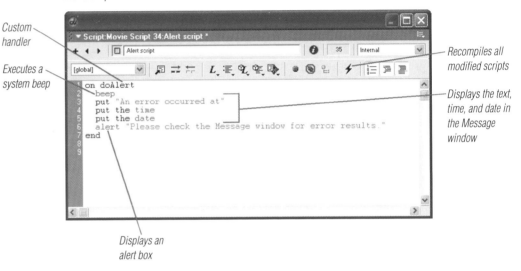

Displays an alert box

FIGURE K-7

Executing Lingo in the Message window

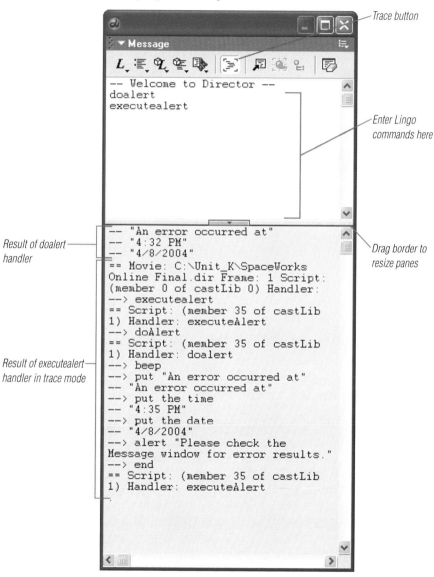

Trace button

Enter Lingo
commands here

Drag border to
resize panes

Result of doalert
handler

Result of executealert
handler in trace mode

Run a script using the Message window

1. Click Window on the menu bar, then click Message to open the Message window with the default message, "Welcome to Director."

2. In the top pane of the Message window, type **doalert**, press [Enter] (Win) or [return] (Mac), then click OK to close the alert box (which you created using a movie script).

   TIP Lingo commands are not case-sensitive. However, most strings in quotation marks are case sensitive.

3. Click at the end of the script (line 9) in the Movie Script window, type **on executeAlert**, then press [Enter] (Win) or [return] (Mac).

4. Type **doalert**, press [Enter] (Win) or [return] (Mac), type **end**, then press [Enter] (Win) or [return] (Mac) twice.

5. Click the Recompile All Modified Scripts button in the Movie Script window. ⚡

6. In the top pane of the Message window, click below the code to display the insertion point (if necessary), then click the Trace button in the Message window to select it. ☰

7. Type **executealert**, press [Enter] (Win) or [return] (Mac), then click OK to close the alert box.

   The Message window appears, as shown in Figure K-7.

8. Close the Message window and the Movie Script window.

9. Save your work.

You executed a movie script in the Message window.

CREATE CAST MEMBER AND FRAME SCRIPTS

What You'll Do

In this lesson, you will create cast member and frame scripts.

Creating Cast Member and Frame Scripts

Cast member scripts are attached to a cast member, not to a behavior. A cast member script is useful when you want an action to occur whenever the cast member appears in the movie. When the cast member is assigned to a sprite, the cast member's script becomes available. A frame script is a behavior and is attached to a frame in the script channel in the Score. Frame scripts are cast members and can be used in any frame.

Finding handlers and text in scripts

When you are working with multiple scripts in a movie, it can be difficult to find the specific handler and text that you want. The Find command is useful for finding a handler or text in scripts and for replacing it with another handler or text, respectively. To find a handler in a script, click Edit on the menu bar, point to Find, click Handler, select the handler that you want to find, then click Find. To find text in a script, open the Script window that you want to search, click Edit on the menu bar, point to Find, click Text, type the text that you want to find in the Find text box, then click Find. To replace text in a script, open the Find Text dialog box, type the text that you want to find in the Find text box, type the text that you want to replace it with in the Replace text box, then click Replace or Replace All.

FIGURE K-8
Cast member script

Event
handler

Erases the
contents of
the cast
member

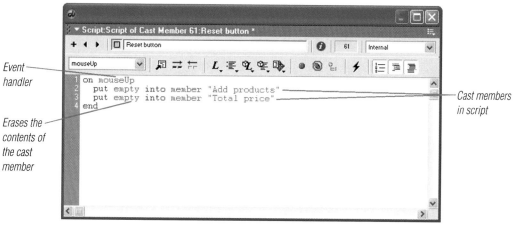

Cast members
in script

FIGURE K-9
Scripts in the Cast window

Drag the Clear
calculation cast
member here

Cast member
script

Frame
script

Create cast member and frame scripts

1. Click frame 25 in the frame channel in the Score to display the Price scene, scroll down the Cast window, then click the Reset button cast member.

2. Click the Cast Member Script button in the Cast window to open the Script window, which displays the start and end statements of the `mouseUp` handler. 🐾

3. Type **put empty into member "Add products"**, press [Enter] (Win) or [return] (Mac), then type **put empty into member "Total price"**, as shown in Figure K-8.

   These commands erase the contents of the Add products and Total price cast members.

4. Close the Script window.

5. Double-click frame 25 in the behavior channel in the Score to open the Script window, displaying the start and end statements of the `exitFrame` handler.

6. Type **put empty into member "Add products"**, press [Enter] (Win) or [return] (Mac), then type **put empty into member "Total price"**.

7. Click the Cast Member Name text box, then type **Clear calculation**.

8. Close the Script window, then drag the Clear calculation cast member (space 17) to space 62 in the Cast window, as shown in Figure K-9.

   When you play the movie and click the Price button sprite, the contents of the Add products and Total price fields will be erased.

9. Save your work.

You created cast member and frame scripts.

USE VARIABLES IN A SCRIPT

What You'll Do

In this lesson, you will use variables in a script.

Using Variables in Scripts

Lingo supports both global and local variables. A global variable can be used by all handlers in a movie. Before you can use a global variable, you need to **declare** it, which lets Director know that the variable is global. To declare a global variable, you use the `global` keyword. For example, you can use the statement `global MyName`, where `global` is a keyword, and `MyName` is the global variable. Local variables exist only within a handler and are no longer available when the handler ends. You don't need to declare a local variable. You can give a local or global variable any name, but avoid Lingo terms and keywords because they create script problems. Before you can use a local or global variable, you need to assign a value to it. To assign a value to a variable, you use the equals operator. For example, in `Temp = 0`, `Temp` is the variable, and `0` is the value. Lingo also comes with a special variable called **me**. The variable me is a keyword that allows you to refer to an object without actually naming it, which comes in handy when you plan to use

the same script many times. An **object** is any part of Lingo scripting that is designed both to receive input and to produce a result. Every event handler is an object.

Look at the details of the script shown in Figure K-10. The first two lines of the script are comments. The next line is the `on mouseDown` handler with a me keyword. The me keyword is needed to define the `spritenum` property, which provides sprite channel numbers for variables. The next few lines of Lingo commands assign values to variables. The next set of commands is called an If-then structure. An **If-then structure** evaluates a statement and then branches to outcomes. If the statement is `TRUE`, the command after `then` is executed. If the statement is `FALSE`, the command after `else` is executed. The Lingo command uses the term `return`, which refers to [Enter] on Windows and [return] on Macintosh. The next set of commands is called a **case statement**, which is used to replace a chain of If-then structures. Lingo compares the case statement with the comparison in the lines below it. If it finds a match, Lingo performs the statement. Each line in the Add products list is associated with a price. The final command puts the product name and the price in the Add products cast member on the same line, separated by a (:) and ($). The operator **&** means to connect, or **concatenate**, the strings that are in quotation marks (""), and **&&** means to connect the strings and add a space between them.

FIGURE K-10

Details of a script with variables

```
1  -- Identifies the line item selected, hilites the line, calls a handler to        ─── Comments
2  -- determine the price, then adds the item and price to the Add products list.
3
4  on mousedown me
5     theMember = the member of sprite me.spritenum                                   ─── Assigning
6     theLine = the mouseline                                                             variables
7     hilite line theLine of member theMember
8     theText = sprite(me.spritenum).member.text
9     theLine = the mouseline
10
11    If the text of member "Add products" = empty then nothing
12    else                                                                            ─── If-then
13       put return after member "Add products"                                           structure
14    end if
15
16    case (theLine)of
17       1: price = 74.99
18       2: price = 14.99
19       3: price = 14.99
20       4: price = 9.75
21       5: price = 175.00                                                            ─── Case statement
22       6: price = 119.50
23       7: price = 5.99
24       8: price = 8.25
25       9: price = 4.50
26    end case
27
28    put line theLine of theText && ":" && "$" & price after member "Add products"
29  end
30
31
```

Concatenate the contents of variables and text

Use variables in a script

1. Click the Product list sprite on the Stage to select it.

2. Click Window on the menu bar, then click Behavior Inspector to display the Behavior Inspector tab in the Code panel.

3. Click the Behavior Popup button in the Behavior Inspector, then click New Behavior to open the Name Behavior dialog box. **+.**

4. Type **Calculation list**, then click OK.

5. Click the Script Window button in the Behavior Inspector to open the Script window for the Calculation list, then type the script shown in Figure K-11.

6. Close the Script window, then minimize the docking channel (Win) or close the grouped panel (Mac) with the Property inspector.

(continued)

FIGURE K-11
Script with variables

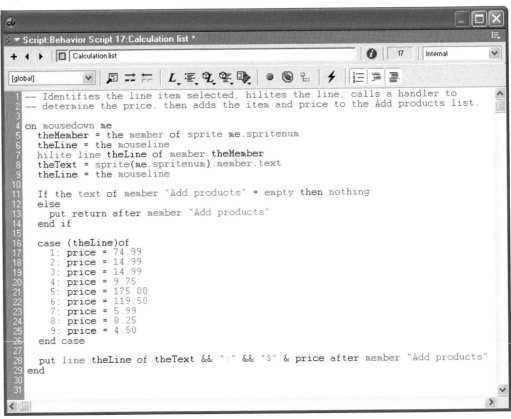

FIGURE K-12
The Stage with script results

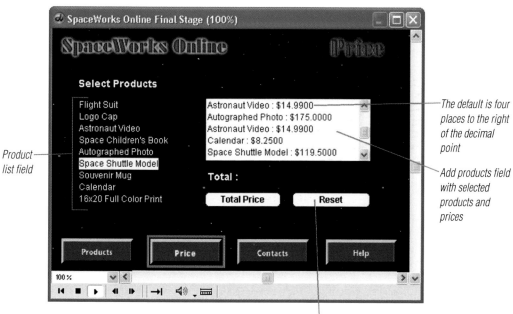

Product list field

The default is four places to the right of the decimal point

Add products field with selected products and prices

Erases the contents of the Add products field

7. Rewind and play the movie, click the Price button on the Stage, then click several items in the Product list on the Stage, as shown in Figure K-12.

8. Click the Reset button on the Stage to erase the contents of the Add products field, then stop the movie. If a script error happens, check the script to make sure it's typed correctly.

9. Drag the Calculation list cast member to space 63 in the Cast window, then save your work.

You used variables in a script.

ADD FUNCTIONS TO A SCRIPT

What You'll Do

In this lesson, you will add a function to a script.

Adding Functions to a Script

A function is a Lingo element that returns a value of a particular state or condition. For example, the `date()` function will display the current date set in the computer, and the function `the number of lines in textParagraph` will display the number of lines in the cast member textParagraph. Parentheses can occur at the end of a function; the function is applied to the variable between the parentheses. Lingo provides a number of functions that can be invoked from any script. You can also design and program custom functions by writing handlers that return values.

Look at the details of the script shown in Figure K-13. The script uses the function the `floatPrecision` to set the number of decimal places to display and set the floating-point numbers (the values below the decimal point). In addition, the script uses the function `the number of`

`lines in` to determine the number of lines with text in the Add products cast member. The script also uses the `repeat with` statement to add the prices for the products. A **repeat with statement** repeats

the commands (between the `repeat with` and `end repeat` statements) a specified number of times. In this case, it determines the number of lines in the Add products cast member.

FIGURE K-13

Details of a script with functions

floatPrecision
function

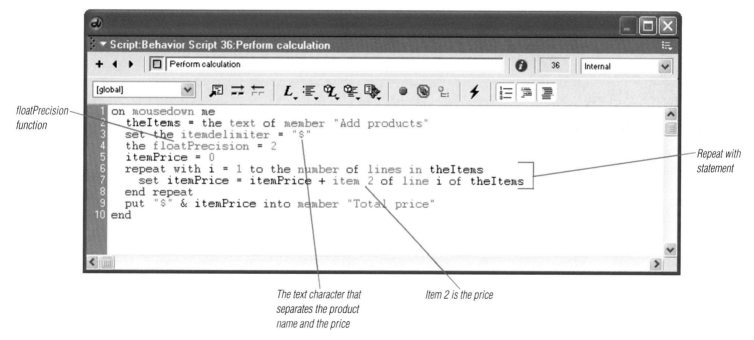

Repeat with
statement

The text character that
separates the product
name and the price

Item 2 is the price

Add functions to a script

1. Click an empty cast member space in the Cast window, then click the Total Price button sprite on the Stage.

2. Click Window on the menu bar, then click Behavior Inspector to display the Behavior Inspector tab in the Code panel if necessary.

3. Click the Behavior Popup button in the Behavior Inspector, then click New Behavior to open the Name Behavior dialog box. **+.**

4. Type **Perform calculation**, then click OK.

5. Click the Script Window button in the Behavior Inspector to open the Script window for the Total Price button sprite, then type the script shown in Figure K-14.

   The script determines the number of lines with text in the Add products field, and adds up the total price of the products in the Total price field.

(continued)

FIGURE K-14

Script to perform a calculation

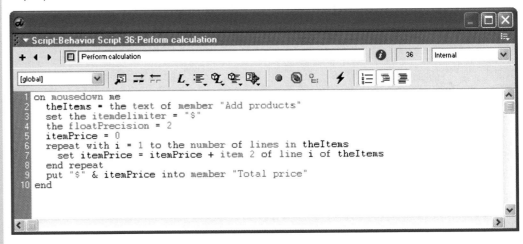

```
on mousedown me
  theItems = the text of member "Add products"
  set the itemdelimiter = "$"
  the floatPrecision = 2
  itemPrice = 0
  repeat with i = 1 to the number of lines in theItems
    set itemPrice = itemPrice + item 2 of line i of theItems
  end repeat
  put "$" & itemPrice into member "Total price"
end
```

Result of calculation with 2 decimal points

Adds the contents of the Add products field

6. Close the Script window, then minimize the docking channel (Win) or close the grouped panel (Mac) with the Property inspector.

   TIP When you close the Script window, Director checks for any problems with the Lingo instructions. If it encounters a problem, an alert box appears with troubleshooting options.

7. Rewind and play the movie, click the Price button on the Stage, click several items in the Product list on the Stage, then click the Total Price button on the Stage, as shown in Figure K-15.

8. Click the Reset button on the Stage, then stop the movie.

9. Drag the Perform calculation cast member to space 64 in the Cast window, then save your work.

You added a function to a script.

USE THE DEBUGGER WINDOW

What You'll Do

In this lesson, you will follow a script in the Debugger window.

Debugging a Script

When Director encounters a problem executing part of a script, an alert box appears and tells you what went wrong with the script. The alert box allows you to click a button to debug the script, open the script, or ignore the problem. The Debugger window helps you use basic troubleshooting techniques to quickly find and fix Lingo code that isn't doing what you want. Using the Debugger window, you can trace a script as it's being executed and locate errors as it progresses line by line or handler by handler. You can cause the Debugger window to open by setting breakpoints in a script. A **breakpoint** is a location in a script where you want Director to stop executing Lingo commands, so you can look at the status of variables in the script. You cannot set a breakpoint in lines beginning with keywords, such as `on` and `global`.

The Debugger window consists of three panes: Handler History, Variable, and Script. The Handler History pane shows the current handler and any handlers from which it may have been called. The Variable pane shows variables and property settings in the current handler as they existed when the breakpoint or problem occurred. The Script pane shows the current handler, including the line of Lingo where the breakpoint or problem occurred. The Debugger window also includes buttons, such as Step Script, Step Into Script, Run Script, Stop Debugging, Watch Expression, and Go to Handler, to help you diagnose script problems. For example, each time you click the Step Script button, Director executes the next line of the script, which is identified by a green arrow.

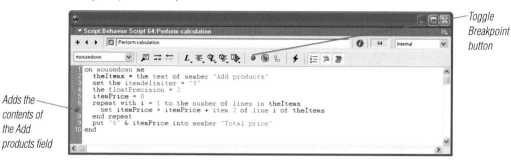

Toggle Breakpoint button

Adds the contents of the Add products field

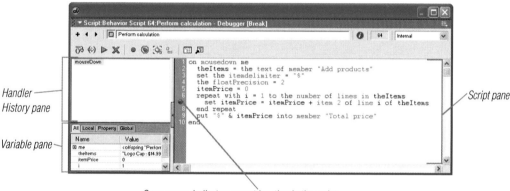

Handler History pane

Variable pane

Script pane

Green arrow indicates current location in the script

Making troubleshooting easier

You can make troubleshooting easier by following some basic guidelines for writing Lingo code. The more comments you add to a script, the easier it will be later to decipher what the Lingo code is doing. If you use meaningful variable names that reflect their function, you will make it easier to understand Lingo code. Additionally, if you make one change at a time, you can isolate problems while avoiding new ones. You should also make a backup copy of a movie before you make significant changes to try to fix a problem.

Follow a script in the Debugger window

1. Click the Perform calculation cast member in the Cast window (if necessary), then click the Cast Member Script button in the Cast window.

2. Click the beginning of the command `set itemPrice = itemPrice + item 2 of line i of theItems` in the script.

3. Click the Toggle Breakpoint button in the Script window, as shown in Figure K-16.

   TIP If a gray circle appears instead of a red one, the Ignore Breakpoints button is turned on in the Debugger window. Click the button to turn it off.

4. Resize the Behavior Script window so that you can see the Stage, rewind and play the movie, then click the Price button on the Stage.

5. Click several items (more than three) in the Product list on the Stage, then click the Total Price button on the Stage, which triggers the breakpoint you set in Step 3 and opens the Debugger window, as shown in Figure K-17.

6. Click the Step Script button two times to execute two commands, indicated by the green arrow.

7. Click the red dot breakpoint in the Script window to remove the breakpoint.

   TIP You can click the blue area to the left of a line in the Script window to set a breakpoint.

8. Click the Stop Debugging button, then close the Script window.

9. Save your work.

You followed a script in the Debugger window.

OPEN A MOVIE IN A WINDOW

What You'll Do

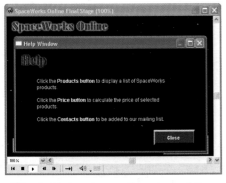

In this lesson, you will open a movie in a window.

Opening a Movie in a Window

You can use a **Movie in a Window (MIAW)** script to open and play one or more movies in a separate window while the main movie plays on the Stage. An MIAW is useful when you want to provide additional material in a movie, such as Help information, without having to incorporate it permanently in the main movie. The main movie and the MIAW can also communicate with each other to create interactive features, such as a status window. Shockwave does not support MIAWs, so only use MIAWs in movies that you intend to package as projectors. The easiest way to create an MIAW is to use the **open window** command, but if you want more control over the appearance of the window, you need to add Lingo commands to set specific window properties. The Lingo Dictionary (accessed from the Help menu) includes a complete list of Lingo commands for MIAWs.

Look at the details of the MIAW script shown in Figure K-18. The first line is the **on mouseUp** handler. The third line creates a global variable called **newWindow**. This will be used to create the MIAW. Next, the variable **newWindow** is assigned to equal **window "Help Window"**, which is the name on the title bar of the MIAW window. The next four lines add properties to the window: assign the name of the window to the movie filename to be opened, specify the movie filename (Online Help.dir) and path location (not specified, which means that the file needs to be located in the same folder as the main movie file), select a window type (see the comment section in Figure K-18 for a list of common MIAW window types), turn on the modal type to prevent interaction with other elements while the window is open, and set the size of the window. The final command is to open the movie in a window.

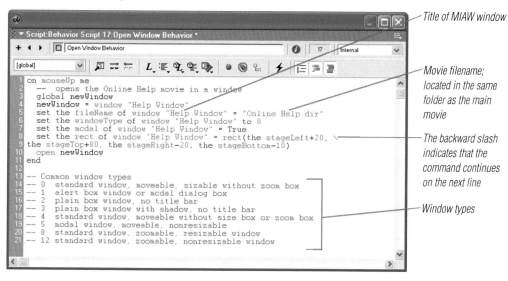

Title of MIAW window

Movie filename; located in the same folder as the main movie

The backward slash indicates that the command continues on the next line

Window types

FIGURE K-19
Movie in a window

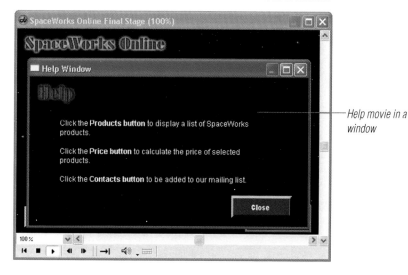

Help movie in a window

Open a movie in a window

1. Click the Help button sprite on the Stage to select it.

2. Click Window on the menu bar, then click Behavior Inspector to display the Behavior Inspector tab in the Code panel if necessary.

3. Click the Behavior Popup button in the Behavior Inspector, then click New Behavior to open the Name Behavior dialog box. **+.**

4. Type **Open Window Behavior**, then click OK.

5. Click the Script Window button in the Behavior Inspector to open the Script window for the Help button sprite, type the MIAW script (except the comments at the end) shown in Figure K-18 (resize the window as necessary), then press [Enter] (Win) or [return] (Mac) twice at the end.

   TIP The continuation symbol (\) continues a long command on two lines. To create a (\), press [Alt] [Enter] (Win) or [option] [return] (Mac).

6. Close the Script window, then minimize the docking channel (Win) or close the grouped panel (Mac) with the Property inspector.

7. Rewind and play the movie, then click the Help button on the Stage to open the Help movie in a window, as shown in Figure K-19.

8. Click the Close button on the Stage to close the Help window.

9. Save your work, then exit Director.

You opened a movie in a window.

Understand scripts.

1. List and describe the four types of scripts.
2. Describe how to create each type of script.

Understand handlers, messages, and events.

1. List and describe the most commonly used types of events.
2. Describe the structure of a handler.

Examine Lingo elements.

1. Start Director, then open the file Parent Scripts.dir from where your Unit K data files are stored.
2. Open the Script window for cast member 3 (the parent script).
3. Read the script comments in red and identify several Lingo elements in the script.
4. Close the Script window.
5. Play the movie, click the plant a flower button two times, then click a flower several times (each instance of a flower is a child object).
6. Exit Director and don't save changes to the movie.

Create and run a script.

1. Start Director, open the file MD K-2.dir from where your Unit K data files are stored, then save it as **Nova Final**.
2. Open the Movie script window.
3. Type a script with the handler on doAccept to sound a beep, display the alert **Congratulations! Your loan has been accepted!**, then end.

4. Type a script with the handler `doDecline` to sound a beep, display the alert **I'm sorry, but your loan has been declined.**, then end.
5. Recompile all modified scripts, then open the Message window.
6. Test the `doAccept` handler and the `doDecline` handler in the Message window, then close the windows.

Create cast member and frame scripts.

1. Select the Reset button in the Cast window.
2. Create a cast member script like the one shown in Figure K-8 and close the Script window.
3. Double-click frame 25 in the behavior channel, type lines 2 and 3 from the script shown in Figure K-8, then name it **Clear calculation**.
4. Close the Script window, then move the Clear calculation cast member to space 56 in the Cast window.

Use variables in a script.

1. Click the Product list sprite on the Stage, then open the Behavior Inspector.
2. Create a new behavior named **Calculation list**, then open the Script window.
3. Type a script like the one shown in Figure K-11, but change the prices, then close the Script window and Behavior Inspector.
4. Move the Calculation list cast member to space 57 in the Cast window.
5. Rewind and play the movie, then click the Calculator button on the Stage.

6. Click several items in the Product list, click the Reset button, then stop the movie.

Add functions to a script.

1. Click the Total Price button sprite on the Stage, then open the Behavior Inspector.
2. Create a new behavior named **Perform calculation**, then open the Script window.
3. Type a script like the one in Figure K-14, but delete the `floatPrecision` statement and change `item 2 of line i of theItems` to `integer(item 2 of line i of theItems)` (which takes out the decimal places in the price and total), then close the Script window and Behavior Inspector.
4. Move the Perform calculation cast member to space 58 in the Cast window.
5. Rewind and play the movie, then click the Calculator button on the Stage.
6. Click several items in the Product list, click the Total Price button, then stop the movie.

Use the Debugger window.

1. Open the script for the Perform calculation cast member.
2. Set a breakpoint for the `set itemPrice = itemPrice + integer(item 2 of line i of theItems)` command.
3. Rewind and play the movie, then click the Calculator button on the Stage.
4. Click several items in the Product list on the Stage, then click the Total Price button on the Stage.

5. Step through the script.

6. Remove the breakpoint, close the window, then stop the movie.

Open a movie in a window.

1. Create a script for the Guide button to open the Loan Guide movie in a window. (*Hint*: the Loan Guide movie needs to be located in the same folder as the main movie that opens it.)

2. Type an MIAW script similar to the one shown in Figure K-18 without setting the rest of the window and adding the comments at the end.

3. Rewind and play the movie.

4. Click the Guide button to open the MIAW, then drag the MIAW window down to the bottom of the screen (drag the title bar).

5. Compare your screen to Figure K-20, then click the Return button to close the window.

6. Stop and save the movie, then exit Director.

FIGURE K-20
Completed Skills Review

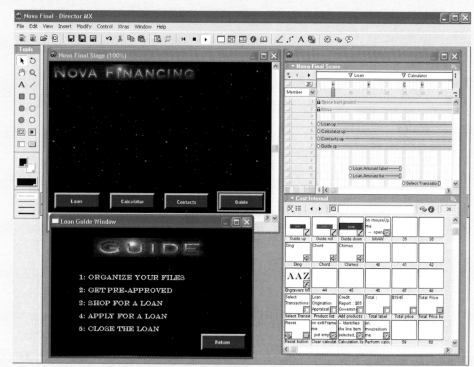

You are an instructor at Silicon Valley College. You are preparing course materials to teach a class on Macromedia Director. You want to develop a class presentation that outlines the basic concepts of Lingo. You use Director to create a movie presentation (like a slide show) that covers Lingo scripts, handlers, messages, and events. Include a description or animation of the handler hierarchy flowchart.

1. Start Director and save the movie as **Lingo Class**.
2. Create a text cast member with the text **Director Lingo Class** and drag it to the top of the Stage; drag the sprite across the entire presentation.
3. Create a text cast member with text describing Lingo handlers, and drag it to the center of the Stage (frames 1 to 30).
4. Create a text cast member with text describing Lingo messages, and drag it to the center of the Stage (frames 31 to 60).
5. Create a text cast member with text describing Lingo events, and drag it to the center of the Stage (frames 61 to 90).
6. Create an animated flowchart summarizing the one in Figure K-3, and add it to the Stage as the last scene.
7. Play the movie, then compare your screen to Figure K-21.
8. Save the movie, then exit Director.

FIGURE K-21
Completed Project Builder 1

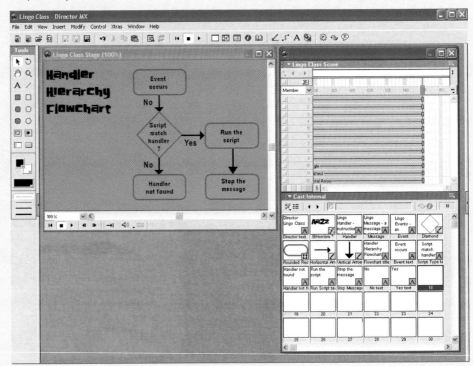

You are a new developer for Casino Games, a small computer game company. You are prototyping a new casino game in Director. You are still learning Lingo, but you want to use the scripting language to become more familiar with its internal workings. To get started, you want to create alerts for the winner and loser of the game. You use Director to create a script to display an alert box and a beep for the winner and the loser, and use the Messenger window to test the script.

1. Start Director and save the movie as **Casino Game**.
2. Create a text cast member with the text **casino game prototype** and drag it to the top of the Stage.
3. Open the Movie Script window.
4. Type a script with the handler on doWinner to sound a beep, display the alert **You have won!**, then end.
5. Type a script with the handler on doLoser to sound a beep, display the alert **You have lost!**, then end.
6. Recompile all modified scripts, then open the Message window.
7. Test the doWinner handler in the Message window.
8. Test the doLoser handler in the Message window, then test it again with the Trace on.
9. Compare your screen to Figure K-22.
10. Close the windows, save the movie, then exit Director.

FIGURE K-22
Completed Project Builder 2

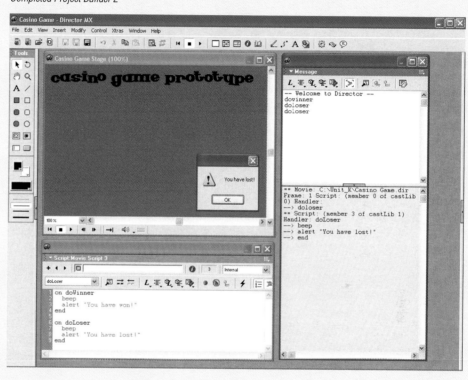

You are the software designer for Sports Genesis, a sports game development company. Sports Genesis is in final production for an upcoming sports trivia game called Score!. You want to create a separate Director movie with information about the software, so you can manage it separately from the sports game. You use Director to create a movie with "about" information and a Close button, then create another movie with an About button to test the process of opening a movie in a window.

1. Start Director and save the movie as **About**.
2. Create a text cast member with the text **Sports Genesis Score!** and drag it to the top of the Stage.
3. Create a text cast member with information about the software (include software name, version, company name, registered user, and product identification number), and drag it on the Stage.
4. Animate the text cast member with the "about" information so that it appears from the bottom of the Stage and moves up under the Sports Genesis Score! text like rolling credits in a movie.
5. In the Paint window, create a button cast member with the text **Close**, add the cast member to the Stage, then attach a script to the Close button on the Stage that returns to the previous movie.
6. Save the movie.
7. Create a new movie and save it as **Sports Trivia Game**.
8. Create a text cast member with the text **Sports Genesis presents** and drag it to the top of the Stage.
9. Create a text cast member with the text **Score!** and drag it below the title on the Stage. You can also add additional text and graphics to individualize your design.
10. In the Paint window, create a button cast member with the text **About**, add the cast member to the Stage, then attach a script to the About button on the Stage that opens the About movie in a window.
11. Set the MIAW to open as a modal window with the title **About Sports Genesis Score!**, and adjust the size of the window to display the About movie properly.
12. Save and play the movie.
13. Click the About button, drag the MIAW down to view the Stage, then compare your screen to Figure K-23.
14. Click the Close button on the Stage, stop the movie, then exit Director.
15. Put a copy of this movie in your portfolio.

FIGURE K-23
Completed Design Project

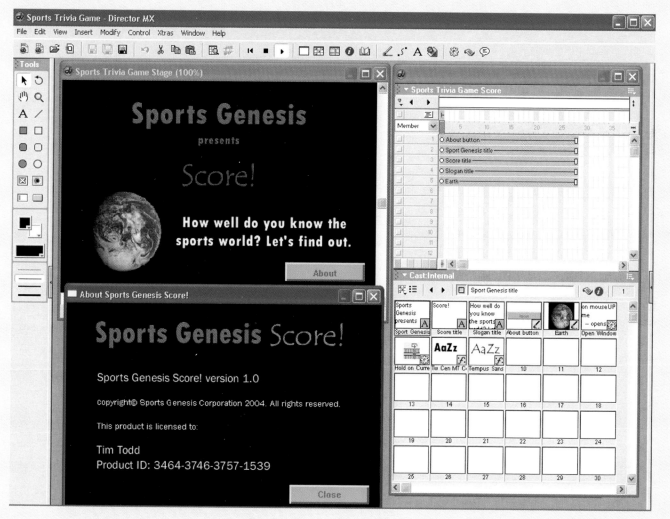

Your group can assign elements of the project to individual members, or work collectively to create the finished product.

You are a new member of the Quality Assurance team at Script It!, a multimedia development company that creates custom applications with Macromedia Director. A developer at the company is working on a new application, which contains custom scripts. In preparation for a new testing project, your boss asks you to carefully review Lingo elements. You are new to testing Lingo scripts, so you practice testing scripts with targeted examples from the Macromedia Director Support Center. You use Director's Debugger window to set breakpoints in the scripts and then test them.

1. Assign each member of the group to debug a script from a sample program from the Macromedia Director Support Center, then write down your results. Choose from the following sample movies: Global variables, Global Pass, MIAW, Debugging, If statements, and Case statements.
2. Start Director, then choose Director Support Center on the Help menu.
3. On the Macromedia Director Support Center Web site, access the Director Examples link and the Sample Source Files link, click a link to a sample movie, read the TechNote about the topic, download the sample movie file, then close your browser.
4. Decompress the file using WinZip (Win) or Stuffit (Mac). See your instructor for instructions or an uncompressed file.
5. Open the movie file, then save it with a new title.
6. Play the movie and test its functionality.
7. Open some of the scripts and set some breakpoints to discover how the scripts work.
8. Play the movie and document your results.
9. Compare your screen to Figure K-24; your file and results may differ.
10. Close the Debugger and Script windows.
11. Save the movie, then exit Director.

FIGURE K-24

Completed Group Project

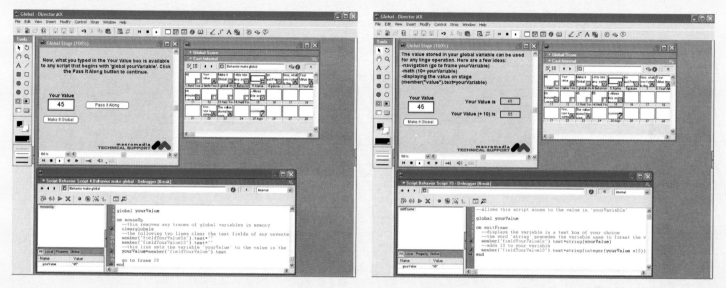

PREPARING AND DELIVERING MOVIES

1. Embed fonts in movies.

2. Manage Xtras for distributing movies.

3. Set movie playback options.

4. Set projector options.

5. Create and launch a projector movie.

6. Create a protected movie.

Understanding Distribution Methods

After you create and fine-tune a movie, you are ready to prepare and deliver it. As you prepare to deliver the movie, you might need to include, or **embed**, unique fonts that are not common on most computers, and package Xtras with the movie so that the movie runs properly on a playback computer. Director provides several different formats to save a movie for distribution to users. You can save your Director movie as a projector movie, a Shockwave movie, a Shockwave projector movie, or a protected movie. You can also distribute a movie in the Director movie format, but this format is not recommended because users can alter the movie using Director. Before you save a movie in any of the distribution formats, it's important to understand how Director plays movies in each of the formats.

A **projector movie** is a stand-alone program that users can play on their computers without having Director installed. A projector movie includes a self-contained movie player known as the **standard player** that plays the Director movie. A projector

movie is intended for play in a window or on a full screen without a browser.

A **Shockwave movie** is a compressed movie that does not include the standard player. A Shockwave movie is intended for play over the Internet in a browser. Users must have the Shockwave player installed on their computers to play the movie. You can download the Shockwave player for free from the Macromedia Web site at *www.macromedia.com*.

A **Shockwave projector movie** is another compressed movie that users can play on their computers without a browser. Shockwave projector movies also use the Shockwave player instead of the standard player, and are much smaller versions of an equivalent projector movie.

A **protected movie** is an uncompressed Director movie that users cannot open and modify in Director. Protected movies do not include any player software to play the movie. They can be played only by a projector, as a movie in a window (MIAW), as a Lingo operation, or by using the Shockwave player.

Tools You'll Use

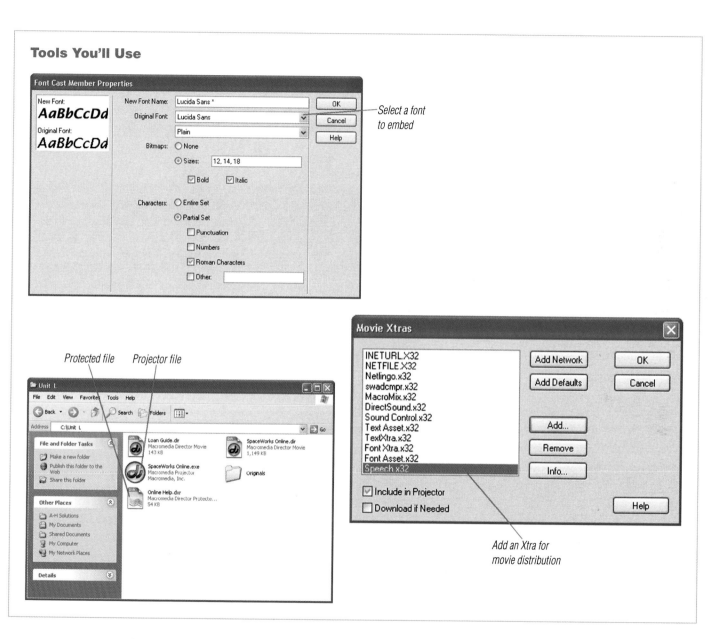

Select a font to embed

Protected file   Projector file

Add an Xtra for movie distribution

EMBED FONTS IN MOVIES

What You'll Do

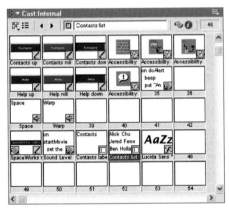

In this lesson, you will embed a font in a movie.

Understanding Fonts

Everything you type appears in a **font**, a particular typeface design and size for letters, numbers, and other characters. Usually, each typeface, such as Times New Roman, is made available in four variations: normal, bold, italic, and bold italic. There are two basic types of fonts: scalable and bitmapped. A **scalable font** (also known as outline font) is based on a mathematical equation that creates character outlines to form letters and numbers at any size. The two major scalable fonts are Adobe's Type 1 PostScript and Apple/Microsoft's TrueType or OpenType. Scalable fonts are generated in any point size on the fly and require only four variations for each typeface. A **bitmapped font** consists of a set of dot patterns for each letter and number in a typeface for a specified type size. Bitmapped fonts are created or prepackaged ahead of time and require four variations for each point size used in each typeface. Although a bitmapped font designed for a particular font size will always look the best, scalable fonts eliminate storing hundreds of different sizes of fonts on disk.

Embedding Fonts in Movies

If you use a font in your movie that is not installed on a playback computer, Director will use a substitute font for the playback computer. To avoid this, you can embed fonts in a Director movie so that the font will be displayed properly even if it is not installed on the playback computer. You use the Font Cast Member Properties dialog box to select the font you want to embed. You can only embed fonts that are already installed on the development computer. (If you embed all the characters in a bitmapped font into the movie, you increase the size of the file. To speed up movie downloading and keep file size small, you can specify a subset of bitmap characters to be embedded.) When you embed a font in a movie, Director stores the font information as a cast member. Embedded fonts work on both Windows and Macintosh computers. After you embed a font in a movie, the font appears on all of the movie's font menus, and you can use it as you would any other font; use the embedded font name with the asterisk. Director compresses embedded fonts, so they usually only add 14 to 25K to a file.

FIGURE L-1
Font Cast Member Properties dialog box

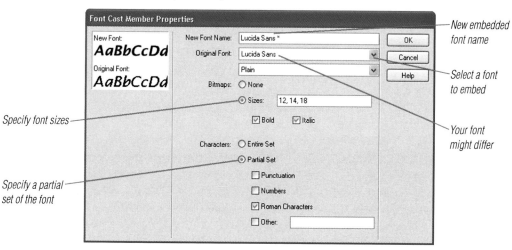

Specify font sizes ——

Specify a partial
set of the font ——

New embedded
font name

Select a font
to embed

Your font
might differ

FIGURE L-2
Embedded font in the Cast window

Embedded font
cast member; your
font might differ

Embed a font in a movie

1. Start Director, open the file MD L-1.dir from where your Unit L data files are stored, then save it as **SpaceWorks Online**.

2. Minimize the docking channel (Win) or close the grouped panel (Mac) with the Property inspector.

3. Click Insert on the menu bar, point to Media Element, then click Font to open the Font Cast Member Properties dialog box.

4. Click the Original Font list arrow, then click an available font.

5. Click the Sizes option button, click the text box to the right, then type **12, 14, 18** to specify the font sizes you want to include with the movie.

6. Select the Bold check box, select the Italic check box, click the Partial Set option button, then select the Roman Characters check box, as shown in Figure L-1, to specify the font style and character set you want to include with the movie.

   TIP To include specific bitmap characters in a movie, select the Other check box, then type the characters (a, b, d, s, t, and so on) in the text box to the right.

7. Click OK to display the font cast member in the Cast window, as shown in Figure L-2.

8. Scroll down the Cast window, double-click the Contacts list cast member, then select all the text in the Text window if necessary.

9. Click the Font list arrow, click the font you selected in Step 4, close the Text window, then save your work.

You embedded a font in a movie.

MANAGE XTRAS FOR DISTRIBUTING MOVIES

What You'll Do

In this lesson, you will add an Xtra to a movie for distribution.

Managing Xtras for Distributing Movies

Many important features in Director are controlled by Xtras, such as creating text and vector shapes, importing different media types, or adding third-party transition effects. If your movie uses an Xtra that is not installed on the playback computer, the movie will not run properly. To fix this problem, when you distribute a projector movie, you need to either package the Xtra with the movie file or give the user the choice to download it. You can use the Movie Xtras dialog box, which includes a list of the most commonly used Xtras, to specify the Xtras you want to include and the ones you want the user to download. (If you see an Xtra listed in the Movie Xtras dialog box that you are not using, it is a good idea to remove it from the movie to reduce the file size and increase the speed of the movie.)

QUICKTIP

If you don't want to package Xtras with a movie, you need to create an Xtras folder in the folder with the projector movie file, copy the Xtras to the folder, select the Xtras in the Movie Xtras dialog box, and then deselect the Include in Projector check box.

FIGURE L-3
Movie Xtras dialog box

Add an Xtra to a movie

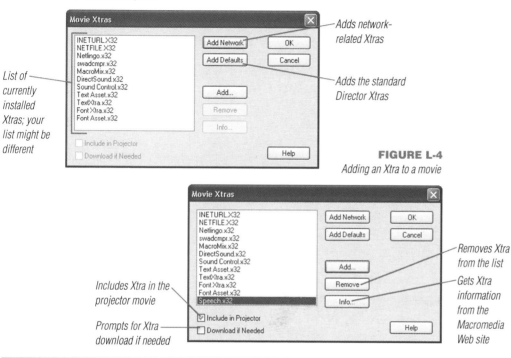

List of currently installed Xtras; your list might be different

Adds network-related Xtras

Adds the standard Director Xtras

FIGURE L-4
Adding an Xtra to a movie

Includes Xtra in the projector movie

Prompts for Xtra download if needed

Removes Xtra from the list

Gets Xtra information from the Macromedia Web site

1. Click Modify on the menu bar, point to Movie, then click Xtras to open the Movie Xtras dialog box, as shown in Figure L-3.

   TIP To add the Xtras required to connect a projector to the Internet, click Add Network.

2. Click Add to open the Add Xtras dialog box, which displays a list of all used Xtras.

3. Scroll (if necessary), click Speech.x32 (Win) or Speech (Mac), then click OK to add the Speech Xtra to the list.

   TIP To restore the default list of Xtras in the Movie Xtras dialog box, click Add Defaults.

4. Scroll to the bottom of the list (if necessary), then click Speech.x32 (Win) or Speech (Mac) to activate the check boxes at the bottom of the dialog box.

5. Verify that the Include in Projector check box is selected (as shown in Figure L-4), which indicates that the Xtra is included when Director creates a projector file.

6. If you have access to the Internet, click Info to open the Macromedia Web site in your browser, then read the information about the Xtra.

7. Close your browser.

   TIP If you delete all Xtras, the default Xtras will be automatically reinserted into your movie.

8. Click OK to close the Movie Xtras dialog box.

9. Save your work.

You added an Xtra to a movie for distribution.

Working with third-party Xtras

You can use six types of Xtras in Director: image filter, importing, transition, cast member, Lingo or scripting, and tool, all of which are external authoring aids. Director comes with a set of third-party Xtras on the Director installation CD-ROM. You can incorporate these and many other Xtras, which you can find on the Macromedia Web site (*www.macromedia.com*), into your movies. To use these Xtras, you need to install them first. To install an Xtra, find the Xtras folder in the Director program folder, place the new Xtra in the Xtras folder, then restart Director. In some cases, you might need to use an installer; check the Xtra documentation. You can access Xtras in Director in different places. The transition Xtras appear in the Frame Properties: Transition dialog box, the cast member Xtras appear in the Cast window, and other Xtras appear as menu commands on the Xtras menu or the Media Element submenu on the Insert menu.

SET MOVIE PLAYBACK OPTIONS

What You'll Do

In this lesson, you will set movie playback options.

Setting Movie Playback Options

You can use the Movie Playback Properties dialog box to set general and streaming playback options for a movie. In the General section of the Movie Playback Properties dialog box, you can select options to lock the movie to its current tempo settings and make the movie pause when its window is inactive. In the Streaming section, you can set the movie to stream using the Play While Downloading Movie check box, and then specify the number of frames downloaded before the movie begins to play. If you have an introductory scene that plays while other media are downloading, you need to set an appropriate download value that will allow for all the required media to be loaded during the introductory scene before the movie begins to play. When you create a movie to stream, you need to make sure all cast members have been downloaded by the time the movie needs them; otherwise, one or more cast members will not appear in the frame. If the Play While Downloading Movie check box is deselected, Director downloads all cast members before the movie starts to play. You can provide placeholders (a rectangle with diagonal lines) for media elements that have not downloaded yet to let users know where media elements will appear in a movie. The options set in the Movie Playback Properties dialog box take effect when you create a projector or Shockwave movie, or preview the movie in a browser.

FIGURE L-5
Movie Playback Properties dialog box

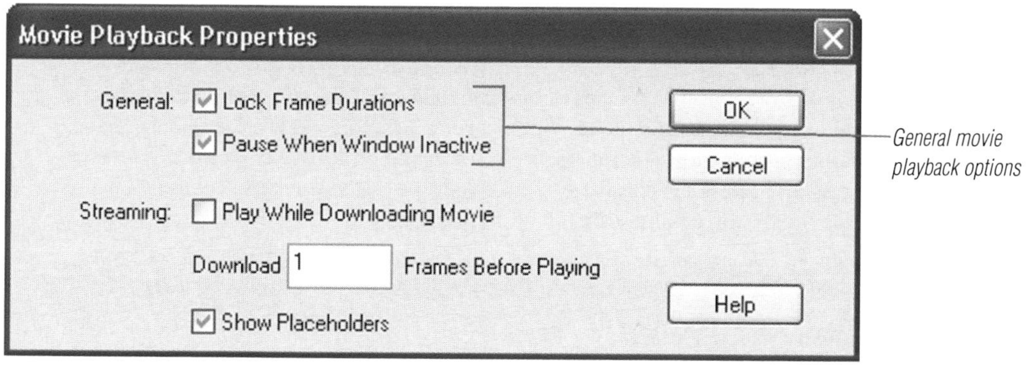

Movie Playback Properties ☒

General: ☑ Lock Frame Durations   [OK]

        ☑ Pause When Window Inactive   [Cancel] — *General movie playback options*

Streaming: ☐ Play While Downloading Movie

        Download [1] Frames Before Playing

        ☑ Show Placeholders   [Help]

Set movie playback options

1. Click Modify on the menu bar, point to Movie, then click Playback to open the Movie Playback Properties dialog box.

2. Select the Lock Frame Durations check box to keep the tempo of the movie steady.

3. Select the Pause When Window Inactive check box to make the movie pause when its window is deactivated.

4. Deselect the Play While Downloading Movie check box to turn off streaming.

5. Select the Show Placeholders check box, as shown in Figure L-5, to display placeholders for media elements that don't completely download before the movie starts playing.

6. Click OK.

7. Save your work.

You set movie playback options.

SET PROJECTOR OPTIONS

What You'll Do

In this lesson, you will set projector options.

Setting Projector Options

Before you create a projector movie, it's important to set the options that will affect the Director movie. Some of the options are specific to the computer on which you create the projector. You can set projector options to play back one or more movies in the foreground or the background, determine which stage settings to use, compress the projector file, and select the player to use. On the Macintosh, you can indicate which target computer, MacOS X or Classic MacOS, you want to run the projector See Table L-1 for a description of the player options. Director retains the option settings after you define them, so you don't have to set them each time. You can include only Director 8 or later movies in projectors. You can use the Update Movies command on the Xtras menu to convert older movies to the latest version of Director.

TABLE L-1: Player Options in the Projector Options Dialog Box

player option	description
Standard	Includes the uncompressed player in the projector file. This option starts the movie faster than other options but creates the largest projector file.
Compressed	Includes a compressed version of the standard player in the projector file. The compressed version significantly reduces the projector file size, but decompressing the player adds a few seconds to the startup time of a movie.
Shockwave	Makes the projector use the Shockwave player installed on the user's computer instead of including the standard player in the projector file. If the Shockwave player is not available when the movie plays, the movie prompts the user to download it.

FIGURE L-6

Projector Options dialog box

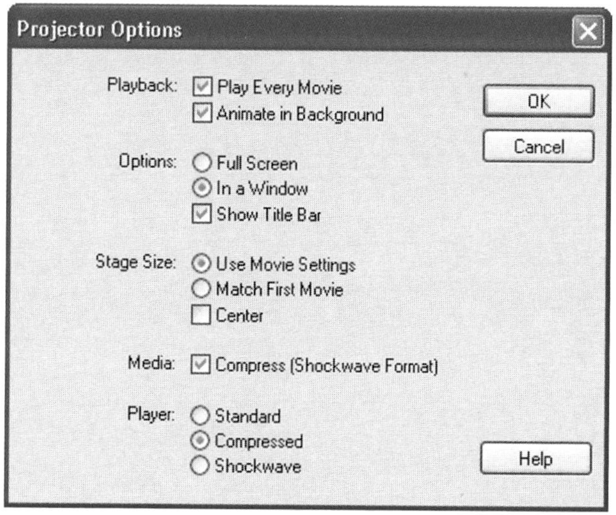

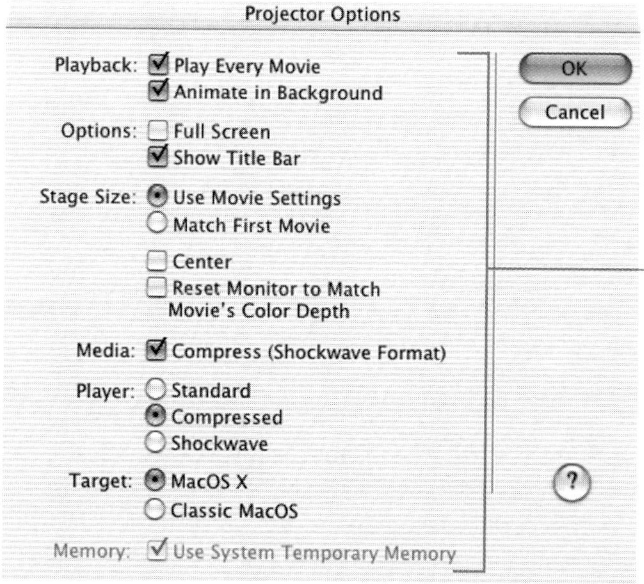

Macintosh projector options

Set projector options

1. Click File on the menu bar, then click Create Projector to open the Create Projector dialog box.

2. Click Options to open the Projector Options dialog box.

   TIP If you want to include more than one movie in the projector, select the Play Every Movie check box.

3. In the Playback section, select the Play Every Movie check box, then select the Animate in Background check box, which plays the movie even when the user switches to another program.

4. In the Options section, click the In a Window option button (Win), then select the Show Title Bar check box if necessary.

   TIP To switch the color depth of your monitor to the color depth of each movie in the projector play list automatically, select the Reset Monitor to Match Movie's Color Depth check box (Mac).

5. In the Media section, select the Compress (Shockwave Format) check box to compress the movie in the Shockwave format, which reduces the projector file size.

   TIP This option does not create a Shockwave movie; it only uses Shockwave technology to compress the projector movie.

6. In the Player section, click the Compressed option button, as shown in Figure L-6.

7. Click OK, then click Cancel.

   The projector options are set, even though you didn't create a projector movie. These settings remain in effect until you change them.

You set projector options.

CREATE AND LAUNCH A PROJECTOR MOVIE

What You'll Do

In this lesson, you will create and launch a projector movie.

Creating a Projector Movie

A projector is a stand-alone play-only version of your movie. You can include as many movies as you want in a projector. When you create a projector, Director embeds all files (such as internal and external casts and Xtras), except linked media, and the standard player into a single program file. The standard player (either uncompressed or compressed) is a self-contained Director movie player that the projector uses to play the Director movie. If you are creating a project with many Director movies that are called by Lingo scripts, such as MIAW, it is not a good idea to package all the movies into one projector because the projector file will become very large and require a lot of RAM. Instead, you should create a projector from the main movie and protect the

Distributing a movie on a disk, to a local network, or to the Internet

When you distribute a movie on a disk, local network, or the Internet, all linked media, such as bitmaps, sounds, and videos, need to be in the same relative folder location as they were when you created the movie. To make sure you don't forget any linked media, it is a good idea to place linked files in the same folder as the projector or in a folder inside the projector folder. If you plan to place a movie on the Internet for playback in a browser, the linked media need to be at the specified URL when the movie plays. If you plan to link media on a local disk only to a Shockwave movie, you need to place the media in a folder named dswmedia. To test movies in a browser, place the movie, linked casts, and linked media in folders within a dswmedia folder, and use relative links instead to refer to them. If you plan to place a movie on a local network, all files must be set to read-only, so that other users cannot change the movie file, and users must have read/write access to their system folder, so that the movie player can access system files.

other movies. If you have linked media, you need to place the files in the same folder as the projector to make sure the movie plays properly. If the linked media is not in the same folder, you need to include Lingo to link the main movie to the other external movies. You can use the Save and Compact command on the File menu to compress and optimize the movie, which creates a faster projector file. After you create a projector movie, you can modify it only by changing the original movie in Director, and then creating a new projector file.

To create a projector for Windows or Macintosh, you need to use Director for Windows or Macintosh, respectively. In other words, you cannot create a projector for Windows using Director for Macintosh, or vice versa. If you want to create a cross-platform movie using either Director for Windows or Director for Macintosh, you must create a Shockwave movie so that users can play the movie created in either platform in their browser.

Launching the Movie in a Projector

After you create a projector movie, the Director file appears in the location where you save it with a distinctive icon. Unless you linked files to the projector, everything the movie needs to play is included in the stand-alone program. As long as the playback computers meet the minimum hardware requirements, the computers can play the projector movie. If you include the standard player in the projector movie, users don't need to install Director or any other player. For the Shockwave projector, the playback computer needs to install the Shockwave player to launch the movie.

Testing a Movie

Before you release your movie, it's important to test the final product on a variety of computer systems to make sure it plays properly in different conditions. During the testing process, make sure that all linked media and fonts appear correctly on the screen, and that the movie plays properly on all computers (such as Windows 95, 98, NT 2000, Me, XP, or later and Mac OS 8.x, 9.x, X, or later) and monitor display settings (8-, 16-, and 32-bit color) that users are likely to use. If you plan to play the movie over the Internet, you need to make sure the movie plays fast enough over a slow Internet connection.

Create a projector movie

1. Click File on the menu bar, then click Save and Compact to save and compress the movie.

2. Click File on the menu bar, then click Create Projector to open the Create Projector dialog box.

3. Navigate to the location where your Unit L data files are stored, as shown in Figure L-7 (Win) or Figure L-8 (Mac).

4. In the list of files and folders, click SpaceWorks Online.dir, then click Add.

   TIP You can click Move Up or Move Down to change the order of multiple movies in the projector.

5. Click the Files of type list arrow, then click Movie Cast Xtra, if necessary (Win).

6. Click Create to open the Save projector as dialog box.

7. In the File name text box, type **SpaceWorks Online**.

8. Navigate to the location where your Unit L data files are stored, if necessary.

   TIP To avoid problems with linked media, create the projector file in the same folder as the linked media.

9. Click Save to save the movie, cast, and included Xtras in a single projector file.

You created a projector movie.

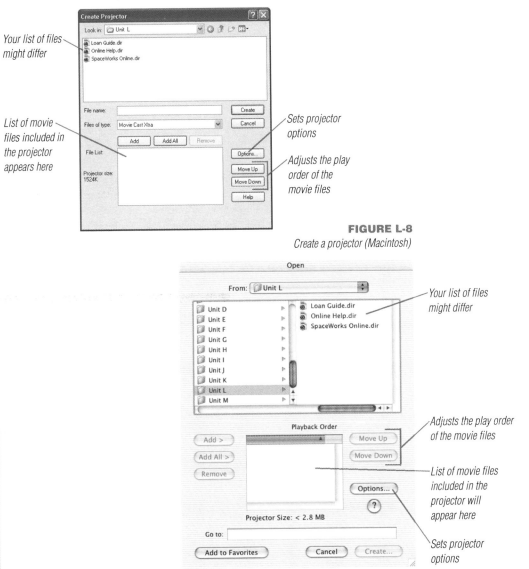

FIGURE L-7
Create Projector dialog box (Windows)

Your list of files might differ

List of movie files included in the projector appears here

Sets projector options

Adjusts the play order of the movie files

FIGURE L-8
Create a projector (Macintosh)

Your list of files might differ

Adjusts the play order of the movie files

List of movie files included in the projector will appear here

Sets projector options

FIGURE L-9

Projector icon in Windows Explorer (Windows)

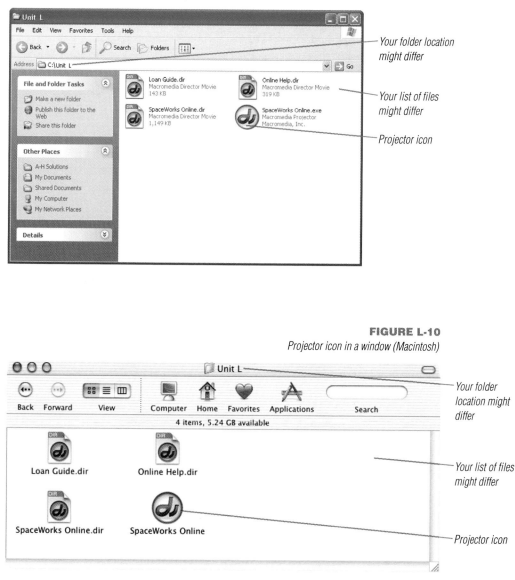

Your folder location might differ

Your list of files might differ

Projector icon

FIGURE L-10

Projector icon in a window (Macintosh)

Your folder location might differ

Your list of files might differ

Projector icon

Launch a projector movie

1. Open Windows Explorer (Win) or Finder (Mac).

2. Navigate to the location where your Unit L data files are stored to display the projector file.

3. Double-click the SpaceWorks Online icon, as shown in Figure L-9 (Win) or Figure L-10 (Mac), to launch the projector movie.

   If the Shockwave player is not installed when you play the movie, it will not work.

4. Click the Price button, then close the projector using the window title bar.

5. Close Windows Explorer (Win) or close all open Director MX related windows in Finder (Mac), then display the Director program window if necessary.

6. Click File on the menu bar, click Create Projector to open the Create Projector dialog box, then click Options to open the Projector Options dialog box.

7. Deselect the Play Every Movie and Animate in Background check boxes, then click the Full Screen option button.

8. Deselect the Compress (Shockwave Format) check box, then click the Standard option button.

   You restored projector options to their original settings.

9. Click OK, then click Cancel.

You launched a projector movie.

CREATE A PROTECTED MOVIE

What You'll Do

Update Movies Options

> In this lesson, you will create a protected movie.

Creating a Protected Movie

When you create a projector file that uses other movie files or external casts, you might want to protect those external files from being modified. When you protect external files, Director changes the files to prevent users from opening and editing them in Director. Before you create a protected movie, make sure you have backup copies of the original because the original movie will be deleted from your computer. You can create a backup copy when you protect the movie using the Update Movies Options dialog box. When you create a protected movie, Director closes the original movie file and adds the .dxr extension to the protected movie file, as shown in Figure L-11, and a .cxt extension to any protected casts. After you create a protected movie, no one will be able to open it in Director. A protected file can be played only by a projector, as a movie in a window, or by using the Shockwave player. Although it is important to protect your external files, there is one disadvantage: Director does not compress the movie into a smaller size.

FIGURE L-11

Protected movie files in Windows Explorer (Windows)

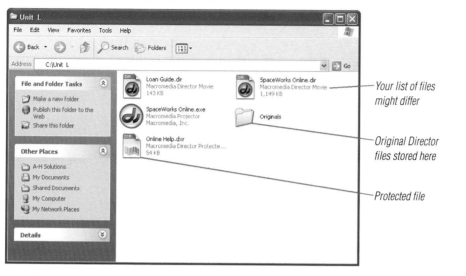

— *Your list of files might differ*

— *Original Director files stored here*

— *Protected file*

FIGURE L-12

Update Movies Options dialog box

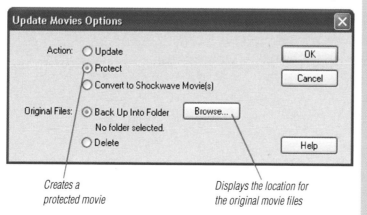

Creates a protected movie

Displays the location for the original movie files

Create a protected movie

1. Click Xtras on the menu bar, click Update Movies, then click Yes (if necessary), to save the movie and open the Update Movies Options dialog box.

2. Click the Protect option button, as shown in Figure L-12.

3. Click Browse to open the Select folder for original files dialog box, then navigate to the location where your Unit L data files are stored if necessary.

4. Click the Create New Folder button (Win), or New folder button (Mac), type **Originals**, press [Enter] (Win) or click Create (Mac), then double-click the Originals folder (Win).

5. Click Select Folder (Win) or Choose (Mac) to return to the Update Movies Options dialog box, then click OK to open the Choose Files dialog box.

6. Navigate to the location where your Unit L data files are stored, click Online Help.dir in the file list, then click Add.

7. Click Proceed to display a warning message, then click Continue to protect the file and store the original file in the Originals folder.

8. Exit Director.

9. Use Windows Explorer (Win) to launch the protected file Online Help.dxr, click OK as necessary to close the alert boxes, then exit Director.

You created a protected movie.

Embed fonts in movies.

1. Start Director, open the file MD L-2.dir from where your Unit L data files are stored, then save it as **Nova**.
2. Change the font for the Loan Amount label text cast member to one available on your computer, and add bold to the text.
3. Embed the font you selected.

Manage Xtras for distributing movies.

1. Add the Speech.x32 (Win) or Speech (Mac) Xtra to the movie.
2. If you have access to the Internet, read the Web site information about the Xtra.

Set movie playback options.

1. Select the playback option to pause when the window is inactive.
2. Select the playback option to show placeholders.

Set projector options.

1. Select the projector option to play every movie.
2. Select the projector option to play in a full screen.
3. Select the projector option to play the movie in the center of the Stage.
4. Select the projector option to compress the movie with the Shockwave format.
5. Select the projector option for the compressed player.

Create and launch a projector movie.

1. Save and compact the movie.
2. Create a projector movie for the Nova movie.
3. Name the projector file **Nova**.
4. Save the projector file where your Unit L data files are stored.
5. Launch the Nova projector movie from Windows Explorer (Win) or Finder (Mac), click the Calculator button, then press [Esc]

or [Alt][F4] (Win) or ⌘[Q] (Mac) to exit the movie.
6. Switch back to Director.
7. Restore the original projector option settings.

Create a protected movie.

1. Protect the Loan Guide.dir movie; back up the original movie file in the Originals folder.
2. Exit Director.
3. Display your Unit L data files folder in Windows Explorer (Win) or Finder (Mac).
4. Compare your screen to Figure L-13.
5. Launch the Nova projector movie, then click the Guide button.
6. Click the Return button, then press [Esc] (Win) or ⌘[Q] (Mac) to exit the movie.
7. Use Windows Explorer (Win) to open the protected file Loan Guide.dxr, close the alert boxes, then exit Director.
8. Close Windows Explorer (Win) or any open windows in Finder (Mac).

FIGURE L-13
Completed Skills Review

Original data file not shown

You are a multimedia instructor at a local college. You are teaching a class on Director and want to explain and demonstrate Director's movie distribution method. You use Director to create a movie with definitions of each distribution method and save the movie as a projector movie.

1. Start Director and save the movie as **Movie Delivery**.
2. Create a text cast member with the text **Director Movie Distribution Methods**, and drag it to the top of the Stage.
3. Create a text cast member with the text **Projector** and its definition, then drag it on the Stage.
4. Create a text cast member with the text **Shockwave** and its definition, then drag it on the Stage.
5. Create a text cast member with the text **Protected** and its definition, then drag it on the Stage.
6. Create a projector movie called **Movie Delivery** in a window (centered and showing the title bar) with compressed media and player.
7. Play the projector movie.
8. Compare your screen to Figure L-14, then close the movie if necessary.
9. Restore projector options, save the movie, then exit Director.

FIGURE L-14
Completed Project Builder 1

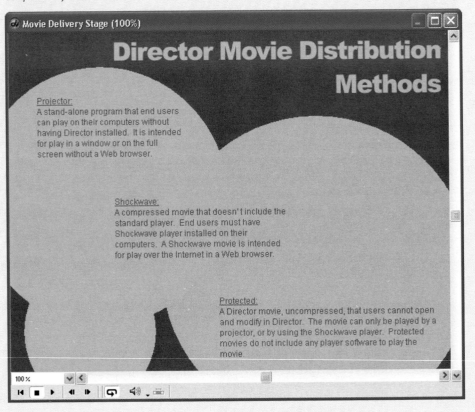

You are the marketing manager at Font Mania, a font development company. You have developed two new fonts for a client. You want to create a simple font viewer for the client to review the fonts. You use Director to display two fonts, embed them in a movie, and create a projector.

1. Start Director and save the movie as **Font Catalog**.
2. Create a text cast member with the text **Font Mania**, and drag it to the top of the Stage.
3. Create a text cast member with the entire alphabet and numbers 1 to 10, using a font, and drag it to the left side of the Stage. (*Hint*: Select a unique font on your computer.)
4. Create a text cast member with the entire alphabet and numbers 1 to 10, using another font, and drag it to the right side of the Stage.
5. Embed the fonts in the movie.
6. Create a compressed projector file called **Font Catalog** with the movie centered in a window.
7. Restore projector options, save the movie, then exit Director.
8. Play the projector movie, then compare your screen to Figure L-15.
9. Close the projector.

FIGURE L-15
Completed Project Builder 2

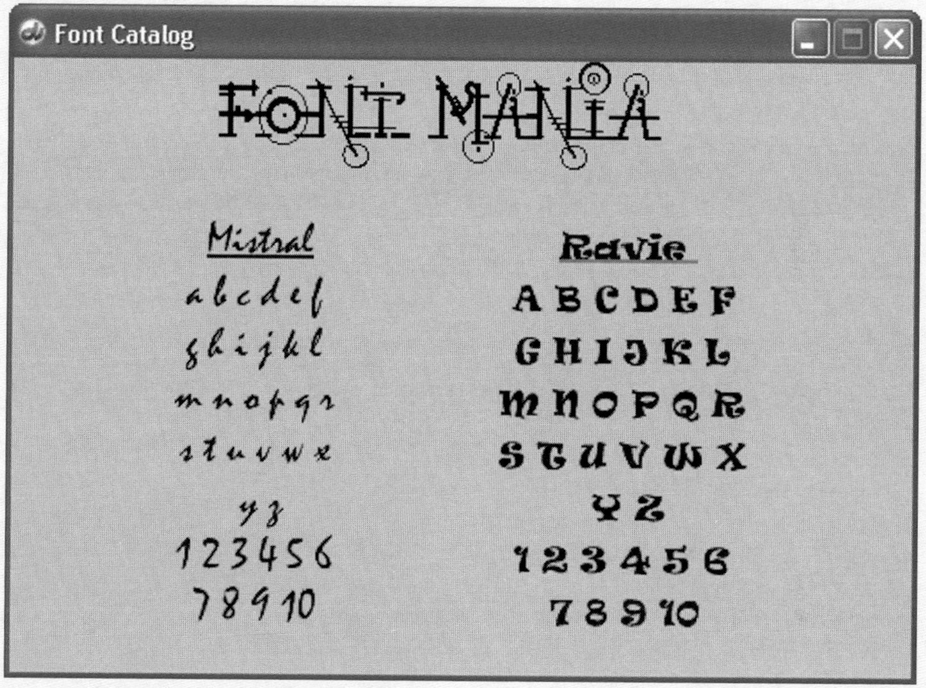

You are the software developer for TigerSoft, an antivirus software development company. As part of the development for the initial release of VirusAlert 1.0, you want to create a separate Director movie with information about the software and the names of the development team. You use Director to create a protected movie with rolling credits for the development team and a Return button, and then create a projector movie with an About button to test the process of opening a separate movie in a window.

1. Start Director and save the movie as **About VirusAlert**.
2. Create a text cast member with the text **TigerSoft** and drag it to the top of the Stage.
3. Create several text cast members with information about the software (include software name, version, registered user, company name, and product identification number), and drag them on the Stage. You can also add additional text and graphics to individualize your design.
4. Create a text cast member with five to ten names and drag it on the Stage, then embed any special fonts used in the movie.
5. Animate the text cast members to appear from the bottom of the Stage to the top, like rolling credits in a movie.
6. In the Paint window, create a button cast member with the text **Return**, add the cast

member to the Stage, and then attach a behavior to the Return button on the Stage that closes the About VirusAlert window.
7. Save the movie.
8. Create a new movie and save the movie as **TigerSoft**.
9. In the Paint window, create a button cast member with the text **About**, add the cast member to the Stage, and then attach a script to the About button on the Stage that opens the About VirusAlert movie in a window.
10. Add text and a graphic to create an About screen and embed any special fonts used in the movie.

FIGURE L-16
Completed Design Project

11. Create a compressed projector file called **TigerSoft**, with the movie centered in the full screen and the Animate in Background playback option selected.
12. Restore projector options, then save the movie.
13. Create a protected movie called **About VirusAlert**; back up the original movie file in the Originals folder.
14. Save the movie (if necessary), then exit Director.
15. Play the TigerSoft projector movie, click the About button, then compare your screen to Figure L-16.
16. Click the Return button, then press [Esc] (Win) or ⌘[Q] (Mac) to close the projector.
17. Put a copy of this movie in your portfolio.

Your group can assign elements of the project to individual members, or work collectively to create the finished product.

You are a member of the technology and design department at In View, a public relations company specializing in movie promotions. The producer of a space documentary called *Earth Unveiled* wants you to create a Director movie with a documentary movie clip in the MPEG format and package it for audiences to view in a projector file. You use Director to install an Xtra, called DirectMedia Xtra, to import the MPEG movie, then create a projector movie. *Note*: For Macintosh, skip Steps 2 and 3. The Macintosh does not need an Xtra to import an MPEG movie.

1. Assign each member of the group to research space movies on the Web for layout ideas, and to obtain earth MPEG movies for the project. Use movies from the Web that are free for both personal and commercial use (check the copyright information for any movie before downloading it).
2. Install the DirectMedia Xtra, located in the Xtras folder where your Unit L data files are stored, using the installer provided by the developer of the Xtra. During the installation, be sure to select the Xtras folder located in the Director MX folder.
3. Start Director, then save the movie as **Earth Unveiled** (Win) or **Earth Unveiledm** (Mac).

4. Add the DirectMediaXtra.x32 to the Xtras list (if necessary), then verify that the Include in Projector check box is selected for the Xtra (Win).
5. Change the background of the Stage to black.
6. Create a text cast member with the text **Earth Unveiled**, and drag it to the top of the Stage.
7. Embed any special fonts used in the movie.
8. Import the earth MPEG movie from the location where your Unit L data files are stored. (*Hint*: Use the DirectMedia Xtra command on the Tabuleiro Xtras submenu on the Insert menu (Win) or the Import command on the File menu (Mac) to import an MPEG movie.)
9. Create a compressed projector file named **Earth Unveiled** using the full screen with the movie centered in a window.
10. Restore projector options, save the movie, then exit Director.
11. Play the projector movie, then compare your screen to Figure L-17.
12. Press [Esc] (Win) or ⌘[Q] (Mac) to close the projector if necessary.

FIGURE L-17
Completed Group Project

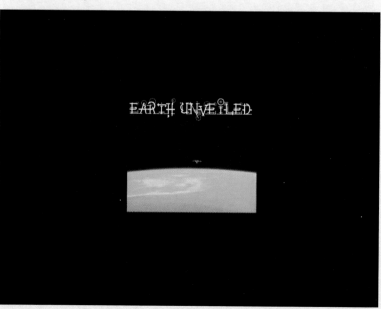

MAKING WEB CONTENT WITH SHOCKWAVE

1. Design Shockwave movies.

2. Install Shockwave Player.

3. Make a Shockwave movie stream.

4. Set Shockwave publishing options.

5. Set Shockwave compression options.

6. Make a Shockwave movie resizable.

7. Preview, publish, and play a Shockwave movie.

Understanding Shockwave

Shockwave is multimedia Web content that you can view in browsers, such as Microsoft Internet Explorer, Netscape Navigator, and America Online (AOL). Web sites use Shockwave content for interactive product training and demonstrations, e-commerce programs, music, multiuser games, and communication. Statistics by King, Brown & Partners Inc. (a market research company) have shown that offering Shockwave Web content increases both traffic and user retention. Shockwave content is created with Director as a compressed movie and viewed on the Web with Shockwave Player.

Shockwave Player is one of the most widely distributed software components on the Internet. Over 300 million users have Shockwave Player installed, and approximately 350,000 users install Shockwave Player daily. Shockwave Player is downloadable free from *www.macromedia.com*. Macromedia also offers Web publishers free licensing to distribute Shockwave Player on the Internet, corporate intranets, and CD/DVD-ROMS. Shockwave Player is installed as a shared system component and includes an automatic software updating feature, which checks to make sure you have the latest version of Shockwave Player. Shockwave Player supports multiple platforms and browsers.

Shockwave content examples are available on the Web. These examples can give you ideas on how you can create Shockwave Web content. You can visit the Shockwave Web site at *www.shockwave.com* or the Macromedia Web site at *www.macromedia.com* to see some of these examples in action.

Tools You'll Use

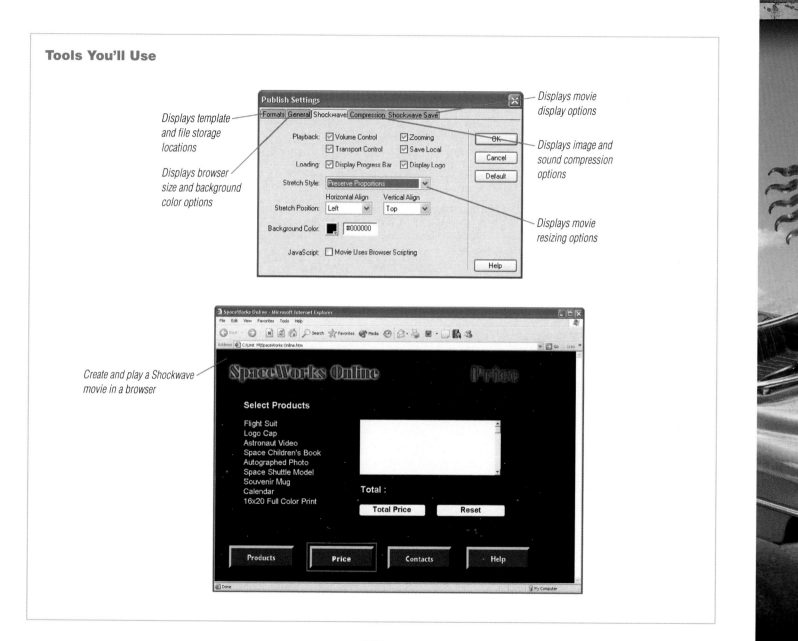

Displays template and file storage locations

Displays browser size and background color options

Displays movie display options

Displays image and sound compression options

Displays movie resizing options

Create and play a Shockwave movie in a browser

DESIGN SHOCKWAVE MOVIES

What You'll Do

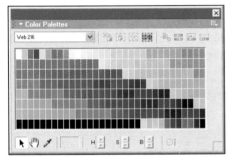

In this lesson, you will learn how to design Shockwave movies.

Designing Shockwave Movies

Designing a Shockwave movie for the Web is slightly different from designing a Director movie for a local computer or CD-ROM. When you publish a Shockwave movie, you should take into account some important design considerations. The main design consideration is to keep the size of the Shockwave movie as small as possible so that you can minimize the download time from the Web. For example, if you have a 70K Director movie file and save it as a Shockwave movie, the file reduces to 25K. If your Internet connection downloads files at 2K per second, it will take 12 seconds to download the file, which can be a long time to wait for today's Web user.

Design Considerations for Shockwave Movies

- Keep the movie size small; smaller movies will download, display, and play faster.
- Keep graphic files as small as possible; use JPEG (Joint Photographic Experts Group) and GIF (Graphics Interchange Format) files. JPEG file format supports millions of colors (24-bit color depth), but loses image quality by discarding image data during the compression process. GIF file format, which is standard in Director, uses only 256 colors, but it doesn't lose any image quality after compression. You use the Image Compression feature for JPEG to reduce file size, as shown in Figure M-1.
- Minimize the number of cast members; delete any unused cast members.
- Do not select the Loop Continuously feature; a movie with a continuous loop ties up computer memory while the Web page is open.
- Use low color depth (8-bit or less); color depth is a measure of the number of colors that an image can contain.
- Use the Compression Enabled feature for Shockwave audio and choose a low setting, as shown in Figure M-1.
- Avoid palette issues such as inadvertent color flashes; use the Web Index

Color Palette (Web 216), as shown in Figure M-2.

- Keep imported sounds as small as possible; use the lowest possible sampling rate.
- Loop small audio files for long background tracks.
- Use short film loops, such as a cast member produced from a sequence of other cast members.
- Use the Tiling feature in the Paint window to create backgrounds.
- Use the Paint window to create objects; objects you create in Director have smaller file sizes than imported graphics.

- Use ink effects to produce different effects using the same cast member.
- Use field cast members instead of text cast members; field cast members require less space.

Excluding Director Features for a Shockwave Movie

Director is a full-featured multimedia program, but Web technology is not full-featured, so not all Director features are available when you publish a Shockwave movie. The following list identifies common features that Shockwave does not support.

Features Not Available for a Shockwave Movie

- Movie in a Window (MIAW), a Director movie running in a window of its own, separate from the Stage of the main movie
- Lingo commands that change system settings, such as Restart or Shutdown, or that run external files
- FileIO Xtra or other Xtras that open external files
- Printing
- Custom menus

FIGURE M-1
Shockwave compression settings

FIGURE M-2
Web Index Color Palette

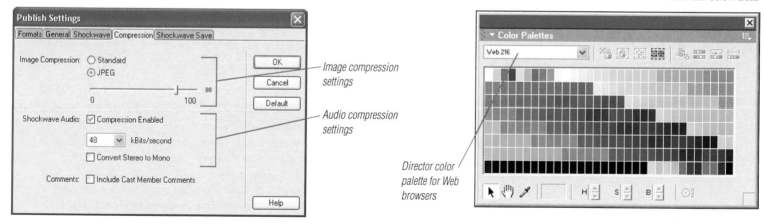

Image compression settings

Audio compression settings

Director color palette for Web browsers

INSTALL SHOCKWAVE PLAYER

What You'll Do

 In this lesson, you will install Shockwave Player.

Installing Shockwave Player

To play Shockwave movies within a browser, you need to install Shockwave Player on your computer. Shockwave Player is a software product developed by Macromedia, Inc. for browsers on Windows and the Macintosh. The Shockwave 8.5.1 Player can play Shockwave movies back to version 5. You can download the latest version of Shockwave Player free from the Macromedia Web site at *www.macromedia.com*. The Director MX CD-ROM also comes with Shockwave Player. To install it from the CD-ROM, open the Shockwave Player folder on the CD-ROM, double-click the installer icon, then follow the instructions. After you install Shockwave Player, you can set the Auto Updates option in the Shockwave Properties dialog box to receive Shockwave Player updates automatically.

QUICKTIP

To turn on Shockwave Player Auto Updates, right-click (Win) or [control]-click (Mac) a Shockwave movie in your browser, click Properties, then select the automatic update check box.

Testing the Shockwave and Flash Players

If you are not sure whether Shockwave Player and Flash Player are installed correctly on your computer, you can test them by using a link on Macromedia's Web site. The test determines if you have Shockwave Player and Flash Player installed on your computer and, if you do, which version. If you have any version of Shockwave Player and Flash Player, two movies appear on the test Web site. To access the test Web site, open your browser, go to *www.macromedia.com/support/shockwave*, then click the Test Macromedia Web Players link.

FIGURE M-3

Download Shockwave Player Web page

Your Web
page location
and display
might differ

Installs the
Shockwave
Player

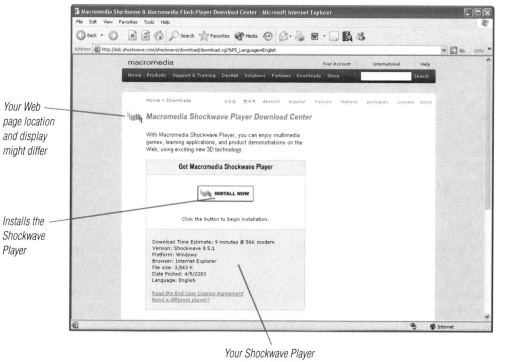

Your Shockwave Player
version might differ

1. Connect to the Internet, then go to *www.macromedia.com.*

2. Click the Products link to display a list of Macromedia products, then click the Shockwave Player link to display the Macromedia Shockwave Player Web page.

   TIP If a link is no longer available, use the search feature on the Macromedia Web site to locate the Shockwave Player download Web page.

3. Click the Download link (your link might be different) to display the installation Web page, as shown in Figure M-3.

4. Click Install Now (your link might be different).

5. Follow the instructions in dialog boxes that appear, if necessary.

   When both the Shockwave Player and Flash Player movies begin to play without comment, the Shockwave Player installation is successful.

6. Close your browser.

You installed Shockwave Player.

MAKE A SHOCKWAVE MOVIE STREAM

What You'll Do

In this lesson, you will set Shockwave streaming options and attach streaming behaviors to a movie.

Streaming Shockwave Movies in Director

Streaming is a process that allows you to view the beginning of a Shockwave movie in your browser while the rest of the movie continues to download from the Web, so you don't have to wait for the entire movie to download before it starts to play. A streaming movie starts to play as soon as Director downloads the Score information and the cast members for the first frame. After the movie starts to play, Director continues to download cast members and any linked media in the background as they appear in the Score. When you create a movie to stream, you need to make sure all cast members have been downloaded by the time the movie needs them—otherwise the cast members will not appear in the frame. Streaming does not decrease the total time needed to download a movie, but it does reduce the time it takes to start viewing the movie.

Setting Shockwave Playback Options

You can use the Movie Playback Properties dialog box to set streaming playback options for the movie. In the Streaming section, you can set the movie to stream, and then specify the number of frames to download before the movie begins to play. If you have an introductory scene that plays while other media are downloading, you need to set the download value so that all of the required media for the introductory scene are loaded before the movie begins to play. The playback option can be set or changed at any time before you publish the Shockwave movie.

Adding Streaming Behaviors to a Movie

Internet bandwidth is the amount of data that can be transmitted in one second. Bandwidth is still limited for Web users; this can affect the ease of downloading or streaming files. Shockwave movies are often too big to stream without complications. One strategy you can use to make streaming more effective is to loop a sequence of your movie while cast member media download in the background. Director comes with built-in streaming behaviors, as shown in Figure M-4, that allow you to control how a movie plays while Shockwave media are downloading from a Web server. The Jump and Loop behaviors wait for streaming media to become available and then move the playback head to the next frame, a specified frame, or a specified marker. These behaviors differ slightly: the Jump behaviors loop the playback head on only a single frame while the media are loading, and the Loop behaviors can loop the playback head over a range of frames while the media are loading. The Progress Bar behavior, when applied to a text or field cast member, shows a percentage that increases (from 0 to 100) as media are loading.

FIGURE M-4
Library palette with streaming behaviors

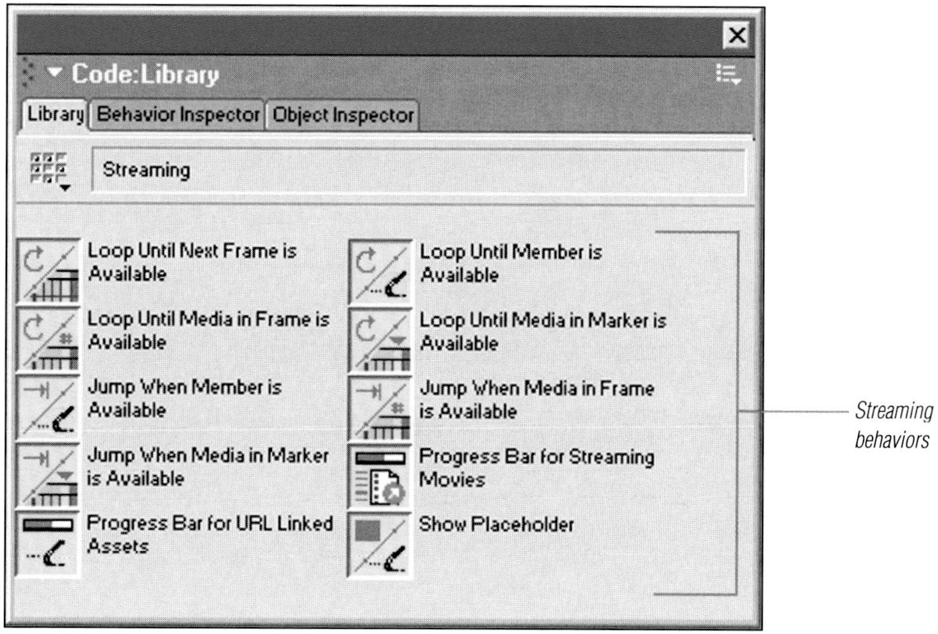

Streaming behaviors

Set Shockwave playback options

1. Start Director, open the file MD M-1.dir from where your Unit M data files are stored, then save it as **SpaceWorks Online.**

2. Click Modify on the menu bar, point to Movie, then click Playback to open the Movie Playback Properties dialog box.

3. Select the Play While Downloading Movie check box (if necessary) to turn on streaming for the movie.

   TIP If the Play While Downloading Movie check box is deselected, Director downloads all cast members before the movie starts to play.

4. Double-click the Download text box to select the current value.

5. Type **30** (if necessary) to specify the number of frames downloaded before the movie begins to play.

6. Select the Show Placeholders check box (if necessary), as shown in Figure M-5, to display placeholders for media elements that did not completely download.

7. Click OK.

   The options you set in the Movie Playback Properties dialog box take effect when you publish a Shockwave movie or preview the movie in a browser.

8. Save your work.

You set Shockwave streaming playback options.

Streaming options

Drag the
Progress
Bar for
Streaming
Movies
behavior to
the Progress
bar sprite

Loop Until
Next Frame
is Available
behavior

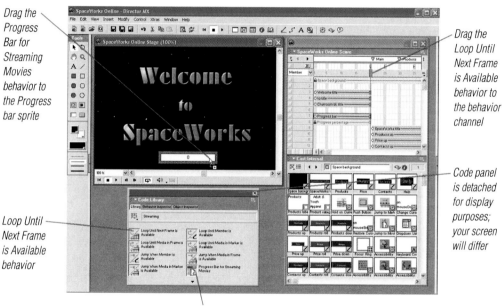

Drag the
Loop Until
Next Frame
is Available
behavior to
the behavior
channel

Code panel
is detached
for display
purposes;
your screen
will differ

Progress Bar for
Streaming Movies
behavior

Add streaming behaviors to a movie

1. Click Window on the menu bar, then click Library Palette (if necessary) to display the Library tab in the Code panel.

2. Click the Library List button, point to Internet, then click Streaming.

3. Drag the Loop Until Next Frame is Available behavior to frame 20 in the behavior channel to open the parameters for "Loop Until Next Frame is Available" dialog box.

4. Click the Loop Type list arrow, click Loop To Specified Frame, then click OK to loop through the introductory animation until the media in frame 21 are available for use.

5. Scroll down the Library palette, then drag the Progress Bar for Streaming Movies behavior onto the Progress bar sprite on the Stage, as shown in Figure M-6, to open the Parameters for "Progress Bar for Streaming Movies" dialog box.

6. Select the Enable Display of Percent Loaded check box.

7. Click the Display Percent Loaded in Member list arrow, click Progress percentage, then click OK.

8. Rewind and play the movie, then stop the movie (if necessary) when it reaches the end.

   The progress percentage changed from 0% to 100% very quickly because the Shockwave movie is not being downloaded from the Web.

9. Save your work.

You attached a streaming behavior to a sprite.

SET SHOCKWAVE PUBLISHING OPTIONS

What You'll Do

In this lesson, you will set Shockwave publishing options.

Setting Shockwave Publishing Options

You can publish a Director movie and its entire linked media as a Shockwave movie, which you can play back in a browser on the Internet or on an intranet. To publish a Shockwave movie, you need first to set Shockwave publishing options in the Publish Settings dialog box using the following tabs: Formats, General, Shockwave, Compression, Shockwave Save, and Image (only shown when an image template is selected). When you publish a Shockwave movie, you also need to create a Hypertext Markup Language (HTML) file (a standard Web page format) so that a browser can play it. You can select an HTML template location for the HTML and Shockwave files using the Formats tab. See Table M-1 for a description of the HTML template options. The Shockwave and HTML files use the same name as the Director movie, unless you change it. On the General tab, the Shockwave movie's width and height are set to match the dimensions of the Director movie, and the background color is set to the one used as the Stage color in the movie, unless you change it. You can also use the Shockwave Save tab to include a context menu that appears when a user right-clicks (Win) or [control]-clicks (Mac) a Shockwave movie. The context menu provides users with volume control and playback options.

TABLE M-1: HTML Template Options

HTML template	description
No HTML Template	Creates only the Shockwave file, without the HTML file
Shockwave Default	Creates an HTML file that runs a Shockwave movie in a browser
Detect Shockwave	Detects whether users have the correct version of Shockwave Player installed
Fill Browser Window	Expands the Shockwave movie to fill the entire browser window
Loader Game	Displays a game with a progress bar while the Shockwave movie loads
Progress Bar With Image	Displays a progress bar and an image while the Shockwave movie loads; the Image tab in the Publish Settings dialog box appears, where you select the image's frame number and an image compression setting
Simple Progress Bar	Displays a progress bar while the Shockwave movie loads
Shockwave With Image	Automatically installs the Windows version of Shockwave Player, if not installed
Center Shockwave	Centers the movie in the browser window
3D Content Loader	Displays movies with 3D content

Set Shockwave publishing options

1. Click File on the menu bar, then click Publish Settings to open the Publish Settings dialog box, which displays the Formats tab, as shown in Figure M-7.

2. Click Default to restore default settings in the Publish Settings dialog box.

3. Click the HTML Template list arrow, then click Detect Shockwave.

4. In the HTML File section, click the Select Output button, navigate to the location where your Unit M data files are stored, then click Select Folder to select a storage folder for the HTML file. [···]

(continued)

FIGURE M-7
Formats tab in the Publish Settings dialog box

Displays HTML templates

Displays folder destinations for the files

Select check box to view movie in a Web browser after you publish it

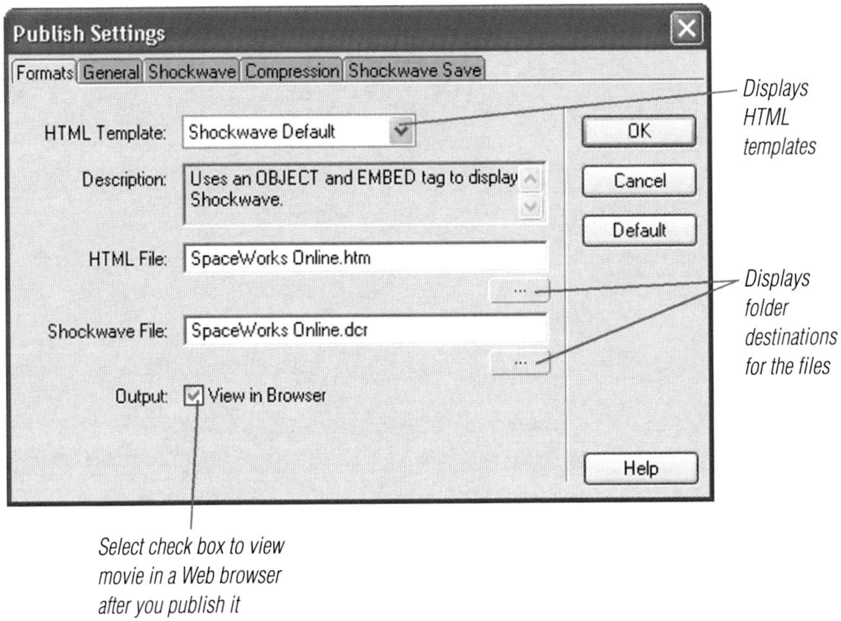

FIGURE M-8

Shockwave Save tab in the Publish Settings dialog box

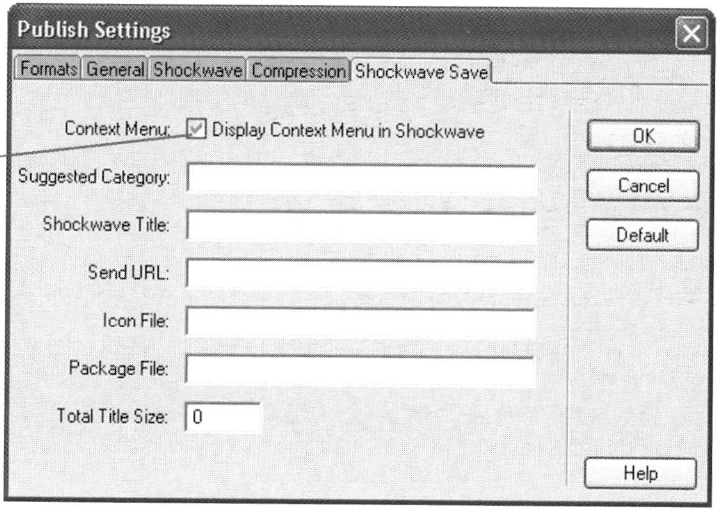

Select check
box to access
a menu in the
Shockwave
movie

Publish Settings ☒

Formats | General | Shockwave | Compression | Shockwave Save

Context Menu: ☑ Display Context Menu in Shockwave

Suggested Category: [   ]

Shockwave Title: [   ]

Send URL: [   ]

Icon File: [   ]

Package File: [   ]

Total Title Size: [0]

[OK]

[Cancel]

[Default]

[Help]

5. In the Shockwave File section, click the Select Output button, navigate to the location where your Unit M data files are stored, then click Select Folder (Win) or Choose (Mac) to select a storage folder for the Shockwave file. [···]

6. Verify that the View in Browser check box is selected.

7. Click the Shockwave Save tab.

8. Select the Display Context Menu in Shockwave check box (if necessary), as shown in Figure M-8.

9. Click OK, then save your work.

You set Shockwave publishing options.

SET SHOCKWAVE COMPRESSION OPTIONS

What You'll Do

In this lesson, you will set Shockwave compression options.

Setting Shockwave Compression Options

The Compression tab in the Publish Settings dialog box allows you to compress all bitmap cast members and sounds when you publish a Shockwave movie. When you compress graphics and sounds in a Shockwave movie, it downloads faster from the Web. The Compression tab allows you to set general compression options for the entire movie. If you want to set individual compression options for a selected graphic, you can use the Compression pop-up menu on the Bitmap tab in the Property inspector. This setting overrides the general settings on the Compression tab in the Publish Settings dialog box. You can use Shockwave Audio (SWA) to compress all internal sound cast members. Shockwave Audio makes sounds much smaller in a Shockwave movie, by a ratio of as much as 12 to 1, without noticeable loss in sound quality.

Converting multiple movies into Shockwave files

If you have multiple Director movies and casts, you can convert them to Shockwave files all at once, instead of converting each one individually The conversion creates a movie file with the .dcr extension and a cast with the .cct extension, which the user cannot modify. You can convert the files while preserving the original files, or convert the files and delete the original files. To convert multiple movies to Shockwave files, click Xtras on the menu bar, click Update Movies, click the Convert to Shockwave Movie(s) option button, click the Back Up Into Folder option button, click Browse, select the folder where you want to put the original files, click Open, click Select Folder, click OK, select the movie you want to convert, click Add for each individual file or Add All, then click Proceed. Director does not automatically save linked external casts. You need to add each external cast that you want to convert. After a movie is compressed into the Shockwave format, you cannot edit the file. You need to change the original Director movie and then convert the movie to Shockwave again.

FIGURE M-9

Compression tab in the Publish Settings dialog box

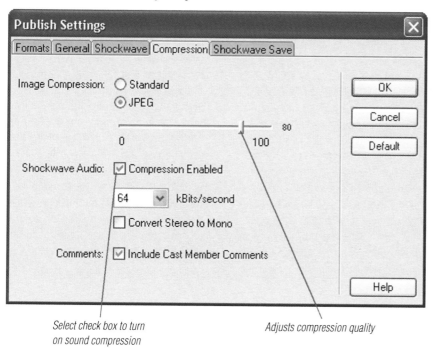

Select check box to turn
on sound compression

Adjusts compression quality

1. Click File on the menu bar, click Publish Settings, then click the Compression tab, as shown in Figure M-9.

2. Click the JPEG option button if necessary.

3. Drag the Image Compression slider to 70.

   The lower the percentage, the more the image is compressed.

4. Select the Compression Enabled check box if necessary.

   TIP If you use Shockwave Audio compression and distribute the movie, you need to include the SWA decompression Xtra. Click Modify on the menu bar, point to Movie, click Xtras, click Add, click swadcmpr.x32 (Win) or SWA Decomp PPC Xtra (Mac), then click OK twice.

5. Click the kBits/second list arrow, then click 56.

   This option sets the sound bit-rate setting. The lower the value, the more the sound is compressed, which produces lower-quality sound.

6. Click OK.

7. Save your work.

You set Shockwave compression options.

MAKE A SHOCKWAVE MOVIE RESIZABLE

What You'll Do

Publish Settings

Formats | General | Shockwave | Compression | Shockwave Save

Playback: ☑ Volume Control ☑ Zooming
☑ Transport Control ☑ Save Local

Loading: ☑ Display Progress Bar ☑ Display Logo

Stretch Style: Preserve Proportions

Horizontal Align   Vertical Align
Stretch Position: Left   Top

Background Color: ■ #000000

JavaScript: ☐ Movie Uses Browser Scripting

OK
Cancel
Default
Help

In this lesson, you will make a Shockwave movie resizable.

Making a Shockwave Movie Resizable

Because computer displays are set to different resolution sizes, which may not match the size of your movie, you need to decide how you want your Shockwave movie to appear in a browser window. You can set the Shockwave movie to stretch with a browser window, or not to stretch so that it remains the same size regardless of a browser window's size. To make a Shockwave movie stretchable, you need to set three options in the Publish Settings dialog box. In the Publish Settings dialog box, you need to set the Dimensions value to Percentage of Browser Window on the General tab, and select the Zooming check box and a Stretch Style option on the Shockwave tab. These options and the size of the browser window determine the size of the Shockwave movie. See Table M-2 for a description of the Stretch Style options. When you are developing a resizable Shockwave movie, you need to be aware that fonts and bitmaps, which are made up of individual pixels or dots, do not stretch well and might become difficult to read or appear skewed.

TABLE M-2: Stretch Style Options

stretch style	description
No Stretching	Makes the movie play at the size specified in the Dimensions pop-up menu on the General tab. Resizing the browser crops your movie if it doesn't fit.
Preserve Proportions	Retains the same aspect ratio of your movie, regardless of the size of the browser window. The movie is aligned with respect to the Horizontal Align and Vertical Align settings.
Stretch to Fill	Stretches the movie to fill the browser window. The aspect ratio of your movie might change, which will distort the appearance.
Expand Stage Size	Expands the Stage size to equal the height and width dimensions in the HTML file. Only the Stage changes size; sprites remain the same size.

Make a Shockwave movie resizable

1. Click File on the menu bar, then click Publish Settings to open the Publish Settings dialog box.

2. Click the General tab.

3. Click the Dimensions list arrow, then click Percentage of Browser Window, as shown in Figure M-10.

   TIP If you use Netscape as your browser, click Match Movie instead of Percentage of Browser Window, then skip to Step 7. The Match Movie and Pixels options set the movie to a fixed size.

   (continued)

FIGURE M-10
General tab in the Publish Settings dialog box

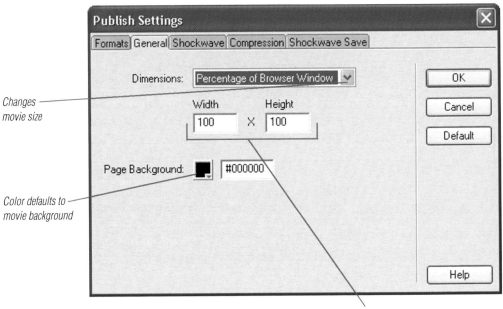

Changes movie size

Color defaults to movie background

Your dimensions might differ

5. Click the Stretch Style list arrow, then click Preserve Proportions, as shown in Figure M-11, to retain the same aspect ratio of your movie regardless of the size of the browser window.

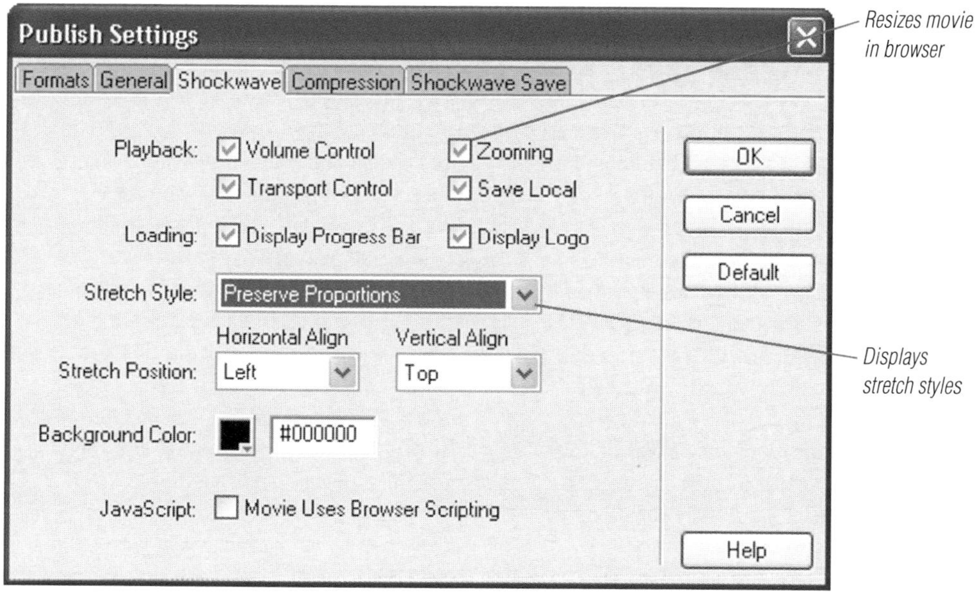

6. Verify that the Zooming check box is selected.

> TIP To set the Dimensions and Stretch Style options automatically, click the Formats tab in the Publish Settings dialog box, click the HTML Template list arrow, then click Fill Browser Window.

7. Click OK.

8. Save your work.

You set Shockwave resizable options.

FIGURE M-11
Shockwave tab in the Publish Settings dialog box

Resizes movie in browser

Displays stretch styles

PREVIEW, PUBLISH, AND PLAY A SHOCKWAVE MOVIE

What You'll Do

In this lesson, you will preview, create, and play a Shockwave movie.

Previewing, Publishing, and Playing a Shockwave Movie

Before you publish a Shockwave movie, you can preview and test it in your browser When you preview a Shockwave movie in a browser, Director creates temporary Shockwave and HTML files, then removes them when you're done. When you preview or publish a Shockwave movie, Director makes sure all of the required Xtras are available. If an Xtra is needed and is not installed (typically in the Plug-in folder), you can set the Download if Needed option in the Movie Xtras dialog box to have Director inform the user that the Xtra is needed, and then download it.

In Director, an Xtra is generally implemented as a plug-in, a software module that adds a specific feature to a program. To publish a Shockwave movie, you use the Publish command on the File menu. When you publish a Shockwave movie, you also create an HTML file so that a browser can play it. After you create the HTML file, you can use other Web page editing programs, such as Macromedia Dreamweaver, to customize the HTML file further. After you publish a Shockwave movie, you can modify it only by changing the original movie in Director, and then creating a new Shockwave file.

Using linked media with Shockwave

If your Shockwave movie uses any linked media or external casts and you want to preview the movie locally on your computer in your browser, you need to place the external files in a folder named dswmedia inside the Shockwave Player folder, along with the Shockwave movie and the HTML file. You only need to place the files once on your local computer; users will not have to place them on their computers to view the movie from a Web site. The dswmedia folder is part of Director's security scheme, which prevents the movie from accessing your local drive and your personal data.

FIGURE M-12
Shockwave movie in a browser

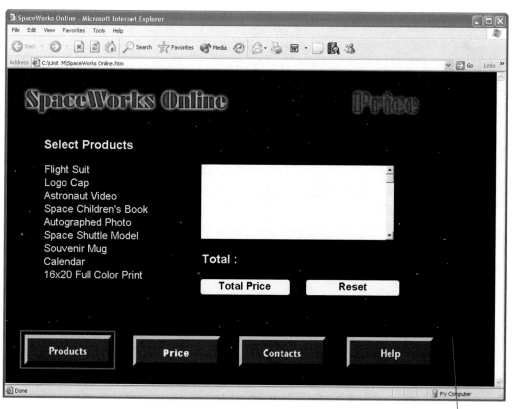

Shockwave movie fills
the browser window

1. Click File on the menu bar, then click Save and Compact to save and optimize the file before you preview it in your browser.

2. Click File on the menu bar, then click Preview in Browser to open your browser, load the movie, and play it.

    Because the Shockwave file is only tempo-rary, it is not centered and the background doesn't match.

    > TIP If a warning about missing an Xtra appears, write down the missing Xtra, then click OK. In Director, click Modify on the menu bar, point to Movie, click Xtras to open the Movie Xtras dialog box, click Add, click the missing Xtra, then click OK twice.

3. Click several buttons in the movie.

4. Close your browser.

5. Click File on the menu bar, click Publish, then click Yes (Win) or Save (Mac) (if necessary) to save the movie.

    Director publishes the Shockwave file with the .dcr extension (Win) and the HTML file with the .htm extension (Win) in the folder where your Unit M data files are stored, and then the movie plays in a browser.

6. Click several buttons in the movie, as shown in Figure M-12.

7. Resize your browser window to resize the Shockwave movie.

8. Close your browser.

9. Exit Director.

You previewed, published, and played a Shockwave movie.

Design Shockwave movies.

1. List and describe five ways to reduce thesize and download time of a Shockwave movie.
2. List five Director features not available for Shockwave movies.

Install Shockwave Player.

1. If you already installed Shockwave Player, test the Shockwave and Flash Players using a link on the Macromedia Web site.

Make a Shockwave movie stream.

1. Start Director, open the file MD M-2.dir from where your Unit M data files are stored, then save it as **Nova**.
2. Turn on the streaming option in the Movie Playback Properties dialog box.

3. Set the Download value to 15, then close the dialog box.
4. Open the Library palette (if necessary), and display the Streaming behaviors.
5. Drag the Progress Bar for Streaming Movies behavior onto the Progress bar sprite on the Stage.
6. Select the Enable Display of Percent Loaded check box.
7. Change the Display Percent Loaded in Member value to Progress percentage.
8. Rewind and play the movie, click the buttons on the Stage, then stop the movie.

Set Shockwave publishing options.

1. Open the Publish Settings dialog box and set the default settings.
2. Set the HTML Template to Shockwave Default.

3. Select the folder where your Unit M data files are stored for the HTML file.
4. Select the folder where your Unit M data files are stored for the Shockwave file.
5. Display the Shockwave Save tab.
6. Select the Display Context Menu in Shockwave check box, if necessary.
7. Close the Publish Settings dialog box.

Set Shockwave compression options.

1. Open the Publish Settings dialog box.
2. Display the Compression tab.
3. Set the JPEG option if necessary.
4. Select the Compression Enabled check box if necessary.
5. Set the sound bit-rate setting to 48.
6. Close the Publish Settings dialog box.

Make a Shockwave movie resizable.

1. Open the Publish Settings dialog box.
2. Display the General tab.
3. Change the Dimensions option to Percentage of Browser Window.
4. Display the Shockwave tab.
5. Change the Stretch Style option to Stretch to Fill.
6. Select the Zooming check box if necessary.
7. Close the Publish Settings dialog box.

Preview, publish, and play a Shockwave movie.

1. Save and compact the movie.
2. Preview the movie in a browser.
3. Close your browser.
4. Publish the Shockwave movie.
5. Click several buttons on the Stage, then compare your screen to Figure M-13.
6. Resize the browser window.
7. Close your browser.
8. Exit Director.

FIGURE M-13
Completed Skills Review

You are a teacher at an elementary school and want to create learning material that students at the school can view through a browser. You are learning how to use Director to create Shockwave content for the Web and want to test out the process. You use Director to open a movie and save the file as a Shockwave movie and HTML file to view in a browser.

1. Start Director, open the file MD M-3.dir from the location where your Unit M data files are stored, then save the movie as **Shuttle Landing**.
2. Open the Publish Settings dialog box.
3. Select the folder where your Unit M data files are stored for the HTML file.
4. Select the folder where your Unit M data files are stored for the Shockwave file.
5. Set the HTML Template option to Center Shockwave.
6. Display the Shockwave Save tab and select the Display Context Menu in Shockwave check box.
7. Display the Compression tab, select the JPEG option, then set the Image Compression slider to 50.

8. Select the Compression Enabled check box, then set the sound bit-rate setting to 48.
9. Close the Publish Settings dialog box.
10. Save and compact the movie.
11. Publish the Shockwave movie and view it in a browser, then compare your screen to Figure M-14.
12. Close your browser.
13. Exit Director.

FIGURE M-14
Completed Project Builder 1

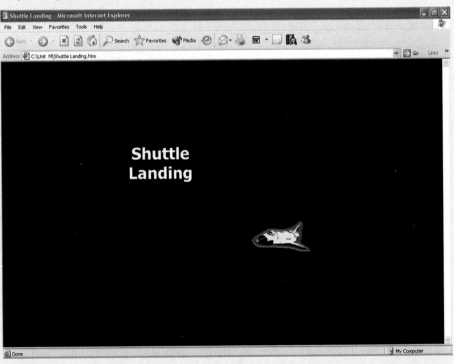

You are the owner of Anywhere Travel, an independent travel agency. You have some new specials that you want to promote on the Web. You use Director to create a movie with travel specials—including locations, extras, and cost—and save it as a Shockwave movie.

1. Start Director, open the file MD M-4.dir from the location where your Unit M data files are stored, then save the movie as **Anywhere Travel**.
2. Open the Publish Settings dialog box.
3. Select the folder where your Unit M data files are stored for the HTML file.
4. Select the folder where your Unit M data files are stored for the Shockwave file.
5. Set the HTML template to Center Shockwave.
6. Display the General tab, set the page background to black, then set the Dimensions option to Match Movie.
7. Display the Compression tab, select the JPEG option, then set the Image Compression slider to 25.
8. Deselect the Compression Enabled check box, then close the Publish Settings dialog box.
9. Save and compact the movie.
10. Publish the Shockwave movie and view it in a browser, then compare your screen to Figure M-15.
11. Close your browser.
12. Exit Director.

FIGURE M-15
Completed Project Builder 2

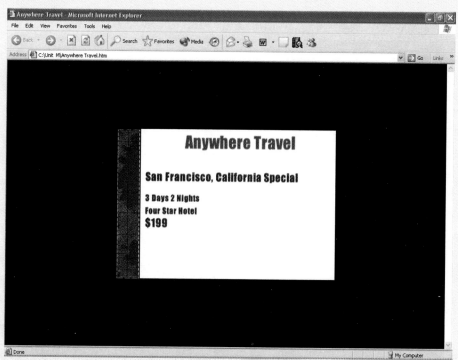

You are a design student at a local college. Your roommate works as a clown at elementary school assemblies. As part of his program, he wants to project an animated clown face that is scared of a computer mouse onto a large screen with his computer. You use the Paint tool to create a clown face and add a built-in behavior that moves the clown face when the pointer gets close to it.

1. Start Director, and save the movie as **Clown Face**.
2. Create a text cast member with the text **Avoid the Clown Face**, and drag it to the top of the Stage. You can also add additional text and graphics to individualize your design.
3. Use the Paint tool to create and name a clown face cast member, then drag the clown face on the Stage.
4. Open the Library palette and display the Interactive list of behaviors.
5. Apply the Avoid Mouse behavior to the clown face on the Stage.
6. Play the movie and move the mouse toward the clown face, then stop the movie.
7. Open the Publish Settings dialog box.
8. Select the folder where your Unit M data files are stored for the HTML file.
9. Select the folder where your Unit M data files are stored for the Shockwave file.
10. Set the HTML template to Fill Browser Window.
11. Display the General tab, then set the Dimensions option to Percentage of Browser Window.
12. Display the Compression tab, select the JPEG option, then set the Image Compression slider to 50.
13. Close the Publish Settings dialog box.
14. Save and compact the movie.
15. Publish the Shockwave movie and view it in a browser, then compare your screen to Figure M-16.
16. Close your browser.
17. Exit Director.
18. Put a copy of this movie in your portfolio.

FIGURE M-16
Completed Design Project

Your group can assign elements of the project to individual members, or work collectively to create the finished product.

You are a member of a literacy project at Cornerstone Books, a small book publishing company. As a team member, you are responsible for promoting the literacy project and helping kids learn how to read. This year's emphasis is on using technology, so you decide to create multimedia versions of popular children's books or original stories. You use Director to create an animated movie depicting a popular children's book or original story.

1. Choose a popular children's book or create your own story, and then assign each member of the group a page to create.
2. Assign each member of the group to browse the Web for layout ideas, and to obtain pictures, drawings, or photographs for the project. Use media from the Web that are free for both personal and commercial use (check the copyright information for any such media before downloading it). If you have a scanner, you can use your own drawings.
3. Start Director and save the movie as **Literacy**.
4. Create a text cast member with the title of your book and drag it to the top of the Stage.
5. Import the images you downloaded or scanned and drag them sequentially in the same channel in the Score, or use one image as a background.
6. Create text cast members that contain the text of the story, and drag them to the Stage.
7. Open the Publish Settings dialog box, and set the default settings.
8. Select the Center Shockwave HTML template.
9. Select the folder where your Unit M data files are located for the HTML file.
10. Select the folder where your Unit M data files are located for the Shockwave file.
11. Display the General tab, change the Dimensions option to Match Movie, then change the page background to a color in the background of the story if necessary.
12. Display the Compression tab, change the Image Compression option to Standard.
13. Display the Shockwave tab, change the Stretch Style option to No Stretching (if necessary), select the Zooming check box (if necessary), change the background color to a color in the background of the story (if necessary), then close the Publish Settings dialog box.
14. Save and compact the movie.
15. Publish the Shockwave movie and view it in a browser, then compare your screen to Figure M-17.
16. Close your browser.
17. Exit Director.

FIGURE M-17
Completed Group Project

Read the following information carefully!

Find out from your instructor the location of the Data Files you need and the location where you will store your files.

■ To complete many of the units in this book, you need to use Data Files. Your instructor will either provide you with a copy of the Data Files or ask you to make your own copy.

■ All of the Data Files are organized in folders named after the unit in which they are used. For instance, all Unit A Data Files are stored in the unit_a folder. You should leave all the Data Files in these folders; do not move any Data File out of the folder in which it is originally stored.

■ If you need to make a copy of the Data Files, you will need to copy a set of files from a file server, standalone computer, or the Web to the drive and folder where you will be storing your Data Files.

■ Your instructor will tell you which computer, drive letter, and folders contain the files you need, and where you will store your files.

■ You can also download the files by going to *www.course.com*. See the inside back cover of the book for instructions to download your files.

Copy and organize your Data Files.

Copy the folders that contain the Data Files to a Zip drive, network folder, hard drive, or other storage device.

■ Find and keep track of your Data Files and completed files.

■ Use the Data File Supplied column to make sure you have the files you need before starting the unit indicated in the Unit column.

■ Use the Student Creates File column to find out the filename you use when saving your new file for the exercise.

■ Depending on where you store the files, you might need to relink any external files, such as a QuickTime (.mov) or AVI (.avi) video file, associated with a Director Data File. When you open a Data File, Director will ask you the location of the external file.

■ Note that Units H and I contain data files that are Macintosh-specific.

Files used in this book

Unit	Data File Supplied	Student Creates File	Used in
A	MD A-1.dir		Lessons/Skills Review
	Fun.dir		Project Builder 2
		Magic_Doc.doc	Design Project
B		SpaceWorks Promotion.dir	Lessons
	Media/ Space Background.bmp Media/Blue Earth.jpg Media/Mwm Logo.tif		Lessons/Skills Review

Unit	Data File Supplied	Student Creates File	Used in
	MD B-1.dir		Skills Review
		Charity Project Plan.doc	Project Builder 1
		ABC123.dir	Project Builder 2
		Resume.dir	Design Project
		Space Pres.dir	Group Project
C		Space Graphics.dir	Lessons
	MD C-1.dir		Skills Review
		Unique Pools.dir	Project Builder 1
		US State.dir	Project Builder 2
		Borderlines.dir	Design Project
		NYC Olympics.dir	Group Project
D	MD D-1.dir	Space Graphics.cst	Lessons
	Space Ships.cst Media/4 Planets.jpg Media/9 Planets.jpg Media/Blue Earth.jpg Media/Colorful Star.gif Media/Jupiter.gif Media/Mostly Space.jpg Media/Saturn.jpg Media/Space Background.gif Media/Space Planet.jpg Media/Uranus.jpg		Lessons/Skills Review
		Space Star.dir Space Backgrounds.cst	Skills Review
		Langford Financial.dir Financial Symbols.cst	Project Builder 1
		Keenen Group.dir Flowchart Symbols.cst	Project Builder 2
		Designer Flags.dir Victory Flags.cst	Design Project
		Only Desserts.dir Dessert Photos.cst	Group Project

Unit	Data File Supplied	Student Creates File	Used in
E	MD E-1.dir		Lessons
	MD E-2.dir		Skills Review
		Design Contest.dir	Project Builder 1
		Shape Matching.dir	Project Builder 2
		Answers Prototype.dir	Design Project
		Animal Matching.dir	Group Project
F	MD F-1.dir		Lessons
	MD F-2.dir		Skills Review
		On Target.dir	Project Builder 1
		Coin Collectors.dir	Project Builder 2
		Bug Be Gone.dir	Design Project
		All Butterflies.dir	Group Project
G	MD G-1.dir		Lessons
	MD G-2.dir		Skills Review
		Shooting Star.dir	Project Builder 1
		Bouncing Ball.dir	Project Builder 2
		Smiley Face.dir	Design Project
		Last Chance.dir	Group Project
H	MD H-1.dir SpaceWorks Pres.dir Media/Blastoff.mov Media/Blastoff.wav (Win) Media/Blastoffm.swa (Mac) Media/Earthvenus.avi Media/Meteor.wav Media/SolarSystem.swf	SpaceWorks Pres.mov	Lessons
	MD H-2.dir Animal Pres.dir Media2/Birds.wav (Win) Media2/Birdsm.swa (Mac) Media2/Dog.aiff Media2/Dog.mov		Skills Review

Unit	Data File Supplied	Student Creates File	Used in
	Media2/Dolphin.swf Media2/Eagle.wav Media2/Lion.au Media2/Monkey.au Media2/Monkey.mov Media2/Tiger.au Media2/Tiger.avi Media2/Wolf.au Media2/Wolf.mov Media2/Zebra.au Media2/Zebra.mov	Animal Pres.mov	Skills Review
	World Travelers.dir	World Travelers.mov	Project Builder 1
		True 2 Life.dir	Project Builder 2
		Chem101.dir	Design Project
		Animal Fun.dir	Group Project
I	MD I-1.dir Media/Color Storm.gif Media/Color Table.act (Win) Media/Color Tablem.act (Mac) Media/Light Blue Storm.gif Media/Orange Storm.gif		Lessons
	MD I-2.dir Media2/Color Meter Table.act (Win) Media2/Color Meter Tablem.act (Mac) Media2/Color Meter.gif		Skills Review
		Family Reunion.dir	Project Builder 1
		L is for.dir	Project Builder 2
		SoHo Art Studios.dir	Design Project
		Woodwork Toys.dir	Group Project
J	MD J-1.dir Help.dir		Lessons
	MD J-2.dir Guide.dir		Skills Review
		Zoom.dir	Project Builder 1

Unit	Data File Supplied	Student Creates File	Used in
		Toy Think.dir	Project Builder 2
		Credits.dir Sports Game.dir	Design Project
		Computer Support.dir	Group Project
K	MD K-1.dir Online Help.dir Sprite Rotation Example.dir		Lessons
	MD K-2.dir Loan Guide.dir Parent Scripts.dir		Skills Review
		Lingo Class.dir	Project Builder 1
		Casino Game.dir	Project Builder 2
		About.dir Sports Triva Game.dir	Design Project
L	MD L-1.dir Online Help.dir	SpaceWorks Online.exe Online Help.dxr	Lessons
	MD L-2.dir Loan Guide.dir	Nova.exe Loan Guide.dxr	Skills Review
		Movie Delivery.dir Movie Delivery.exe	Project Builder 1
		Font Catalog.dir Font Catalog.exe	Project Builder 2
		About VirusAlert.dir About VirusAlert.dxr TigerSoft.dir TigerSoft.exe	Design Project
	Xtras/DirectMediaXtra150.exe	Earth Unveiled.dir Earth Unveiledm.dir Earth Unveiled.exe	Group Project

Unit	Data File Supplied	Student Creates File	Used in
M	MD M-1.dir Help.dir	SpaceWorks Online.dcr SpaceWorks Online.htm	Lessons
	MD M-2.dir Guide.dir	Nova.dcr Nova.htm	Skills Review
	MD M-3.dir	Shuttle Landing.dcr Shuttle Landing.htm	Project Builder 1
	MD M-4.dir	Anywhere Travel.dcr Anywhere Travel.htm	Project Builder 2
		Clown Face.dir Clown Face.dcr Clown Face.htm	Design Project
		Literacy.dir Literacy.dcr Literacy.htm	Group Project

&
An operator that connects strings in quotation marks ("").

&&
An operator that connects strings and adds a space in between.

Animation path
A track a sprite moves along to create an animation.

Arguments
Placeholders that pass values to scripts.

Authoring tool
A software program, also known as a development platform, that allows you to create your own software.

Behavior
A ready-made script.

Behavior channel
A row in the Score used to write frame scripts, also known as the script channel.

Behavior Inspector
A panel used to create, view, and change behaviors of a selected object in a movie.

Behavior scripts (sprite and frame)
Lingo scripts that add interactivity to a movie. Behavior scripts can use over 100 built-in library behaviors.

Bézier curve
A type of vector shape curve.

Bit depth
A measure of how much data space is available to store a given moment of sound or a particular image. The higher the bit depth, the better the sound or image quality.

Bit rate
The degree of compression in an audio file.

Bitmap
A pixel-by-pixel representation of a graphic.

Bitmapped font
A font that consists of a set of dot patterns for each letter and number in a typeface for a specified type size.

Blend value
Makes a sprite more or less transparent. A blend value of 100% makes a sprite completely opaque and a blend value of 0% makes a sprite completely transparent.

Breakpoint
A location in a script where you want Director to stop executing Lingo commands.

Brightness
A measure of how much black is mixed with a color.

Bullet mark
An identifying symbol indicating that an option is enabled (Win).

Case statement
Commands used to replace a chain of If-then statements.

Cast library
Useful for storing any type of commonly used cast members, especially behaviors.

Cast member
Media element in the Cast window.

Cast member script
Script attached to a specific cast member that cannot be shared.

Cast window
A storage area that contains media elements, such as graphics, images, digital videos, sounds, animations, text, color palettes, film loops, and scripts.

Channel
A row in the Score.

Channel separator bar
A thin line along the edge of a docking channel used to quickly minimize a docking channel.

Check mark
An identifying symbol indicating that a feature is currently selected.

Child object
A child script that is executed only when a rule is met for its parent script.

Closed shape
A shape in which points connect.

Color depth
The number of colors that an image or a computer monitor and display adapter can display.

Color mode
Director specifies color in RGB (red, green, blue) and palette index color modes. The RGB color mode identifies a color by a set of hexadecimal numbers that specify the amounts of red, green, and blue needed to create a color. The palette index color mode identifies a color by the number (0 through 255) of its position in a color palette.

Color palette
A set of colors used by a movie or cast members.

Command
A directive that accesses a program's feature.

Comments
Information, such as notes or instructions, that you can add to a script.

Compression
Reduces the size of a file. The higher the compression ratio, the smaller the file size.

Constants
Elements that never change, such as TRUE and FALSE constants.

Context-sensitive help
A help function that specifically relates to what you are doing.

Control handles
Vector shape components that determine the degree of curvature between vertices.

Control Panel
A tool that controls the playback of a movie using DVD-type controls, including Rewind, Stop, and Play buttons.

Cue point
A marker in a sound or video used to trigger an event in Director.

Cycle value
Determines how many times a gradient repeats from the start color to the end color within a vector shape.

Declare
A statement that lets Director know that the variable is global.

Destination color
The ending color of gradient blends that starts with the foreground color.

Development platform
A software program, also known as an authoring tool, that allows you to create your own software.

Diamond
An identifying feature indicating that an option is enabled (Mac).

Dithering
Blends the colors in a new palette to approximate the original colors in a bitmap.

Docking channel
A region located on the left and right side of the Director window to which you can temporarily attach and detach panels (Win).

Document panel
A panel related to a movie, such as the Score and Cast window.

Dot syntax
A Lingo writing style that is a more concise, shorter form of verbose.

Dynamic color management
The use of a changeable color palette in Windows that lets the program define all but 16 colors, which Windows reserves for its interface elements, in the 256-color palette.

Effects channels
The upper rows in the Score.

End frame
The last frame in a sprite, denoted by a small bar.

Event
An occurrence, such as a key press, that Director detects and responds to by sending a message.

Expressions
Parts of a Lingo statement that generate values.

External cast
A cast that is saved in a separate file outside a movie.

Field text
The text created using the Field tool or Field window.

File
A collection of information stored together as an individual unit.

File extension
A three-letter extension at the end of a file-name that identifies the file type for an operating system.

Film loop
Combines many sprites and effects over a range of frames into a single cast member.

First line indent marker
Sets the indent for only the first line of text in a paragraph.

Focus ring
A colored rectangle around the boundaries of a sprite that a user selects using [Tab].

Frame
A column in the Score.

Frame-by-frame animation
A series of cast members placed in the Score one frame at a time. The process involves altering cast members slightly from frame to frame to build an animated sequence.

Frame channel
A shaded row in the Score, also known as the timeline, which contains numbers to identify each frame.

Frame script
A script—attached to a frame—that adds interactivity and extended functionality to a movie.

Functions
Operations that return a value.

Gradient
Shading from one color to another color.

Grid
A set of rows and columns of a specified height and width that are used to help place sprites on the Stage.

Guides
Horizontal or vertical lines you can either drag on the Stage or lock in place to help you align sprites.

Handler
A script that responds to messages triggered by a specific event during a movie's playback. A handler starts in the Behavior Script window with the word *on* followed by the name of a trigger message.

Hanging indent
Indent where the first line left margin starts at 0" while the margin for the remaining lines starts at 1".

Hexadecimal number
An internal computer numbering scheme that is used to identify colors in a color palette.

Hue
The color created by mixing primary colors (red, blue, and yellow).

If-then
A structure that evaluates a statement and then branches to outcomes. If the statement is TRUE, the command after *then* is executed. If the statement is FALSE, the command after *else* is executed.

Indent markers
Marks displayed on the ruler that show the indent settings for a paragraph containing the insertion point in the Text window.

Interactive multimedia
Software produced with Director that combines elements of interactivity and multimedia.

Interactivity
A software program's ability to include user feedback and navigation.

Internal cast
An internal storage area for cast members that is saved as part of a movie.

Internet bandwidth
The amount of data that can be transmitted over the Internet in one second.

Irregular shape
A freeform object.

Java applet

A movie converted to Java. Java applets created in Director provide extended functionality to play simple movies in a browser where plug-ins, such as the Shockwave Player, are not allowed or don't provide the needed functionality.

Kerning

A specialized form of spacing between certain parts of characters; kerning improves the appearance of text in large sizes but does very little to improve the appearance of small text.

Keyframe

The first frame or an animation point in a sprite; denoted in a sprite by a circle.

Keyframe indicator

A symbol that indicates a frame is a keyframe.

Keywords

Reserved words in Lingo that have special meaning.

Lasso tool

A tool in the Paint window that selects anything that is surrounded by it.

Left indent marker

Sets the indent for all the text in a paragraph.

Library palette

A panel with over 100 built-in behaviors that you can drag onto sprites and frames.

Linear gradient

Shading from one color on one side of a shape to another color on the other side.

Lingo

Director's programming language.

Lingo script

Simple scripts that can be attached to sprites or frames to navigate to a specific location in a movie. You can create a script by double-clicking a frame in the Behavior channel, and then typing one or more Lingo instructions.

List

An effective way to store, track, and update a set of data, such as a series of names or numbers.

Luminosity

A measure of how much black is mixed with a color.

Marquee tool

A tool in the Paint window that selects everything within its rectangular bounds.

Me

A keyword in a Lingo command that refers to an object without actually naming it.

Memory Inspector

A window that displays the amount of system memory available to Director for a movie and indicates the amount of memory used by the entire movie as well as different parts of the movie, such as the cast window and score (Win).

Menu

A list of commands used to accomplish certain tasks.

Menu bar

Organizes commands into groups of related operations. You can choose a menu command by clicking it or by pressing [Alt] plus the underlined letter in the menu name (Win), or by pressing [command] plus the designated letter (Mac).

MIAW

A Movie in a Window that plays in a separate window while the main movie plays on the Stage.

Moveable button

Sets a sprite's moveable property on the Sprite tab in the Property inspector.

Moveable property

Allows users to drag a sprite on the Stage while the movie is playing.

Movie

A Director file.

Movie script

A script that is available during playback of an entire movie; it's not attached to any object.

Multimedia
A combination of graphics, images, digital video, sound, text, and animation.

Object
Any part of Lingo scripting that is designed to both receive input and produce a result.

Open shape
A shape in which the starting point and the ending point do not connect.

Operator
A term that changes values using arithmetic symbols, compares two values and determines whether the comparison is true or false, or combines text strings together.

Palette channel
A row in the Score used to set the available colors for a movie.

Palette index color mode
A color palette that identifies a color by the number (0 through 255) of its position in a color palette.

Panel
A window you can collapse, expand, and group to improve workflow.

Panel group
A collection of panels in a window.

Parent script
A script that contains Lingo statements used to create and control child scripts.

Pixel
An individual point in a graphic with a distinct color.

Playback events
Events related to what happens when the playback head moves to another frame and when a movie is launched.

Playback head
An object in the frame channel that moves through the Score, indicating the frame that is currently displayed on the Stage.

Preload value
Determines when cast members are loaded into memory as a movie plays.

Projector movie
A stand-alone program that users can play on their computers without having Director installed.

Properties
The various attributes of an object.

Property inspector
A panel used to view and change attributes of any selected object or multiple objects in a movie.

Protected movie
An uncompressed movie that users cannot open and modify in Director. Protected movies do not include any player software to play the movie.

QuickDraw graphic
A shape created with the Tool palette.

Radial gradient
Shading from one color in the center of a shape to another color on the outside.

Real-time recording
Records the movement of a cast member on the Stage. The process involves setting up the recording attributes and dragging a cast member around the Stage.

Registration point
Adjusts the location of a sprite on the Stage by entering a horizontal (X) and vertical (Y) value measured from the top-left corner of the Stage.

Regular shape
An oval, rectangle, or rounded rectangle.

Remapping
Replaces the original colors in a bitmap with the most similar solid colors in a new palette.

RGB color mode
A color palette that identifies a color by a set of hexadecimal numbers, which specifies the amounts of red, green, and blue needed to create a color.

Right indent marker
Sets the indent for the text from the right margin in a paragraph.

Sampling rate
The frequency with which recordings are taken per second, measured in kilohertz, or kHz.

Saturation
A measure of how much white is mixed in with a color. A fully saturated color is vivid; a less saturated color is washed-out pastel.

Scalable font
A font that is based on a mathematical equation.

Schematic flowchart
A chart that sketches out the navigational structure of a movie and makes sure each section is properly connected.

Score
A window that organizes and controls media elements over a linear timeline.

Script
Tells the story of a movie production in text form. In Director, a script is simply Lingo code.

Script channel
A row in the Score used to write frame scripts, also known as the behavior channel.

Scripting
Writing programming code to add custom functionality to a movie.

Shockwave
A program that lets you play, collect, and manage Shockwave movies, especially games, offline.

Shockwave movie
A compressed movie that does not include the standard player. A Shockwave movie is intended for play over the Internet in a browser.

Shockwave Player
A software product developed by Macromedia for browsers on the Macintosh and Windows platforms. Plays movies created in Director.

Shockwave projector movie
A compressed movie that users can play on their computers independent of a browser.

Shortcut key
A keyboard alternative to using the mouse.

Sound channels
Two rows in the Score used to add music, sound effects, and voice-overs.

Span duration
A default duration of 28 frames that each new sprite contains.

Spread value
Controls whether the gradient is weighted more toward the start color or end color. Values greater than 100 weight the gradient toward the starting color, and vice versa.

Sprite
A representation of a cast member that has been placed on the Stage or in the Score.

Sprite bar
A line in a sprite in the Score that connects the beginning and end of a sprite.

Sprite channels
Rows in the score where sprites are placed.

Sprite label
The text that identifies the sprite in the Score.

Sprite Overlay panel
Displays important sprite properties directly on the Stage.

Sprite span
The range of frames in which a sprite appears.

Stage
Serves as the viewing area for the visual elements of a Director movie.

Statements
Complete Lingo instructions executed when a handler is triggered.

Step recording
A process of real-time recording of one frame at a time that involves setting up the recording attributes, moving the playback head forward one frame, changing the sprites' attributes, and moving the playback head forward again one frame.

Storyboard
Tells the story of a movie in visual form.

Streaming
A process that allows users to view the first part of a Shockwave movie in a browser while it continues to download the rest of the movie from the Web.

Stroke width
Determines the thickness of lines and outlines.

Tab
Used to position text at a specific location in the Text window.

Tab stop
A predefined position in the text to which you can align tabbed text. By default, tab stops are located every ½" from the left margin.

Tempo
The speed of a movie.

Tempo channel
A row in the Score used to adjust the speed or time of a movie as it plays.

Thumbnail
A Cast window view that displays a small image of each cast member.

Time events
Events related to the operating system and the user when nothing is happening.

Timeline
A shaded channel in the Score, also known as the frame channel, which contains numbers to identify each frame.

Title bar
Displays the filename of the open file.

Tool palette
Contains a set of tools used to create shapes, such as lines, rectangles, rounded rectangles, and ellipses.

Tool panel
A panel related to tools and options settings, such as the Tool palette and Property inspector.

Toolbar
Contains buttons for the most frequently used commands.

Tooltip
A help tag that displays the button name and a keyboard shortcut (Win).

Transition channel
A row in the Score used to set screen transitions, such as fades, wipes, dissolves, and zooms.

Tweening
An animation technique that makes a sprite move from one position to another.

Unload value
Determines which cast members stay in memory and which ones are removed when the movie plays.

User feedback events
Events related to mouse and keyboard actions performed by the user.

Variable
A storage container in which you name and assign values.

Vector shape
A mathematical description of a geometric form.

Verbose
A Lingo writing style that is similar to English.

Vertices
Fixed points of a vector shape.

Window events
Events related to the times when multiple Director movies are running in multiple windows.

Xtra
A software module you can add to Director, which extends the capabilities of Director.